THE
COMPLETE HISTORY
OF AMERICAN
FILM CRITICISM

JERRY ROBERTS

SANTA
MONICA
PRESS

Published by: Santa Monica Press LLC
P.O. Box 1076
Santa Monica, CA 90406-1076
1-800-784-9553
www.santamonicapress.com
books@santamonicapress.com

Printed in the United States

Santa Monica Press books are available at special quantity discounts when purchased in bulk by corporations, organizations, or groups. Please call our Special Sales department at 1-800-784-9553.

ISBN-13 978-1-59580-049-7

Library of Congress Cataloging-in-Publication Data

Roberts, Jerry.
  The complete history of American film criticism / Jerry Roberts.
     p. cm.
  Includes bibliographical references.
  ISBN 978-1-59580-049-7
  1. Film criticism--United States--History. I. Title.
  PN1995.R595 2010
  808'.066791--dc22
                            2009039715

Cover and interior design and production by Future Studio

THE COMPLETE HISTORY OF AMERICAN FILM CRITICISM

JERRY ROBERTS

CONTENTS

DEDICATION

This book is dedicated to my lifelong friends
Kevin Morris and Doug List

ACKNOWLEDGMENTS

Although this was the most one-man band operation among my books, I want to first thank Doug List for providing me with his clip file on film critics, which he had collected through two decades. James Robert Parish's daily, unofficial, and often surprising cyberspace clearinghouse of Hollywood information has also been a great gathering source for 21st-century data.

Of critics, I was particularly glad to have made the acquaintances of and shared some time with George Anderson, Yardena Arar, Gary Arnold, Joe Bensoua, Joey Berlin, Edward L. Blank, Ron Brewington, Duane Byrge, Jorge Camara, Charles Champlin, Dean Cohen, Bruce Cook, Michael Dare, Manohla Dargis, Roger Ebert, Douglas Edwards, David Ehrenstein, David Elliott, Jim Emerson, Harold Fairbanks, Juan Rodriguez Flores, Brandy French, Steve Gaydos, Peter Henne, Kirk Honeycutt, David Hunter, Andy Klein, Arthur Knight, Helen Knode, Sandra Kreiswirth, Don Lechman, Emanuel Levy, Doug List, Lael Lowenstein, Herbert G. Luft, Rod Lurie, Leonard Maltin, Willard Manus, Joe McBride, Todd McCarthy, Myron Meisel, Dale Munroe, Jean Oppenheimer, Robert Osborne, Barry Paris, John Powers, Peter Rainer, Harriet Robbins, Dorothy Rochmis, Robert Rosen, Dean Sander, David Sheehan, Henry Sheehan, Gene Siskel, Charles Solomon, Bob Strauss, Ella Taylor, Myra

Taylor, Bob Thomas, Kevin Thomas, Kenny Turan, Marylynn Uricchio, Barbara Vancheri, Ron Weiskind, Glenn Whipp, and Michael Wilmington.

Critics and film writers in general often engage in studio bashing, and this book does its fair share of that. But the studios can take it—easily. However, critics and writers often can't get along without the aid of publicists, those employed by the studios or the independent agents. Among the very best of these individuals are or have been: Jennifer Allen, Vivian Boyer, Greg Brilliant, Andre Caraco, Harry Clein, Mickey Cottrell, Jan Craft, Steve Elzer, Suzanne Fritz, Flo Grace, Margaret Grohne, Eddie Hill, Cece Horwitch, Stacy Ivers, Angela Johnson, Laura Kim, Pat Kingsley, Melody Korenbrot, Susan Levin, Frank Lomento, Arlene Ludwig, Vivian Mayer, Pat McQueeney, Harry Medved, Carol Stone Morrison, Julian Myers, Dawnette Norris, Catherine Olim, Mark Pogachefsky, Fredell Pogodin, Anne Reilly, Michelle Robinson, Ed Russell, Tammy Sandler, Lisa St. Amand, Heidi Schaefer, Robin Sherr, Gail Silverman, and Elizabeth Wolfe.

Of the folks who worked at Copley Los Angeles Newspapers in my 11 years there, I was pleased to have worked and been friends with Don Lechman, and worked alongside Laura Accinelli, Joe Bensoua, Torin Burgess, Diana Chapman, Bill Cizek, Betty Czachowski, Sam Gnerre, Jeannie Grand, Meredith Grenier, Andrea Hayashi, Alan Janson, JoLene Krawczak, Sandra Kreiswirth, Steve Marconi, Lisa Messinger, Dan McLean, Jan Molen, Terry Moore, Leilani Nishida, Bea Nyburg, Gary "Palmer" Palmer, Verne Palmer, Chris Richard, Warren Robak, Cathy Schwier, Tim Scoggins, Frank Suraci, Rebecca Jo Tubb, and Tim Woodhull.

Without Ramino Zahed, Jim Emerson, Stu Levine, Steve Chagollan, Tomm Carroll, and especially Steve Gaydos and Ted Elrick—all of whom hired me as a freelance writer on Hollywood and the movies—my career would have been even more checkered, and perhaps my outfits striped. Others who deserve theirs for prolonging my Hollywood stay include Alex Ben

Block, Anne Bergman, Howard Burns, Elif Cercel, Bob Fisher, Bob Hofler, Kirk Honeycutt, Darrell Hope, Noela Hueso, Ross Johnson, Matt King, Doug List, Paula Parisi, Chris Purcell, Jay Roth, Pat Saperstein, Gregory Solman, Nancy Spielvogel, Tom Tapp, Randy Tierney, and Chuck Warn.

In 25 years of covering Hollywood, I enjoyed and learned from my conversations with many film directors. Among those past and present who helped me understand the filmmaking process are: Paul Bartel, John Boorman, Jack Cardiff, Jack Clayton, Roger Corman, Clint Eastwood, Blake Edwards, Milos Forman, John Frankenheimer, Lasse Hallström, Monte Hellman, Walter Hill, Agnieszka Holland, Peter Jackson, Burt Kennedy, Sir David Lean, Delbert Mann, Ronald F. Maxwell, John Milius, Phillip Noyce, Alan J. Pakula, Ivan Passer, Mark Pellington, Daniel Petrie, Joe Pytka, Harold Ramis, Carl Reiner, John Sayles, Paul Schrader, Joel Schumacher, Quentin Tarantino, Gus Van Sant, Andrzej Wajda, John Waters, and Robert Wise.

My conversations with the following actors helped shape my understanding of films: Claude Akins, John Carradine, Willem Dafoe, Matt Damon, Robert Davi, Sammi Davis, Clint Eastwood, Morgan Freeman, James Garner, Ben Gazzara, Danny Glover, Gene Hackman, Tom Hanks, Richard Harris, Kathryn Harrold, Arliss Howard, Barnard Hughes, Holly Hunter, Raul Julia, Arthur Kennedy, George Kennedy, Deborah Kerr, Ben Kingsley, Bruno Kirby, Kay Lenz, Joe Mantegna, Lee Marvin, Roddy McDowall, Elizabeth McGovern, Helen Mirren, Christopher Mitchum, Robert Mitchum, Gary Oldman, Chazz Palminteri, River Phoenix, Joan Plowright, CCH Pounder, Oliver Reed, Kurt Russell, Theresa Russell, Gary Sinise, James Stewart, Sharon Stone, Imogen Stubbs, Meg Tilly, M. Emmet Walsh, and Alfre Woodard.

Among the friendships that have been constant through the life of this project have been those with Doug List, Don Lechman, Kevin Morris, and Wil Haygood. I also thank my wife, Joanne Mallillin, and my family, including my late father, Alexander Roberts, who kept tabs on the books I was doing;

my mother, Ann L. Roberts; brother and sister-in-law, Mark and Patty Roberts of Staunton, Virginia; my sister-in-law, Maria Kolfschoten; my nephews Kyle and Tyler Kolfschoten; and my cousin, Dr. Carol Grabowski of Long Beach, California.

I would also like to thank the patient Jeffrey Goldman at Santa Monica Press. His knowledge of this subject matter, support of this project, and understanding of its prescience carried inspiration. Thanks also go to Breanna Murphy and Brittany Yudkowsky of Santa Monica Press.

I also have to thank my associates at Arcadia Publishing, whose understanding, good humor, and good will have been truly appreciated: Devon Weston, Christine Talbot, Scott Davis, John Poultney, Julie Albright, Debbie Seracini, Katie Kellett, Richard Joseph, Kelly Reed, Hannah Carney, Kristie Kelly, Jared Jackson, David Mandel, Luke Cunningham, Sarah Higginbotham, Alison Yoder, Tim Killian, Davey Thomas, Rob Kangas, Ryan Easterling, Jim Kempert, Ariel Richardson, Mark Weisman, Jane Elliot, and Frank Travell.

Ned Comstock in USC's Doheny Library's Cinema Studies Department deserves special mention as does Claudia Weissberg, Web Manager of the Pulitzer Prizes. Measures of inspiration to stay the course on this project came from my memory of conversations about films with Bob Schwerin in Pittsburgh, and from incremental status checks from Chris Epting.

When the idea for this book first germinated, several people showed kindness at that time in my life, when I was grateful for it, and they include Teddy Cohen; Carl DiOrio; Sandy Dreger; Cathy Dunkley; Dorothy Mitchum; Ralph Nelson, Jr.; Eddie Rivera; Marc Starr; Tricia Thomas; and David Valdes.

INTRODUCTION

In the first decade of the 21st century, the drastic contraction of cultural news and feature coverage at newspapers and magazines put many print film critics out of business while newspapers and magazines retrenched in the face of an industry-wide economic crisis. Meanwhile, new blogs and Web sites devoted to judging movies popped up seemingly each week. There were seismic changes in the presentation of film reviews as the movie culture continued to turn away from the so-called "expert" and proclaimed anyone a critic who had an opinion and Internet access. Articles in 2008 by Anne Thompson in *Daily Variety*, David Carr in *The New York Times*, and Patrick Goldstein in the *Los Angeles Times* tolled the death knell for print film critics. Reactions on blogs and elsewhere on the Internet in 2009 fanned the notion that the era of the informed critic was over.

More than 30 newspaper and magazine critics vacated their posts since 2006. They were fired, laid off, retired, bought out by management, or saw the critic's post terminated. Some accepted reassignments. Michael Wilmington quit at the *Chicago Tribune*. The list of casualties included David Ansen of *Newsweek*, Jack Mathews and Jami Bernard of the *New York Daily News*, David Elliott of the *San Diego Union-Tribune*, and the troika of Michael Atkinson, Dennis Lim, and Nathan Lee at *The*

Village Voice, formerly one of the nation's central forums of film criticism as the pulpit for more than two decades of the great auteur proponent, Andrew Sarris.

Critics have educated generations of discriminating moviegoers on the difference between good films and bad, and, more importantly, pointed out what was good in bad films and was bad in good films. They resurrected prematurely dismissed pictures or those that could not find immediate audiences. They called attention to great directors, often emphasizing the contributions of their collaborators—cinematographers, production designers, screenwriters, costumers, and actors.

Critics heralded foreign films, especially in the postwar era. Critics such as Manny Farber, Robert Warshow, and Sarris studied the bodies of work of the long-tenured Hollywood directors. Their revisions of these directors' reputations helped establish the notion that film was the 20th century's most significant art form.

Critics put up the signposts for us to understand as much as we do about the aesthetic visions, storytelling sensibilities, and emotional intent inherent in movies created by such artists as John Ford, Howard Hawks, Alfred Hitchcock, George Stevens, William Wyler, John Huston, Frank Capra, Anthony Mann, and hundreds of other filmmakers. Many critics continued in this tradition of showing the way, analyzing, probing, praising, and griping: Pauline Kael, Judith Crist, Roger Ebert, Vincent Canby, Gene Siskel. . . .

Several out-of-print and academic titles have told pieces of the American film critics' story, such as Myron O. Lounsbury's *The Origins of American Film Criticism, 1909–1939*, Stanley Kauffmann and Bruce Henstell's *American Film Criticism: From the Beginnings to Citizen Kane*, Alistair Cooke's *Garbo and the Night Watchmen*, and Edward Murray's *Nine American Film Critics*. These piecemeal, relatively obscure volumes are informational and helpful in telling the whole story, which expanded significantly with the explosion of film culture in the 1960s and 1970s. The advent of television critics, and eventually Internet reviewers, and the concurrent studio efforts to drown the voices of the true critics, then diluted the power and significance of many print film critics in the 1990s.

Dozens of film critics have had their reviews packaged into volumes, notably Pauline Kael, Roger Ebert, Richard Schickel, Dwight Macdonald, Otis Ferguson, John Simon, James Agee, Manny Farber, Andrew Sarris, and Stanley Kauffmann. Book-length studies have been written on certain critics, including Ferguson, Agee, and Bosley Crowther. David Denby, Ebert, and Phillip Lopate independently edited big anthologies that repackaged notable reviews by certain critics.

This book is intended as a narrative history to explain who was who in film criticism, when they wrote, what publications they wrote for, and why these people were important, not just in their day, but also to their venues and outlets, and to film history as well. his book was written as a general, accessible, fact-packed compilation concerning the nature and scope of, and changes and controversies in, film criticism in the United States.

The easy analogy is that this book is a road map to film criticism history. For those who already know a lot about the subject, this book provides chronological perspective and functions as a framework with a continuum of mini-biographies placed within the contexts of their times and movie history.

First and foremost, this book chronicles the important and influential critics throughout the 20th century and into the 21st century. It tells the stories of the creation of such groups as the National Board of Review of Motion Pictures (1909), New York Film Critics Circle (1935), Hollywood Foreign Press Association (1943), National Society of Film Critics (1966), and Los Angeles Film Critics Association (1975), and touches on the many groups that proliferated in the 1990s and beyond.

The book places the important critics writing for big newspapers in certain cities within the context of film criticism's overall history. It covers film critics who became filmmakers (Frank S. Nugent, Quinn Martin, Peter Bogdanovich, Paul Attanasio, Paul Schrader, Rod Lurie, et al.). It details the main critics in the cultural epicenter of New York who presided through the years at *The New York Times*, *New York Herald-Tribune*, and *The New Yorker*, as well as at other significant periodicals.

The critics at *Time* and *Newsweek*, and *The New Republic* and *The Nation*, are covered, as well as those at the significant film journals (*Film Culture*, *Film Heritage*, *Film Quarterly*, etc., and up through the late 20th-century era of *Film Comment*, *American Film*, *Premiere*, and *Movieline*), and also the trade papers, particularly *Daily Variety* and *The Hollywood Reporter*.

The book recalls and illuminates various battles: between auteur theorists and their opposition, as well as between the critics and studios (Judith Crist vs. Twentieth Century-Fox, Joseph McBride vs. Paramount), critics and filmmakers (Kael vs. Orson Welles, Kenneth Turan vs. James Cameron), and critics and themselves (Kael vs. Sarris, Kael vs. Macdonald, Kael vs. Siegfried Kracauer, Kael, et al. vs. Bosley Crowther, John Simon vs. Rex Reed, Simon vs. Charles Champlin, Raymond Carney vs. Vincent Canby, Ebert vs. Richard Corliss, Ebert's love-hate relationship with Gene Siskel), and details the legend of Ms. Kael's devoted "Paulettes."

This book is intended for the more committed moviegoer or passionate movie buff. It is not being written for critics, although many critics could learn their profession's history from this book. It is not being written for the amorphous "industry," although many in Hollywood might understand the role of the critic much better than they had by giving it a read.

While great reference work by Anthony Slide preserved the writings of film critics, scant historical framing of film critics' influence has been written to place them within the context of their times and their publications, and within the scope of film history. No narrative thread pulls together the pioneering talents of the silent era critics (Frank E. Woods, Robert E. Sherwood, Gilbert Seldes) who wrote about D.W. Griffith, Charlie Chaplin, and Mary Pickford, with the significant prewar reviewers (Otis Ferguson, Frank S. Nugent, Cecelia Ager) who examined the Marx Brothers, Frank Capra, and Marlene Dietrich, and the great postwar arbiters (Agee, Farber, Sarris) with their insights into film noir, Alfred Hitchcock, and foreign films.

The arrival of the great age of film criticism in the 1960s included the meteoric rise of Pauline Kael as well as the advent of Judith Crist, Roger Ebert, Stanley Kauffmann, and Richard Schickel, the creation of the National Society of Film Critics and the beginnings of the film critic on television (Crist, Kauffmann, John Simon, Gene Shalit, and Rex Reed). The proliferation of outstanding critics occurred in the 1970s as Hollywood's product also experienced a renaissance from such protean talents as Francis Ford Coppola, Steven Spielberg, and other filmmakers.

Hollywood's attention to the blockbuster syndrome after *Jaws* (1975) produced the critical malaise of the 1980s and 1990s. Sequels, teen films, and copycat films led into the doldrums of the 1990s. The depression over consistently poor movies that found big audiences through saturation marketing—despite critical drubbings—proved time and again that critics had little influence. The studio marketing departments invented and nurtured the "Blurb Mill"—reviewers in marketing departments' pockets. Depression among film critics was expressed by David Denby, Richard Corliss, Peter Rainer, J. Hoberman, Jonathan Rosenbaum, and others.

Film criticism has traditionally been looked upon as an exotic and privileged occupation. Ebert estimated in the 1980s that perhaps 100 people in America made their livings as film critics. A head count in 2009 put the number at about the same. People interested in what Kael or Crist had to say—Canby or Denby, Schickel or Champlin—have usually been short-changed as to their backgrounds, and just why they should sit in judgment. This book attempts to provide some of that information as well. With these mini-biographies, placed within a chronological framework, this book's intent is the biography of a profession.

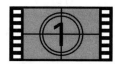

THE BEGINNINGS: THE SILENT ERA

I*he New York Dramatic Mirror* introduced a page dedicated to the moving pictures in May 1908, for which Frank E. Woods solicited advertising and wrote copy. The page became a section, sometimes eight pages in length, into which Woods eventually inserted the column, "Review of Late Films." By 1912, the section included features and Woods embarked on a commentary column, bylined "The Spectator," which often centered on film aesthetics. Even after Woods left the paper in August 1912, *The New York Dramatic Mirror* remained an influential publication, and in 1914 its circulation was reported at 17,500.

Woods was an adman by trade who became fascinated by movies. He is invariably referred to by historians as "probably" the first American film critic. The inexact qualifier is usually added because, due to the dearth of material available on publications of the times, it is difficult to pinpoint exactly who started writing informed criticism first. "He revealed a rare understanding of the creative efforts of early filmmakers and, in particular D.W. Griffith," Eileen Bowser wrote. Woods penned scenarios for the Biograph film company and film producers before becoming a director for Kinemacolor, then for Carl Laemmle's Independent Motion Picture Company.

Woods went to work for Griffith in 1912 and became

general manager and head of the scenario department, a position he held years later at Famous Players-Lasky. Woods eventually was a credited writer on 90 silent films, including Griffith's *The Birth of a Nation* (1915), and was one of the 36 founding members of the Academy of Motion Picture Arts and Sciences. Woods eventually became something that is rarely associated with film critics or most screenwriters along any portion of the movies' continuum: wealthy. Griffith's wife claimed that Woods came to "own" a town near Barstow, California. This was the Mojave Desert hamlet in San Bernardino County known as Lenwood.

Woods exerted some influence on Griffith. In the spring of 1914, when he worked as a scenarist for the Biograph Company, Woods urged the director to read or re-examine *The Clansman*, a novel by Thomas W. Dixon. Griffith had already been aware of the play derived from the novel, but Woods was enthusiastic about transferring the Civil War-era book to the screen. Griffith read the book, formulated his own thoughts, and went on to develop *The Birth of a Nation*. A great advancement in cinema storytelling and action direction, this Civil War-era movie upheld the Ku Klux Klan as a mighty organization of righteousness, and is obscenely racist regarding African Americans. It remains as divisive a great film as the American cinema has ever produced.

"Woods is, indeed, a most problematical figure in Griffith's career," Richard Schickel wrote in his biography of Griffith. "He was a sensible and perceptive critic, perhaps the first more or less responsible journalist to comment more or less responsibly (and regularly) on the developing art of film. As such, his widely read column was largely responsible for spreading the reputation of Biograph films, building up Griffith in the process—a crucial element in the creation of a 'genius,' with immediate benefits and long-term hazards for his subject. Yet Woods might already have been selling scenarios to Griffith, and definitely would be within the year. In short, he had an undeclared interest in puffing Griffith."

Woods probably created a conflict of interest by earning money from Griffith while he was writing about the director for *The New York Dramatic Mirror*, before he went to work
for Griffith. Schickel points out that Woods also wrote as "The
Spectator" these words on Griffith's *The Red Man's View* (1909),
a film about Native Americans: "The injustice that the red race
has suffered at the hands of the white, is held up to our eyes
in convincing picture language, and the conclusion is conveyed
that they are now receiving as wards of the nation only scant and
belated attention." As Schickel wrote: "Curious! Griffith could
sympathize with, and romanticize, a race he did not know, yet
was full of unconscious racism toward blacks, whom he knew
better. Similarly, his critic."

Griffith was the product of a border state, Kentucky, and
born a decade after the Civil War ended. Woods was born the
year before the war started, in 1860, more than 100 miles north
of the Mason-Dixon Line, in Linesville, Pennsylvania. Of Griffith's *His Trust* (1911), The Spectator wrote that the battle scenes
were "managed with a skill that baffles criticism." Historian
Lewis Jacobs claimed that Woods was eventually known as "the
film's major critic. . . . From the outset, Frank Woods impressed
the movie makers: they read his column steadily, respected his
opinions and often acted upon his advice."

As an adman, Woods was at first writing copy that would
draw studio advertising to *The New York Dramatic Mirror*. But
that mission was usurped by an obvious love for film itself and
an investigation of the medium. "What started as an apology
for the film manufacturers became the earliest exploration into
a number of important esthetic and social issues concerning the
motion picture," Myron O. Lounsbury wrote.

The very first instance of The Spectator was published
in *The New York Dramatic Mirror* on May 1, 1909. "Motion
pictures are at least gaining recognition as an institution of immense value to mankind," was Woods's lead sentence to a piece
that set the stage for future columns on the business and art
of motion pictures, and the paper's role in supporting them.

Woods consistently urged filmmakers to upgrade the form. "In his later writing, Woods increasingly considered criticism as a constructive appreciation of new and significant developments in motion picture technique and content," wrote Lounsbury in the seminal 1973 study, *The Origins of American Film Criticism, 1909–1939.*

"Reviewing," Woods wrote, "is not merely finding fault and picking flaws: it is more properly the bestowal of praise where it is deserved—the recognition of merit where it exists."

The style and tone of the unsigned reviews in *The New York Dramatic Mirror* suggest that they were written by the same person who wrote The Spectator. Woods used the column to enlarge on themes that improved the stature of pictures. "Probably the most marked change that has taken place in the style of picture acting in the last year or two has been in the matter of tempo," The Spectator declared on June 4, 1910. "In the old days the pictures were literally 'moving' pictures, and lively moving at that. Everything had to be on the jump.

"The more action that could be crowded into each foot of film the more perfect the picture was supposed to be. Some of this manner of picture acting still survives, usually when an old-timer does the acting or directing, but, generally speaking, it has given place to more deliberation. People in the pictures now move about somewhat after the style of human beings, and not jumping jacks. For all of which let us give due thanks to the special divinity that rules over motion picture affairs.

"One producing company," Woods continued in his admiration of Griffith's production outfit, "the Biograph, was a pioneer among American producers in this reform, and its films have long been distinguished by deliberation and repose, to such an extent that at one time it was a matter of much comment and criticism on the part of those who looked on the innovation as a little short of sacrilege."

While Woods is seen as the first notable individual regularly judging movies for one publication, he didn't write the first review. The first film review in *The New York Times* reported on the first public exhibition of a moving picture at Koster and Bial's Music Hall in New York. The celluloid compendium included images of girls dancing, surf breaking on a beach, and comedians in a boxing match.

The unsigned writer of the April 23, 1896, piece reported "buzzing and roaring heard in the turret and an unusually bright light fell upon the screen." After brief descriptions of the images, he concluded they "were all wonderfully real and singularly exhilarating."

"Film reviewing, like the industry it represented, was in its infancy in these years," wrote historian Anthony Slide in the initial volume of his *Selected Film Criticism* anthology series, *Selected Film Criticism, 1896–1911.* "What passed for a 'review' then might not be considered a review by the standards of the teens or the twenties. Criticism of films was chiefly limited to the film trade papers, such as *The Moving Picture World,* and to the theatrical trade papers, such as *The New York Dramatic Mirror.* The non-trade periodicals paid scant attention to the cinema." *The Readers' Guide to Periodical Literature* during these incubation years also paid little attention to cinema reviews, referencing nearly exclusively feature articles.

Views and Film Index, one of the earliest trade papers, began publication on April 26, 1906, but its "New Films" column of plot synopses didn't become a regular feature until June 16, 1906. Throughout the early silent era, information on new films, usually in the form of brief plot capsules, carried little or no opinions.

Variety, which Sime Silverman began publishing in 1905, started reviewing movies as portions of vaudeville acts in 1907. Except for a gap lasting from March 1911 to January 1913, *Variety* has provided nearly a century of unbroken film reviewing. *Variety* began publishing the section "Moving Picture News and Reviews" in January 1908. Initially edited by Alfred Saunders, the "Moving Picture News" supported the independent companies operating outside New York's mainstream studio system. Saunders left the publication, which tended to not give bylines, in 1912, and the paper's focus became exhibition, coverage of theatres and the films shown in them rather than production. The section merged with *Exhibitors' Times* in 1913 and emerged as *Motion Picture News* and lasted until 1930, edited by William A. Johnston.

The Moving Picture World, which began publishing in March 1907, first printed film criticism on January 18, 1908, in a column called "Our Visits." The *World* "quickly surpassed *Views and Films Index* (which it bought out in 1911) as the most important trade weekly in the industry," wrote historian Richard Abel in *Encyclopedia of Early Cinema*. "The *World* staked out a middle ground between the Motion Picture Patents Company and the Independents."

"Too much credit for the improvement of the movie art cannot be given to the trade paper critics of this period," historian Lewis Jacobs wrote, mentioning W. Stephen Bush, Louis Reeves Harrison, Epes Winthrop Sargent, and Frank E. Woods.

Moving Picture World editor J.P. Chalmers recruited writers Bush, Harrison, Sargent, and Thomas Bedding to contribute reviews and feature articles. The *World*'s circulation reached 15,000 by 1914, but its influence waned in the 1920s, and it ceased publication the following decade. Bush wrote articles and reviews for the *World* from 1908 to 1916, and through most of 1917 served as editor of *Exhibitors Trade Review*. He championed adaptations of the classics to promote lofty aesthetic values and high educational standards.

"The skill of a talented and ardent master of the cinema silent drama is apparent at every turn," wrote Bush in the *World* on March 1, 1913, about *The Prisoner of Zenda*, directed by Edwin S. Porter, who had distinguished himself as the director of the granddaddy western for Edison, *The Great Train Robbery* (1903). "Mr. Porter knew the possibilities of his instrument and made the conquest quite complete. He has disarmed and delighted the most captious critics by the daring but entirely successful use of all those advantages which are peculiar to the motion picture."

Harrison worked for the *World* from 1908 to 1920, writing most of the film reviews, heading a contributors list that included George Blaisdell, James McQuade, and Hanford C. Judson. Historian Madeline F. Matz wrote that Harrison also composed "editorials that exhorted screenwriters to be sensitive to the moods of the public, encouraged cooperation between producer and exhibitor, advised producers to draw on current events for screen material, urged honesty in film criticism, condemned salacious films as pernicious, and celebrated the merits of color photography and sound effects." Harrison also wrote one of the first books about film production and screenwriting, *Screencraft*, published in 1916.

"*Ramona*, as played, is a powerful drama of natural love," Harrison wrote in the *World* of one of D.W. Griffith's first California-lensed films, in 1910. "It is set amid scenes of surpassing beauty, so sympathetically chosen as to lend the whole play a pure spirit of poesy; scene and dramatic art are so harmoniously blended that the picture play is a veritable poem. The producers have advanced a step in the evolution of a new art and blazed the way for additional, greater achievement."

Harrison, like Otis Ferguson two decades later, and few others, realized that the movies were growing up before his eyes, like the cliché of infants who sprout to teens unnoticed by their families. "The new art was without tradition," Harrison wrote in 1913 in *The Moving Picture World*. "None of us could go back to masters of other days and learn the rules of what had never been. . . . No man could look deeply into the subject without realizing that motion pictures were about to become a power in working upon the human spirit and no man of heart would desire that influence to be an evil one." Harrison urged films to take an inspirational role to benefit the human condition: "Let us go deep into the social problems that are deeply affecting us at this moment! Let us probe the ignominy of our political system! Let us search for truth even if it is as deep as a well! For truth is truth to the end of reckoning!"

Epes Winthrop Sargent was a former music and vaudeville reviewer who helped Silverman cofound *Variety* in 1905. He wrote magazine fiction as well and sold stories to film companies. Sargent became the story editor for producer Sigmund "Pop" Lubin in 1909. From 1911 to 1919, Sargent wrote a screenwriting advice column for *Moving Picture World*. His book, *Technique of the Photoplay*, went through three editions (1912, 1913, and 1916). From 1928 to 1938, Sargent wrote film reviews signed "Chic." for his friend Sime Silverman's *Variety*.

Bush, Harrison, Sargent, and Woods found the medium advancing along with their appreciation. In the mid-teens, feature films became a regular reality. "The move to longer films was inevitable," Stanley Kauffmann wrote in 1972. "A confluence of forces brought it about. First, foreign films of one or two reels were having success that showed the public appetite for longer work. Second, the Independent companies, eager to do things differently from the Licensed companies, opted for the longer films that the licensed companies had resisted.

"Third, there was a growing impulse in film artists themselves to burst the twelve-minute bond. Griffith made a few two-reel films toward the end of his Biograph days and, in mutiny against his employers, made one four-reel film, *Judith of Bethulia* [1914]. This outraged the executives, who saw no reason for tampering with a successful formula; so, in order to grow, Griffith left Biograph. (Which soon sank.)

"From the viewpoint of criticism, this general move to the feature film was absolutely crucial," Kauffmann contended in his anthology, *American Film Criticism: From the Beginnings to Citizen Kane*. "Now there was not only more substantial work to write about, it *had* to be written about. The reportorial function of criticism was needed as longer films played longer engagements in any one place; and the evaluative functions had greater play." The success of Erico Guazzoni's European-produced *Quo Vadis?* (1912), which Adolph Zukor imported and exhibited in a dollar-a-head, road-show arrangement, opened the door for features.

Among the more personal industry periodicals of the silent era was *Wid's Films and Film Folk,* first published by Wid Gunning in 1915. It became *Wid's Daily* in 1918. Absent advertising, it sold itself on the basis of Gunning's enthusiastic reviews. Joe Dannenberg assumed the editorship in 1922 and changed the name to *Film Daily,* and *Wid's Yearbook* to *Film Daily Yearbook of Motion Pictures,* which published the names of local newspaper reviewers and contact editors—even in small towns—for industry press agents for decades.

Whereas Gunning's cozy style endorsed a William S. Hart western with, "Tell 'em this is Bill's latest and oil up the ticket machine," other trade organs in the personal vein could be caustic. P.S. Harrison's *Harrison's Reports,* which began publishing in 1919, considered Erich von Stroheim's *Greed* (1924) as "the filthiest, vilest, most putrid picture in the history of the motion picture business."

More professionally polished trade sheets arrived during the Jazz Age. Tamar Lane edited *Film Mercury* from 1924 to 1933. One of film criticism's ancillary missions, to save the memory of box-office failures that paradoxically were worthy films of artistic merit, was part of Lane's modus operandi in the silent era. Victor Seastrom's *The Tower of Lies* (1925) never found wide public acceptance, but Lane felt compelled to characterize it as "one of the finest of the past decade—[it] seems doomed to fade silently into motion picture oblivion, unheralded and unsung." Lane also recognized the technical advances of filmmaking in the service of artistry. Writing in *Film Mercury* about Paul Fejos's *The Last Moment* (1928), which was photographed by Leon Shamroy, Lane pointed out that the film "is composed of a series of camera tricks, camera angles, and various motion picture devices which for completeness and novelty have never before been equaled upon the screen."

The *New York Morning Telegraph* was the first American newspaper to publish a page devoted to motion pictures in its Sunday edition, beginning at the earliest, according to historian Richard Abel, in January 1910. *Morning Telegraph* editor George Terwilliger, who later became a major screenwriter of the silent era, oversaw his paper's 1912 split of vaudeville and motion pictures into their own separate sections. The motion pictures section sometimes ran to eight pages and included reviews, articles, news items, and advertisements. Supporting independent filmmakers, the *Morning Telegraph* reported a circulation of 70,000 in 1914 and, as Abel judged, its Sunday supplement became a weekly source of news for the film industry, and was the "most widely read trade paper, certainly by its core readership of exhibitors."

As a subject for coverage in the first decades of the 20th century, film "proved especially attractive to the more aggressive papers of the day," wrote Richard Koszarski in *An Evening's Entertainment: The Age of the Silent Feature Picture, 1915–1928*. "In this regard it is an unfortunate accident of history that the one newspaper whose film reviews are the most easily accessible, *The New York Times*, was never very interested in motion pictures and gave them extremely low priority through the silent period. . . . The level of criticism in the *Times* was so shallow that many historians, looking here first and assuming that it represented the current journalistic standard, dismiss newspaper reviews of the period out of hand." Myron O. Lounsbury virtually ignored newspapers in *The Origins of American Film Criticism, 1909–1939*, a masterful chronicle of the magazine film critics of that period.

Newspapers' broad market penetration in the years before radio "suggests that their coverage of film was of real significance in shaping the way their readers approached the phenomenon of motion pictures," Koszarski wrote. These early "reviews" consisted mostly of press advance material, few opinions, and, in the manner of the day, few bylines, so that any criticism was generally anonymous.

By the 1920s, when movies became a part of the national leisure fabric, newspapers' criticism amounted to journalistic coverage—getting essentials into the paper. Aesthetics were rarely considered or understood. However, some distinct newspaper voices "used their columns as literary sounding boards for pontificating, amusing, cajoling, or otherwise entertaining their growing readership," Koszarski wrote. He cited W. Ward Marsh of the *Cleveland Plain Dealer*, Harriette Underhill of the *New York Tribune*, Kitty Kelly of the *Chicago Examiner*, and Carl Sandburg, who wrote about the movies from 1920 to 1927 for the *Chicago Daily News* as examples of this journalistic style. Sandburg's impressionistic pieces included interviews with filmmakers and players, often described the filmgoing experience, and the particular theatre.

While the movie business grew ferociously on the West Coast into the 1920s, Harry Carr became an in-town connoisseur of the product. "With *Intolerance*, David Wark Griffith has made his place secure as one of the towering geniuses of the world," Carr wrote in the *Los Angeles Times* in 1916. "As a medium for expressing art, moving pictures may not stand the test of time, but *Intolerance* is greater than any medium. It is one of the mileposts on the long road of art, where painting and sculpture and literature and music go jostling eagerly along together. [*Intolerance* makes *Birth of a Nation*] look like a fishing shack when a dreadnaught sweeps into a harbor."

Carr took note of Charlie Chaplin, writing in 1921 in the *Times*, "To my mind *The Kid* is by long odds the best motion picture comedy ever made. It has more than humor; it has tenderness and literary charm." Carr's boss, *Times* drama critic Edwin Schallert, also marked Chaplin's artistry, writing in 1925, "The first comedy of epic proportions has reached the screen. Charlie Chaplin's *The Gold Rush* sets a pace for length . . . in the blighter sort of entertainment, and although it is not all gay by any means, its premier appeal is for merriment."

Walter Prichard Eaton, drama critic of the *Boston Evening Transcript*, was cited by Lounsbury only because Eaton's articles appeared in *American Magazine*, *Atlantic Monthly*, and other monthly periodicals, and for the fact that Eaton, like George Jean Nathan and others later, appeared to be on a mission to prove the inferiority of movies through his condescending reviews. Eaton was among the drama critics of the day who were convinced that movies were a passing fad.

Like Eaton, several other writers attempted to sort out the meaning of movies and their place in the cultural landscape in the silent era's magazines, particularly Robert Coady, Kenneth Macgowan, Vachel Lindsay, and Gilbert Seldes. Victor Freeburg saw movies as representations of visual beauty and viewed them in terms of composition and other pictorial qualities, much the same way an art critic would consider a painting, often disregarding the actors, actions, and story. Attempts by these various writers to analyze movies and derive and articulate their cultural meaning illustrated the medium as an art form of fascination and organic growth.

Motion Picture Story and *Photoplay*, the first fan magazines, began publishing in 1911. *Motion Picture Classic* arrived in 1915 and *Shadowland* in 1919. Short fiction connected to films, star profiles, and synopses of two-reelers comprised their contents at the outset. James R. Quirk is credited with revising *Photoplay*'s vision when he arrived in 1915 as the publication's vice president.

Quirk hired Julian Johnson as editor, then assumed full control himself in 1920. Quirk eliminated most of the gush from the magazine, and ran it as if it were a balancing act, bringing stars to the public while using film criticism as an educational tool for the industry and the general readership. Johnson, according to Anthony Slide, "introduced criticism to fan magazines" with his "Department of Comment and Criticism of Current Photoplays" in the November 1915 issue of the magazine.

"Depressingly few of those critics who wrote seriously about film in its infancy and adolescence ever had the inclination or opportunity to write films themselves," Richard Corliss wrote in *Talking Pictures: Screenwriters in the American Cinema*. "Julian Johnson, a generous and far-sighted critic for the early *Photoplay*, wrote titles for some of the finest late silent films: *Manhandled, Moana, The Sorrows of Satan, Wings, The Patriot, Beggars of Life, Docks of New York*, and others." Johnson became story editor of Fox and remained with Twentieth Century-Fox, retiring in 1957 as the head of the Story Department. He died in 1965 at age 79.

Johnson and Quirk's efforts launched a major step in film evaluation in the silent era. "The effort toward artistic quality in motion pictures was further quickened by the critical comments of a fan magazine of the day, *Photoplay*," wrote Lewis Jacobs. "Under the [guidance] of James R. Quirk from 1915 on, it praised genuine artistry in films." A typical editorial remarked, "Will you think of your art as a business or your business as an art? Will you say, 'make this picture because it will sell?' or 'make this picture because it deserves to sell?'"

Koszarski claimed that Quirk's standards "were too idiosyncratic for any reader to fully comprehend," and his more infamous reviews included the contention that Erich von Stroheim's *Foolish Wives* (1922) was an "insult to every American." Be that as it may, *Photoplay*'s top writers included the very best of the era, including two who went on to frame early film history with dexterity, Adela Rogers St. Johns, and Terry Ramsaye, who wrote the seminal history, *A Million and One Nights*, published in 1926, the year before the movies started to talk.

The first notable group of movie reviewers was unified against the possible censorship of movies. The National Board of Review of Motion Pictures was founded in 1909 in New York City to protest Mayor George McClellan's revocation of motion picture exhibition licenses on Christmas Eve 1908. The mayor, the son of one-time Union Army chief of staff, General George Brinton McClellan, believed that the new medium degraded the morals of the community. To protest this arbitrary abrogation of constitutional freedoms, theatre owners, including Marcus Loew, and film distributors, including Edison, Pathe, Biograph, and Gaumont, turned to John Collier and Charles Sprague Smith of the People's Institute at the old Cooper Union and established the National Board of Censorship of Motion Picture Shows. Members joining this board included those from the Women's Municipal League, Public Education Association, League for Political Education, Federation of Churches, and the

Association of Motion Picture Exhibitors of New York State.

The joint mission of this collective was to protect children from images in films that might be detrimental to them without restricting what adults could see. This mission corresponded to the goal of the Motion Picture Association of America (MPAA) in the 1960s with its rating system. Lacking power and the will beyond disapproval of salacious films, the group had no clout.

To stave off governmental censorship of films, the committee became an unofficial clearinghouse for judging the merits of movies. In 1915, the group changed its name to the National Board of Review of Motion Pictures. It began giving out awards to films that it felt upheld moral standards. In the late teens, as the motion picture industry gradually relocated to California, the New York-centric NBR lost much of its power, especially after the Hays Office was established in Los Angeles in 1922 by the Motion Picture Producers and Distributors of America (MP-PDA) as an industry-cozy watchdog of motion picture content.

Despite its creation in a no man's land where the pressures came from the film industry seeking growth, respect, and freedom, and the government agencies listening to what might be termed the early 20th century's moral majority, and having its purpose undercut by another office as the lion's share of the business vacated New York, the NBR has lived a long, consistent life. From 1916 into the 1950s, the statement, "Passed by the National Board of Review," became a generally accepted signifier of merit for a picture.

The NBR's activities were the subject of coverage in *The New York Times* and other newspapers, and its publications had influence on filmmakers and filmgoers, including *Film Program* (1917–1926), *Exceptional Photoplays* (1920–1925), *Photoplay Guide to Better Movies* (1924–1926), *National Board of Review Magazine* (1926–1942), and *Films in Review* (1950–present). Contributors to these publications through the years included Alfred Hitchcock, Fritz Lang, Tennessee Williams, Dore Schary, William Saroyan, and Pearl S. Buck.

"In 1929, the NBR was the first group to choose the 10

best English language movies of the year and the best foreign films, and is still the first critical body to announce its annual awards," the NBR's Web site says. *The New York Times* began selecting a world aggregate "10 best" list in 1924. Critics who wrote for NBR publications included Iris Barry, Alfred B. Kuttner, Harry Alan Potamkin, William K. Everson, James Agee, Manny Farber, Alistair Cooke, and the regular reviewer through the Depression Era, James Shelley Hamilton.

"The NBR's two journals made a serious attempt to understand and criticize movies without necessarily hoping they would perform some moral or aesthetic magic on the public," wrote Raymond J. Haberski, Jr., in the 2001 study, *"It's Only a Movie": Films and Critics in American Culture.* "In a world in which aesthetic judgment seemed progressively less important, the NBR had decided to consider popular taste within its cultural criticism. Such an approach would enable the board to deal with the movie industry and the public on their own terms without Progressive Era expectations.

"At the same time, the editors of *EP* and *NBRM* sought to bridge the gap between the art form and the popular movie," Haberski wrote. "The board wanted to explore the possibilities of a movie aesthetic for both popular as well as artistic pictures. Its editors would consider the popularity of a picture as well as its contribution to the technical development of the film. Ultimately, such an approach would make it easier to redefine movies as art and redefine art within mass culture."

Actors and directors of the early silent era weren't acknowledged in reviews. Films carried scant credits, and the studios wanted to avoid having to adjust contracts for the popularity of potential "stars" and the successes of exceptional filmmakers. From the arbiters' theatre seats, there were stark and subtle advancements in quality as well. Anthony Slide noted the "superior quality of the rank reviews published in the early teens by *The New York Dramatic Mirror*, under the guidance of Frank Woods. Another is the excellent work of Frederick James Smith in *Motion Picture Classic*." After a stint with the *New York Dra-*

matic Mirror, Smith joined *Motion Picture Classic* in 1918. "His comments," wrote Slide in 1982, "are probably the closest to those by exponents of current popular film criticism."

Among the reviewers for *The New Republic* in the silent era were Frances Hackett, George Soule, Alfred B. Kuttner, Bruce Bliven, renowned literary critic Edmund Wilson, longtime drama critic Stark Young, and Evelyn Gerstein. Gerstein was the theatre and film critic of the *Boston Herald*, then New York film correspondent for the *Boston Evening Transcript*, and later film editor of *Theatre Guild Magazine*. Critics who occasionally contributed pieces to *The Nation* included Kuttner, Gerstein, and drama critic Joseph Wood Krutch.

Occasionally writing essays on the movies in this period were humorist Ted Shane, who also wrote for *The New Yorker*, as well as drama critic Burns Mantle of the *New York Evening Mail* (1911–1922) and *New York Daily News* (1922–1943), and columnist Heywood Broun, who reviewed D.W. Griffith's *Intolerance* (1916) in the *New York Tribune* by beginning, "David W. Griffith is an immature philosopher, a wrongheaded sociologist, a hazy theologian, a flamboyant historian, but a great movie man. As a picture *Intolerance* is quite the most marvelous thing which has been put on the screen, but as a theory of life it is trite without being true." For openers, Broun cited the film's presentations of lost causes, drinking, juvenile court, and organized charity as being "unduly harsh or incorrectly portrayed."

Trends in reviewing became evident as the teens gave way to the Roaring Twenties. "It is interesting to note that in some publications, such as *The New York Dramatic Mirror*, the quality of the reviews deteriorated as the decade progressed," wrote Slide, a premier scholar of the silent era. "In others, such as *The Moving Picture World* and *Variety*, the standards became higher; *Variety* in particular has grown in strength through the years. The quality in film reviewing in fan magazines reached its zenith about 1919, when one had [Frederick James] Smith in *Motion Picture Classic* and Julian Johnson and Burns Mantle in *Photoplay*, while Adele Whitely Fletcher and Hazel Simpson

Naylor were not doing too bad a job in *Motion Picture Magazine*, and Peter Milne had left *Motion Picture News* to take the critical helm at *Picture-Play*.

"Standards in fan magazine reviewing went slowly downhill in the twenties and have steadily declined," Slide wrote. "As far as the non-film periodicals are concerned, it has been an uphill trend. It could not be much else simply because few general periodicals bothered to recognize the cinema's existence in the teens, let alone to take its product seriously. *Life*, with its occasional film reviews by the drama critic in the late teens, had particularly high standards, which it carried through into the twenties, when Robert E. Sherwood and Robert Benchley were its reviewers. There is no comparison between reviews in, say, *Life* and those mediocre early efforts in *The New York Times*."

Lounsbury pointed out that in the second decade of the 20th century, the greatest body of significant material in film journalism "is discovered on the trade journals and entertainment periodicals, while both the well-established and avant-garde magazines of art, literature and politics exhibit only sporadic enthusiasm for the motion picture. The literature broadens considerably in the twenties: permanent reviewing columns appear for the first time outside the trade press; frequent essays are contributed to the journals of political opinion and to the periodicals of art, literature and the drama. By the ends of the decade, the first specialized magazine of film aesthetics, *Experimental Cinema*, is published.

"In the thirties, the complexion of serious literature changes once again," Lounsbury continued. "The flurry of critical activity in the twenties, found in almost every type of magazine and newspaper, gradually subsides. By the middle thirties, film criticism has become established on a more permanent basis within periodical literature: reviewers now contribute regularly to mass-circulated magazines such as *Esquire*, to the journals of political opinion—*The New Republic*, *Nation*, and *New Masses*—and to the drama magazines, such as *New Theatre*."

But before film criticism became more firmly established

during the Great Depression, when producing movies of escapism was very much on Hollywood's mind, the 1920s found some reviewers in a state of uncertainty. "The optimism and ideals of the pioneer film critics did not survive the war," Lounsbury wrote of World War I, which ended in 1918.

Some film critics were looking for more meat on Hollywood's repetitious bones, more artistic merit in screen stories and treatments. Gilbert Seldes, Alfred B. Kuttner, and Robert E. Sherwood each shared the notion that his own critical vision needed to extend beyond the Hollywood product. Between 1919 and 1924, Lounsbury wrote, "the American critic, dissatisfied with the assembly-line production in Hollywood, examined the nature of the foreign photoplay and re-evaluated the contributions of the native movie pioneers. The encounter with commercialism gave film literature its first international and historical perspective."

After returning from service in World War I, Sherwood secured a job as a rewrite man for *Vanity Fair*. Born on April 4, 1896, in New Rochelle, New York, and educated at Harvard University, Sherwood was a cofounder of the famous Algonquin Hotel Round Table discussion group. He resigned from *Vanity Fair* along with Robert Benchley when Dorothy Parker was fired for writing caustic theatre reviews. This trio of friends was hired within a week at the old *Life*, a former sister publication of the *Lampoon*, and worked together for a decade. Sherwood's first significant job at *Life* was as associate editor of motion-picture criticism.

"In 1920 there were few motion-picture critics and those who were writing did little more than present plot summaries," wrote Sherwood scholar R. Baird Shuman. "However, Sherwood reviewed films critically in terms of the writing, direction, production, and acting."

"Praise is difficult to compose, for it is always easier to be harsh than it is to be ecstatic," Sherwood wrote in *Life* in his review of Rex Ingram's *The Four Horsemen of the Apocalypse* (1921). "The reviewer's task would be much simpler if every movie was of the calibre of Man-Woman-Marriage, for instance. Nevertheless, we have told our story, and we stick to it. *The Four Horsemen of the Apocalypse* is a living, breathing answer to those who still refuse to take motion pictures seriously. Its production lifts the silent drama to an artistic plane that it has never touched before."

Several months later, Sherwood found the Fred Niblo-directed Douglas Fairbanks vehicle *The Three Musketeers* (1921) much to his liking. "In apportioning the praise for the success of *The Three Musketeers*, one is inclined to overlook the fact that a considerable share of the credit belongs to Edward Knoblock, who adapted the story, and has made an intelligent if free translation of Dumas. All things considered, *The Three Musketeers* is the superior of any of the German pictures that have been brought to this country. It ranks with *The Four Horsemen of the Apocalypse* and *The Kid* as one of the great achievements of the movies."

Sherwood's perceptive analyses and articles were soon being printed on the pages of the *New York Herald*, *McCall's*, *Photoplay*, and other magazines. Shuman reported that Sherwood received up to $300 a review. Sherwood was promoted to editor of *Life* in 1924, and was also an editor for Scribner and eventually a speechwriter and advisor to President Franklin D. Roosevelt, as well as a special assistant to the Secretary of War and Secretary of the Navy before and during World War II. In the 1930s, Sherwood shifted his focus to the stage, especially after forging a friendship with playwright Sidney Howard. Sherwood was awarded four Pulitzer Prizes, for the plays *Idiot's Delight* (1936), *Abe Lincoln in Illinois* (1938), and *There Shall Be No Night* (1940), and for the historical biography, *Roosevelt and Hopkins* (1940). He won an Academy Award for adapting MacKinlay Kantor's novel *Glory for Me* into William Wyler's Oscar-winning best picture, *The Best Years of Our Lives* (1946).

"The future of the theatre depends on one consideration," Sherwood wrote after shifting to playwriting, "its ability to give its audiences something which they can't obtain more cheaply and more conveniently, in the neighboring cinema palaces." Sherwood's plays included *Waterloo Bridge* (1930), *Reunion in Vienna* (1931), and *The Petrified Forest* (1935). He died of a heart attack in 1955.

The Art of the Moving Picture by Vachel Lindsay was the first book-length contemplation of film criticism. This 1915 examination of the trade is both an amazingly accurate and absolutely wrongheaded set of analyses and theories about a medium that was rapidly becoming one of the great pastimes, cultural influences, and evolving arts. Lindsay's was the first book to treat the movies as art, formalizing film criticism in appreciation of the films of D.W. Griffith, Cecil B. DeMille and others, equating them with revered museum pieces.

The Art of the Moving Picture was written by a man set in his ways. Lindsay, an Illinois native who died in 1931 in the same Springfield home in which he was born in 1879, was a poet steeped in a strong sense of morality. He studied art in Chicago and traveled widely in the United States as a young man, walking through the Midwest, South, and Southwest. His poetry, which he first published himself, caught the attention of John Dos Passos and included paeans to film stars.

In *The Art of the Moving Picture*, Lindsay comes off as eccentric and bombastic. His insistent prose used literary and biblical references, tossing in the names of great poets, inventors, civilizations, and saints amid stilted comparisons and contrasts. If read aloud, the book would be suitable for a blustery oratory delivered at a chautauqua for the hearing-impaired. The cover photo of the 2000 Modern Library reissue, which depicts the fuzzy image of a man with a megaphone, seems both apt and caustic. Although Lindsay lacks the crankiness of the fictional nabob, Sheridan Whiteside, the intolerant critic at the center of the 1939 George S. Kaufman/Moss Hart play, *The Man Who Came to Dinner*, he offers a similar brand of righteousness. Lindsay's one earthy characteristic, evident almost as asides, was infatuations for screen heroines, particularly Mary Pickford, Lillian Gish, and Mae Marsh.

Lindsay was centrally fixated on a mission to make readers believe that the movies were an honorable gift of art. "I have said that it is a quality, not a defect, of the photoplays that while the actors tend to become types and hieroglyphics and dolls, on the other hand, dolls and hieroglyphics and mechanisms tend to become human," Lindsay wrote. "By an extension of this principle, non-human tones, textures, lines and spaces take on a vitality almost like that of flesh and blood.

"It is partly for this reason that some energy is hereby given to the matter of reinforcing the idea that the people with the proper training to take the higher photoplays in hand are not veteran managers of vaudeville circuits, but rather painters, sculptors and architects, preferably those who are in the flush of their first reputation in these crafts. . . . Let the thesis be here emphasized that the architects, above all, are the men to advance the work of the ultra-creative photoplay."

Had Lindsay's theories been put into practice, Frank Lloyd Wright might have been a founding father of the Directors Guild of America. Some of Lindsay's tangents, which often spring from his theological and patriotic ideals, are pure corn pone. Among his chapters are: "The Motion Picture of Fairy Splendor," "The Motion Picture of Religious Splendor," and "The Substitute for the Saloon."

Lindsay's essays border on the ridiculous from the 21st century view. But as Stanley Kauffmann, the great longtime film critic for *The New Republic*, points out in the introduction to the reissued edition in 2000, Lindsay foresaw film culture, film education, the Hollywood star system, the marketing power of the movies, and, in essence, the auteur theory. "But with all the oddities, the bad guesses, the exaggeration of prose and of bad judgment, the embarrassing touches of a much lesser Whitman, this book is a considerable marvel," Kauffmann wrote.

Lindsay's prescient stab toward the auteur theory came nearly a half century before the French critics firmed it up in *Cahiers du cinéma*. "An artistic photoplay . . . is . . . the product of the creative force of one soul, the flowering of a spirit that has the habit of perpetually renewing itself," Lindsay wrote, even though his auteurs would be taking T-squares and tilted tables behind their Mitchell cameras.

The Art of the Moving Picture can be read the way D.W. Griffith's *The Birth of a Nation* can be viewed—as a huge precedent, but with glaring flaws. *The Art of the Moving Picture* was widely praised. Francis Hackett, the editor of *The New Republic*, concluded his 1915 review of the book by writing, "[Lindsay] has initiated photoplay criticism. That is a big thing to have done, and he has done it, to use his own style, with Action, Intimacy, Friendliness and Splendor."

The second significant book analyzing the influence of the movies was Hugo Münsterberg's 1916 volume, *The Photoplay: A Psychological Study*. The author, a leading intellectual of his time, was a native of Germany who met William James in Paris and later was invited by James to assume the leadership at Harvard University of what was then called the Philosophical Department. Developing theories, writing books, making friends in high circles, including Presidents Woodrow Wilson and Theodore Roosevelt, Münsterberg wasn't drawn to the flickers until 1915, the year before *The Photoplay* was published in April 1916.

Münsterberg saw an exhibition of director Herbert Brenon's *Neptune's Daughter* (1914), starring Australian swimming champion Annette Kellerman. Münsterberg was so taken by Ms. Kellerman's charms that he saw the film many times, circumstances which engaged his thinking about the power of motion pictures. He spent the summer of 1915 in nickelodeons and was entreated to write for the magazine *Paramount Pictograph* by its publisher, Paramount Pictures founder Adolph Zukor. *The Photoplay: A Psychological Study* covered broad territory by explaining the contemporary making of movies, equipment, duties of filmmakers, the depth and emotional force of onscreen images, and the aspects that the individual viewer brings to the motion picture experience: attention span, emotions, memory, and imagination.

"Depth and movement alike come to us in the moving

picture world, not as hard facts, but as a mixture of fact and symbol," Münsterberg wrote. "They are present yet they are not in the things. We invest the impressions with them." Münsterberg arrived at the notion that the viewer's personal experience and psychological involvement commingle with the film's images and ideas, and complete the film experience. Münsterberg emphasized that an artwork may be the product of an artist, but it is also art in the individual perceptions of the viewer. To extend that notion into the discussion of critics, that hypothetic viewer, any viewer, can be his or her own critic, whether that criticism becomes public discourse or not. Part of Münsterberg's thinking emphasized that the work of art, or film in this case, must to some degree replicate reality. But it also must be removed from reality so that it interprets that reality—so that the work can be identified as art.

Münsterberg's book became partially buried with his reputation, which was tarnished by a public relations problem. *The New York Times* labeled him "Dr. Hugo Monsterwork" for his lie-detection methods used in a murder trial. Suffragettes were irked by his opinion that women did not make good jurors. His unsuccessful efforts to be a voice advocating a peaceful solution during World War I was still a Germanic one; meanwhile, the U.S. contemplated the eventual 1917 mobilization that defeated the Hun. Münsterberg was marginalized, even at Harvard. He died eight months after *The Photoplay* was published, in December 1916, during a classroom lecture.

THE SOUND ERA

The movies began to talk in 1927 when Warner Bros. released Alan Crosland's *The Jazz Singer*, a mostly silent film with synchronized sound passages. Al Jolson starred in a Jewish show-business story derived from a Samson Raphaelson play, infamously singing "My Mammy" in blackface and famously declaring, "Wait a minute, wait a minute, you ain't heard nothing yet. Wait a minute, I tell you. You ain't heard nothing yet. Do you want to hear 'Toot, Toot, Tootsie?'" A year later, Bryan Foy's rackets melodrama, *Lights of New York* (1928), became the first "talkie" to use Warner Bros.' Vitaphone Company process developed through Western Electric.

Eventually Fox's Movietone process refined sound recording on film and the movie business went through a sea change. Static cinematography resulted from the bulky soundproof housings needed to suppress the mechanized noises of the cameras. The sound era meant ruined careers for actors whose voices were deemed somehow inappropriate for talkies. Staginess returned as actors spoke whole scenes into fruit bowls and other centerpieces where hidden microphones could record their voices. The import of international films suffered as camera movement and montage regressed while specific language on soundtracks became prerequisite.

"With the arrival of the talking pictures, the pictorial effectiveness, the dynamic movement, the ingenious camera work, the characteristic fade-outs and lap dissolves of the screen, the definite techniques of histrionic pantomime and the ability to range all over the outdoors—all these were lost to the film," wrote film critic Richard Watts, Jr., in the *New York Herald-Tribune*.

Welford Beaton, the editor of the *Film Spectator*, was among the critics who felt that sound was a passing fancy. "It is the fact that the present age is becoming overcanned," Beaton wrote in 1929 in the *Saturday Evening Post*, dismissing sound in all the entertainment media. "We stood for the phonograph and the radio, but talking pictures carry the thing a little too far. Now we are promised television and a third screen dimension. . . . We are never going to be entertained by hearing Jack Barrymore read *Hamlet* to us from one of our living room walls."

Beaton's erroneous contention was more proof that critics usually had no sway against the popular tide. But after he saw *The Jazz Singer*, Beaton changed his tune, writing, "*The Jazz Singer* will have a definite place in screen history and Warner Bros. are to be congratulated upon blazing a trail along which all other producers soon will be traveling." *Film Spectator*, founded by Beaton in Hollywood in 1926, and renamed the *Hollywood Spectator* in 1931, was an attempt to launch a critical journal in the movies' backyard during the years before *Daily Variety* and *The Hollywood Reporter*. In 1972, Stanley Kauffmann judged Beaton's and his contributors' criticism a throwback to the *New York Dramatic Mirror* and *The Moving Picture World*, "where American film criticism had begun: that is, that there was a great consciousness that the trade critic's best way to help the industry was to write the most rigorous and informed criticism that he could, emphasizing expertness about films and studios and picture people, without slavishness to business criteria."

While the sound revolution caught on, America and the world experienced financial doldrums after the Stock Market Crash of October 1929 financially crippled U.S. banks and international trade, putting millions out of work. The international unrest fostered by the Great Depression also coincided with Adolf Hitler's rise in Nazi Germany, and the advent of World War II. Hollywood's product during the 1930s was certainly escapist— characterized by Busby Berkeley's elaborate musicals, tales of the western frontier, and champagne romances in the high tax brackets. But the underbelly of the era was portrayed as well, especially by Warner Bros., in "torn from the headlines" movies about racketeers, fringe operators, and the disenfranchised.

Mervyn LeRoy directed *I Am a Fugitive from a Chain Gang* (1932), while William A. Wellman caught the brutal essence of the Depression-era mood with *Heroes for Sale* (1933) and *Wild Boys of the Road* (1933). Frank Capra tackled the bank-crash catastrophe head-on three years after the fact with *American Madness* (1932), and John Ford crafted the finest film ever made about the Great Depression, *The Grapes of Wrath* (1940), about displaced "Okies" and the disintegrated American dream.

Movies were far from being recognized as the 20th century's most important art form, even as some of the great representatives of film were being rolled out to a mostly undiscerning audience. However, coteries of film fans who saw deeper into the developing movie medium than did the masses became established in some urban areas in the 1920s and 1930s. The "Little Cinema" movement took its general tack from the Little Theatre movement of the 1920s, which rejected melodramas and pageants in favor of plays about individual dilemmas, epitomized by the early work of Eugene O'Neill. While conspiracy theories led to some notions that movies were censored by the influence of the governing aristocracies of the other performance arts—theatre and vaudeville—who were jealous of the explosive growth of the movies, the Little Cinema movement and the aficionados who supported it formed the first vestiges of the cinema's avant-garde. The National Board of Review of Motion Pictures, which in later decades would be considered the musty old guard of film criticism, was at the forefront of promoting pictures of aesthetic merit over the run-of-Hollywood melodramas during the 1920s. The NBR's executive secretary, Wilton Barrett, mulled over art-vs.-commerce arguments at annual meetings and on the pages of NBR's magazine, *Exceptional Photoplays*, which was renamed the *National Board of Review Magazine* in 1926.

"Between 1927 and 1933, short-lived film museums, repertory film theatres, and film lending libraries appeared in Paris, London, Moscow, and New York," wrote Peter Decherney in *Hollywood and the Culture Elite: How the Movies Became American* (2005). "To some extent, these short-lived endeavors followed the international explosion of art cinemas and film journals in the 1920s. In a prescient observation, Gilbert Seldes dubbed the art cinemas of the mid-twenties 'cinema museums,' because they gave life to older or unprofitable films." Critics extolling the Little Cinema movement included Seldes, Alexander Bakshy, Evelyn Gerstein of the *Boston Evening Transcript* and later *Theatre Arts*, and Seymour Stern of the *New York Sun* and *Quill*.

Gerstein consistently expressed dismay at Hollywood's product, often in backhanded style, presaging the anti-studio tenor inherent in critics to come. Sergei Eisenstein's *The Battleship Potemkin* (1926), for instance, was appreciated by her for its merits, which included not being an "anemic and picaresque dumb show patented in Hollywood." The anti-studio bias, so ingrained in film critics by rote in all phases of the sound era, was fully operational before that.

The Museum of Modern Art Film Library was founded with a grant from the Rockefeller Foundation in June 1935 on the recommendation of a special committee of its board, including John D. Rockefeller and John Hay Whitney. Its purpose was to collect all examples of the burgeoning art form, not just those deemed especially of merit, or especially "arty" in one way or another. The Film Library's first curator was Iris Barry, the film critic of the London *Spectator* from 1923 to 1929, and founder of the London Film Society in 1924. Film critic William Troy of *The Nation* was particularly delighted by MoMA's Film Library. "Such academic recognition marked, for Troy, a positive and valuable gain in motion picture prestige," historian Myron O. Lounsbury wrote, especially in light of the anti-intellectualism that Troy perceived as growing during the Depression.

In October 1932, Harvard classmates Julien Levy and Lincoln Kirstein, a future dance impresario and central figure in New York arts circles for several generations, started a film society. At an organizational meeting, Harry Alan Potamkin stood up and, as witnesses recalled, "vehemently urged that we show Communist films and Communist films only." Supporting Potamkin in this endeavor was the young Dwight Macdonald, a political radical who mellowed a little through the years and became *Esquire*'s film critic in the 1960s. Potamkin held little sway this time, but became the all but ordained rabble-rouser among early sound-era critics.

Potamkin, an eccentric Marxist who wrote strikingly informed reviews for small New York-based magazines, was unlike most movie reviewers in the 1930s, who weren't equipped to detect genre gains, artistic leaps, or rudimental technical advances of the medium even as they were thrilled by them or otherwise affected by their seamless incorporations into the filmmaking processes. Almost all reviewers usually just pointed out whether the new Gary Cooper western, Shirley Temple romp, or Fred Astaire/Ginger Rogers whirl was just swell, so-so, or a real stinker. Descriptions of plot developments often made up large portions of "reviews," which were placed in most newspapers near the comics. Movie critics in general weren't considered at all on a par with the critics who covered theatre, books, and art.

Potamkin expressed frustration with the state of his contemporaries in the essay, "Film Novitiates, Etc." in *Close Up* in 1930. Potamkin wrote that film criticism suffered from the presence of "the perennial novice." More than a decade later, in 1942, film critic Otis Ferguson complained in *The New Republic* in "Case of the Critics," that no standard for film criticism had been established or adopted. Potamkin and Ferguson were both singular crusaders for the movie medium and film criticism, but both died young—Potamkin at 33 in 1933 from ulcers, Ferguson at 36 in 1943 from Nazi warplanes—never to see such standards developed. Had they lived long lives, they still wouldn't have witnessed film criticism standards. If their spirits are alive today, they understand that the ghost was given up long ago.

Potamkin's forgotten legacy was resurrected by historian and filmmaker Lewis Jacobs in 1977. Jacobs compiled *The Compound Cinema: The Film Writings of Harry Alan Potamkin*, which was published by Columbia University's Teachers College. Potamkin's essays and critiques in a wide variety of publications—*The Daily Worker, Hound & Horn, Close Up, American Cinematographer, New Freeman, National Board of Review Magazine*—evolved from his impressions in the 1920s of basic movie unity, that a film is created and developed and given emphasis by many people and edited together. But Potamkin felt that the medium itself had to grow. This unity, or "compound cinema," in Potamkin's terms, required evolutionary catalysts to keep it fresh, for which he was always on the lookout. Otherwise, the Hollywood product, Potamkin could see, was repeating itself, forcing "the movie constantly into its simplest form," keeping it "forever simplistic, a lisping, sputtering idiot."

Potamkin wanted to see the medium progress artistically, and emphasized that "intensiveness" went hand in hand with that. The intensiveness was inherent in his own reaction to Carl Theodor Dreyer's *The Passion of Joan of Arc* (1929). As Russell Campbell explained in 1978, progressive for Potamkin meant the dominant ordering of most films, mostly in the Hollywood tradition of sequential time. Intensiveness was the quality of the edited or clustered images, whether or not they corresponded to a plot, time sequence, or Potamkin's notion of "the interferences of theme."

To Potamkin, even the great D.W. Griffith, who had invented the flashback as a narrative film device, had succumbed to the stasis of the Hollywood line of sequential films. "Observe how the American director, including Griffith himself, has relapsed completely into the chronological film," wrote Potamkin, "rather than developed the associative, constructed, back-and-forth reference film." In a later era, Potamkin might have been a fan of writer-director Quentin Tarantino, whose films often move back and forth in time.

Potamkin was born in 1900 in Philadelphia and studied at the University of Pennsylvania and New York University. He wrote poetry, edited a literary magazine, and operated a children's theatre. His twin passions for film and communism, especially in its 1920s framework as an idealistic movement among New York intelligentsia, made Potamkin unique among film critics. "Potamkin's writing . . . came out of a milieu the likes of which has no parallel today," Campbell wrote. "It was a milieu in which the radical critic could be sustained by the actual existence, small but active, of a revolutionary labor movement in the United States."

When Potamkin died in 1933, his body lay in state at the Workers' Center in New York. As Campbell noted, Potamkin was undoubtedly the only U.S. film critic to have been sent off with a Red funeral. "As the thirties progressed, and until his death in 1933, Potamkin's writing in the *New Masses* increasingly assumed the tone of the doctrinaire Communist," Myron O. Lounsbury wrote. Potamkin was also one of the few critics whose political convictions informed his avocations. He contributed "The Aframerican Cinema" to a surprising and enlightened 1929 edition of *Close Up* devoted to "The Negro in the Film." *Close Up* was a short-lived magazine published in Switzerland in English and distributed in New York and London.

In his essay, Potamkin advocated assimilation of African art and dance into films and formulated aesthetic principles for the cinematic treatment of African-American lives, and also surveyed the treatment of blacks in art, literature, and the theatre, recommending Eugene O'Neill's *The Emperor Jones* as film material. (The play was adapted into a United Artists film in 1933 by director Dudley Murphy, starring the actor who helped make it a stage hit, Paul Robeson.)

A progressive thinker on multiple subjects, Potamkin was an anomaly of film criticism as a communist, a crusader on issues of race at a time when such advocacy got people killed, a vital promoter of alternatives for the narrative film, and a minority voice whose emphases occasionally ran contrary to the mainstream—he eventually quibbled in print with Matthew Josephson, Gilbert Seldes, and even his former hero, Alexander Bakshy (over a theory of "dynamics" that didn't include Potamkin's ideas on intensiveness and progressive cinema).

Potamkin's career arc had very little in common with the other notable film critics of his day—if "career arc" could be used regarding critics. Film criticism certainly wasn't established as a firm vocation in the 1930s, and considered barely beyond something in which to dabble. Mainstream newspapers became inured to movie reviews by stringers, copy editors, and society and feature writers. On the bigger papers, these writers only assumed the movie reviewer's post as a place to tread water until a reporter's spot or the drama critic's position became available.

Various writers, artists, critics in other disciplines, and academics saw the medium's enormous potential, but still considered it as a stepchild in American culture. Whatever they had to say about the movies was usually diversionary for them. They rarely brought anything new to the discussion. For most of them, a good movie equaled a good play, and their film reviews might as well have been about the latest theatre piece. They didn't see movies as careful pictorials created and defined by the coordinating intelligence of a director, who coalesced the work of writers, actors, cameramen, set designers, and film editors.

But, then, there were Harry Alan Potamkin, Alexander Bakshy, Gilbert Seldes, Pare Lorentz, Otis Ferguson, and a few others who thoroughly examined the uniqueness of cinema, and grasped its potentialities. They tried their best to explain the movies' effects on them and why those effects were idiosyncratic to the medium. Thus, Potamkin's terms such as "intensiveness" and "compound cinema" illustrated his unique efforts in the language to get his points across to the reader. Not only were these critics persuasive enough to get their general points across about specific films, they were pathfinders for the generations of film critics to come.

"These reviewers, essayists and authors were attempting

to describe and evaluate an aesthetic experience comparatively new to mankind, to answer charges that the motion picture was simply a photographic record of actuality," Lounsbury wrote. "The film critic worked under the assumption that the medium contained artistic elements beyond the mechanical reproduction of dull, literal facts. Each writer sought in his own way to describe the nature of these elements in relationship to music, drama, painting, science, humanitarianism and public taste."

The commonalities between the stage and screen—people acting a story within a frame before your eyes—led to stage-styled criticism moved whole-cloth to the realm of movie criticism. "Analogies between the stage and the screen assume that they deal with the same material. But they don't," wrote Alexander Bakshy, film critic of *The Nation* from 1927 to 1933. "The material of the screen is not actual objects but images fixed on the film. And the very fact that they have their being on film endows these images with properties which are never found in actual objects. For instance, on the stage the actor moves in real space and time. He cannot even cross the room without performing a definite number of movements.

"On the screen an action may be shown only in terminal points with all its intervening moments left out," Bakshy wrote. "Similarly, in watching a performance on the stage the spectator is governed by the actual conditions of space and time. Not so in the case of the movie spectator. Thanks to the moving camera he is able to view the scene from all kinds of angles, leaping from a long-distance view to a close-range inspection of every detail. It is obvious that with this extraordinary power of handling space and time—by elimination and emphasis, according to its dramatic needs—the motion picture can never be content with modeling itself after the stage."

Bakshy, who also wrote drama criticism and translated Russian literature, was one of the first critics to break down the distinctions of cinematic art. Bakshy's importance as a critic wasn't lost on Harry Alan Potamkin. Pointing out Bakshy's early writings about movie pantomime as cinematic rhythm and the medium's use of color tones rather than Technicolor flash, Potamkin declared, "No American has captured in the written word the qualities of cinema so well as has Alexander Bakshy." Bakshy was one of the more progressive cultural critics of the years between world wars, who did his part in easing the movies toward acceptance as an art form. However, he quit film criticism in 1933, fed up with the quality of the movies.

"Not only are there woefully few [films] that are worthy of serious consideration, but if you happen to be a film critic you are obliged to stop and analyze the incessant flow of bilge issuing from the film factories in Hollywood and elsewhere as if it were really to be measured by the standards of intellectual and artistic achievement," Bakshy wrote in his last column in *The Nation*. "The whole procedure becomes unspeakably grotesque, resembling in a way what the Russians describe as shooting sparrows with cannon balls. Worse still, it becomes wearisomely repetitious, for in the films originality is found in virtues, not, as in real life, in sins."

Notable writers on literature and culture who occasionally penned opinion pieces on the movies prior to World War II included Clifton Fadiman, Mark Van Doren, Lincoln Kirstein, Edmund Wilson, Louise Bogan, William Troy, and Paul Goodman. Most of these critics wrote seriously about things other than the movies. Wilson, one of the great essayists in American letters, and a light of *The New Yorker*, famously wrote books on the Russian Revolution and the Dead Sea Scrolls. He was also enamored of Charlie Chaplin's *The Gold Rush*, and wrote one of the seminal essays on the filmmaker in *The New Republic* in 1925.

Bogan was a major poet, and Goodman a noted psychotherapist. Kirstein, an heir to a retail fortune who became a dance impresario, was also a poet and critic, financier, publisher, and theatrical gadfly. He founded the quarterly *The Hound & Horn*, which published from 1927 to 1938, and included pieces by Harry Alan Potamkin and Dwight Macdonald. Kirstein was an editor along with Jay Leyda, Lee Strasberg, Mary Losey, and Robert Stebbins (aka Sidney Meyers) on the short-lived *Films*, published from 1939 to 1940. Van Doren was a novelist, literary critic, and Pulitzer Prize-winner for *Collected Poems* (1939). He wrote major studies on Shakespeare, Nathaniel Hawthorne, and Henry David Thoreau, and served as the literary editor and off-and-on film critic for *The Nation* in the 1920s and 1930s.

William Troy and Van Doren accepted responsibility for film coverage in stints during the Depression for *The Nation*. Neither stayed long in the post and the film criticism they did write is almost forgotten. Stanley Kauffmann and Bruce Henstell compiled a film criticism anthology in 1972 and included a Troy review, but felt compelled to note that "when a selection of William Troy's literary essays was published posthumously in 1967, neither of the eulogists who provided the introductions saw fit to mention that Troy had ever written a line of film criticism." That Troy compilation and homage, *William Troy: Selected Essays*, won the National Book Award.

Some of these writers contributed pieces to the *National Board of Review Magazine*. The National Board of Review of Motion Pictures, which mostly was (and still is) known for publishing the film buff magazine, *Films in Review*, had been publishing lists of recommended films in the periodical since 1920. The first-string reviewer for the magazine was James Shelley Hamilton, but the board was mostly made up of New York society figures. Among its officers were book publisher Robert Giroux, illustrator Lynd Ward and Sigmund Freud's translator, A.A. Brill. The New York-based NBR put out its first top-10 list of best American films in 1929, and the set was comprised of *Applause*, *Broadway*, *Bulldog Drummond*, *The Case of Lena Smith*, *Disraeli*, *Hallelujah!*, *The Letter*, *The Love Parade*, *Paris Bound* and *The Valiant*.

Hamilton succeeded Alfred B. Kuttner as the head of the Exceptional Photoplays Department of the *National Board of Review Magazine*. Hamilton subsequently published many reviews as well as career analyses, particularly of directors Jean Renoir and Ernst Lubitsch. Hamilton had a knack for relating information about exactly why a certain picture was novel, such as one about scientific discovery. "To have taken a life story of this kind, so far removed from the romantic tangles and physical activities of the usual popular entertainment," Hamilton wrote of William Dieterle's *The Story of Louis Pasteur* (1936), "and made it vivid, engrossing and thrilling for the mass audience, is a step that may lead the motion picture along a path some of its best friends have long wished to see it tread."

Hamilton, who was born on January 17, 1884, in Orange, Massachusetts, and died on his Vermont farm in 1953, was a silent-era screenwriter for Pathe, William Fox, and Famous Players-Lasky who also wrote the English titles for V.I. Pudovkin's *Storm Over Asia* (1928) and Aleksandr Dovzhenko's *Arsenal* (1928). Hamilton became a book editor in New York for publisher Appleton, then G.P. Putnam. He had been the drama critic of *Everybody's* and editor of the short-lived *Cinema*. Hamilton was "a man of taste and discrimination, ironical and witty in conversation, and his appetite for films was infinite," Robert Giroux wrote in 1982.

Hamilton was also a clear voice against movies with a homily, a problem he saw in Howard Hawks's *Scarface* (1932): "The only really troublesome weaknesses in the story are in the extraneous moralizing speeches, unexceptionable in their morals but quite out of place in the drama, indubitably thrown in for whatever they might be worth as a 'lesson.' The lesson of such films is never taught by incidental sermons, but by the life we see being lived."

Hamilton wrote the majority of the reviews in the 1930s for the *National Board of Review Magazine*. Richard Griffith succeeded Hamilton as the executive director of the NBR and changed the magazine's format and name to *New Movies*. Shortly thereafter, Griffith succeeded Iris Barry at the Museum of Modern Art's Film Library. The new joint editors for the NBR, Henry Hart, an editor at Scribner's and former editor-in-chief at Putnam, along with Quincy Howe, the news analyst of early television and an editor at Simon & Schuster, inaugurated *Films in Review* in 1950.

The unmitigated movie lovers among the critics of the
1930s—Gilbert Seldes, Pare Lorentz, and Otis Ferguson—maintained lengthy movie-reviewing posts along with their abiding
affections. While Lorentz and Ferguson were both interrupted
by World War II—the former became a colonel in the Army Air
Corps and stopped reviewing, the latter was killed in the Mediterranean—Seldes wasn't stopped on any front. Like Edmund
Wilson and Lincoln Kirstein, he was a high-brow cultural critic
with observations on many arts and venues enough to keep him
busy. These included the monthly "Lively Arts" column in *Esquire*, the film critic's post at *The New Republic*, and columns in
the *Saturday Evening Post* and the *New York Evening Journal*, and
later, TV criticism for the *Saturday Review*.

Seldes was a happy investigator of popular culture. His
enduring classic is *The Seven Lively Arts* (1924), in which he
argued that pop culture forms—comic strips, movies, musical
comedy, vaudeville, radio, popular music, and dance—were as
important as the dramatic theatre. Film critics who would follow Seldes's lead and keep abreast of pop culture, weaving it in
and out of reviews, included James Agee, Manny Farber, Robert
Warshow, and Pauline Kael.

"The motion picture chapters in *The Seven Lively Arts*
embraced almost every type of critical reaction to the Hollywood film of the early twenties," Lounsbury wrote. "The book
condemned the unimaginative display of ostentation encouraged by the movies of Cecil B. De Mille. It regretted the loss of
inventive spontaneity which had established the universal appeal
of the Keystone Kops. It urged the examination of film principles discovered within the German cinema. Although Seldes
did not speak in terms of refinement or pictorial beauty, he did
share with Alfred Kuttner and Robert Sherwood a distaste for
recent trends within the film industry."

If Agee became the Renaissance man of film critics in
America, Seldes was the Renaissance man across the general cultural landscape. As Christopher Berkeley pointed out, Seldes
helped establish T.S. Eliot's *The Waste Land* and James Joyce's

Ulysses in the modernist canon in the 1920s, and in the 1960s wrote a favorable review of *The Beverly Hillbillies* in *TV Guide*.

Seldes's friendships are often mentioned to establish his wide acceptance and influence, and an abridged list includes Ernest Hemingway, Jack Benny, Van Wyck Brooks, Edward R. Murrow, Jimmy Durante, F. Scott Fitzgerald, and Paul Whiteman. If Harry Alan Potamkin might be called the brooding, ultra-intellectual, obscurantist, tragic tortured soul of early film criticism, Seldes was the opposite, the multidimensional, democratic sunshine boy.

"Groucho's is the first voice I have heard from the screen in swift chatter—not as swift, not as crisp as his wisecracking on stage, but better in these respects than all the other deliveries I have encountered." Seldes wrote about the Marx Brothers' first film, Robert Florey and Joseph Santley's *The Cocoanuts* (1929). Seldes, whose books included *The Movies Come from America* (1937), also wrote drama criticism and books about the Great Depression, drinking in America, and World War I. His style was straightforward, accessible, and enthusiastic. Biographer Michael Kammen summed up Seldes as a "vulnerable" critic in *The Lively Arts: Gilbert Seldes and the Transformation of Cultural Criticism in the United States.*

"It seems to me beyond question that in *City Lights* Charlie Chaplin has created one of his masterpieces," Seldes wrote in *The New Republic* in 1931. "I do not know whether to rank it before this or after that; it is a completely organized and a completely created whole which exists for itself without question and without comparison. The immediate effect of the picture is that it is funnier than many things he has done and infinitely inventive; the second effect is that it is magnificently organized, deeply thought out and felt, and communicated with an unflagging energy and a masterly technique. Chaplin is the only artist whose pictures always give the impression of being created before your eyes, with this extraordinary result, that when you see them you cannot believe that they have ever been shown before, and that when you see them a second time you are constantly surprised and elated by their perfection."

Gilbert Vivian Seldes was born on January 3, 1893, and raised in a communitarian atmosphere in Alliance, New Jersey. The younger brother of noted journalist George Seldes, Gilbert attended Harvard College and also became a journalist. After a stint as music critic of the *Philadelphia Evening Ledger* and an editor of *Collier's*, Seldes accepted a Harvard classmate's invitation to edit *The Dial*, one of the enduring "little magazines." These so-called "little" periodicals were usually commercial enough to keep publishing in limited circulation, experimental writings and arts observations with unconventional social ideas and political theories, later identified as literature of the modernist movement. In the Jazz Age, *The Dial* had become a guiding light of the modernist literary tradition. Seldes's editorship at *The Dial* helped establish and strengthen his enthusiasm for pop culture, leading to *The Seven Lively Arts*. He eventually wrote more than 20 books.

For the stage, Seldes adapted Aristophanes' *Lysistrata* in 1930, and it was revived in 1946 with a cast including Violet Kemble-Cooper and Sidney Poitier. In a rather protean collaboration in 1939, Seldes wrote the book for a teaming of Agnes de Mille, Walt Disney, and Benny Goodman on *Swingin' the Dream*, a jazz version of Shakespeare's *A Midsummer Night's Dream* featuring Louis Armstrong and Butterfly McQueen as Puck. A novelist and radio scriptwriter, Seldes also wrote the pioneering how-to book, *Writing for Television* (1952), became the first programming director of CBS Television, and was the founding dean of the Annenberg School for Communication at the University of Pennsylvania. He died in 1970.

"It is surprising that no one has yet pointed out the simple and astounding reason for the success of Mae West in the movies," Seldes wrote in *Esquire*. "In the thousands of columns written about her two things have been said again and again: that she is voluptuous and that she is vulgar, one of which is hardly true, the other hardly important. She has been treated as the 1934 harder, more sophisticated version of the old movie vamp, as if she weren't exactly at the opposite pole, in technique and intent, from the whole Theda Bara school; and the revolution she may cause in the movies' morals and appeal has not yet been suspected, least of all in Hollywood. Miss West constitutes, in my opinion, a threat to the Hepburns, the Crawfords, the Garbos, the Shearers (lumping in these plurals themselves and those who aspire to be like them)." Seldes concluded that, unlike women portrayed in most of Hollywood's chastened product, West portrayed sex as a pleasure, and that was why she was successful. Another critic who found Ms. West a fresh personality during the Depression was Pare Lorentz.

"What most producers will fail to understand," Lorentz cheerfully advised in *Vanity Fair* about Lowell Sherman's Mae West vehicle, *She Done Him Wrong* (1933), "is that this picture is not just smutty, and that, although definitely a burlesque show, it has a certain beery poignancy and, above all, a gusto about it which makes it a good show." Lorentz eventually became a filmmaker himself, a pioneer documentarian in the dexterous use of music and narration, in presenting themes of grand-scale ecology, and in the blending of fact-based dramatizations with other documentary material. While Mervyn LeRoy's *I Am a Fugitive from a Chain Gang* impressed most of Lorentz's cotemporaries with its brutal portrayal of a Southern prison system, he considered it clumsy and peopled with caricatures. "I don't hold with the radical school of critics that indignation *per se* is art," he wrote in *Vanity Fair*. "However, I don't join hands with the arty boys, either, who maintain that all indignation is cheap, inartistic simply because it attempts to grind an ax. Actually, *I Am a Fugitive* is not a moralizing treatise. But you can't see it without feeling that it is a savage document against existing penal systems, nor can you ignore daily evidence that such systems are operating in our great commonwealths every day of the week."

Born Leonard MacTaggart Lorentz in Clarksburg, West Virginia, on December 11, 1905, Lorentz attended Buckhannon High School, West Virginia Wesleyan, and West Virginia University. He adopted his father's first name as his own, and edited *Moonshine*, a humor magazine in Morgantown. He quit school at age 19 to try a journalism career in New York, where he edited the General Electric Company's house organ, then was hired as film critic of *Judge*, a post he held for a decade. He was film critic for the *New York Evening Journal* from 1930 to 1932 and subsequently reviewed for *Vanity Fair, Town & Country*, and *McCall's* while he wrote a political column, "Washington Sideshow," for King Features Syndicate, and scattered short stories and news features to the prevailing periodicals of the day, including *Harper's, Scribner's, Fortune*, and *Story* magazine. He married actress Sally Bates, conned William Randolph Hearst into financing his 1931 European honeymoon, as the story goes, and was eventually fired twice by the newspaper tycoon.

The Roosevelt administration, having assessed Lorentz's book, *The Roosevelt Year* (1933), a photo-history of FDR's first year in the Oval Office, asked him to inject the government's dry filmmaking program with engaging technique. This led to the documentaries *The Plough That Broke the Plains* (1936), about the Depression-era drought in the Midwest; *The River* (1938), about the Mississippi, and *The Fight for Life* (1940), on childbirth in America. A significant critic, Lorentz was also a significant filmmaker. "The documentary films by Pare Lorentz have pointed the way to lyrical blending of narration and music, and to a contrapuntal relation of sound and image," wrote Lewis Jacobs in *The Rise of the American Film*.

Lorentz burned brightly and quickly as both a critic and as a filmmaker. After serving as chief of the U.S. Film Service, he received a presidential appointment to the Army Air Corps, attaining the rank of lieutenant colonel from 1943 to 1946. He was awarded the Legion of Merit in 1945. After the war, he lived what's been described as a quiet life, devoid it seems of any lingering public notoriety or published writings, and died in 1992 in Armonk, New York.

Lorentz adopted a fogey's dissatisfaction early, prior to the war, and lodged this complaint in *McCall's* in 1939: "Youngsters go to the movies when they have nothing else to do. . . .

After fifty years, it is time, not for history, but for an obituary. There never again can be the excitement over movies as there was in the early days because they went with automobiles, electricity, good roads, long-distance telephone, and the general mechanical development of the age."

While in the midst of his reviewing life, Lorentz could not find contemporaries who lived up to his idea of his own calling. "I am constantly amazed by the lack of intelligent, informed writing about motion pictures in this country," he wrote in *Judge* on August 29, 1931. ". . . There are few men working on New York daily papers who have good, critical judgment, but . . . the manifold importance of pictures is reduced by them to casual comment. . . . Outside of New York, I have been unable to find a newspaper movie critic unharnessed by his advertising department." This backhanded libel at the still shaky profession of film critic would be replicated in both the mainstream and entertainment industry press for several generations.

In New York, around the time Lorentz departed for Washington, one contemporary, Otis Ferguson, was gaining headway toward becoming the leading film critic of his time. Lounsbury found it instructive to talk about Otis Ferguson by comparing—for all intents and purposes—the dueling critics on the two deep-discussion newsweeklies of the day, *The Nation* and Ferguson's *The New Republic*.

"Van Doren and Ferguson, the reviewers of the two leading magazines of liberal opinion, differed greatly in their attempts to describe the significance and immediate impact of the film medium in the thirties," Lounsbury wrote in 1973. "Van Doren, although he retained a certain degree of seriousness expressed by his predecessors in *The Nation*, failed to extend the nature of film criticism beyond the prose style found in the typical book review. Rarely did Van Doren's greater preoccupation with the foreign screen, film traditions, and significant literary content enable him to surpass Ferguson's more light-hearted yet perceptive analysis of the movie medium." Andrew Sarris concurred in 1971: "In fact, Ferguson was one of the few professional reviewers of his time with more than a rudimentary interest in the history of the medium."

Ferguson maintained his forum at *The New Republic* by embracing the medium and coaching it, sternly rebuking it when he thought the movies were overly coy, unduly petulant, or trotting out the same song and dance. Writing for *The New Republic* beginning in 1934, Ferguson became a singular light, expressing wit, style, and occasionally not much tolerance for Hollywood studio product. Alexander Korda's landmark British import, *The Private Life of Henry VIII* (1933), transformed Charles Laughton into an international star, especially after he won his Academy Award for best actor as Henry. But Ferguson felt that the film contained "on each inch of celluloid its trademark, which is the word ham."

Like other critics of his day, Ferguson reviewed the stars and the stories on the screen. But he was also predisposed to look into the nature of films and try to understand methods and tricks, the parts of the process that created mood and effects. He was the first long-tenured critic of the sound era about which one could say that when the cinema fascinated him, he was doubly fascinated as to why.

Ferguson was born in Worcester, Massachusetts, in 1907, and worked at odd jobs beginning at age 15, but persisted with studies until he graduated high school. He joined the navy and, after four years, was promoted to seaman first class. He obtained an A.B. from Clark University in Worcester in three years, wrote for the *Clark Quarterly*, and won a writing contest put on by *The New Republic*. In 1934, he wrote his first film reviews for the magazine and a year later became an assistant editor. An avid music fan, Ferguson haunted jazz clubs and became an aficionado of the form, often reviewing the great live entertainers of the day.

After the attack on Pearl Harbor, Ferguson joined the merchant marine. He was eventually assigned to a cargo ship supplying the Allies, which made a run to Archangel, supplying the Soviets via the Barents Sea, and then to the Mediterranean

Theatre. Ferguson was killed in 1943 during the beginnings of the Italian campaign when his ship was bombed in the Bay of Salerno. He was 36.

Long neglected as an influential figure in film criticism, Ferguson's work was resurrected by Robert Wilson through an anthology of his criticism, published in 1971 by Temple University Press. However, Ferguson was a direct influence on the styles and tones of the two film criticism masters of the war years and after, James Agee and Manny Farber. The latter inherited Ferguson's job at *The New Republic*. "Americans seem to have a special aptitude for allowing History to bury the toughest, most authentic native talents," complained Farber in his famous essay, "Underground Films," in which he cited Ferguson first on a list of forgotten artists that included photographer Walker Evans and film producer Val Lewton.

Ferguson's conversational tones, his populist sentiments, and his succinct, punchy writing style established him as a thinking man's proletariat with his cerebral gears usually engaged on the how and the why certain movies worked. He fit his forum, *The New Republic*, as his tone seemed to court cineastes and intellectuals as well as the politically aware and literarily minded casual readers. His opinions were provocatively and often amusingly presented.

Norman Taurog's version of *The Adventures of Tom Sawyer* (1938), which was produced on a large scale by David O. Selznick, moved Ferguson to remark that it "should make Mark Twain circulate in his grave like a trout in a creel." H.C. Potter's *The Cowboy and the Lady* (1938) worked for Ferguson like "just a lot of chestnuts pulled out of other people's dead fires." He gave Fritz Lang some credit for *Western Union* (1941), writing, "It's impossible to know what clichés the director may have prevented, but it is enough and all too much to see those he left in."

Vigilant for cinematic advances, Ferguson pointed out his impressions of these developments as they moved past him. "No one can study the deceptive effortlessness with which one thing leads to another without learning where the true beauty of this medium is to be mined," he wrote, admiring Alfred Hitchcock's *The Lady Vanishes* (1938). The critic tried to enlarge on this notion with his assessment of Hitchcock's *Foreign Correspondent* (1940), writing, "If you have any interest in the true motion or sweep of motion pictures, watching that man work is like listening to music. . . . If you would like a seminar on how to make a movie travel the lightest and fastest way, in a kind of beauty that is peculiar to movies alone, you can see this once, and then again to see what you missed, and then study it twice."

This quest to establish the medium as an art form was later picked up by Agee, whose fervor became a crusade. Ferguson's watch included this evaluation of Frank Lloyd's *Mutiny on the Bounty* (1935): "Incidents are made vivid in terms of the medium—a swish and pistol crack of the lash, the sweating lean bodies, the terrible labor, and the ominous judgment from the quarterdeck." Ferguson was likely as not to identify incremental gains made by the movies in terms of maturation. Carol Reed's *Night Train to Munich* (1940) was a "very nice triumph of skill and maturity in films, and thus a pleasure to have." John Ford's *The Grapes of Wrath* (1940) was for Ferguson "the most mature motion picture that has ever been made, in feeling, in purpose, and in the use of the medium."

Ford had impressed Ferguson on previous occasions. "*The Prisoner of Shark Island* is a powerful film," Ferguson wrote of the 1936 Ford picture about Abraham Lincoln's assassin's physician. It was "rarely false or slow, maintaining the relentless cumulative pressure, the logical fitting of one thing into another, until the audience is included in the movement and carried along with it in some definite emotional life that is peculiar to the art of motion pictures at its best."

Ferguson recognized that film art is based in the primary aspects of dialogue writing, acting, camera framing and camera movement, and film editing. And he felt that the more seamless that these and other ingredients were combined by the director, the more effective any film would be. Ferguson felt that if he could detect showboating in a filmmaker, the less effective the final result would be. Unlike critics who would zero in on directors as distinctive stylists with persistent themes—Von Sternberg and Lubitsch—Ferguson argued that direction should parallel musical composition and should show little or no sign of itself. He praised William Wyler's direction of *The Little Foxes* (1941) for its "omniscience."

Ferguson was a willing participant, ready to be affected by filmmaking techniques, but he didn't want to detect their overt signifiers. The main reason Ferguson felt that Orson Welles's *Citizen Kane* (1941) amounted to "retrogression in film technique" was that it was unnecessarily showy, a movie that brandished technique. "In the line of the narrative film, as developed in all countries but most highly on the West Coast of America, it holds no great place," he wrote of *Citizen Kane*. Ferguson felt that the best films and their makers operated much like magicians and made sure that "the devices for illusion [were] always and necessarily hidden in the natural emergence of the illusion itself." Ferguson was contrary to a point, wanting to be transported by movies into their worlds by methods that did this without revealing themselves, and, at the same time, was utterly fascinated by those same, seemingly magical methods that did so.

Ferguson was often deeply affected by the canvas of particular films, of being overwhelmed or transported into, say, the MGM brand of effusive Americana displayed in Clarence Brown's version of Eugene O'Neill's *Ah, Wilderness!* (1935). "A job of picture making, in craftsmanship and feeling, that is wonderful to see," Ferguson wrote. John Cromwell's *Algiers* (1938) also captivated him: "Few films this season, or any other," Ferguson wrote, "have sustained their mood more brilliantly." If a movie's mood could possess him, he had the talent to convey that to audiences. Sam Wood's version of Thornton Wilder's *Our Town* (1940) moved him to write, "You can nearly smell things cooking, and feel the night air."

In the opening paragraph of his review of Sam Wood's *A Night at the Opera* (1935), Ferguson evinced a range of characteristics that were consistent throughout his career: a sense of humor, appreciation for vitality, references to other films—all expressed engagingly to the reader. His sense of humor was such that he could bear the mundane, the trite, and the outright bunk and not care as long as the way to the mirth or the punch line was spirited and in good fun.

"In terms of rhyme, reason, good taste and formal plot structure, *A Night at the Opera* is a sieve, a leaky ship, and caulked to the guards with hokum," Ferguson wrote in *The New Republic*. "It has three of the Marx Brothers and absolutely no pride. It seems thrown together, made up just as they went along out of everybody's else's own head—it steals sequences from René Clair, it drives off with whole wagonloads of the Keystone lot without so much as putting the fence back up; it has more familiar faces in the way of gags and situations than a college reunion—it has even got a harp-and-piano specialty, which it goes through with dead solemnity for about fifteen minutes. In short, *A Night at the Opera* is a night with the Marx Brothers, who have a zest for clowning and a need to be cockeyed that are either genius or just about enough to fit them all out with numbers and a straight jacket."

For a critic who was so much a lover and supporter of the medium, Ferguson also operated behind one of its all-time fraud detectors. Like Evelyn Gerstein and Harry Alan Potamkin before him, and Manny Farber a generation later, Ferguson was ever suspicious of Hollywood gloss. Ferguson was even more suspicious of the great artist calling foul as a way to gain attention. Critics such as Edmund Wilson and Lincoln Kirstein wrote about Sergei Eisenstein's problems getting his supposedly brilliant documentary, *Que Viva Mexico!* (1932), released. "A way to be a film critic for years was to holler about this rape of great art," Ferguson wrote about *Que Viva Mexico!*, siding with William Troy and others who saw middling merit in the picture, "though it should have taken no more critical equipment than common sense to see that whatever was cut out, its clumping repetitions and lack of film motion could not have been cut in."

Aside from Agee and Farber, other critics have looked

back to Ferguson as the first truly great American film critic, despite those who came before him. "I think a strong claim can be made for Ferguson as the writer of the best and most subtly influential film criticism ever turned out in America," Andrew Sarris wrote in the introduction to Robert Wilson's compilation, calling Ferguson the "one American critic who most closely resembles [André] Bazin," the great French film critic. "No other film critic has come as close as Ferguson to x-raying the connective tissue—physical, visual, soniferous, psychological—that binds isolated images into an organic narrative on the screen. . . . Ferguson was very much in tune with the technocratic spirit of the thirties, and very much in sympathy with the working stiffs who were both the subjects and the labor force of so many movies. His instinctive populism, however, never degenerated into crudity, vulgarity, or philistinism. And he was deadly serious about the craft of film criticism even when he was poking fun at its pedantic excesses."

The notion in film history of 1939 as Hollywood's greatest banner year during the so-called Golden Age of the studios finds no corroboration in a retrospective look back on Ferguson's reviews of the great movies. For MGM in 1939, the great Victor Fleming was the credited director on two of the most enduring masterworks, *Gone with the Wind* and *The Wizard of Oz*.

Of *Gone with the Wind*, Ferguson wrote, "It moves, just as I suspected it would, and it is in color, just as I heard it was, and the Civil War gets very civil indeed and there is a wonderful bonfire . . . young love and balls and plantations and practically everything. . . . They threw in many good things, and everything else but the towel, and they got them in line and added them up to one of the world's imposing cancellations." Ferguson felt that *The Wizard of Oz* had more dead weight than a musical fantasy ought to. "It has dwarfs, music, Technicolor, freak characters, and Judy Garland," he wrote. "It can't be expected to have a sense of humor as well—and as for the light touch of fantasy, it weighs like a pound of fruitcake soaking wet."

The 1939 combination of director Frank Capra and

James Stewart and Jean Arthur in *Mr. Smith Goes to Washington* rankled Ferguson: "[It's] going to be the big movie explosion of the year, and reviewers are going to think twice and think sourly before they'll want to put it down for the clumsy and irritating thing it is," he wrote against the tide of popular sentiment. "Politically, the story is eyewash. . . . One scout leader who knows the Gettysburg address by heart but wouldn't possibly be hired to mow your lawn can throw passionate faith into the balance and by God we've got a fine and free country to live in again."

Ferguson's voice was one of the clearest and most distinct in criticism: He was a man often opposing convention, studio press relations, and an undemanding public who bought tickets to be entertained and emotionally moved at a time when the movies were, by and large, a diversion from problems, or a fun weekly ritual, and not food for thought. His was often a lonely voice.

Ferguson understood the youth of the art he was writing about, and sought to help others comprehend the quick advances in the technology that drove the art. "In their 40-odd years, the movies have developed their high craftsmen, and gradually out of the craftsman's effects, an art," he wrote. "The movies were upon us before anyone had time to grow up and become a professor in them.

"They literally grew out of the people, the hundreds of thousands of people who jumped in to produce, distribute, exhibit, write for, or act in a popular commodity; and the millions and millions whose demand for some kind of excitement or relaxation as available and easy as the funnies, has made the whole sky-high fantasy not only real but inevitable." Anyone can excel, he wrote, "a grip can become Darryl F. Zanuck, a gas jockey can be the next big star."

While the art form was finding boundaries and great practitioners were rising through Hollywood in all the disciplines, Ferguson also was one of the first major film critics to understand that some of these practitioners were expressing themselves within the contexts of melodrama, genres, and on the ragged fringe. In this, he had great kinship to Farber, who later fully comprehended the significance of the American action-genre films, notably westerns and crime films. Clive James connected this influence all the way through to Pauline Kael by using her well-established term "trash" in a definition of Ferguson's understanding.

"Ferguson could see that there was such a thing as a hierarchy of trash," wrote James in *The New York Times* in 2006. "He enjoyed *Lives of a Bengal Lancer* even where it was corny, because the corn ('execrable . . . and I like it') was being dished out with brio. This basic capacity for delight underlay the vigor of his prose when it came to the hierarchy of quality, which he realized had its starting point in the same basement as the trash. A Fred Astaire movie was made on the same bean-counting system as a North-West frontier epic in which dacoits and dervishes lurked treacherously on the back lot, and Astaire wasn't even a star presence compared with a Bengal lancer like Gary Cooper." James quoted Ferguson's assessment of Astaire: "As an actor, he is too much a dancer, tending toward pantomime; and as a dancer he is occasionally too ballroomy. But as a man who can create figures, intricate, unpredictable, constantly varied and yet simple, seemingly effortless . . . he brings the strange high quality of genius to one of the baser and more common arts."

Jonathan Rosenbaum, decades after Ferguson's death, called the *New Republic* critic a "punchy slangmeister" for his appropriation of trendy terms and terse jabs with them— "ballroomy," for instance. Manny Farber would go deeper into jazz-like riffs of his own idiom, pulling sentences occasionally through a Kerouac-like prism, and heaping on the multicolored adjectives and adverbs. But Ferguson was the first notable film critic to not cleave close to Webster's. He also had his favorites, including a preference for Margaret Sullavan vehicles, which Andrew Sarris pointed out. Proclivities aside, Ferguson was the singular stylist of the pre-World War II era to go the deepest into film-craft's direct relationship to what was seen onscreen. Ferguson pushed film criticism further than the rest of his contemporaries, the ones writing accessibly for mass-market periodicals and, presumably, the discerning common man.

In a career roughly parallel to Ferguson's, Meyer Levin reviewed films for *Esquire* from 1933 to 1939. The Chicago-bred author of *The Old Bunch* (1937), *Compulsion* (1956), *The Architect* (1981) and many other novels, Levin served as associate editor of the magazine, which was published and edited as a racy men's magazine in the pre-*Playboy* era by David A. Smart and Arnold Gingrich. Levin's monthly column was "Candid Cameraman," in which he expressed a populist tendency and extolled stories that illuminated the politics of complex contemporary human interactions, in films as varied as Alfred Santell's version of Maxwell Anderson's *Winterset* (1936) and John Ford's *The Informer* (1935). "An exposure of the atrocious social compulsions, created by man's own civilization, which result in the destruction of such good hearts as that of Gyp Nolan must be accepted as within the best uses of human art," Levin wrote about the Ford film.

Smart felt a rivalry with *Time* that was partly based on the publisher's sense that his magazine was too Jewish and that *Time* was the epitome of Waspishness, as detailed by Hugh Merrill in his history of *Esquire*. Smart received Madison Avenue advice to eliminate the Jewish-sounding bylines in his magazine, so "Meyer Levin" was one of the first to go. At the same time, Levin attempted to persuade the *Esquire* office and shop to become members of the Book and Magazine Guild.

Weary of arguing with Smart, Levin quit the magazine in 1939. His final movie review appeared under the byline of "Patterson Murphy." Despite the more pronounced anti-Semitism of the 1920s and 1930s, no one has yet explained the subtle differences of this being perhaps too possibly Irish a byline and less of an off-putting ethno-signifier than Meyer Levin. Levin's final review, of Frank Capra's *Mr. Smith Goes to Washington*, concluded that the film "goes beyond entertainment" and is "a pure lesson in civics" and "it is one of the great triumphs of the democratic method that such a film of self-criticism can be made, and universally shown, in our land." The bitter irony of that assessment by Patterson Murphy needs nothing further. Levin moved on to write many well-received books, and remains an important figure in Judaic American letters.

Other slick magazines began a tradition of film reviewing around the time that the movies began to talk. The first movie reviewed by *The New Yorker* was a silent classic, F.W. Murnau's *The Last Laugh* (1924). The review was by Will Hays, Jr., which appeared in the first issue of the magazine on February 21, 1925, in a column of criticism and celebrity gossip called "Moving Pictures." Hays (not the deviser of the Motion Picture Production Code of ethics, or any relation) deemed the movie "a superb adventure into new phases of film direction . . . a splendid production." Hays wrote four total movie columns for the magazine. The column was also written in the mid- and late 1920s by Theodore Shane (signed "T.S.") and Oliver Claxton ("O.C.").

Occasionally, the reviews ran unsigned. The first long-term reviewer, John C. Mosher, took over in 1928 and held the post until his death in 1942. David Lardner, one of the four renowned literary sons of the great sportswriter and humorist Ring Lardner, succeeded him during the war years when David's son, John Lardner, and the great theatre critic, Wolcott Gibbs, also reviewed films. John McCarten assumed the post as *The New Yorker*'s top critic in 1945 and served to 1960, when Brendan Gill and, briefly and concurrently, Roger Angell, took over the beat.

Mosher was the author of a collection of sketches, *Celibate at Twilight*, and was among the "Talk of the Town" compilers for *The New Yorker*. He had an appreciation of the Marx Brothers, calling *Monkey Business* (1931) "the best the family has given us" upon its release. He complained about drab photography and "shoddy" sets, but found the picture enjoyable, with the brothers' antics ingrained into the story instead of welcomed piecemeal intrusions into "morass."

In a review of Howard Hawks's *Scarface* (1932), Mosher assessed it as a protracted johnny-come-lately in the gangland sweeps: "It has obviously been shaved and trimmed a bit here and there, which you notice at times uncomfortably; although it is unusually long and has so many killings, as it is, you wonder what violence on earth could have been omitted. In general, too, I should say it lacks the brilliance of acting and detail that *The Public Enemy* and *Little Caesar* both had, and that it now seems a sort of resume of all the gunmen pictures we have seen, surpassing the average film of this sort only in the matter of length and the quantity of gore."

Mosher was one of the critics swept up by the originality of Orson Welles's *Citizen Kane* (1941). Welles's well-advertised independence, granted by RKO Radio Pictures to make the movie about a newspaper tycoon, was evident from the opening, which eschewed credits through the revelation of the title character's mysterious utterance, "Rosebud." This independence, Mosher wrote, "like fresh air, sweeps on and on throughout the movie, and in spite of bringing to mind, by elaborately fashioned decoration, a picture as old in movie history as [*The Cabinet of Dr.*] *Caligari*, the irregularity of the opening sets a seal of original craftsmanship on what follows." Mosher declared: "Something new has come to the movie world at last."

Occasional fill-in reviewers during Mosher's tenure at the urbane magazine included E.B. White and Russell Maloney, who, in writing about Victor Fleming's *The Wizard of Oz* (1939), claimed that it "displays no trace of imagination, good taste, or ingenuity. . . . I say it's a stinkeroo. The vulgarity of which I was conscious all through the film is difficult to analyze. Part of it was the raw, eye-straining Technicolor, applied with a complete lack of restraint."

Harold W. Ross, the esteemed founding editor of *The New Yorker*, was one of the most notable early editors to establish ground rules for movie critics' comportment. In fact, he rebuked the magazine's cofounder, Raoul Fleischmann, heir to the yeast fortune, for compromising Mosher's integrity in a 1932 memo. As a standard of journalistic principles as they apply to film criticism, the memo is probably archetypal:

Mr. Fleischmann,

May I respectfully call your attention to the fact that in asking Mr. Mosher to get you an extra ticket for the opening of the movie *Grand Hotel* you violated a very important rule of the office, or two or three. We have a rule, definitely iron-clad, that we do not ask managements for free tickets except for critics or other writers or artists actually on assignment. Everybody in the editorial office has been advised of this, repeatedly if necessary. We frequently ask managements direct for extra tickets, but always insist upon paying for them. . . .

Moreover, I have made a strenuous fight to keep the critics and other writers aloof from the press-agent, ballyhoo, special-favor gang. I have been especially anxious in this respect about the movies department, as it happens, for a systematic and powerful effort is made to bring the movie critics into line. I have repeatedly warned Mosher against falling into a rut. . . . Won't you please help me out . . . by not requesting such favors of writers, as it runs directly counter to my efforts?

Across town, the film coverage of *The New York Times* matured while the self-styled paper of record solidified itself as the be-all and end-all of journalism. The paper's historical coverage of the movies' artistic merits through the latter portions of the century was generally top-notch, and the *Times* has remained a major source on all aspects of industry growth and artistry. But during the silent era, the *Times* treated movies shabbily, if at all.

The variably catalogued and microfilmed newspapers through the century make it impossible to get a sense of film coverage and reviewing styles of many of the main newspaper critics working in the first half of the 20th century. After movie coverage became a regular beat at the *The New York Times* in 1924, the persons assigned the dual roles of motion picture editor and chief film critic were in themselves distinctive and tough to please.

The pioneer, Mordaunt Hall, retired after a decade on the job at age 56 and then came back to journalism on radio, then on another newspaper, and lastly for a press syndicate. His replacement, Andre Sennwald, worked for two years in the job, admirably by all accounts, and then was killed in a gas explosion so powerful it blew out the side wall of his apartment building. The third man, Frank S. Nugent, became such a thorn in Hollywood's side with unfavorable critiques that Twentieth Century-Fox hired him away ostensibly as a screenwriter, effectively eliminating him from what was viewed as the top position in the reviewing ranks. Nugent's replacement, Bosley Crowther, became the longest-serving chief film critic in the paper's history, settling into the post during the World War II years and lasting into the Vietnam War era.

Frederick William Mordaunt Hall, aka Frederick Wentworth Mordaunt Hall, known casually as "Freddie," was the first regularly assigned movie critic for the *Times*, holding the post from October 1924 to September 1934. He was born on November 1, 1878, in Guildford, Surrey, England, the son of a school headmaster in Tottenham. Hall worked extensively on both sides of the Atlantic before and after World War I, during which he was commissioned a lieutenant in the Royal Naval Volunteer Reserve and assigned to intelligence duties. He wrote of his wartime experiences in *Some Naval Yarns* (1917), and remained in the service until 1919.

By this time, Hall, 41, already had worked as an advance agent in 1907 for William Frederick Cody's "Buffalo Bill's Wild West Show." In his eventful year of 1909, Hall joined the staff of the *New York Press*, married Helen Rowe, and was accused, along with another reporter, by Oscar Hammerstein I of assaulting the theatrical impresario outside New York's Hotel Knickerbocker. The charges were dropped when Hammerstein left on a European journey. Hall stayed with the *Press* until 1914, when he jumped to the *New York Herald*.

After the war, Hall wrote inter-titles for films, designing and lettering them with the young Alfred Hitchcock at the Famous Players-Lasky studio in Islington, England. Hall's byline first appeared in *The New York Times* in 1922. After he retired from the *Times* in 1934, Hall hosted a radio program on the movies, and served as drama critic for the *Boston Evening Transcript* from 1936 to 1938. On December 10, 1941, three days after the Japanese bombing of Pearl Harbor, Hall became a U.S. citizen. He worked for CBS Radio in New York in 1942, and later as a copy editor and feature writer for Bell Syndicate, one of the newspaper features suppliers owned by John Neville "Jack" Wheeler, who founded the North American Newspaper Alliance. Hall died in New York City on July 2, 1973, at age 94.

Hall's decade as the film critic for the *Times* was not the career pinnacle that the post became for such successors decades later as Bosley Crowther and Vincent Canby, after film culture deepened in the U.S. But Hall's reviews and reports bridged the silent-to-sound era, and provided an identifiable voice to bring the paper's film coverage out of the wilderness. In 1924, the *Times* published its first 10-best films list: *The Dramatic Life of Abraham Lincoln*, *The Thief of Bagdad*, *Beau Brummel*, *Merton of the Movies*, *The Sea Hawk*, *He Who Gets Slapped*, *The Marriage Circle*, *In Hollywood with Potash and Perlmutter*, *Peter Pan*, and *Isn't Life Wonderful*.

"Although there are several adroitly directed passages in this production," Hall wrote about G.W. Pabst's *Pandora's Box* (1929), starring Louise Brooks as Lulu, a newspaper magnate's consort, "the narrative is seldom interesting. One is not in the least concerned as to what happens to any of the characters whose nonchalance during certain junctures is not a little absurd. . . . Miss Brooks is attractive and she moves her head and eyes at the proper moment, but whether she is endeavoring to express joy, woe, anger or satisfaction it is often difficult to decide."

Chaplin's war film, *The General* (1926), did not seem to

be what Hall expected, either. "The production itself is singularly well mounted, but the fun is not exactly plentiful. . . . Here he is more the acrobat than the clown, and his vehicle might be described as a mixture of cast iron and jelly." If the subtleties of Brooks's interpretation escaped him, and Chaplin was more serious than normal, Hall admired F.W. Murnau's *Sunrise* (1927). "It is filled with intense feeling, and in it is embodied an underlying subtlety . . . exotic in many ways, for it is a mixture of Russian gloom and Berlin brightness." Hall was on solid ground describing Mervyn LeRoy's *Hard to Handle* (1933), starring James Cagney as a publicist: "A violent, slangy, down-to-the pavement affair which has many a mirthful moment."

Sennwald joined the *Times* as a reporter in 1930 and became a film critic in October 1934. Phillip Lopate, in his extensive 2006 anthology, *American Movie Critics*, identified Sennwald as the first daily reviewer at *The New York Times* "with a deep grasp of film culture." Sennwald evinced a liberal posture as well as some of the same social responsibility in his reviews that came to characterize his longest-serving successor, Bosley Crowther. Sennwald was moved by the Depression-era drama of a farm collective, *Our Daily Bread* (1934).

"King Vidor, who gave us *The Crowd* and *Hallelujah*, has plunged his camera boldly into vital American materials in *Our Daily Bread*," Sennwald wrote in 1934. "His new work, which he wrote, produced and financed himself, is a brilliant declaration of faith in the importance of the cinema as a social instrument. In richness of conception alone, Mr. Vidor's attempt to dramatize the history of a subsistence farm for hungry and desperate men from the cities of America would deserve the attention and encouragement of intelligent film-goers. But *Our Daily Bread* is much more than an idea. Standing in the first rank of American film directors, Mr. Vidor has brought the full power of a fine technique and imagination to his theme. *Our Daily Bread* dips into profound and basic problems of our everyday life for its drama, and it emerges as a social document of amazing vitality and emotional impact."

Sennwald pointed out overt racism in films during a time when many critics failed to call it debasing—or call any attention to it whatsoever—upholding it as if it were standard behavior. "The stereotypical treatment of black characters in *The Littlest Rebel* is more offensive than usual," Sennwald wrote of David Butler's 1935 Shirley Temple vehicle, "with 'happy darkies' nervously pondering the prospect of being freed from slavery and shivering in their boots when the Yankees arrive."

A curious macabre fascination with violence in films was expressed by Sennwald in one of his final pieces. The *Times* published his essay, "Gory, Gory Hallelujah," on the cinematic trend toward violence that he found in the midst of the Great Depression. This piece speculated that brutality might be inherent in the national mood. Sennwald described scenes from Frank Lloyd's *Mutiny on the Bounty* (1935), Lloyd Bacon's *Frisco Kid* (1935), Howard Hawks's *Barbary Coast* (1935), Tay Garnett's *China Seas* (1935), and Henry Hathaway's *Lives of a Bengal Lancer* (1935) to illustrate his point. Sennwald wrote of his personal reaction to these scenes: "The result is that I am now . . . striving to convince myself that I am representing a profound universal emotion rather than a private aberration when I gloat lingeringly over these scenes of violence."

Time reported: "The theory that the most noteworthy trend of the cinema in 1935 was towards scenes of 'physical torture and brutality,' and that the trend 'may be related very distinctly to the national state of mind' was suggested last fortnight by Andre Sennwald, brilliant 28-year-old cinema critic of *The New York Times*, in an article called 'Gory, Gory, Hallelujah.' Same day the article appeared, the mangled corpse of Critic Sennwald was discovered in the living room of his penthouse. An explosion was caused by a spark in a gas-filled room in which he had apparently committed suicide." Detectives investigating the death learned that Sennwald may have been losing his eyesight.

"While we were not always in agreements with his comments and contentions, we admired his fascinating style and have quoted him freely in these columns," wrote L.F. Guimond, associate editor of *Boxoffice* magazine. "The death of Andre Sennwald is a distinct loss not only to his thousands of readers, but also to the motion picture industry, because he ranked high among the constructive critics, whose opinions were read and respected by producers seeking to create the type of entertainment which appeals to the majority of theatre-goers."

Frank Stanley Nugent, born on May 27, 1908, in New York City, replaced Sennwald as motion picture editor and chief film critic. Nugent earned a degree in journalism at Columbia University, and in 1929 he joined *The New York Times* as a reporter. He covered, among other events, the Lindbergh baby kidnapping and the trial of Bruno Hauptmann. Nugent worked as a summer replacement on the film beat prior to becoming a film critic under Sennwald in 1934. In the four years in which Nugent was the *Times*'s main film critic, he "became recognized as a leading commentator on the artistic and business aspects of the industry," according to his 1966 obituary in *Variety*. He died at age 57 in December 1965, after suffering a heart seizure following aorta transplant surgery.

"He was known as a tough and demanding critic, one who championed quality and freedom of expression in pictures at a time when sponsor pressures were constant and powerful," the *Variety* obit elaborated. "He had no patience with the potboiler pix Hollywood turned out by the bushel to accommodate the double and triple bills that theatres offered in the Depression Era."

Taking into account Tyrone Power's omnipresence in a string of hits during the late 1930s as one of Twentieth Century-Fox's biggest stars, and not predisposed to see that as a forward development, Nugent reviewed Fox's big production of *The Story of Alexander Graham Bell* (1939), starring Don Ameche, and noted its absence of Power. The prickly Nugent wrote, "If only because it has omitted Tyrone Power, the Twentieth-Fox production . . . at the Roxy, must be considered one of that company's more sober and meritorious contributions to the historical drama."

Both Fox and the Roxy colluded in pulling their advertising from the *Times* for more than six months, meaning more than $50,000 in sure revenue went unearned. The *Times*, interested in keeping Nugent as impartial as possible, didn't tell the critic about the covert financial issue at the time, which also had as an ancillary rift a hiccup in the friendship of *Times* publisher Arthur Ochs Sulzberger and Roxy operator Howard Cullman. It was only later that Sultzberger wrote Nugent a memo that *Variety* described as an enlightening "it might interest you to know."

Nugent recognized the great stride made in the western genre by John Ford's *Stagecoach* (1939), the adaptation by Dudley Nichols of Ernest Haycox's story, "Stage to Lordsburg." Nugent understood the advances that Ford provided in character depth with a game cast of actors and in the action photography by Bert Glennon and Ray Binger to propel forward an adventure journey in a genre that was usually denigrated for its juvenile plots and one-dimensionality.

"In one superbly expansive gesture . . . John Ford has swept aside ten years of artifice and talkie compromise and has made a motion picture that sings a song of camera," Nugent wrote. "It moves, and how beautifully it moves, across the plains of Arizona, skirting the sky-reaching mesas of Monument Valley, beneath the piled-up cloud banks which every photographer dreams about." The story might be familiar, Nugent wrote, but it was Ford's rousing interpretation that made the film great. "His attitude, if it spoke its mind, would be: 'All right, you know what's coming, but have you seen it done like this?' And once you've swallowed your heart again, you'll have to say, 'No, sir! Not like this!'"

Nugent's ecstatic review of *The Grapes of Wrath* is among the most quoted passages on Ford's films: "In the vast library where the celluloid literature of the screen is stored, there is one, small, uncrowded shelf devoted to the cinema's masterworks, to those films which by dignity of theme and excellence of treatment seem to be of enduring artistry. . . . To that shelf of screen classics, Twentieth Century-Fox yesterday added its version of

John Steinbeck's *The Grapes of Wrath*. . . . Direction, when it is as brilliant as Mr. Ford's has been, is easy to recognize, but impossible to describe. . . . *The Grapes of Wrath* is just about as good as any picture has a right to be."

After that review, Nugent was hired by Twentieth Century-Fox as a screenwriter. Back-room wisdom held that Nugent had been bought out of the film review business, his critical voice silenced by industry cash—bigger money than *The New York Times* had to pay. This was identified by Joseph McBride as a "cynical move by Zanuck to get rid of a critic who frequently panned the studio's films," in a footnote to McBride's massive biography, *Searching for John Ford* (2001).

Zanuck offered Nugent less than $1,000 a week, a modest studio screenwriting salary at the time, but nearly three times what the *Times* paid him, according to Nugent's 1966 obituary in *Variety*. "When word got out, critics on both coasts quickly broadcast that the critic was being taken out of circulation by the old 'if you can't fire him, hire him' strategy," *Variety* said, an assumption also printed in the *Times* obit on Nugent. "He was assured by Bill Morris, of the William Morris Agency, and Zanuck that the offer was genuine," *Variety* added.

Before Nugent accepted the job, he discussed the matter with Nunnally Johnson, who had also been a New York newspaperman at the *Brooklyn Daily Eagle* and *New York Herald-Tribune*, before he went to Hollywood. Johnson encouraged Nugent to take the job. Nugent did, and became the highest-profile film critic to not only accept the bigger money in Hollywood but also to work in the art form that he had always appreciated from afar. More critics no doubt envied Nugent than blamed him for such a shift within the writing occupations.

While the motion picture editor's position at the *Times* was assumed by Bosley Crowther in 1940, Nugent spent the next four years under his Fox contract critiquing screenplays. Nugent, who also freelanced articles during his Fox servitude to the *Saturday Evening Post*, *Collier's*, *The New York Times Magazine* and other periodicals, wasn't given the opportunity to write films of his own.

The notion that Zanuck buried Nugent in the script-critiquing post has abided. "That the pix people generally were happy to see Nugent leave the *Times* was no secret, for many regarded him as an assassin," *Variety* judged. Nugent didn't receive a screen credit until Ford surprised him by offering him the opportunity to research and write *Fort Apache* (1948). Eventually, Nugent wrote more sound-era films for Ford, 11, than anyone except Dudley Nichols, who wrote 15. Nugent was Ford's primary screenwriter during the director's autumnal period, comprising the first cavalry trilogy, the evocative portrayals of romanticized Ireland, and his revisionist considerations of a Wild West that he helped invent on the screen.

Nugent's films directed by Ford include five westerns, most importantly *The Searchers* (1956), Ford's enduring masterpiece about embittered racism against Native Americans, specifically John Wayne's Ethan Edwards versus the Comanche during a years-long quest across the Southwest, ostensibly to bring back a kidnapped relative. Adapted from an Alan Le May novel, Nugent's screenplay was named in 2005 as one of the "101 Greatest Screenplays" by the Writers Guild of America. The American Film Institute named *The Searchers* in 2007 as one of the "100 Greatest American Films," and in 2008 the AFI named it the greatest western of all time.

Nugent's other films for Ford are: *3 Godfathers* (1948), *She Wore a Yellow Ribbon* (1949), *Wagon Master* (1950), *The Quiet Man* (1952), *Mister Roberts* (1955), *The Rising of the Moon* (1957), *The Last Hurrah* (1958), *Two Rode Together* (1961), and *Donovan's Reef* (1963). Nugent wrote films for other directors as well, and they include Otto Preminger's *Angel Face* (1952), Raoul Walsh's *The Tall Men* (1955), and pictures for Robert Wise, Stuart Heisler, Phil Karlson, and J. Lee Thompson.

Nugent served as president of the Screen Writers Guild, the forerunner of the Writers Guild of America, from 1957 to 1958. He received an Academy Award nomination for adapting *The Quiet Man* from a Maurice Walsh story and received Screen

Writers Guild Awards for *The Quiet Man* and *Mister Roberts*. Nugent was one of the most successful Hollywood screenwriters, and filmmakers in general, to have first forged a successful career as a film critic. "On the wide horizon of Hollywood history," Richard Corliss wrote in 1973 in his pioneering study of movie writers, *Talking Pictures: Screenwriters in the American Cinema*, "only Nugent's sail stands out among those reviewers who have dared put their critical vision to the test of ungrateful producers and aggrandizing directors." Others have left film criticism, some briefly, for industry jobs—from Frank E. Woods to Rod Lurie—but none established longtime Hollywood success on a scale tantamount to Nugent's.

New York's other great newspaper during the middle 20th century, the *Herald-Tribune*, created a staff position to cover movies the year after the 1924 merger of the Republican-leaning *New York Herald* and the former powerhouse of Horace Greeley in 1800s, the *New York Tribune*. Installed in the newly created post was Richard Watts, Jr., who was born in Parkersburg, West Virginia, in 1898, and studied at Columbia University before joining the *Brooklyn Times* in 1922 as a reporter, then the *Herald-Tribune* in its formative year.

Watts covered the movies for 11 years, or until Percy Hammond retired as the *Herald-Tribune* drama critic in 1936. The natural succession for reporters or critics covering the performing arts in the first half of the 20th century was to aspire to the drama critic's chair or drama editor's position, especially in New York, where Broadway was the cultural cauldron. This was only one reason why the film critic's post at many periodicals changed personnel so often.

Watts was the drama critic from 1936 to 1942 for the *Herald-Tribune* and also served as a war correspondent, covering the Spanish Civil War in 1937 and 1938, as well as World War II, filing from Europe, South America, and the Far East. He worked for the Office of War Information from 1942 to 1944. After the war, Watts resumed drama criticism, this time for the *New York Post*, where he was a mainstay from 1946 until his 1974 retirement, after which he wrote a weekly column for two years. He died of a heart attack in New York in 1981 at the age of 82.

As a movie reviewer, Watts became enamored of the attractive actress that famed Swedish filmmaker Mauritz Stiller brought to America when he accepted an offer by Metro-Goldwyn-Mayer. "In the leading role, Greta Garbo, Swedish screen star, makes her American debut," Watts wrote of Monta Bell's *Torrent* (1926) in the *Herald-Tribune*. "She seems an excellent and attractive actress, with a surprising propensity for looking like Carol Dempster, Norma Talmadge, ZaSu Pitts, and Gloria Swanson in turn. That does not mean she lacks a manner of her own."

Watts followed the Garbo phenomenon as it encountered the sound era, when many silent film idols were falling by the wayside after opinions that their voices somehow detracted from their appeal. "The most eagerly and fearfully awaited cinema event since the talking pictures got into their stride took place yesterday, when the voice of that fascinating, inscrutable, almost legendary personage, Miss Greta Garbo, was heard upon the screen for the first time," Watts wrote in the *Herald-Tribune*. "It is pleasant to report that, in a day when so many tragic blows are being delivered at the prestige of some of the most appalling of film stars, Miss Garbo appears entirely triumphant in her defiance of the microphone."

Watts wrote that Garbo's voice resembled that of Katharine Cornell, one of the era's great Broadway stars. "[Garbo's] voice is revealed as a deep, husky, throaty contralto that possesses every bit of that fabulous, poetic glamour that has made this distant Swedish lady the outstanding performer of the motion picture. There is the vague, intangible, mythical, poetic quality in her tones that only the incomparable Miss Cornell offers upon the stage, and there is combined with it the same strange, paradoxical mood of realism that her stage parallel offers. It is impossible to believe that any Garbo addict will be made unhappy by hearing his heroine speak."

Among the filmmakers championed by Watts was Ernst

Lubitsch, the German-born director of Paramount's early sound-era operettas starring Maurice Chevalier, *The Love Parade* (1929) and *The Smiling Lieutenant* (1931). "All the shrewd delights that were promised in *The Love Parade* all realized with an economy and sureness that give it a luster which no other American-made comedy-satire has achieved," Watts wrote about *The Smiling Lieutenant*. "One must look to *Le Million* to find its peer," he added, citing René Clair's 1931 French-made soufflé for a comparison.

When Watts moved to the drama editor's chair in 1936, he was succeeded as *Herald-Tribune* film critic by Howard Barnes, who had joined the paper in 1929. Barnes was the younger brother of the *Herald-Tribune*'s notable foreign correspondent and foreign editor during and after the war, Joseph Barnes. Howard Barnes shared the film reviewing with Otis L. Guernsey, Jr., through the war years and after. From 1948 to 1951, Barnes was both film and drama critic.

Barnes kept New York abreast of Hollywood's considerations of men in uniform while World War II brewed and erupted. He found Mitchell Leisen's Army Air Corps anthem *I Wanted Wings* (1941) "far more a poster than a drama." But Barnes expressed deep affection for the British naval effort dramatized in Noel Coward and David Lean's directing collaboration, *In Which We Serve* (1942), writing, "Never at any time has there been a reconstruction of human experience that could touch the savage grandeur and compassion of this production."

Barnes could be cynical about Hollywood and yet go overboard for a fantastic deep-sea saga, as two of his reviews of John Wayne movies exhibit. Of Jules Dassin's *Reunion in France* (1943), Barnes remarked of Wayne's costar, "Miss [Joan] Crawford isn't making all of the sacrifices implied in the script. . . . Dressing like a refugee certainly is not in her contract." In his review of Cecil B. DeMille's *Reap the Wild Wind* (1942), which pitted Wayne against a giant squid, Barnes canonized the director's contributions as "the essence of all his experience, the apogee of all his art, and as jamfull a motion picture as has ever played two hours upon the screen."

The Grapes of Wrath touched Barnes the way it did many critics of the day, and he found a means to glom onto its glories in his *Herald-Tribune* review. "A genuinely great motion picture," he wrote, "which makes one proud to even have a small share in the affairs of the cinema."

Theodore Strauss claimed that Barnes had been compromised by Hollywood. A former second-string film critic for *The New York Times* who was later identified by the red-baiting *The Hollywood Reporter* as a communist, Strauss quit the paper in the 1940s to become a screenwriter. "Mr. Barnes's friendships seem to have led him occasionally into undue praise or softened damns, and in recent years his reviews have become increasingly pompous, written with a dean-like resonance that clips off clichés at a monotonous rate," Strauss wrote. "Fuzziness has crept into his reviews which resembles the speech of a man talking without his teeth." Barnes was replaced as the main drama critic on the *Herald-Tribune* by Walter Kerr in 1951, and Otis L. Guernsey, Jr., assumed more control over the film beat around the same time.

The nation's widest-read daily newspaper in the post-World War II era was the *New York Daily News*, with a two and a half million circulation and an estimated six or seven million daily readers. Three "ladies," as they were called, reviewed the movies: Kate Cameron, Wanda Hale, and Dorothy Masters. Cameron was actually the nom de plume for female critics at the *Daily News* after the paper's founder, Captain Joseph Medill Patterson, transferred movie critic Paul Gallico to the sports section in the late 1920s due to consistently unfavorable reviews. "Kate Cameron" put in nearly a half century as the *Daily News*'s lead critic.

Her start also marked one of the first notable episodes of the softening of film-review coverage by a major newspaper. "I think women film critics are more intuitive and understand movies better," Patterson said. According to historian Gerald Peary, "Kate Cameron" was derived from "Camera on!" In a similar manner, the *Chicago Tribune*'s Mae Tinee, derived from "matinee," stood as the pen name of several women film critics in the decades before Gene Siskel's reign.

The first Kate Cameron was Irene Thirer. The second was Thirer's former assistant and Patterson's sister-in-law, Loretta King, who judiciously applied the four-star rating system for films that her paper popularized, and which was adopted decades later by many newspapers as well as cinema guidebooks. As Kate Cameron, King praised Barbara Stanwyck's "charm and earnestness" in George Stevens's *Annie Oakley* (1935), gave three and a half stars to Ernst Lubitsch's comedy *To Be or Not to Be* (1942), and the full four stars to Robert Wise's *The Sand Pebbles* (1966), even though she warned that the Steve McQueen picture about an American gunboat on the Yangtze River in China "has several torture scenes that women will find hard to bear." King's 32 years as Kate Cameron ended in 1967, overlapping Kathleen Carroll's three decades at the newspaper from 1962 to 1992.

Among the other film critics to have presided over the transition from silent pictures into the sound era was Quinn Martin of the *New York World*. He was also one of the first film critics to land a Hollywood job. No relation to the famous television producer of the same name who later worked for Paramount Television, Quinn Martin joined Paramount Pictures in 1931. This was after he lost his job, along with 3,000 others, when Roy Howard of the Scripps-Howard chain bought the *World* from the heirs of Joseph Pulitzer, amortized it, and added its name to his *New York Telegram*, becoming the *New York World-Telegram*.

"The major thrill of this autumn in the cinema has come to town as Eliza, that lorn and harried slave mother, crosses the ice at the Central," Martin wrote of director Harry A. Pollard's sound version of Harriet Beecher Stowe's *Uncle Tom's Cabin* (1927), made in Arkansas by Carl Laemmle's Universal Pictures. "Mr. Laemmle's new film—long in the making and painstakingly pointed in trimmings of menace and sentiment, put together with all the broad, bold strokes which a resourceful and showman-like director could summon—this first movie version of Uncle Tom and Little Eva and Simon Legree appears to be a promising hook upon which the Universal Company may hang high hopes of rich revenue." Like many reviewers, Martin indiscriminately named Laemmle as the film's director, when in fact his role was as the studio head who oversaw the production on an agenda of many films. Pollard directed. Also, like some reviewers of the silent era other than the trade paper reviewers, Martin wrote first of the film's potential monetary gain and secondarily in terms of his view of its aesthetic success. Like many reviewers, Martin's prose read like the Universal company line. "*Uncle Tom's Cabin* is nicely photographed, smartly charged with business designed to sharpen its audience interest, and will, I am confident, prove to be as grand and glorious a show upon the screen as ever it was underneath a tent," Martin wrote.

Unlike the film beat elsewhere, for reporters and critics at the trade papers *Daily Variety* and *The Hollywood Reporter*, covering the movie industry was, and still is, a way of life. The economically worded flip and slangy evaluations of movies in *Variety* were devised to inform the industry quickly about the pictures' economic expectations. *Variety* began publishing film reviews in 1907 and its reviews were at first unsigned, then signed cryptically by the 1930s and after with monikers such as "Mosk," "Tube," "Hift," and "Brog." *Variety*'s critics emphasized the financial potential of films in their capacities to become audience pleasers, and were often blunt and always intent on pointing out the technical aspects, catering as they did to an industry clientele. They also used *Variety*-speak, lingo the trade invented or adopted, such as "hoofology" for dancing, "oater" for western, "moppet" for child, "slugfest" for fight, "warbling" for singing, "thespically" for performance-wise, and so on.

Always on the lookout for big box-office returns, aka "socko b.o.," or "smacko boffo," *Variety*'s critics often reported their impressions of films in dime-novel-like quips. The *Variety* assessment of Ray Enright's *Blondie Johnson* (1933), was: "After she departs for the pen, she lets the public in on the fact that crime doesn't pay. Neither will the picture." The trade paper's readers often followed the clearly described assessments of particular movies' merits in sometimes sing-song terms. William Dieterle's *The Hunchback of Notre Dame* (1939) was a "super thriller-chiller" while Erle C. Kenton's Universal franchise entry *House of Frankenstein* (1944) was a "chiller-diller meller." And Marion Gering's *Rose of the Rancho* (1934) qualified as a "fandango mustang meller . . . a tango version of a bronc opera."

But *Variety* could also be eloquently blunt when the situation called for it, and possessed of a social consciousness. Its reviews could carry a smacko emotional response. The *Variety* critic considering Lewis Milestone's *All Quiet on the Western Front* (1930) was moved to write: "The League of Nations could make no better investment than to buy up the master-print, reproduce it in every language to be shown to every nation every year until the word war is taken out of the dictionary." Of Vincente Minnelli's African American musical *Cabin in the Sky* (1943), the trade looked past potential earnings to opine, "Whatever its box-office fate, [it is] a worthwhile picture for Metro to have made, if only as a step toward Hollywood recognition of the place of the colored man in American life."

In 1933, *Variety* opened an office in Los Angeles, and *Daily Variety* was created to cover the movie business while *Variety* in New York became *Weekly Variety* in name, and still covered the domains of Broadway, radio, and other entertainment forms in the Big Apple. The 1935 headline, "Sticks Nix Hick Pix," is only the most famous example of *Variety*'s idiosyncratically slang approach. Meaning that rural-themed movies weren't doing much business in small towns, the headline was famous enough to have been interpreted onscreen by James Cagney as playwright and impresario George M. Cohan in Michael Curtiz's *Yankee Doodle Dandy* (1942). Among the terms invented by the magazine are "sitcom," "payola," and "striptease."

On September 3, 1930, William R. "Billy" Wilkerson, a Nashville, Tennessee, native who had aspired to the medical field and been wiped out by the 1929 Wall Street crash, founded *The Hollywood Reporter* on a song. Using an outrageous style to gain attention, printing the most scandalous information his report-

ers could confirm on studio figures, Wilkerson devised a must-
read industry hot-sheet. He penned some of the top stories in
his own column, "Tradeviews." By 1936, after warring with the
studios, which tried to shut out his muckraking reporters, Wilkerson prevailed, becoming a powerful figure whose paper was
anticipated beyond Hollywood. President Franklin D. Roosevelt
had his copy flown daily across the country.

Wilkerson used his newspaper's proceeds to become a
nightclub owner, controlling the Café Trocadero and Ciro's on
the Sunset Strip and the Flamingo Hotel in Las Vegas. A notorious gambler, Wilkerson cultivated business relationships
with aviation tycoon and movie producer Howard Hughes and
West Coast racketeer Benjamin "Bugsy" Siegel. With Siegel,
Wilkerson was one of the first entrepreneurs to realize the gambling and entertainment possibilities of Las Vegas. Driven by
virulent anti-communist sentiments during the McCarthy era,
Wilkerson determined that the Screen Writers Guild was hon-
eycombed with "Reds," and was a leading figure in publicizing
the anti-communist witch hunts in Hollywood. The Hollywood
blacklist was often referred to simply as "Billy's list." A heavy
smoker, Wilkerson died of a heart attack in 1962 at his Bel Air
home, after which his fifth wife, Tichi Wilkerson, took over the
editorship of *The Hollywood Reporter*.

During its formative years in the 1930s, *The Hollywood
Reporter* printed a brand of film criticism that lacked the verve
of its rival, *Daily Variety*. Since then, *Daily Variety* and *The Hollywood Reporter* evolved apart together, so to speak, as entertainment industry institutions, lasting longer than most studios,
competing for the industry dollar and readership through editorship changes, and surviving staff defections, corporate reconstitutions, and the myriad industry power shifts on the Hollywood
landscape each year. Without both sheets keeping score, many
so-called insiders would find themselves nearer the outside.

"Howard Hawks has, in *Only Angels Have Wings*, a tremendously engrossing picture," claimed *The Hollywood Reporter*
in a typical 1939 review. "When clipped judiciously to the top of

the bill playing time it will prove topnotch screen fiction of that particular brand which sets up a merry jingle at the cash register. The picture is more than packed with 'atmosphere,' thrills and action, plus a goodly portion of romantic stuff."

Getting a bead on the "romantic stuff" and other things in pictures that appealed to the ladies was Cecelia Ager. She was the first important female film critic to rise from trade paper journalism, recognized as a shrewd judge of Hollywood product, an astute student of developing film art, and a sharp and entertaining writer. Richard Corliss would remark nearly half century after Ager's career that she "established the bright, brittle tone that [Pauline] Kael would later make her own."

Ager transcended the treatment of film criticism by mostly male and sexist newspaper managements as a suitable domain for women—something for them to do along with "sob-sister" columns and the society pages. Sexism in newspapers was a byproduct of the times, when big city editors were almost exclusively male; a rare exception being Agnes Underwood at the *Los Angeles Examiner*. Howard Hawks's prescient *His Girl Friday* (1940), a remake of Lewis Milestone's version of the Ben Hecht-Charles MacArthur play, *The Front Page* (1931), changed the sex of the enterprising reporter, Hildy Johnson, to a woman. As played by Rosalind Russell in one of her finest performances, Hildy was more talented than her competition, as quick on the wisecrack as the boys in the city room, and as tough-minded as her editor.

Ager had not the brass and pluck of Russell's Hildy in the film, according to contemporaries, but she had the style and poise. She was born Cecelia Mayer on January 23, 1902, in Grass Valley, California. She was married to songwriter Milton Ager in a 1924 ceremony presided over by New York mayor Jimmy Walker after a four-month courtship. Milton Ager penned "I'm Nobody's Baby," "Hard Hearted Hannah," "Happy Days Are Here Again" and other tunes.

At a party thrown by singer Sophie Tucker, Cecelia goaded publisher Sime Silverman into providing a woman's voice in

Variety. He hired her in 1933 to report on fashion in films—what actresses were wearing on the screen and who designed the outfits—then to report on and review the films themselves. Cecelia Ager was a monitor of couture in the early decades of celebrity journalism, when columnists such as Hedda Hopper, Louella O. Parsons, and Sheilah Graham covered Hollywood. Ager freelanced stories for *The New York Times*, *Vogue*, and *Harper's Bazaar*, many of them about fashion. After editor Ralph Ingersoll and bankrolling silent partner Marshall Field III launched *PM*, the leftist New York City daily newspaper of the 1940s, Ager was hired as film critic by entertainment editor John T. McManus. She shared the movie reviewing with McManus, who had occasionally reviewed movies for *The New York Times* in the 1930s and had served as motion picture and radio editor of *Time*.

Ager's boss and partner was one of several film critics—Harry Alan Potamkin, Pare Lorentz, and Dwight Macdonald among them—who found politics as much of a vocational pull as pictures. McManus served as the president of the Newspaper Guild of New York from 1943 to 1947, and held several other labor organization posts. McManus ran for governor of New York several times, twice as the candidate of the American Labor Party. He pled the Fifth Amendment right against self-incrimination to questions about the Communist Party before a 1956 U.S. Senate subcommittee investigation into communism in the media. McManus died in 1961.

Ager stayed with *PM* through its 1948 demise, and reviewed for its successor, the *New York Star*, which folded in 1949. One of her daughters was Shana Alexander, the first female reporter and columnist for *Life*. Alexander followed in her mother's journalistic footsteps and later became known as the outspoken liberal advocate facing off weekly against conservative pundit James J. Kilpatrick on CBS's *60 Minutes*. Ager's reviews were known for pithy quips and smooth style. Summing up Orson Welles's *Citizen Kane* (1941), she wrote, "Seeing it, it's as if you never really saw a movie before."

Alistair Cooke took notice. A British-born journalist educated at Harvard and Yale, Cooke had been film critic for the BBC in the 1930s, and reported news as NBC's London correspondent. Later the host of CBS-TV's *Omnibus* and PBS's *Masterpiece Theatre*, Cooke included Ager's writing in his anthology of film criticism, *Garbo and the Night Watchmen* (1937), which highlighted both British and American critics. After the book's publication, Cooke met Ager and later told Alexander his impressions of her mother, which she recounted in the memoir *Happy Days*. Cooke was surprised, he told Alexander, to find her mother "a gentle, reserved woman not given to small talk. What stayed in my memory was the striking contrast between her quiet, almost melancholy manner and the wonderfully cynical brashness of her writing. I had expected a variation on Anita Loos, Dorothy Parker, or at least, Clare Boothe Brokaw (later Luce). They were the female literary gadabouts of the day. By contrast, Cecelia Ager might have been mother superior on her day off."

On the page, Ager was often superior to other critics, but a mother superior she was not, despite the esteemed Cooke's personal assessment. She had a knack for inferring the naughtiness in films in clever passages that worked like conspiratorial asides at cocktail parties. "Except perhaps for the showgirls in a Metro musical, there has never been assembled for one movie a greater and more delightfully varied number of female knockouts," Ager wrote of Howard Hawks's *The Big Sleep* (1946). "But whereas Metro showgirls at least look content, every woman in *The Big Sleep* is feverishly hungry for love . . . and though every one of them would prefer Humphrey Bogart, they settle instantly for anybody."

The smarts and sass that came through in Ager's prose did so from a levelheaded point of view. Her assessment of George Cukor's *Our Betters* (1933), a dalliance in posh surroundings with impeccable people, begins: "Constance Bennett flings herself into the hoity-toity, snobsy-wobsy elegance of *Our Betters* like the prodigal hot-footing it home. . . . She's so sure in her characterization, she makes it practically an autobiography. *Our Betters* is terribly smart, violently upper class. Insistently it shrieks toniness. . . . Miss Bennett wears ropes of black pearls with a dark crepe dress, that's how up in blatant luxury she is. Every detail is so painstakingly indisputable it sets up a positive nostalgia for the other side of the railroad tracks."

With *Daily Variety* and *The Hollywood Reporter* competing for the dollars of entertainment industry workers throughout the Los Angeles area, the *Los Angeles Times* and other newspapers developed entertainment departments as well. Among the staff writers on the *Times* dedicated to reporting on and reviewing the movies were Harry C. Carr and Edwin Schallert in the silent era. Philip K. Scheuer was hired in 1927, and Norbert Lusk also reviewed films. "If there are to be gangster pictures, let them be like *The Public Enemy*, hard-boiled and vindictive almost to the point of burlesque," wrote Edwin Schallert in the *Times*. "There is the scene, for instance, where, irked by his sweetheart, [James Cagney's gangster character] crushes a cantaloupe in her face. An odd variation this of the old pie-throwing gag." Actually, and very famously, the face-massaging fruit was a grapefruit.

Lusk, citing apparently light coffers as a reason to not abide Katharine Hepburn in a screwball comedy, Howard Hawks's *Bringing Up Baby* (1938), wrote, "RKO's mistake in casting Katharine Hepburn in goofy comedy is proved by the poor, single week of *Bringing Up Baby*. It seems that almost any star, including Irene Dunne, Carol Lombard, and Myrna Loy, may attempt antic comedy and make a go of it, but that medium is not for Miss Hepburn in the theater where she is accepted as an important dramatic actress." Schallert acted as the corrective conscience of the paper regarding the Great Kate in his review of *The Philadelphia Story* (1940): "Miss Hepburn, as a comedienne, is perhaps a greater star than she ever was at any prior cinema period, as a serious actress. This comes near being her champion achievement."

The crossing of genre lines was often the only way that pigeonholed talent could make a go of it as an all-around performer. The segregation lines were more pronounced for others in Hollywood. Racism being what it was through the mid-20th century, gains for film criticism in the black community seem to have been minimal, following the general tack of social suppression for black performers in white productions. Moreover, critics such as Harry Alan Potamkin, Peter Noble, Walter White, Hay Chowl, Kenneth MacPherson, and other black and white writers were still dealing with issues of equality in films. Evaluation was yet down the line, even as reporting on entertainers and the arts was on the upswing in the black press, including the *Chicago Defender*, *Amsterdam News* in New York, *Baltimore Afro-American*, *California Eagle*, and the nationally distributed *Pittsburgh Courier*. Historian Donald Bogle cited the efforts of Earl Morris of the *Pittsburgh Courier* and Fay Jackson of the *Los Angeles Sentinel* as significant in terms of gains made by the black press covering entertainment. Morris, as well as actress Hattie McDaniel, successfully campaigned producer David O. Selznick to keep the word "nigger" out of the screenplay of *Gone with the Wind*.

Phillip Lopate's 2006 film criticism anthology, *American Movie Critics*, swung wide to include an assessment of *Gone with the Wind* in the black newspaper the *Washington Tribune* by the African-American poet Melvin B. Tolson. As Clive James wrote in *The New York Times Book Review*, Tolson reviewed the film "in terms that could have been expanded into a handbook for the civil rights movement 20 years before the event. One look at the relevant piece will tell you why a critic has to know about the world as well as the movies: Tolson could see that *GWTW* was well made. But he could also see that the script was a crass and callous rewriting of history, a Klan pamphlet in sugared form, a racial insult."

The first solidarity among film critics occurred in 1935 when the New York Film Critics Circle was formed, comprised of the critics on the city's daily newspapers. Donald Lyons, a *Wall Street Journal* writer, wrote in *Film Comment* more than half a century after the group's formation that it was the "corrective conscience" of the Academy of Motion Picture Arts and

Sciences. A newspaper strike in 1962 forced the group to expand to include magazine critics. Some years later, when *Time* film critic Richard Schickel departed New York for Los Angeles, the NYFCC decided that its geographic fence had to come down.

The Academy Awards, beginning in 1927–28, were initially skewed toward the films released by the two studios that were operated by the Academy's most influential guiding forces, Louis B. Mayer of Metro-Goldwyn-Mayer and Jack L. Warner of Warner Bros. But the New York critics selected John Ford's *The Informer*, released by RKO, for best picture of 1935 while the Oscar went to Frank Lloyd's *Mutiny on the Bounty* (MGM). When the best picture Oscar went to Victor Fleming's *Gone with the Wind* (MGM) in 1939, the NYFCC selected William Wyler's *Wuthering Heights* (Goldwyn). At least in the first four years of the 1940s, the corrective conscience was at work. The best picture selections in those years were: 1940, Alfred Hitchcock's *Rebecca* (Oscar), Ford's *The Grapes of Wrath* (NYFCC); 1941, Ford's *How Green Was My Valley* (Oscar), Orson Welles's *Citizen Kane* (NYFCC); 1942, Wyler's *Mrs. Miniver* (Oscar), David Lean and Noel Coward's *In Which We Serve* (NYFCC); and 1943, Michael Curtiz's *Casablanca* (Oscar), Herman Shumlin's *Watch on the Rhine* (NYFCC).

The NYFCC in the late 1930s and early 1940s included the critics at *The New York Times* and *Herald-Tribune*, Archer Winsten of the *New York Post*, Eileen Creelman of the *New York Sun*, Alton Cook of the *World-Telegram*, Rose Pelswick at the *Journal-American*, Cecelia Ager and John McManus at *PM*, Leo Mishkin at the *Morning Telegraph*, and the all-femme troika of Dorothy Masters, Kate Cameron and Wanda Hale at the *Daily News*.

The NYFCC received awards-season competition from the Hollywood Foreign Press Association, which began awarding the Golden Globes in 1943. Like many members of the National Board of Review, who tended to film culture in New York long after the movie business left for Los Angeles, most of the HFPA constituents couldn't be called film critics. They were often part-time news correspondents working for overseas publications or simply representing their nations.

The first Golden Globe for best picture went to Henry King's *The Song of Bernadette* (1943). But any expectation that the Foreign Press's bid to be another barometer of tastes differing from the Oscars didn't come to pass; the group joined the Hollywood party. The only year in the 1940s when its best picture choice wasn't also awarded the Oscar was 1948, when John Huston's *The Treasure of the Sierra Madre* and Jean Negulesco's *Johnny Belinda* tied for the top honor, and Laurence Olivier's *Hamlet*, Oscar's eventual best picture, was awarded the globe for best foreign film. The Golden Globes were perceived almost immediately as harbingers of Oscars.

The early Golden Globes ceremonies were nothing like the TV extravaganzas that they became in the 21st century. "The only people in the room were a few South American and British journalists and the winners," remembered Angela Lansbury of her Golden Globe for best supporting actress in 1946, for Albert Lewin's *The Picture of Dorian Gray*. "It was a very insignificant group, like a cottage industry, but I, as a young actress, was thrilled to be given anything."

Of the prewar books that called attention to film aesthetics for aficionados and the public at large, Lewis Jacobs's *The Rise of the American Film* (1939) left a lasting impact. Arthur Knight, the great film critic for the *Saturday Review*, called it in 1957, "a detailed, superbly documented history . . . revealing the inter-action between the public, the businessman and the film artist—all set firmly against the economic and social history of the period." Alistair Cooke edited *Garbo and the Night Watchmen*, a 1937 compendium of British and American film criticism by Otis Ferguson, Cecelia Ager, Graham Greene, Meyer Levin, Robert Forsythe, John Marks, Don Herold, and Robert Herring. The book culminated with all nine critics' assessments of Charlie Chaplin's *Modern Times* (1936).

THE POSTWAR ERA

Domestic box-office movie receipts reached an all-time high of $1.5 billion in 1946. Three years later, the take fell off by 70 percent. The generation that had won World War II prospered as auto production and travel within America increased, sports attendance grew, and more disposable income meant that the movies suddenly were no longer America's primary leisure-time activity as the parents of the future "baby boomers" got busy, and suburbia expanded. As the 1950s advanced, television gradually became an essential part of most American lives as an information source and a window to daily and nightly entertainment.

Americans had more choices or learned that they did. Families and businesses, which had survived on patchwork arrangements to get through the Great Depression and then the war years, reestablished senses of normalcy and continuity, themes of strength in the nation's social and economic fabric, even as the ominous Cold War loomed over foreign policy. This continuity became firmly established or renewed for two generations as periodicals re-entrenched in the 1950s along with other businesses. At the midcentury and even decades later into the television age, "the paper" remained either the main or a secondary news source in American lives.

Genuine film criticism appeared in the larger-circulation

dailies, usually written by a regular reviewer. He or she often doubled as the drama editor or drama critic or feature writer. Covering the movies and caring about Hollywood was off the radar of regular newspaper coverage in the 1950s. Most of the smaller and medium-sized U.S. papers used syndicated information from Hollywood in the form of "gossip columns," in many cases, to suffice for their full range of national entertainment coverage, which was usually ghettoized near the amusements page or "funny papers." These columnists included such powerful and long-serving scribes as Sidney Skolsky, who wrote for the *New York Daily News*, then the *New York Daily Mirror*, and, eventually, the *New York Post*, and for 30 years through United Features Syndicate; Hedda Hopper, writing for the Esquire Feature Syndicate in the late 1930s and later the Los Angeles Times Syndicate, and eventually the Chicago Tribune Syndicate; Louella O. Parsons for William Randolph Hearst's *New York American* and Universal News Service; and Sheilah Graham for the North American Newspaper Alliance.

Like such in-town Hollywood columnists as Ezra Goodman at the old *Los Angeles Daily News*, the syndicated columnists often conveyed press-agent material and relied on close relationships with stars' personal press agents and studio public relations departments for tidbits the way news reporters relied on inside sources, often through "legmen" as go-betweens. The business of selling movies relied on selling stars, so the studios and press agents relied on the columnists to convey much of what they wanted. Hollywood reporters such as Bob Thomas for the Associated Press and, later, Vernon Scott for the United Press International wrote lively feature articles and human-interest profiles, but they, like the columnists, felt the studio pressure to give their reporting a positive spin, or at least a light touch.

Thomas called the 1940s the "era of wonderful nonsense." One of Thomas's first stories was to take a tape measure to Warner Bros. to gauge Bette Davis's measurements after she had a baby, because she was to have had the perfect female figure. "Oh, she loved it," Thomas remembered from a 1999 perspective. "Can you imagine doing that with Michelle Pfeiffer today?" Even the news reporters on Hollywood participated in the studio-nurtured coziness.

The only other sources for film information for most newspapers during the midcentury were publicity materials created and sent by the studios in the form of press releases and stills depicting the films. These materials were eventually packaged into essential-sounding "press kits," which were shipped to entertainment editors and departments and film critics. "In volume, such stuff creates a fraudulent and hypnotic haze of mock evaluation, and it is unfortunate that it is circulated so widely," wrote Ernest Callenbach, writing what he termed a "sociological study" on the state of U.S. film journalism in 1951 for the *Hollywood Quarterly*. "The situation assumes importance when we remember that many American filmgoers are reached only by these surreptitious plugs—and the fan magazines." Some two dozen fan magazines included *Photoplay*, *Silver Screen*, and *Modern Screen*.

Information in the form of press materials, stills, and "news" releases of all sorts were scattered by Hollywood to periodicals at a rapid rate. Film criticism could not keep up with the PR machines, and the general assumption from half a century later is that, even if it could, it still wouldn't have made that much difference. The audience wasn't educated to the state of films as an art form. Going to the show at the Stanley or the Rialto or the Loews was a ritual rather than a choice. If the week's pick by a single person, between couples, or for a family outing was a John Wayne western or an Esther Williams escapade, then something different would be offered next week. In the smaller towns with one theatre, the week's movie was often a main conversation piece.

Moreover, the critics didn't have the training, persuasiveness, and knowledge to help the average reader discern what was good or bad, significant or overrated, let alone be a factor in defining an art form. The general opinion of film critics up until the 1960s was that they were, by and large, composers of plot précis with an opinion tacked on, and all with the depth of a loved-her, hated-him quip.

"There is no hope for film reviewing in New York or any place else as it is presently constituted," John Lardner wrote in 1945. "The reviewers and their heirs-apparent of the moment, will never be any better than they are because they have no choice or desire to learn, because they are recruited for every reason but the right one, because film reviewing is regarded in the trade as a spot for a hack or a venial biddy, because practically all the present critics would jump to something else if it looked better—and safe—economically."

Lardner saw the post of film critic from the inside as one of the fraternity, having written movie criticism for *The New Yorker*, and eventually from the outside as the screenwriter of Alexander Hall's *Up Front* (1951) and other films. The son of the great humorist and sportswriter Ring Lardner and brother of the eventual Academy Award-winning screenwriter for *M*A*S*H* (1970), Ring Lardner, Jr., John Lardner was most notable as a sports and at-large columnist and war correspondent for *Newsweek* and the North American Newspaper Alliance.

Lardner advised that groups of screenwriters and film reviewers swap jobs for a year to learn the problems and peculiarities of the other group's working lives. He suggested screenwriters would find that reviewers tend "entirely apart from their qualifications and natural gifts, to grow stagnant, sulky, superficial, pedantic, or a little larcenous around the edges." Furthermore, they would understand the professional hazard of watching dreck day in and day out. "They would see how ordinary or downright bad a year's motion picture product still looks in the total view, how much hack work remains in it today, how much shoddiness, how many clichés.

"In hundreds of cases, perhaps a majority, the platitudinous quality of finished pictures is not their fault, but even so, working in the factory itself, in touch with no other patterns, they become adjusted or resigned and fail to sense completely a condition which smacks the innocent victim between the eyes," Lardner wrote.

With some regular critics ineffectual and the public unresponsive to whatever enlightened or enlightening material was being written about the movies, the studios kept supplying the pictures, even as television viewing replaced much filmgoing, reducing box-office revenues. Moreover, the major Hollywood studios were found guilty by the U.S. Supreme Court of violating antitrust laws in 1948. Their monopolies controlling all aspects of the business were broken, and they were found guilty of price fixing, block booking, and other trade restraints. Paramount Pictures and four other studios were ordered to divest themselves of their theatre chains.

"Whether it is lucky or unlucky—possibly because most of the 100,000,000 people who go to the movies every year either can't read or don't—the critics have a relatively slight effect upon the screen, beyond raising the blood pressure of Hollywood eyes," wrote Richard G. Hubler in 1946. "There is no symptom of an influence comparable to that which the critics of the New York stage now wield. . . . As a result, Hollywood has no mirror. The public is hypnotized so that the box office is useless as a standard. The critics are either scornful or subjugated. . . . This is a ruinous state of affairs for any art," claimed Hubler, the screenwriter of Byron Haskin's *Man-Eater of Kumaon* (1948) and Stuart Heisler's *Beachhead* (1954).

In the newsrooms of the 1930s and 1940s, the editorial managements and staffs treated the flicks like secondary sports coverage—collegiate track and field or industrial league bowling. To newshounds, the Hollywood fluff from Hopper or Parsons about celebrity marriages and new movies deserved to be placed with the crossword puzzle, horoscopes, and "Gasoline Alley." "For every newspaper that doesn't debase its movie pages to the moronic level, there are dozens that do," wrote Robert Shaw in *Screen Writer* in 1945. "[Readers] get trash, boiler plate, press agentry [sic], or the tired and gushing insincerity of overworked reviewers."

On postwar newspapers, the writing and editing posts were resumed by ex-servicemen or maintained by older scribes and 4Fs as lifelong habitats, enduring like jobs at the bank, the insurance broker, and the deep-mining coal company. The continuum in American professional lives had its journalistic dinosaurs, whose longevity was usually conferred with a master's status.

Philip K. Scheuer joined the *Los Angeles Times* in 1927 as an entertainment department jack-of-all-trades. The Newark, New Jersey, native went west as a writer on a movie for which he also was pressed into service as an assistant cameraman to Burnett Guffey, who eventually won Academy Awards as the cinematographer on Fred Zinnemann's *From Here to Eternity* (1953) and Arthur Penn's *Bonnie and Clyde* (1967). The picture Scheuer and Guffey made was never released. The year Scheuer joined the *Times* was the same in which Alan Crosland's *The Jazz Singer*, starring Al Jolson, paved the way for talking pictures to transform the medium.

Scheuer retired as the *Times*'s main film critic in 1967 when marquees boasted *Bonnie and Clyde*, which paved the way for more permissiveness in American films regarding violence. Scheuer became the *Times*'s main film critic in 1958, when Edwin Schallert retired. Schallert, who joined the paper in 1915, left his post as entertainment editor once in 43 years—to fight in World War I.

At the other end of the country, Archer Winsten reviewed movies for a half a century for the *New York Post*. He retired in 1986. Winsten took "a no-nonsense meat and potatoes approach to his work, telling readers what he felt they would want to know in deciding whether they would enjoy a movie and making no effort to assess its artistic merit," wrote Robert McG. Thomas, Jr., in Winsten's 1992 obituary in *The New York Times*. "Indeed, Mr. Winsten detested the term 'critic' and insisted on being called a 'reviewer,' rejected the very notion that motion pictures were some ineffable form of high art rather than a plausible alternative to, say, an evening at the wrestling matches. As a result, Mr. Winsten, who had a special fondness for westerns of the Roy Rogers ilk, concentrated on what he regarded as the substance of a movie, its actual plot and what it had to say, and generally dismissed the stylistic touches that could sometimes move other critics to the point of paroxysm."

In the working-class cities, the efforts to gain and keep a good job were part and parcel of the ingrained culture. Harold V. Cohen joined the *Pittsburgh Post-Gazette* in 1929 and was *Variety*'s reporter in the Steel City for four decades as well as the *Post-Gazette*'s main film critic until his death in 1969. Cohen's cross-town counterpart, Kaspar "Kap" Monahan, joined *The Pittsburgh Press* as entertainment editor from the *Denver Post* in 1932, and remained the main film critic until his retirement in 1967, when Edward L. Blank replaced him. In Cleveland, W. Ward Marsh, once called "the dean of Ohio film critics," joined the *Plain Dealer* in 1915, began reviewing movies after World War I, and wrote 23,000 film reviews, according to *The Encyclopedia of Cleveland History*. He died at 87, less than a year after he stopped reviewing in 1971.

The sense of permanence for newspapermen and newspaperwomen after the war went hand in hand with their role in the establishment and their by-rote adoption of standard American family values. Their newspapers were often among the bedrock establishments of their cities, and they were representative of those institutions. Loretta King wrote reviews for 32 years as "Kate Cameron" of the *New York Daily News*, and Anna Nangle was the *Chicago Tribune*'s "Mae Tinee" in the post-World War II years. Marjorie Adams was a mainstay of levelheaded discernment at the *Boston Globe*, who was dubbed "the queen of the pack" by Kay Bourne, the arts editor of the *Bay State Banner* for four decades. Adams was also called the "prototype" of the "Boston Bloomer Girls," the mostly female midcentury movie press corps in Boston.

Sam Lesner of the *Chicago Daily News* covered movies and nightclubs in a nearly 50-year career, paralleling the Chicago newspaper era of columnists Mike Royko and Irv Kupcinet. An aspiring opera singer in his youth who took a clerk's job at the *Daily News* to pay for classes at the Chicago Conservatory of Music, Lesner never left the paper. He developed a Rat Pack-brand of toss-off vernacular that could consider Barbra Streisand a "kook" who was a "cross between a sweet-voiced canary and a whooping crane," and figure Stanley Kubrick "flipped his lid" by directing *2001: A Space Odyssey* (1968)—until he saw it a second time and found it a masterpiece.

Doris Arden of the *Chicago Sun-Times* and Ann Marsters of *Chicago's American* (and then *Herald-American*) shared Windy City cultural coverage with Lesner. Each became annoyed at particular Billy Wilder films. "If you wish to see how far Hollywood can sink in mental and spiritual decay for a buck, *Sunset Boulevard* is your source of study," Arden wrote in 1950. "[It is] a sordid melodrama so extravagantly and disjointedly put together that you have the feeling it was turned out by a dozen different authors working independently of each other in a psychopathic ward. . . . Miss Swanson as Norma Desmond emotes all over the lot—to the point where you yourself feel like screaming. . . . Frankly, as we watched Miss Swanson gild this dilly (a burping brain child of the otherwise capable Billy Wilder), we found ourselves asking: How mad can you get working over a script or a cash register?"

A decade later, Wilder won Academy Awards for writing, directing, and producing the best picture, *The Apartment* (1960), about New York executives who stash their building's elevator operator (Shirley MacLaine) in the title flat for sexual sharing. Marsters, a former sports writer for the *Boston American* who eventually wrote the lyrics for "Chicago, the Most Beautiful City," went so far as to reportedly protest to Wilder in person that he had made "a dirty film."

While many critics didn't respect loosening morality in films, they themselves were occasionally disrespected as the specific post of film critic itself was impugned. What little that was written about the profession in the immediate postwar era was almost all derogatory.

"We were and are the bastards in the field of criticism," W. Ward Marsh wrote. "We have no background; that is, ancestry . . . and we are loved when we praise, hated when we damn. Too often we have been the stepchildren not only of the film industry but also of the newspaper we represent. In many instances, we, as individuals, have failed to make good in other departments and have been relegated to the movie reviewing chair where we are torn between the demands of sensitive theater managements and an editor who knows that only advertising will keep him alive." Marsh claimed that he was never pressured by the *Plain Dealer* management to soften his reviews for the paper to cater to studio or theatre advertisers.

The general feeling in Hollywood was that film critics didn't understand films and filmmaking. The misunderstanding on the filmmakers' side included the contention that if the critics comprehended the effort, cost, and artistic or intricate decisions in the making of films, they wouldn't be so critical. In the words of Orson Welles, "You highbrow critics writing about movies are nuts! In order to write about movies, you must first make them." And, of course, the prevailing wisdom abided on the other side that filmmaking decisions, as interesting as they may be, had nothing to do with what was presented as the finished product.

The periodicals themselves often had economic systems that worked against film critics. "The business office does not like objective, competent movie criticism," former Hearst Newspapers reviewer Robert Shaw wrote in 1945. "On hundreds of American dailies, where the editorial budget is on a shoestring basis, there is not sufficient salary available for a person able to write such criticism. And anyway, the business office and the publisher, usually pretty synonymous, share the curious but general concept that movie reviews are a form of lagniappe metered out to the advertising customers. The editorial space allotted to a picture is measured largely by the inches of advertising bought by the exhibitor. This lineage system of movie criticism adhered to by the bulk of our daily newspapers is not especially conducive to the development of any sane standard of movie values in the mind of the newspaper public."

Powerful publishers with axes to grind or political agendas also meddled in the individual opinions presented by their critics. If a journalistic demagogue such as William Randolph Hearst became personally offended by films, his newspapers often did, too. Hearst objected to the portrayal of the Soviet Union in Lewis Milestone's *The North Star* (1943) and Michael Curtiz's *Mission to Moscow* (1943). The celebrated *Citizen Kane* (1941), which was based by screenwriters Orson Welles and Herman J. Mankiewicz on Hearst's life, at first received "a full tide of insensate fury" from Hearst's papers, according to Shaw. "Then it ebbed suddenly. With one brain cell working, the Chief realized that such hysterical barking by the trained seals would attract too much attention to the picture. But to this day [1945] the name of Orson Welles is on the official son-of-a-bitch list of every Hearst newspaper."

Theodore Strauss explained the gap between screenwriters and film critics without any apparent interest in bridging it. Strauss was a film critic for *The New York Times* from the late 1930s to 1944, when he followed the career path of his former boss, Frank S. Nugent, and left the *Times* for Hollywood, joining Paramount Pictures as a screenwriter. Although he eventually wrote the screenplays for Frank Borzage's *Moonrise* (1948), Norman Z. McLeod's *Isn't It Romantic?* (1948, and answered by Leonard Maltin's full, capsule review, "No.") and other films, Strauss had not yet registered a screen credit when he wrote an opus about members of the New York Film Critics Circle for the inaugural edition of *Screen Writer*, the magazine of the Screen Writers Guild, explaining his former fraternity to his new one.

Strauss's attempt was hampered by his lofty regard for his new colleagues, whom he described as "the one body of film craftsmen in Hollywood . . . most intent on raising the level of films to a maturity commensurate with the greatest responsibilities any art has ever faced." Any détente was also hindered by his awful interpretation of the screenwriters' set view of the average New York critic, which was, he said, "some monstrous abortion, the illegitimate offspring of a Coney Island cretin, a cynical sycophant whose palm is regularly crossed with silver in return for laudatory reviews, a talentless man who compensates for his own sense of inferiority by attacking the work of others, a corrupt idiot who—by some whimsical wand of fortune—has been given the power to influence millions of moviegoers."

The Strauss piece did little to dissuade the screenwriters that hacks were judging their work. Overwritten and snobbish, the Strauss article was still one of the few of its era that saw the profession both from inside and from without. Strauss stressed that, "The miracle is not how venal or easily corrupted the reviewers are, but rather how independent they have been able to remain. To be sure, there are several obvious members of the fraternity who have been so opaque as to take this fawning flattery [from studio flacks] at its face value. . . . As for the others they survive their seductions reasonably intact. . . . On the whole, they are an earnest, conscientious, honest, and tolerably intelligent group whose power is debatable. Unfortunately these powers would also suffice the senior clerk in a trading house. It is probable that even movie reviewing makes more complex demands."

Strauss divided the New York critics into three groups: low-, middle-, and highbrow, with the tabloid and Hearst critics in the low category, the reviewers on the major dailies in the middle group, and the critics for *The New Republic*, *The Nation*, *Time*, and *The New Yorker* in the highbrow camp. Strauss had little tolerance for the critics he termed highbrow and, more informally, longhairs, particularly James Agee and Manny Farber, whom he considered together and independently. "Their reviews, filled with an erudition as spurious as it is sterile and critical niceties calibrated to ten-thousandths of an inch," Strauss wrote, "resemble some of the bearded badinage that used to pollute Greenwich Village gatherings in the days when the Swiss Itch was the intellectuals' ambrosia and art was a big word."

Of Wolcott Gibbs at *The New Yorker*, Strauss wrote, "He hardly aspires to review films at all. He merely tolerates them with as much forbearance as he can muster. He writes with the gentle, slightly peevish ennui of an old bachelor condemned for a couple of hours to the company of nose-picking urchins." Gibbs, the magazine's celebrated drama critic from 1940, when he succeeded Robert Benchley, until his death in 1958, spent much of 1945 reviewing films. "The cinema resists rational criticism almost as firmly as a six-day bicycle race, or perhaps love," Gibbs decided, and left for posterity one of the more often-cited quotes about the ills of movie reviewing: "It is my indignant opinion that ninety percent of the moving pictures exhibited in America are so vulgar, witless, and dull that it is preposterous to write about them in any publication not intended to be read while chewing gum."

Of the lowbrow reviewers, Strauss singled out Kate Cameron of the *New York Daily News*, because her reviews reached the largest audience of any newspaper critic. Strauss characterized her as a "sweet and suburban lady who might have stepped out of a Helen Hokinson cartoon," referring to the plump and ditzy society dowagers that Hokinson drew for the pages of *The New Yorker*. Strauss called Cameron's reviewing "not far above the level of advice to the lovelorn columns," and was an early disparager of her paper's four-star rating system. "They are as un-complex, as uncritical, but not quite as accurate," Strauss claimed, "as the carnival contraptions which test how much wind a man can blow out of his lungs."

Strauss deemed the "most homogenous and collectively most influential" group the middlebrow critics: John McManus of *PM*, Bosley Crowther of *The New York Times*, Howard Barnes and Otis L. Guernsey, Jr., of the *New York Herald-Tribune*, Eileen Creelman of the *New York Sun*, Leo Mishkin of the *New York Morning Telegraph*, Archer Winsten of the *New York Post*, and Alton Cook of the *New York World-Telegram*. Strauss's figurative pass in front of this line-up proceeded like a superior officer's inspection for rumpled epaulets.

"And though his judgments have a normal quotient of human erraticism," Strauss wrote of Winsten, "he is totally devoid of pretention or journalistic bow-wow." Predictably, Strauss rated his former boss at the *Times*, Bosley Crowther, as the best of the lot. "Mr. Crowther comes closer than any of his colleagues to fulfilling the requirements of a true critic," Strauss wrote. Callenbach's survey six years later in the *Hollywood Quarterly* also flattered Crowther, whose backups in the 1950s were Eugene Archer, Thomas M. Pryor, and A.H. Weiler. "The most respectable newspaper reviews, from the standpoint of film analysis rather than simple value judging, are beyond doubt those in *The New York Times*," Callenbach wrote.

One observer who did not accept this view of *The New York Times* was John Lardner, who agreed with Strauss on the highbrow and lowbrow critics. "He was in the groove up until then," Lardner wrote, "but he mistakenly went on to speak words much too gentle for what he called the center group. Maybe this is because he used to be a *Times* man. *Times* men have a special kind of myopia toward the distinctive, nay, spectacular, defects of the *Times*." Occasionally, similar opinions glanced off the paper's reputation like golf balls off a tank.

The jaundiced view of film critics in the postwar era inside the entertainment community in narrowly circulated periodicals such as *Hollywood Quarterly*, *Journal of the Screen Producers Guild*, and *Screen Writer* was one thing, but the vitriol spilled into the mainstream. An unsigned 1958 *Time* broadside stopped short of recommending the banishment of newspaper film critics by torchlight beyond the city limits—they weren't deemed consequential enough. The piece was especially pejorative regarding critics "outside New York," with the exception of Philip K. Scheuer of the *Los Angeles Times*; Scheuer was labeled "loftily independent."

The average movie review, the magazine generalized, was written by a shill for the studios. That average review, it said, "has descended to the level of the press agent's blurb—a blurb commonly reprinted by newspapers too idle or strapped to staff a reviewer. A few perceptive, readable critics are still at critical work. But many papers leave the job to worn-out deskmen, middle-aged ladies . . . or unqualified cubs, or else, like the *Des Moines Tribune*, spread it through the city room, at $3 a review. . . . Critics have transformed . . . into a group dispensary of tasteless, colorless, and odorless critical treacle, ignored on a wholesale basis by the moviegoer, sampled only by the movie industry itself . . . merely vigilant for any sign of recalcitrant tartness." With copy editors, mature women, and rookie reporters jumbled into this unopposed libel of an ill-defined profession, at least the critics weren't alone.

"Film criticism is at best a thankless task," wrote Eric Larrabee in *Harper's*. "No one pays it more than a minimum of attention. Though drama critics enjoy an unparalleled tyranny over their readers, and while the influence of book reviewers is at least subject to debate, there can be no question about the powerlessness of the movie critics. The correlation between their opinion of a film and the public's attendance at it is normally a flat negative, and their job has naturally come to be regarded with a certain good-natured contempt.

"On a newspaper," Larabee concluded, "the job of film critic is likely to be held by the restaurant-and-travel editor while he waits for the drama critic to retire." It's true that the film critic's hat was often only one of several worn by the central writer in an entertainment or features department. A generalist, he or she covered symphonies, theatre, radio, and the advent of TV. The plum role for which to strive for such a writer was often theatre criticism, and the main post to attain was drama critic or drama editor. John Beaufort reviewed movies for two generations for the Boston-based *Christian Science Monitor* even as his title shifted from New York bureau chief to theatre critic to features editor to arts and entertainment editor. Howard Barnes and Otis L. Guernsey, Jr., at the *New York Herald-Tribune* wrote hundreds of movie reviews in the postwar era, but both never strayed far from Broadway, and both ended their careers among the 20th century's prominent drama critics.

Callenbach and two researchers talked to film critics on 11 newspapers: Five in New York (Otis L. Guernsey, Jr., of the *Herald-Tribune*, Archer Winsten of the *Post*, Alton Cook of the *World-Telegram*, Bosley Crowther of the *Times*, and Dorothy Masters and Kate Cameron of the *Daily News*), four in Chicago (Sam Lesner of the *Daily News*, Ann Marsters of the *Herald-American*, Doris Arden of the *Sun-Times*, and Mae Tinee of the *Tribune*), and two in Los Angeles (Ezra Goodman of the *Daily News* and Philip K. Scheuer and Edwin Schallert of the *Times*). Callenbach gauged their reading habits on material pertaining to films, and their general methods of communicating to their audiences.

While he named the critics up front in his study, Callenbach treated them anonymously thereafter, as "Critic A," "Critic B," and so on through "Critic J," and generally amalgamated their comments to come to consensus results. "Most of them imagine themselves to be writing from the standpoint of the common man, but a discouraging proportion don't think that their work has any marked effect on their readers," Callenbach wrote. He analyzed their columns for content and determined that all of them uniformly pay attention to three aspects of films:

1. General remarks on the film as a whole, its overall qualities, unity, significance, or appeal.
2. Summaries of plot or story, sometimes in abbreviated synopsis form.
3. Comments on performances.

Callenbach also discovered other categories of discussion by the critics, and listed those as well:

4. Mentions of production staff: director, producer, writer, composer, original author, etc.
5. Breakdown of technical qualities: camera, script (dialogue or situation), music, etc.
6. Remarks on relationships between films: noting remakes, suggesting comparisons.
7. Reports on current production activities, gossip, etc.

Callenbach concluded that the reviewers were mostly plot capitulators who often showed fondness for the overall product if it appealed to their personal sensibilities. He found that the reviewers had very little comprehension of cinematic language and the meaning in what was conveyed by the director or screenwriter. "Other aspects suggested by film literature in general (attitudes manifested in films, influences of films upon audiences, meaning 'behind' films, etc.) received practically no treatment in the sample(s) studied," Callenbach wrote.

The reading between the lines, to take a metaphor from the page to the screen, did not concern these critics, Callenbach found. The language of cinema, the *mise en scène*, the semiology, the signposts carefully prepared by directors, the inner worlds of films, seemed to escape them.

"These comments," he wrote of the reviews analyzed, "are almost all of the type which would be equally applicable to stage drama; there is little consciousness of the film as a form different from the theater. Reviews seldom display awareness of the film as a medium. The film is a *fait accompli*; it is subjected to critical scrutiny only over a restricted area. Evaluations are made only within the familiar machinery of theatrical tradition: plot, character, theme, diction, and also, occasionally, music and spectacle, to round out the Aristotelian hexad.

"The film as a peculiar genre, marked by mobility, ellipsis, and material symbolism, is nowhere discerned. It is startling to perceive the extent which films are thought of as canned theater; the considerable variety of the product, both domestic and foreign, is largely ignored. Audience expectations are narrowed and the flexibility and vitality of the film industry suffer in the long run."

Callenbach also profiled the main magazines in which film journalism appeared, including *Life, Newsweek, Commonweal, Library Journal, The Nation, The New Republic, The New Yorker, The Rotarian, The Saturday Review of Literature, Theatre Arts*, and *Time*. These, he said "provided rather more varied critical fare than does the metropolitan daily press," but that wasn't enough to stem his final pessimistic outlook toward film criticism as a whole. "The present state of film journalism in the United States, then," he concluded, "is no great comfort to those who believe in the potentialities of the domestic cinema."

But by the 1950s, the notions of seeing films as art and film critics as essential staff writers had taken root at most widely circulated national general periodicals. Both *Time* and *Newsweek* devoted ample space to the new releases, but the reviews still went unsigned. John McCarten reviewed for *The New Yorker*, Arthur Knight and Hollis Alpert for *The Saturday Review*, Philip Hartung for *Commonweal*, and Manny Farber and later Richard Hatch for *The Nation*.

Bosley Crowther of *The New York Times* especially upheld his and his paper's high standards, to which he emphasized social responsibility and moral merit in the columns of the 20th century's paper of record. His unchanging values in changing times eventually led to his removal as the *Times*'s main film critic in the late 1960s, but his place at the head of the American critics' table in the 1940s and 1950s was completely assured and unassailable.

"Of all the reviewers functioning in New York today, Bosley Crowther of the *Times* is probably the most balanced, the most consistent, the most penetrating," Theodore Strauss elaborated candidly on his former coworker, who was chairman of the New York Film Critics Circle from 1940 to 1944 and from 1951 to 1967. "Although he writes in the didactic, unexciting tones of a New England schoolmaster, he approaches the task of evaluating films with seriousness and conscience. . . . For all his essential seriousness and staidness of mind, Mr. Crowther . . . has had the simple common sense to realize that the movies, like any popular art, embrace many levels, that they can be cheap and noble, gaudy and splendid, useless and useful."

"In an era when television was growing up and movies were still the major cultural force in American life, Crowther was perhaps the most influential commentator in the country on the art and industry of motion pictures," wrote Robert D. McFadden in Crowther's *Times* obituary in 1981.

F. Bosley Crowther was born in Lutherville, Maryland, on July 13, 1905. He attended high school in Winston-Salem,

North Carolina, and Washington, D.C., and prepared for his 1924 entry to Princeton University at the Woodberry Forest School near Orange, Virginia. Intending to pursue law or a diplomatic career, he instead became editor of the *Daily Princetonian*, won a *New York Times* intercollegiate current events contest, and earned enough money to spend four months traveling in Europe. Crowther received his B.A. in history, and publisher Adolph S. Ochs hired him on the *Times* in 1928 based on the contest victory.

Crowther dabbled at playwriting, but earned his peers' respect as a deadline reporter, covering, among other things, the 1932 gangland-style murder of Vincent "Mad Dog" Coll, an enforcer for the Dutch Schultz mob. Crowther married fellow *Times* staffer Florence Marks in 1933 and was asked to join the drama department the same year by legendary drama critic Brooks Atkinson. Crowther pioneered nightclub coverage at the *Times* as the assistant drama editor through 1937, when he became assistant screen editor. When Frank S. Nugent left the paper in 1940 to write screenplays, Crowther succeeded him as screen editor and lead film critic.

Among the many instances in which Crowther's judgment of a film's morality overrode his impression of its aesthetics is that of Alfred Hitchcock's *Lifeboat* (1944), written by John Steinbeck. Set in the title craft, it concerns the wartime survivors of a ship that had been torpedoed by a U-boat, one of whom is the German commander responsible for the sinking. Crowther, who believed in the wartime function of films as items of propaganda, condemned the film for the morality that would save this Nazi killer. The notion abided that Crowther didn't miss his U.S. diplomatic mission, he just occasionally incorporated it into his criticism.

Crowther opposed censorship by nongovernmental groups. He defended films on the basis that the filmmakers' freedom of expression should not be abridged, an argument he stressed in print regarding Otto Preminger's *Forever Amber* (1947), Roberto Rossellini's *Stromboli* (1950), and other films.

"Throughout my career as a film critic, I was a persistent opponent of film censorship and thus an ardent advocate of freedom of the screen, and I strongly urged and applauded the distribution of worthy foreign-language films in the United States," Crowther stated.

Crowther's support of foreign films was not insignificant, and not without its controversies. American film culture, which was still primarily New York-based in the postwar era, was influenced by the influx of foreign films by the re-energized European film industries after World War II. Roberto Rossellini's *Open City* (1945) and Vittorio De Sica's *The Bicycle Thief* (1949) brought Italian neorealism to art houses. The films of Federico Fellini, including *La Strada* (1954), *Nights of Cabiria* (1957), and *La Dolce Vita* (1960), have had an enormous international impact. The singularly brilliant Ingmar Bergman's films came from Sweden, and Crowther deemed the master's *Wild Strawberries* (1957) an "exquisitely poetic picture" and "a film to soothe the mind and warm the heart." Many other film critics adopted the cause of these European imports as if they were needy refugees.

Akira Kurosawa's *The Seven Samurai* (1954) and other Japanese films arrived, but Crowther could not abide Kurosawa's *Throne of Blood* (1955), a graphic and forceful reconstitution of *Macbeth* in a Samurai setting, calling it "ludicrous." Michelangelo Antonioni's *L'Avventura* (1960), about the effect on a group of yachting adventurers of the disappearance of a young woman on a remote island, for Crowther was "like trying to follow a showing of a picture at which several reels have got lost."

Crowther made stands, but usually for what he believed was the *Times*'s role in social responsibility. For him, Fred Zinnemann's *High Noon* (1952), with Gary Cooper standing up to mob violence, was "thrilling and inspiring," and Edward Dmytryk's *Crossfire* (1947), with Robert Ryan as a murderous anti-Semite, was "a frank and immediate demonstration of the brutality of religious bigotry."

In the postwar climate of midcentury America on the self-

styled paper of record, Crowther was a man of his times working to maintain the status quo as he saw it. Other newspapers
operated as if they were in the public trust. John Beaufort of the
Christian Science Monitor approached films with specialized radar
to detect their morality and ethics for families that depended on
his paper to live up to its name and point out what might be
offensive to a Christian audience. "Being a newspaper for the
family," he wrote, "the *Monitor* takes notice of what it considers
excessive violence, vulgarity, suggestiveness, and sensationalism."

William Hogan of the *San Francisco Chronicle* was symptomatic of the homogenization and streamlining of American
culture after the war that went hand in hand with social responsibility. This prevalence occasionally underestimated the sophistication of the American public, even in such artistically protean
and cosmopolitan cities as San Francisco. "I cover foreign films,
but rarely promote those over the Hollywood variety as a personal enthusiasm," Hogan wrote. "I feel an American cross-sec-
tion might be bored, might not even understand *Wages of Fear*
or *One Summer of Happiness* no matter how deftly or artistically
they are put together. I try to state clearly what foreign films
mean and whom they will interest."

Foreign films arrived as a godsend to some and a problem
to others, mostly one of language, precipitating either dubbing
into English or subtitles, which also divided critics. Crowther
was an ardent booster of dubbing over subtitles. His August 7,
1960, piece, "Subtitles Must Go!" was one of his more trenchant
diatribes. "Artistry, commerce, and the public's eyesight will best
be served" by dubbing, Crowther wrote, complaining of "dart-
ing the eyes back and forth from the images to the subtitles."

Other proponents of foreign films would have liked to
see the actual words intended by the filmmakers and spoken by
the actors on the screen.

Many French critics who, under the editorship of André
Bazin, wrote about American films in the influential *Cahiers du cinéma* elucidated and defined film noir, extolling dark films of the
bleak American city at night, filled with racketeers, avarice, and

shame. Directors who presented such films—Howard Hawks, Anthony Mann, Sam Fuller, Nicholas Ray, and Robert Aldrich— became their pathfinders. Some of these French critics eventually became internationally celebrated filmmakers themselves in the 1960s and 1970s, including François Truffaut, Claude Chabrol, Jacques Rivette, Eric Rohmer, and Jean-Luc Godard.

Cahiers du cinéma's guiding editorial principle was that directors were the authors of their films. This notion of *politique des auteurs* was applied by Andrew Sarris to American directors of the 1950s and 1960s in his groundbreaking 1962 article in *Film Culture*, "Notes on the Auteur Theory" (see the following chapter).

One reason for the popularity of foreign films in America, Crowther wrote, was that the specific imports were the best productions of their nations. Had each country shipped representative films to America, they no doubt would have been on a par or worse than the run of Hollywood. Another reason for foreign films' popularity was their unselfconscious approach to sex that included cavalier treatments of extramarital sex, nudity, wanton lust, and prostitution.

Critics including Andrew Sarris and Richard Schickel advanced this notion from time to time. The great popular success of Roger Vadim's original French version of *And God Created Woman* (1956), starring Brigitte Bardot (without much of a wardrobe) as a seductress in St. Tropez, was the largest factor in the American market's receptivity to films from abroad. This success was boosted by the condemnation of the film by the Catholic Legion of Decency, attention that piqued public interest. "Let me put this as dryly as I can," Schickel wrote, "We must never underestimate how much the insinuating power of movies derives from their eroticism."

Crowther's voice, and others at major papers, espoused an even keel, a stern moral compass, common sense, and Middle-American values. They were so representative of the status quo that they became predictably culpable in Hollywood salesmanship. The studios still lived by the Production Code and believed in the influence of the Catholic Legion of Decency, even as the permissiveness, sexuality, and ambiguous morality in foreign films began to influence studio filmmakers in the late 1950s and early 1960s.

Film critics' influence and standards became codified in one way by the Screen Directors Guild. From 1953 through 1965 (except for 1962), the labor union that became the Directors Guild of America in 1960 bestowed individuals with the annual Critics Award for distinguished film criticism. The inaugural winner was Bosley Crowther of *The New York Times*. He was followed in 1954 by Harold V. Cohen of the *Pittsburgh Post-Gazette*; 1955, John Rosenfield, *Dallas Morning News* and *Evening Star*; 1956, Frances J. Carmody, *Washington Daily News*; 1957, Hollis Alpert and Arthur Knight, both of the *Saturday Review*; 1958, Philip K. Scheuer, *Los Angeles Times*; 1959, John E. Fitzgerald of the Catholic publication, *Our Sunday Visitor*; 1960, Paul V. Beckley, *New York Herald-Tribune*; 1961, John Beaufort, *Christian Science Monitor*; 1963, Paine Knickerbocker, *San Francisco Chronicle*; 1964, James Meade, *San Diego Union*; and 1965, Sam Lesner, *Chicago Daily News*.

Crowther and some similarly minded apostles, as well as the majority of well-established reviewers, often saw themselves as, above all, day-to-day consumer advocates. Crowther looked out for the upper and upper-middle classes while many of the others looked out for the working stiff, his housewife, and their two growing children—the average middle-class family. "The reviewer's first duty is to the public," Loretta King wrote as Kate Cameron, "and my own responsibility as a reporter has always been to tell the reader where . . . he may be able to get the best return on the money he intends to spend at the box-office, either in amusing entertainment, esthetic satisfaction, or the therapeutic shedding of a tear."

Few film-related magazines existed outside of fan periodicals like *Silver Screen* and *Photoplay*, the trade papers, and scandal rags. Mainstream magazines such as *Life* and *Collier's* increasingly paid attention to film stars and occasionally to trends, but the homogenization of culture in the 1950s resulted in the remedially informed Middle-American home subscribing to the local or big city paper, and perhaps *Time* and *Reader's Digest*, while the television set received increased attention.

"As a critic for *The Saturday Review*, I know that I have an audience quite different from the critic for, say *Seventeen* or *Redbook*," Arthur Knight wrote in 1955. "I can address myself to a hypothetical reader whose education, taste, and background may be assumed from the fact that he reads this particular magazine. In practice, this is less a matter of practical adjustment than, I should say, a merging of identities. It would be difficult to imagine Bosley Crowther reviewing films for the *Daily News*, or Philip Hartung writing for *Time*. Each writes on a level that is comprehensible and significant to the readers of his own publication."

One of the reports to explain the critical voices of the hinterlands to Hollywood's establishment was written for the *Journal of the Screen Producers Guild* by William C. Thomas in 1955. He and his producing partner at Paramount Pictures, William H. Pine, were known as "the Two Dollar Bills" for either their frugality or the fact that their line of B-pictures never lost money. These were often genre items starring Sterling Hayden, John Payne, Ronald Reagan, or Rory Calhoun, including Lewis R. Foster's *Manhandled* (1949) and *The Last Outpost* (1951), Phil Karlson's *Hell's Island* (1955), and Robert Stevens's *The Big Caper* (1957).

A method in the Two Dollar Bills' modus operandi was to precede their pictures in various cities with advance publicity. This meant pressing the flesh in relationships forged partially on the fact that drama editors and film critics such as Hubert Roussel of the *Houston Post*, Norman Clark of the *Baltimore News-Post*, Karl Krug of the *Pittsburgh Sun-Telegraph*, and others enjoyed visitors from Hollywood, who offered first-person column fodder from Tinseltown.

Thomas's report was written in the manner of a how-to address to producers on press manipulation by a man obviously used to the practice. It was composed in happy-dash prose, including anonymous references to "Mr. Oddfellow" and a "confused zany [who] writes drivel under the impression that it's deathless prose." Only some of this otherwise insightful piece is condescending, punctuated by undertones of a tavern travelogue. "You will find [Paul] Hochuli [of the *Houston Press*] battling valiantly for frontage at the Shamrock bar. . . . 'Hock' is a haughty customer," Thomas judged. "After two or three paregoric flips, he may insist that you approach him formally through his agent. You break that down by mentioning football and Rice University, where 'Hock' used to drive great holes through the opposition. . . . Later that day you'll see your movie in print, and so glowingly it will be hard to believe you've [not] done it yourself. . . . John Rosenfield of the [*Dallas*] *Morning News* . . . a nice double-domed Falstaff who knows more than Shakespeare and the Encyclopedia Britannica, and can prove it when pressed. . . . After that you talk music and have some beer. . . .

"Buck Herzog of the *Milwaukee Sentinel* is a gregarious rounder and a good news-hawk," Thomas wrote after a tour through scribes in Pittsburgh, Baltimore, Cleveland, and Fort Worth. "Soon after the introduction, Buck will take you by the arm and lead you across the street to the Plankinton Hotel bar, of which you'll think he is the sole owner and overseer. . . . Marjorie Adams of the *Boston Globe* is an independent lady, rotund, grinning, and full of talk. An excellent interviewer, she will get full meaning and flavor out of your words, and what's more, will print them. In a general way, Marjorie is a prototype of the other Boston Bloomer Girls—Peggy Doyle, Alta Maloney, Mary Sullivan, and Prunella Hall. If you have any funny stories, tell them. But be careful if the austere lady of the *Boston Herald* is present. That's Eleanor Hughes, a fine lady, like the others, but not for borderline stories."

Thomas expressed respect for several critics, particularly Kap Monahan of *The Pittsburgh Press* and Donald Kirkley of the *Baltimore Sun*. The latter is labeled as "an intelligent critic and writer," who "will do all he can to help [the] right man on advance material, but don't try to muscle in on his review of the picture. That, he feels, is his inalienable domain."

Among press critics, Thomas was no A.J. Liebling, but he developed his opinions out of first-person experience. Despite his prejudices and embellishments, his tour for the Screen Producers Guild was a measure of the reality of the times. The face of press ethics in the midcentury certainly wasn't the stern visage it became in the 1960s and especially 1970s, when a paper as mighty as the *Los Angeles Times* was completely overhauled into a bastion of ethical journalism and *The Washington Post* pursued the Watergate issue all the way to the toppling of the President of the United States.

As film culture deepened in the 1950s with the arrival of foreign films and voices of persuasive reason rising from the smaller journals, film critics and their position in general began to accrue some higher regard. The fringe operators on newspaper and magazine staffs began to be seen as "serious" critics in their own departments, and not on a level commensurate with the second-tier sportswriters. Their beat was always more popular than the realms of the art, music, dance, and architecture critics. It just took time for the papers themselves to regard the film beat in the same esteem.

"In the late 'Forties and early 'Fifties, Otis Guernsey had functioned with critical integrity as the *Tribune*'s movie reviewer, although he endured hectoring from executive vice president William Robinson for allegedly costing the paper substantial advertising linage from the Hollywood studios because he was often too negative in his opinions," wrote Richard Kluger in *The Paper: The Life and Death of the New York Herald-Tribune*. "Guernsey was finally asked to switch jobs with drama section editor William Zinsser, who turned out to be even bolder in his naysaying."

William K. Zinsser, who went on to author more than a dozen books, including the enduring literary how-to guide, *On Writing Well*, served as the main film critic of the *Herald-Tribune* from 1955 to 1958. Zinsser felt that producer David O. Selznick and director Charles Vidor's epic remake of Ernest Hemingway's

A Farewell to Arms (1957) was "vulgar to the point of nausea." He wrote that Joshua Logan's musical, *South Pacific* (1958), was "arty and distracting." Zinsser was reassigned to writing editorials about the time his book of collected film criticism and essays, *Seen Any Good Movies Lately?*, was issued by Doubleday.

Zinsser claimed that his move from the entertainment department to the paper's editorial desk was by mutual consent of the hierarchy, even as the *Herald-Tribune* issued a new policy of leniency toward Hollywood. "It is generally assumed in New York motion picture circles," Zinsser wrote without specifics in his book, "that a movie studio can soften an adverse review—in advance—by bringing pressure on a newspaper. Unhappily, there is some truth in this belief."

Elia Kazan's introduction to the book was addressed to Zinsser, and read like a farewell to the soldier who had fought the good fight, and lost. The general assumption from readers was the worst, that Zinsser had been labeled a poison pen by the studios and then kicked upstairs by a *Herald* brass who had colluded with angered moguls during their 1950s war with upstart TV.

Nearly three decades later, Kluger concluded in *The Paper* that Ogden Mills Reid, who had assumed editorial control of the *Herald*, ordered underling George Cornish to replace Zinsser as film critic. "Among the garbage that George Cornish tolerated," Kluger wrote, "was Brown Reid's 1958 order to him to remove William Zinsser as the *Tribune* film critic because his caustic comments on some of Hollywood's more flatulent extravaganzas were believed to be costing the paper advertising revenue. . . . When Brown Reid had Zinsser retired to the editorial page—an event followed instantly by an increase in the paper's movie advertising by perpetrators of some of the most ridiculous blockbusters ever committed to film—the new critic, Paul Beckley, took the hint, and the *Tribune's* historically stringent critical standards in the arts were compromised in the movie department."

The *Time* magazine report on the Zinsser episode mentioned that film critic Justin Gilbert of the *New York Mirror* had also been told to pull his punches by publisher Charles McCabe after the latter received a telegram in Rome from Twentieth Century-Fox. The cable expressed "shocked regret shabby dismissal of our very important ambitious costly above all sincerely patriotic film." This flag-waver was Dick Powell's *The Hunters* (1958), about Korean War flyboys, starring Robert Mitchum. The reportedly unanswered cable also elaborated, "extensive advertising campaign in *Mirror* including two full three-quarter pages over and above regular space."

The New York Film Critics Circle convened on the issue of pressure on newspapers. The critics decided that the Zinsser and Gilbert episodes weren't ones on which to make a stand. "Nothing was done by the critics," Archer Winsten complained in the *New York Post*, "and nothing will be done." Five years later, the *Herald-Tribune* would face a boycott by a studio over its film critic's words, with a different outcome (see the TV chapter).

Despite all the midcentury disrespect for film critics in general, such quirky and mighty talents such as James Agee, Manny Farber, Robert Warshow, Vernon Young, and Andrew Sarris wrote in a different vein, often pursuing aspects of films that the mainstream critics did not see or chose to ignore. These critics and others wrote from odd and fresh angles and recognized trends. The movies began to pique intellectual curiosity and spawn new ways of expression. Space was allotted in intellectual and political journals for think pieces—*Hudson Review*, *Partisan Review*, *New Leader*, *Kenyon Review*—and new film-specific journals were born.

Hollywood Quarterly began publishing in 1945, taking a scholarly approach to the broad spectrum of foreign and domestic movies. Based at the University of California Press, in Berkeley, it was renamed *The Quarterly of Film Radio and Television* in 1951, and its enduring title, *Film Quarterly*, in 1958. Ernest Callenbach has, from time to time, surveyed film critics for *Film Quarterly*, conducting interviews to pin down trends and highlight professional idiosyncrasies.

Film Culture was founded in New York in 1954 by the

filmmaking brothers Jonas and Adolfas Mekas. This journal covered Hollywood movies and evolved into the primary voice of independent and avant-garde cinema, spanning a total of 79 issues between 1955 and 1996. Critics and filmmakers who wrote regularly included P. Adams Sitney, Stan Brakhage, Andrew Sarris, and Parker Tyler. Nontraditional filmmakers such as Brakhage, Maya Deren, Ron Rice, and Paul Sharits found in *Film Culture* a forum to further the understanding of their art.

These were the filmmakers that Parker Tyler later profiled in the book *Underground Film* (1971). Occasionally politically radical, they were an offshoot of intelligentsia's ragged fringe and remained marginalized. As youth culture infused Hollywood in the late 1960s and 1970s and invigorated sweeping social and cultural changes as large as the civil rights movement and the end of the Vietnam War, criticism found a like brashness in liberal, arts-oriented, city-based weeklies in the 1970s and 1980s. Their antecedents carried the words of Agee, Young, and Manny Farber, and a few others who could have been swept into Theodore Strauss's cadre of "longhairs." Innovators, they went unnoticed in their time. Agee was the one who edged toward the spotlight in his final years, then was found by it in premature death.

Agee has been viewed as the great Renaissance man of film criticism. He composed verse, including the Yale collection *Permit Me Voyage* (1934); collaborated with photographer Walker Evans on the landmark book about sharecroppers in rural Alabama, *Let Us Now Praise Famous Men* (1941); wrote the serialized *Mr. Lincoln* (1952–1953) for CBS Television's *Omnibus*; adapted the screenplays for John Huston's *The African Queen* (1952) from the C.S. Forester novel and Charles Laughton's *The Night of the Hunter* (1955) from the Davis Grubb novel; posthumously won the 1958 Pulitzer Prize for fiction for the semiautobiographical *A Death in the Family*, which was adapted by Tad Mosel into the 1960 Pulitzer Prize-winning play, *All the Way Home*; was nominated for National Book Awards for fiction for *The Morning Watch* (1951) and *A Death in the Family*; and was also posthumously honored in 1958 by the publishing of one of the most celebrated anthologies of film criticism, *Agee on Film*.

"He was superbly intelligent, informed, sensitive, witty; and he could write like an angel," averred Arthur Knight in the *Saturday Review*. "He was the best movie critic this country ever had." Some still hold that sentiment to be true. When Agee died in 1955, the films for Huston and Laughton and the movie reviews accounted for much of the literary significance accorded him. *Let Us Now Praise Famous Men*, which was an outgrowth of an assignment for *Fortune* magazine, sold a little more than 1,000 copies in Agee's lifetime; it had not yet become a touchstone of Southern agrarian reform and civil rights victories initiated during the Kennedy and Johnson administrations. The book sold 60,000 copies after Agee's death.

Agee was the unsigned film critic for *Time* from 1938 to 1948 and the film columnist for *The Nation* from 1941 to 1948. All of his columns in *The Nation* and some of his *Time* reviews were collected into *Agee on Film* along with other articles he wrote for *Life*, *Partisan Review*, and *Sight & Sound*. For aficionados of film criticism, he may well be the greatest American critic, or at least the greatest until Pauline Kael became established in the 1960s.

Agee was also the pivotal critic in sensibility, tone, and deep film appreciation in the politically savvy newsweeklies through the World War II years who linked the prewar era of Otis Ferguson to the postwar times of Manny Farber. All three wrote with instinctively expressed common sense in distinctively smart prose using complex comparisons to the other arts and pop culture, and all relied on inveterate senses of humor. This continuum was unwittingly established in the Depression-era by Otis Ferguson, and it continued after Agee into the 1960s in the compositions of Manny Farber. These three were extremely distinct voices and brilliant critics, but their commonalities were an abiding love of the movies and a personal approach to the effect and meaning of films that was often in concert with the changing times and other arts. Occasionally chummy or conspiratorial in their reviews, composed with riffs and slang, rife with direct connections to the reader, Ferguson, Agee, and then Farber had the ability to make the readers believe that they were in on the conversation. The three critics were also linked directly: when Ferguson was killed in World War II, Farber took his place at *The New Republic*; when Agee left *The Nation* in 1948, Farber replaced him.

"The fact that James Agee was such a *personal* critic—and artist—when kept in mind, is a key to most of what is important and worthy in his writing," wrote Donald Phelps in *Film Culture* in 1955. Describing Agee's writing as precise and honest, Phelps continued, "It was this personal element in his film criticism which shocked and held me when I first read Agee's column in *The Nation* in 1946—as the same element did in the columns of Manny Farber in *The New Republic* when I went back to them in the light of Agee's writings, and as I did still later when I finally read the columns of Otis Ferguson, from whom both men must have learned something."

Agee, however, seemed to create the fiercest readership allegiance, as well as a more lasting reputation among film critics and the literati in general. His palpable affection for the medium was ever present. "It is sometimes hard to keep in mind that his monotonous denunciations of purblind Hollywood spring from a love of the movie medium so fierce as to make him want to remold it nearer to his heart's desire with his own hands," wrote Richard Griffith in *The New York Times Book Review* in 1958 when *Agee on Film* was first published. "It was that love that gave him a deeper insight into the nature of the movie medium, *in esse* and *in posse*, than any other American with the possible exception of Gilbert Seldes."

James Rufus Agee was born on November 27, 1909, in Knoxville, Tennessee. His father, Hugh Agee, was killed in an automobile accident when James was six, a circumstance that became the basis for the autobiographical novel *A Death in the Family*. He attended Saint Andrew's School for Mountain Boys in Franklin County, where in 1919 he met his lifelong spiritual mentor, Father James Harold Flye, an Episcopal priest. Agee attended public high school in Knoxville, then Phillips Exeter Academy in Exeter, New Hamphshire, where he became president of the Lantern Club and editor of the *Monthly*. He was admitted to Harvard University despite underachieving grades, and became editor-in-chief of the *Harvard Advocate*. He delivered the class ode at commencement for the Class of 1932.

In New York, Agee was hired by the Luce empire largely through the agency of his friend, Dwight Macdonald, after he had composed a parody of *Time* magazine. Agee reported for *Fortune* and then *Time*. His two months among tenant farmers in rural Alabama with Walker Evans during the summer of 1936 eventually produced *Let Us Now Praise Famous Men*. Agee married Olivia Saunders in 1933 and divorced her in 1938, when he married Alma Mailman. Agee shared the book-reviewing duties for *Time* with Whittaker Chambers, and in the fall of 1941 began reviewing films. He moved to Bleecker Street in Greenwich Village as Houghton Mifflin released *Let Us Now Praise Famous Men*.

Agee's first column for *The Nation* was published in December 1942, in which he called himself an "amateur critic" who hoped to be "stimulating or illuminating." His third marriage, to Mia Fritsch, was in 1945. After varied documentary film work with Helen Levitt in the 1940s, Agee was commissioned by Huntington Hartford to write scripts, and in the autumn of 1950 relocated to California to adapt *The African Queen* with John Huston. Agee suffered his first of a series of heart attacks in Santa Barbara. In 1954, he adapted the nightmarish *The Night of the Hunter*, and in 1955, while riding in a New York City taxi to see his physician, Agee died of a heart attack. Father Flye presided over the funeral rites. Agee was buried on a farm owned by his family in Columbia County, New York, near the Massachusetts border.

"Few general readers will be interested in every word here, but many will be moved by the central figure this book creates," wrote Stanley Kauffmann in *The New Republic* about *Agee on Film*. "The sternest criticism that can be made of these

collected articles is that, from them, emerges not so much a critical intelligence or a Promethean appreciator of an art as a lov-
able and admirable man. Sometimes his lines soar; sometimes
they merely gush. Sometimes his rhapsodic stabs penetrate to
the heart; sometimes they flounder. He is given to meaningless
distinctions. . . . But he has what is missing from most criticism
today—of films and all arts: fierce intensity. The bitter image
he leaves is not of a facile, corrosive cynic but of a blazing pes-
simist." Kauffmann felt that *Agee on Film* helped define 1958
as "a year that marks a beginning of change in general attitudes
toward serious film criticism."

Agee's review of William A. Wellman's *The Story of G.I.
Joe* (1945) was as representative of his considerations of premium
Hollywood movies as any of his criticisms. The film concerned
a U.S. infantry outfit in World War II fighting in Italy, while
the famous North American Newspaper Alliance war correspondent, Ernie Pyle (played by Burgess Meredith), tagged along,
writing of their exploits. "Many things in the film itself move
me to tears," Agee wrote. "The closing scene seems to me a war
poem as great and as beautiful as any of Whitman's. . . . In a
film so excellent there are many things to honor. . . . It would
be impossible to say enough in praise of the performance of Bob
Mitchum as the captain and Freddie Steele as the sergeant. . . .
It is also the first great triumph in the effort to combine 'fiction'
and 'documentary' film. . . . It seems to me a tragic and eternal
work of art."

Agee saw sheer genius in Laurence Olivier's Shakespear-
ean films, *Henry V* (1944) and *Hamlet* (1948). "*Henry V* is one
of the great experiences in the history of motion pictures," he
wrote. ". . . A major achievement—the perfect marriage of
great dramatic poetry with the great contemporary medium for
expressing it. . . . Olivier's films set up an equilateral triangle
between the screen, the stage, and literature. And between the
screen, the stage, and literature they establish interplay, a shim-
mering splendor, of the disciplined vitality which is art."

Agee's abiding passion for the most manipulative of media was tempered by his honesty. The complexities inherent in thinking about the emotional impact of movies, and communicating that impact, often came un-distilled onto the page in Agee's reviews. He sometimes ended up writing about his own writing. "*The Miracle of Morgan's Creek*, the new Preston Sturges film, seems to me funnier, more adventurous, more abundant, more intelligent, and more encouraging than anything that has been made in Hollywood for years," Agee wrote. "Yet, the more I think of it, the less I esteem it. I have, then, both to praise and defend it, then attack it."

He did the same soft-peddled brand of Jekyll-Hyde routine on John M. Stahl's *The Keys of the Kingdom* (1944). Agee lauded the film at first for sincerely presenting a "hero whose heroism is moral." Then he vacillated: "As I think it over, much of the sincerity, and of the ethics, seems beefy, over-comfortable, love-your-fellow-mannish, and in general rather uninteresting."

John Simon, who decades later was the film critic for *The New Leader*, *Esquire* and other publications, penned an essay for *Film Heritage* in 1967 that pinpointed Agee's chief characteristics as "the incoherent love of truth combined with almost sickly humanity and scrupulousness that forced him to see the other side of every view, every statement, every sentence even as he was writing it, and that had him forever qualifying, amending and stalemating himself."

Simon's piece appeared 13 years after the subject's death, in a special edition of *Film Heritage* dedicated to Agee. Editor F. Anthony Macklin's publication was, in 1967, amid an intellectual discussion in editorials, articles, and readers' letters on the merits of Pauline Kael when it took a look back at Agee, calling him "Critic of Honor," and running pieces by his old friend and coworker on *Fortune* in the 1930s, Dwight Macdonald, as well as Joel Siegel.

"If any single aspect of Agee's writing can be found most distinctive, it is surely his sense of humor," wrote Siegel, who years later reviewed for ABC. "The playfully succinct word portraits of performers are but one example of the wit which informs all of his work. Of Irene Dunne: 'she would probably keep her tongue in cheek uttering the seven last words.' Of Esther Williams: 'Wet and peeled, as she slithers her subaqueous charms before underwater cameras, she suggests a porpoise amused by its own sex appeal.' Movie reviewing has always been an arena for public wit-honing demonstrations, from the wise-guy quips of *Time* to my-elbow-in-your-rib punning of Andrew Sarris, but Agee's carefully phrased, good-natured witticisms are merely an extension of his essentially serious sensibility."

Agee's enormous writing talent often outdistanced the talent that could be evidenced in the films he was critiquing—"A fatal defect in a reviewer," decided Dwight Macdonald in *Film Heritage*. Macdonald, who served as film critic of *Esquire* in the 1960s, also averred that "Agee was in fact the most copiously talented writer of my generation. . . . I can think of no other writer of my generation who could when he was in the vein, rise to a more powerful, original style, formally; or a style more flexibly adapted to express the particular subject. Agee was a 'natural' writer, as Honus Wagner and Shoeless Joe Jackson were 'natural' ballplayers. He also had something not common in American writers—a peculiar ability . . . to combine emotion and thought. . . . In his best writing the conventional antithesis between 'feeling' and 'intellect' disappears, merging into something beyond talent or craft, something which only the old-fashioned word 'genius' adequately describes."

Kael, writing one of her first reviews in *The New Yorker* in February 1968, ostensibly on Claude Berri's *The Two of Us*, spends half of her space wondering about Agee, elbowing her way deep into the critical fray. "Was Agee's movie-going so virtuous, or did he, perhaps, now and then, like the rest of us, enjoy decadent, slick, sleazy commercial pictures?" Kael wrote. "We ought to be able to see a reasonably lousy picture without feeling we've been violated. Agee always seemed to be personally betrayed by synthetic elements in a movie, by 'sophistication.'

"Because Agee was so great a critic, there is a tendency to take over his terms, but his excessive virtue may have been his worst critical vice. Agee's demands were, in some ways, both impossibly high for the movie medium and particularly child-like," Kael thought. "As a result, we may need to be liberated from guilt both for enjoying irresponsible movies and for failing to respond to works of such impeccable moral character as *The Two of Us*, but a movie that, to use Agee's language, is tender and full of 'reverence for reality' and all can still seem pretty thin." Kael wrote.

Kael must have forgotten that Agee adapted the novel, *The Night of the Hunter*, about a murderous preacher stalking two children for stolen loot across West Virginia landscapes. Starring Robert Mitchum as the despicable psychosexual cleric, it was one of the most audacious films of the postwar era, mis-understood in its time, becoming, by the 1970s and after, one of the most infamously neglected great films resurrected by re-visionist film criticism. And Kael must have skipped some of Agee's reviews, like the one for Edmund Goulding's lowdown *Nightmare Alley* (1947), starring Tyrone Power amid blackmail in a crummy traveling carnival. "In any mature movie context these scenes would be no better than all right, at that," Agee wrote, "but this kind of wit and meanness is so rare in movies today that I had the added special pleasure of thinking, 'Oh, no; they *won't* have the guts to do *that*.' But they do; as long as they have any nerve at all, they have quite a lot."

Kael, like most major critics in Agee's time and after, paid him attention and at least some homage. Agee considered film "the greatest art medium" of the 20th century, as film scholar Edward Murray wrote in his 1975 study, *Nine American Film Critics*. Like Ferguson before him and Farber in his own time and later, Agee never believed he was writing about amusements. "He felt that, in any given year, the average film could hold its own with the average novel or play," Murray wrote.

Farber may have had more insight into Agee than any-one. Filtered through his own tempered honesty, his review of *Agee on Film* was titled "Nearer My Agee to Thee," published in *The New Leader*. It was a piece that Richard Schickel later called "tormented," because Agee had been Farber's mentor.

"As he shellacked the reader with culture," Farber wrote, "Agee had one infallibly charming tool in his kit: an aristocratic gashouse humor that made use of several art centuries, a fantastic recall of stray coupons—like old song lyrics and the favorite thing people were saying in February 1917—and a way of playing leapfrog with clichés, making them sparkle like pennies lost in a Bendix."

After Agee had landed his column in *The Nation*, Farber observed, he made a strenuous effort to elevate the public's general idea of the movies beyond mere entertainment. Agee sought their placement on a higher plane, treating them as an art form. The effort in this mission showed, but in the process Agee became in and of himself a beacon for like-minded lovers of the cinema. He charmingly conveyed this insistence; it's central to his enduring reputation.

"Suffering from happy-plexis and booming emphasis, Agee's deep-dish criticism in *The Nation* was motivated by a need to bridge Hollywood with the highest mounts of art," Farber wrote. "Like Gilbert Seldes, he had a dozen ways to move films into the museum. Agee was a master of critics' patter, the numbers racket, and the false bracket. He used other critics' enthusiasms ('Winsten and McCarten think it is one of the best ever made. I don't quite care that much for it, but . . .'), expanded petty courage into infinity (Wilder's courage in making *The Lost Weekend*), and maneuvered in a pinch with the one-eyed emphasis. 'June Allyson, who seems incapable of a superficial performance' is a typical Agee periscope of an actress' one trait, a minor sincerity, at the expense of an immobile, rangeless cuteness."

In his mission, Agee may or may not have overrated Charlie Chaplin, Billy Wilder, Laurence Olivier, John Huston, Ingrid Bergman, or dozens of other favorites, but he helped American readers comprehend the talent and importance of these powerful cinema artists. He rose to the occasion with fervor when he felt he recognized a genuine classic. Farber, a lifelong appreciator of the achievements of more workaday filmmakers, felt that

Agee oversold his heroes.

"Though he occasionally lapsed into salesmanship through brilliantly subtle swami glamour (*Henry V*, the Ingrid Bergman cover story), Agee would be wisely remembered for quick biographies and reviews, particularly about such happy garbage as June Haver musicals and an early beatnik satire, *Salome Where She Danced*, where his taste didn't have to outrun a superabundant writing talent," Farber wrote. "Agee was a brick wall against pretense in small movies, but, on Big Scale work, where the Boulevard is made of National Velvet and the Limelight's as stunning as the Sierra Madre, Agee's reviews suggested a busy day at Muscle Beach: flexing words, bulging rumps of talent, pyramidal displays of filming cunning."

Farber concluded that Agee was a literary seducer, and "perhaps as bewitching as his bandwagon believes, if his whole complexity of traits is admitted in the record. Seldom has more personality walked through American criticism with such slyly cloaked over-possessive manners."

Schickel went further, delineating other faults. "Agee's trick was to rationalize purely subjective responses in a confidential language that seemed to show a smart, good-natured fellow riffing casually on a subject everyone, in his day, was pretty casual about," Schickel wrote. "He liked or disliked actors and directors because they did or did not speak to something deep and inchoate in his nature. . . . Mostly, he praised movies that agreed with his liberal, humanistic, and essentially literary biases. He rarely investigated imagery or editing, the visual language that sets film apart from the other narrative arts. He was like a music critic who attends operas for their plots. This is, of course, a besetting sin of movie critics, doomed to write about an art that most entrancingly speaks in an un- (perhaps even anti-) written idiom."

Agee inspired fierce loyalty in his friends as well as his readership. Wiry and handsome, unless he smiled, he usually was a rumpled presence eschewing the suit-and-tie norm of the era. A compulsive libertine to whom marriage vows weren't particularly binding, and an alcoholic, chain-smoker, and insomniac,

Agee wrote about the great unwashed, and became representative as well, with "teeth rotting in his head and dress so slovenly and odoriferous he was banned from eating in the Twentieth Century Fox commissary," Schickel wrote.

John Hersey, another Agee friend, wrote a long tribute to him that was published in *The New Yorker* 33 years after the man's final cab ride. "Through the years of these various lives, Agee's behavior and his body were both abrading badly. Mia bore him four children; the first of them died in an incubator, forty hours old. Jim was repeatedly and carelessly and grossly unfaithful to her, and grew more and more violent in his frustrations and guilt and feelings of failure, but Mia cleaved to him, buoyed him, and, after his heart began to fray, nursed him. He could detect—and he hated—the frittering away of his gifts.

"Angina seemed a kind of punishment," continued Hersey, who won the Pulitzer Prize for fiction for *A Bell for Adano* (1945), and also penned the nonfiction World War II histories "Hiroshima" (1946, published in book format in 1985 by Alfred A. Knopf) and *The Wall* (1950). "In low times all through his life, self-loathing and suicide had hung at the edge of his mind. In the end, as it turned out, he jumped to his death by indirection; he was defenestrated from the upper stories of life, as if in slow motion, by alcohol, nicotine, insomnia, overwork, misused sex, and searing guilt, and—above all, we can guess— by his anger and despair at finding that with all his wild talent he had never been able to write the whole of the universe down on the head of a pin. On May 16, 1955, James Rufus Agee died of a broken heart in a New York taxi-cab. He was only forty-five years old."

His legend calcified in the next decade. The posthumous stamp of the Pulitzer Prize, endurance of *Agee on Film*, and the latent success of *Let Us Now Praise Famous Men* helped generate a cult of appreciation around Agee's memory. "Paradoxically, Agee was lucky mainly in his early death," Schickel wrote, "which permitted people to mourn the works unwritten and which assured his status as an object of the movie world's largely unexamined reverence." And yet *Agee on Film* endures as a classic on the top shelf of film criticism, where the words of Ferguson, Farber, Warshow, Macdonald, Sarris, Kauffmann, Kael, and Simon remain.

Agee was something of an influence in that newfound respect for movies as art through the 1950s—even as film criticism wasn't dealt much respect at all. Writers and actors who had felt that employment in Hollywood was tantamount to slumming largely shook off that notion after the war. Method acting came west with bravado when Elia Kazan directed Marlon Brando in the film of Tennessee Williams's *A Streetcar Named Desire* (1951). Despite all of the references to the contrary in America, film criticism was making some headway as a specific, honorable, definable craft in Great Britain, where the critics had included Graham Greene and Iris Barry in the 1930s, as well as John Grierson, Penelope Houston, Catherine de la Roche, Lindsay Anderson, Roger Manvell, Forsyth Hardy, Dilys Powell, and Ernest Lindgren.

In the Autumn 1956 edition of *Sight & Sound*, Lindsay Anderson's influential article "Stand Up! Stand Up!" urged that critics be socially and politically committed to causes and ideas. Two years later, at the 25th anniversary of the British Film Institute, Anderson, Houston, Paul Rotha and Basil Wright convened, judging that there was an overbalance of witty but snobbish criticism by mostly long-established men who were seeing through old-fashioned eyes.

In America, younger critics were well aware of Bosley Crowther's place at the head of the critical table as the main voice at *The New York Times*. As the top critic for the American newspaper of record, Crowther's words reached beyond New York to cosmopolitan audiences everywhere and studio publicists who accepted the notion of his influence. Despite Crowther's influence as a socially conscious critic who upheld the virtues of good taste and morality, and despite the public recognition of film criticism to have focused on Agee, then Kael and Roger Ebert through the 20th century, a gritty undertow came to life in the critical establishment after the war. His name was Manny Farber. Occasionally during his 91 years, latterly spent as an artist at Leucadia, California, and in eulogies since his death in 2008, Farber has been pegged as the greatest of all American film critics.

Farber called attention to Hollywood's assembly line of B-pictures, something that hadn't theretofore happened. *Variety* reviewed everything, including Hopalong Cassidy and Tex Ritter westerns, but only occasionally did Agee or any other front-rank critic dip into a programmer such as *When Strangers Marry* (1944). Farber was the first critic to take action-genre films seriously. His appreciation of directors such as Howard Hawks, Raoul Walsh, William Keighley, Sam Fuller, Anthony Mann, John Farrow, and Don Siegel dovetailed with the identification of film noir in the early 1950s. French critics gave that name to darkly themed and photographed American studio films dealing in deceit, crime, and urban nightscapes.

"Manny Farber is one of the very few movie critics who have mattered in this country," Schickel wrote, tending more assiduously to his profession than most contemporaries. "[Farber] has shaped and sharpened the sensibilities of two generations of people who care about film. Certainly, he was the first to think seriously and coherently about the American action film, thereby creating an aesthetic that allowed us to fully apprehend, for the first time, our native genius for movie-making. Farber set in motion a revolution in our tastes and perceptions that is still proceeding. How many critics can you say that about? He is the father of us all."

"Ugly Spotting," a representative Farber essay, which was published in *The Nation* in 1950, shows that at least one American critic was as savvy as the French in discovering, even if he didn't name it, film noir. "Hollywood has spawned, since 1946, a series of ugly melodramas featuring a cruel esthetic, desperate craftsmanship, and a pessimistic outlook," he wrote. "These super-tabloid, geek-like films (*The Set-Up, Act of Violence, Asphalt Jungle, No Way Out*) are revolutionary attempts at turning life inside out to find the specks of horrible oddity that make puzzling, faintly marred kaleidoscopes of a street, face, or gesture.

"Whatever the cause of these depressing films—the television menace, the loss of 24 million customers since the mid-1940s—it has produced striking changes in film technique. Writers over-pack dialogue with hackneyed bitterness, actors perfect a quietly neurotic style, while directors—by flattening the screen, discarding framed and centered action, and looming the importance of actors—have made the movie come out and hit the audience with an almost personal savagery. The few recent films unmarked by the new technique seem naive and obsolete."

Emanuel Farber was born on February 20, 1917, to Russian Jewish parents, store owners in Douglas, Cochise County, Arizona, across the border from Agua Prieta, Mexico. The youngest of three sons, he once identified himself as the class clown, and was fond of drawing caricatures of sports stars depicted in newspapers. Farber attended Stanford University, the California School of Fine Arts, and the Rudolph Schaeffer School of Design in San Francisco before moving to Washington, D.C., in 1939 with his first wife, Janet Terrace. He made ends meet as a carpenter.

Farber moved to New York in 1942 and ingratiated himself into the Greenwich Village arts community. He began writing a monthly art column for *The New Republic* in 1942. After the weekly's film critic, Otis Ferguson, was killed aboard a cargo transport in the Mediterranean, Farber coveted and won the movie beat, privately reasoning that four columns a month meant four times the money. Farber wrote through the war years, and contributed reviews and essays to *Time* (1949–1950), *The Nation* (1949–1954), *New Leader* (1958–1959), *Cavalier* (1966), *Artforum* (1967–1971), and to *Commentary*, *Film Culture*, *Film Comment*, and *City Magazine*.

Extolling Howard Hawks was one thing. "Howard Hawks is a bravado specialist who always makes pictures about a Group," Farber wrote. "Fast dialogue, quirky costumes, the way a telephone is answered, everything is held together by his weird Mother Hen instinct." And recognizing the harsh energy in Sam

Fuller's movies was another: "Though he lacks the stamina and range of Chester Gould or the endlessly creative Fats Waller, Sam Fuller directs and writes an inadvertently charming film that has some of their qualities: lyricism, real iconoclasm, and a comic lack of self-consciousness."

But Farber's tastes also scraped the pavement where the threadbare Hollywood fringe met the hardscrabble road. He admired Phil Karlson, the director of *Kansas City Confidential* (1952), *The Phenix City Story* (1955), and the pilot for *The Untouchables* (1959, released theatrically in 1962 as *The Scarface Mob*). "His movies are remarkable for their endless outlay of scary cheapness in detailing the modern underworld," Farber wrote. "Also Karlson's work has a chilling documentary exactness and an exciting shot-scattering belligerence."

Farber found meaning in items that the critical establishment found cheap, tawdry, and unworthy. In a way, he was the antithesis to Bosley Crowther, whose social consciousness would never have allowed him to extol anything remotely "geek-like" or to consider belligerence exciting. Farber was referred to by other critics as "perverse," "original," and "unfathomable." With a hoboish magazine career in the wake of his artist's bloom, Farber had accumulated the qualifications for Schickel's notion that he was the paterfamilias of film criticism's oft-let bloodline, without ever becoming, well, presentable or respectable.

A big city artist and carpenter raised in cowhand country, Farber's pen was a crowbar against pretense for four decades at a dozen publications. But as a paternal figure, he more resembled the renegade stepfather who returned intermittently with some wild-haired story of adventures seen since he last shambled in. Farber could be imagined across the street from Crowther and minions, who might be lock-stepping past Macy's, while he ambled the other way, against the wind toward the other side of town, later grinding the gears on the back blocks, ordering the hash. His reviews identified with action-genre heroes caught in tough binds, and with the filmmakers who regularly put them there. In the world of film criticism, Farber was akin to the solitary protagonists sifting narrow possibilities, with capability in reserve.

Dwight Macdonald considered Farber "as perverse and original a film critic as exists or can be imagined." The *Esquire* critic read Farber's legendary 1957 essay, "Underground Films," published in *Commentary*, and found the "connoisseurship" of the action-genre items described "so acute that, while he included in his underground pantheon John Ford and William Wellman, he excluded from the strict canon their more ambitious (and most generally admired) efforts, such as *The Informer* and *The Public Enemy*. He found them slightly bogus.

"To his impeccable taste, even Ford's *Stagecoach* was infected with Art—he reserved his enthusiasm for 'the pre-*Stagecoach* Ford,'" Macdonald interpreted. ". . . The non-artist, indeed the anti-artist, was his hero." As Farber wrote, "Hawks and his group are the perfect examples of the anonymous artist who is seemingly afraid of the polishing, hypocrisy, bragging, fake educating that goes on in serious art." These anti-artists, Farber maintained, "accept the role of hack" and work best "with material that is hopelessly worn-out and childish."

"There is something in this idea," Macdonald concluded, "so long as it is not pushed too far. Like most ideas, however, it was pushed too far, first by the *Cahiers du cinéma* group in Paris—independently of Farber, as far as I know—and then by their Anglo-American epigones who, after the most delicate calibrations on the *politique des auteurs* yardstick, concluded that Hitchcock's *The Birds* and Preminger's *The Cardinal* were masterpieces."

John Simon recalled voting to admit Farber into the National Society of Film Critics. Simon wrote that he "almost always disagreed" with Farber and found him "on top of that . . . unfathomable by any rational means." Simon said that he voted Farber into the group because the new member's "selfless dedication to film deserved some kind of recognition." Farber was conditioned against the grain. His third wife, Patricia Patterson, wrote that Manny was rejected by the Communist Party in his twenties, by the U.S. Army during World War II, and by the

New York Film Critics Circle after one meeting, and after the group had *asked him* to join.

"They fired me," he told her. He went so against the grain that when Hollywood appeared to also go against its own grain, he went against that grain, too. In the 1957 essay "Hard-Sell Cinema," published in *Perspectives*, Farber complained that "avant-gardism has fallen into the hands of the businessman-artist." Many of the filmmakers that he specified as "ultrasmooth 'radicals'" came out of television, although he didn't say so, and named screenwriters Rod Serling, Paddy Chayefsky, Budd Schulberg, Reginald Rose, and Ernest Lehman, and directors Delbert Mann, Martin Ritt, Robert Mulligan, Sidney Lumet, John Frankenheimer, Fielder Cook, and Jack Garfein.

The general notion of the times was that these writers and directors were bringing stories of everyday people living gritty lives to the screen with expressive integrity. Farber would have none of it. He detected prefabrication, lack of authenticity, and flimsy screenplays, and went on the attack. Their cinema, Farber generalized, "featured words that are anchored to the page by lead weights, characters who are wobbly, unrecognizable reconstitutions of chic art attitudes, and ideas impossible to understand because they come out of a fog of stupidity."

Farber claimed that the "Ice Age started to set in with another weird combination of forces (giving up the experimental 'B,' the ultraconservative turn of big shots like [John] Huston, the decline of the action directors, and explosion of the gimmick: big screen, the 'liberal' insight, Freudian symbols, arts-and-crafts Wellesian photography)." Farber concluded that true artists in the prevailing atmosphere were "hidden by a fantastic army of commercial fine-artists, little locust-like creatures who have the dedication of Sammy Glick, the brains of Happy Hooligan, and the joyful, unconquerable competitive talent of the Katzenjammer Kids."

Farber tapped his reservoir of humor as much or more than his forebears Ferguson and Agee, but he also injected more of a free-form riff into his prose, more adjectives, more made-up signifiers with suffixes ("beaverish," "hoboish," etc.), more barbs and eye gouges without resorting to the venom-pumping, fang-latch-until-the-heart-stops-beating methodology of, say, John Simon. Farber was a righteous judge and not an executioner. He once compared Gregory Peck to an ironing board.

"No ordinary sentences here," Foster Hirsch wrote in 1971. "There is hardly one, in fact, that does not subvert conventional notions of syntax, rhythm, and diction. Farber's is a racy, metaphor-laden, hyphenated, adjective-packed, incredibly dense prose. He discovers new relationships between words, he constructs sentences as launching pads for his tricky, herky-jerky verbal pyrotechnics . . . he backs into a sentence or idea, sideways, obliquely."

"I loved the way Farber wrote," said J. Hoberman in an interview. "I liked the fact that he was all over the place. . . . He didn't seem to be imprisoned, dogmatic, or narrow, confined to what was commercially viable at the time. He had a vast vocabulary and a set of references to draw from—comic strips, photography, painting, and so on. . . . I wasn't only interested in narrative films, and I saw this was true of Farber. He was really the first critic to write from this point of view, and he was a pleasure to read. He didn't have a pretentious or academic style."

Accessibility was in his expressive nature, and his opinions often came with traces of egalitarianism and faith in the uncommon qualities in the common man—in the reader to get what he was saying, in the protagonist to get out of the fix, and in the Wellman or Walsh who put him there.

Farber was taciturn by nature and appreciated it in others. Once in Colorado, in the company of a loquacious Richard Corliss, waxing on some forgotten, high-toned subject, Farber "stared dreamily into the middle distance," Corliss recalled, "and wondered aloud, 'do you think that if I broke your jaw they'd have to wire it shut?'" Rangy, with a high forehead and a piercing gaze, Farber was, in his later years, fully engaged in art, and only occasionally faced with his status as a film guru.

In a profession in which critics are always on the prowl

for new cult favorites, certain critics themselves qualify for that status for varying reasons: Potamkin, Ferguson, Ager, Warshow, Young, Sarris, Hoberman, etc. But Farber ranks as the hardcore cult favorite of them all. While Kael was the breakout critic to assail sanctimony, proper comportment, and status quo morality in films—especially American films—and to extol the visceral qualities of movies, often in their sexual content, and to excite the senses, Farber was the pioneer in this vein.

He was also the first film critic who stayed a film critic for more than a generation, who truly exhibited outsider ethos by rote and managed to survive in the profession—if not for long on many of the periodicals for which he wrote. When a later generation of film critics gravitated to the profession after the 1960s, magnetized by the renegade creativity that was alive in Hollywood at the time, their own maverick sensibilities were fed by whatever knowledge was available about the first fringe dwellers. Manny Farber had gone before them.

When Farber died in 2008 at age 91, the eulogies choked cyberspace. Having lived more than twice as long as Agee, he qualified as the great-grandfather of them all. Susan Sontag was only one of the commentators to call him the best, precisely, "the liveliest, smartest, most original film critic this country has ever produced." Film critics from Donald Phelps to Jonathan Rosenbaum, Richard Corliss to Richard Schickel, expressed their respect and admiration.

Farber's evolving sensibility as an artist helped him draft the manifesto, "White Elephant Art vs. Termite Art." It was published in the same Winter 1962/1963 watershed edition of *Film Culture* as Andrew Sarris's "Notes on the Auteur Theory," and Pauline Kael's appreciation of François Truffaut's *Shoot the Piano Player* (1960). Farber defined white elephant art as pretentious and prize-seeking perfectionism, "reminiscent of enameled tobacco humidors and wooden lawn ponies bought at white elephant auctions decades ago." In past essays, he named George Stevens, Fred Zinnemann, and David Lean as overblown and self-important filmmakers. In the white elephant discussion,

Farber described Truffaut's qualifications, as well as films by Ralph Nelson, Tony Richardson, and Michelangelo Antonioni.

Conversely, Farber defined termite art as having "no ambitions toward gilt culture" and "involved in a kind of squandering-beaverish endeavor that isn't anywhere or for anything." He elaborated that "a peculiar fact about termite-tapeworm-fungus-moss art is that it always goes forward eating its own boundaries, and, likely as not, leaves nothing in its path other than the signs of eager, industrious, unkempt activity." His examples of termite artists included Stan Laurel and Oliver Hardy, John Wayne in John Ford's *The Man Who Shot Liberty Valance*, Jason Robards and Myron McCormick in Sidney Lumet's television version of *The Iceman Cometh* (1960), and detective mystery writers Raymond Chandler and Ross Macdonald.

Of course, the termite tenet applied to Fuller, Karlson, Boetticher, and early Aldrich and Siegel on a frugal level, and to some of the best work of Hawks, Ford, Walsh, Mann, and Wellman on another. These directors were always reapplying, re-streamlining, and readjusting their themes—in screwball comedies, cavalry westerns, mountain pursuits, flyboy melodramas, dogface anthems, rackets pictures, and other genre variants. Farber brought their termite art to our attention, even if he didn't become generally recognized for it until decades later, and even as it apparently differed from locust-like activity that, in his personal brand of entomology, received his consternation in "Hard-Sell Cinema" in 1957.

In 1971, Farber's essays and reviews were packaged into one of the most influential collections of film criticism, *Negative Space*, which was reprinted in the mid-1970s as simply *Movies (by Manny Farber)*, and under its original title and in an expanded edition in 1998 by Da Capo Press. Its impression has been lasting. "And the more carefully I read Farber's pieces throughout the years—well over 20 at this point," wrote Kent Jones in *Film Comment* in 2000, ". . . persistence was what made his work so thrilling (and lasting: how many film critics do you find yourself going back to over 20 years?). Every adjective and every reference point opens up new territory." Persistence, of course, is the hallmark of termite art.

The notion exists that Farber's film criticism was so biting and idiosyncratic that it would have been resurrected without having been collected into *Negative Space*. But that book's endurance, mostly in dog-eared paperback editions, kept Farber's status as an original thinker on movies alive into later generations, after he had shifted his vocation to artist. While other critics have put out dozens of books each, Farber's one volume remains a powerhouse essential. "It's amazing how often it's been quoted, borrowed from, strip-mined, or used as a launching pad," John Powers recalled for National Public Radio.

Farber was but one of several postwar film critics whose reputation was sustained or enhanced by book publishers. The explosion in film literature in the 1970s included anthologies of specific critics, including the collected criticism of the elusive Vernon Young and the perplexing word labyrinths of Parker Tyler, offering both critics newfound readership.

But between *Agee on Film* and the film book publishing phenomenon more than a decade later that brought us *Negative Space* and dozens of other film criticism volumes—even before Pauline Kael and John Simon began to package their reviews and essays on a regular basis in the mid-1960s—Doubleday published Robert Warshow's *The Immediate Experience* (1962). Most of Warshow's essays dealt with movies, while others considered other aspects of popular culture, such as Clifford Odets, *The New Yorker*, and the fates of Julius and Ethel Rosenberg.

Warshow wasn't a traditional movie critic in the sense that he regularly covered films for a periodical; he was an editor for *Commentary*, not a film critic. But the wide-ranging essays in *The Immediate Experience*, preceded by an introduction by Lionel Trilling, made an impact. Included are incisive examinations of William Wyler's *The Best Years of Our Lives* (1946), Laslo Benedek's *Death of a Salesman* (1951), and Leo McCarey's *My Son John* (1952).

Farber's fascination with westerns, crime films, and other

genre pictures was shared by Warshow, whose pieces also appeared in *American Mercury* and *Partisan Review*. Warshow wrote in the tradition of sociological critics who pointed out the social, political, and moral implications of movies in the basic belief that art and society shaped each other. Warshow's two most notable essays were "Movie Chronicle: The Westerner" (1954) and "The Gangster as Tragic Hero" (1948). Like Agee, he died young in 1955, from a heart attack at age 37.

"For Warshow the problem of the American film was an aspect of a larger problem," concluded Edward Murray, "namely, the problem of American popular culture, which had been brought about by industrial capitalism." Before 1929, Warshow argues in "The Legacy of the Thirties," the role of the intellectual involved a search for truth and justice; after 1929, he was corrupted, directly or indirectly, by the communist movement. Warshow called the times a decade of "organized mass disingenuousness," when every act and every idea had some "larger consideration," behind it which destroyed its honesty and meaning. Washow complained that standards were lowered, that John Ford's *The Grapes of Wrath* (1940), portraying a family disenfranchised by the Great Depression, and Anatole Litvak's *Confessions of a Nazi Spy* (1939), about the FBI's investigation of a spy ring in America's heartland, became recognized as artistic, that truth was replaced by propaganda, justice by expediency.

Warshow's essay on gangster films, particularly Mervyn LeRoy's *Little Caesar* (1931) and Howard Hawks's *Scarface* (1932), emphasized their reaction to and against other films' cheerful views of American life. The treatise on westerns, including Henry King's *The Gunfighter* (1950) and Fred Zinnemann's *High Noon* (1952), pointed out that no matter how much the heroes detest violence, violence becomes the clearest expression of their style. Because of his emphasis on sociology, Warshow had little interest in movies' aesthetics.

Vernon Young was a bit of a mystery man. A brilliant critic with original insights and an exceptional writing style, Young is one of only five film critics to have been nominated for the National Book Award if dabblers William Troy and Susan Sontag are included with John Simon and 1974 winner Pauline Kael (for *Deeper into Movies*). Young was nominated in 1972 for *On Film: Unpopular Essays on a Popular Art*. His description of himself, written for Quadrangle Books, was: "I am English by birth, American by citizenship, and I feel most at home in Europe—preferably south of Scandinavia and north of the Alps." When he died in 1986 in Philadelphia, Pennsylvania, his obituary in *Weekly Variety* reported that he was married and divorced three times.

Describing his voracious movie appetite in the 1950s and 1960s, Young recalled difficult and depressing experiences during his comings and goings to and from theatres in London, Rome, Milan, and Rochester, New York. "After listening to other anecdotes similar to those above, someone asked me, 'Is it worth it?'" Young wrote. "Great heavens, what a preposterous question! Life under any conditions is filled with idiotic excursions, false goals, prodigal waste, disappointed loves, galling personal insufficiencies, half-witted associations. Is it worth living?"

Young was a fiction critic beginning in 1949 and then the film critic for the literary quarterly *The Hudson Review*. He occasionally wrote for that periodical and was a freelance essayist for *Film Quarterly, Arts Magazine, Accent, Perspectives on the Arts*, and other publications into the 1980s. As Edward Murray wrote, Young relished the aesthetics of movies and consistently examined their ethnological properties. "All art is a game played with ethnic rules," he wrote.

His fascination for the films of Ingmar Bergman led to his book, *Cinema Borealis: Ingmar Bergman and the Swedish Ethos* (1971). In fact, Young lived in Stockholm for a time and regularly put down Hollywood films when compared to European-made movies. His review of Jan Troell's *The Emigrants* (1971) opened with "the Great American Film has now been made—in Sweden." Young also wrote, "There is always someone announcing that the American movie has come of age. The announcement is always premature."

Young seemed to prefer obscurity, "if not the very oblivion that so many of the films he chose to italicize have suffered," Dan Harper wrote, citing such Young-reviewed fare as *The End of the Great War* (1957) from Poland, *The Golden Fern* (1963) from the former Czechoslovakia, and *The Priest and the Girl* (1966) from Brazil. Conversely, Young never had any respect for Alfred Hitchcock. His career-long denigrations of the director include, "that deck steward among the diabolists."

"I have never, or rarely, known for whom I am writing," Young stated. "It was made pretty clear to me for whom I was not writing—among others, most 'film people,' who never read opinions expressed outside the film publications or the columns of the wide-circulation press. As I was principally published in *The Hudson Review* or in magazines with a comparable, if not identical, readership, I could infer the status of my reader up to a point. . . . Then I began to discover that numerous people read my criticism (not just mine, of course) who never, or seldom, went to a movie! They simply liked to read about movies if they found the critic's point of view interesting and the content vividly re-created. I felt better after that."

The spiritual lineage for practitioners of convoluted and cluttered prose for film journals, who multiplied after the 1960s, can be traced to the prolific Parker Tyler, whose many books include poetry, studies of Vincent van Gogh and Paul Gauguin, and volumes on movies: *The Hollywood Hallucination* (1944), *Magic and Myth of the Movies* (1947), and later volumes dealing with sexuality in films as well as the magnum opus *The Shadow of an Airplane Climbs the Empire State Building: A World Theory of Film* (1973). "Tyler's method of writing is so obtuse, and he is so personally in love with the sound of his own words that it frequently becomes impossible to follow his line of reasoning," film critic Philip T. Hartung wrote in *Commonweal*.

Tyler's work suggested a man of ideas without the facility to express them clearly. *The Hudson Review* printed a 1962 Tyler letter claiming his own "merger of psychoanalysis, myth, free plastic analogies, unconscious syndromes in the film industry, and straight technical criticism, has already won recognition precisely for establishing new criteria of integrity and coherence." Had Tyler not used that final word, the statement might have stood on some vestigial merit.

"Both Parker Tyler and Manny Farber have many times showed us," averred William S. Pechter in *The Kenyon Review*, "there are many ways of not writing film criticism while allegedly writing film criticism." The lifelong companion of underground filmmaker Charles Boultenhouse, Tyler was mentioned 10 times in Gore Vidal's sensational novel *Myra Breckinridge* (1968), after which his books were reexamined and *Hollywood Hallucination* was republished by Simon & Schuster.

Associated with the surrealist movement in the art world of the 1940s, Tyler maintained that movies were not art, but myth, and that because movies are made by so many collaborators, they express the lowest common denominator among their makers. A pessimistic view to be sure, but the effect, according to Tyler, is that the masses tap into a collective hallucination and enjoy a therapeutic release through the emotions played on the screen. He believed in the psychological healing properties in movies. "I believe film is not an isolated art," Tyler once said, "but a universal medium having laws in common with the other arts."

Tyler's initial volumes came out at a time when few book-length analyses existed on the most popular art form. Iris Barry, a former film critic for *The Spectator* and the *Daily Mail* in London, and the curator of the Museum of Modern Art in New York in the 1930s and 1940s, called *Hollywood Hallucination* "the first book in its field to deserve the name of creative criticism." Tyler was fond of deconstructing films such as Billy Wilder's *Double Indemnity* (1944) and John Sturges's *The Great Escape* (1963) and reassigning homosexual identities or other Freudian applications to key characters, coming up with subtexts to the actions that often spun away on a brand of sheer fancy that escaped the movies' intended escapism.

Among other books in the first decades of the postwar era, cineastes were treated to Paul Rotha and Richard Griffith's

The Film Till Now, cinematographer John Alton's *Painting with Light*, and documentary filmmaker Raymond Spottiswoode's (father of director Roger Spottiswoode) *Film and Its Techniques*. Film world fascination was broadening. Lillian Ross's *Picture* repackaged several long articles in *The New Yorker* that followed director John Huston's efforts to adapt Stephen Crane's *The Red Badge of Courage* (1951). Anthropologist Hortense Powdermaker studied the film colony in *Hollywood: The Dream Factory*.

One of the most significant, authoritative, and popular books on the movies was Arthur Knight's *The Liveliest Art: A Panoramic History of the Movies* (1957). "His book is an important critical history of the movies, written by one who is practically a member of the family," Otis L. Guernsey wrote in the *New York Herald-Tribune*. A monumental undertaking beginning with Edison's experiments, the book managed to gracefully digest the range of its subject.

Knight shared the movie beat with Hollis Alpert at the *Saturday Review* when the magazine was a standard of American cultural survey. They alternated reviews into the 1970s, comprising one of the most enduring tandems of informed traditionalists in American film criticism history. Knight, who died in 1991 in Sydney, Australia, also reviewed movies for *The Hollywood Reporter* and *Playboy*, and taught at the University of Southern California, where his students included future directors George Lucas, John Carpenter, and John Milius.

Despite a wide-ranging career in television for such prestigious shows as *Omnibus* and the short-lived *The Seven Lively Arts*, and writing later in life on sex in the movies for *Playboy*, Knight achieved his apotheosis with *The Liveliest Art*, a starting point for many later historical studies. "When the book is read and Knight has finished his recollections of the Marx Brothers, his hearty appreciation of W.C. Fields, of the imagination of Orson Welles, of the directing of John Huston and Elia Kazan, of the war documentaries of the British, of the challenges films have successfully met, one is indeed persuaded that Knight's title for his book is not an exaggeration," Paine Knickerbocker wrote in the *San Francisco Chronicle.*

Steven H. Scheuer's *TV Movie Almanac & Ratings*, the first capsule-review guide for watching movies on television, was published in 1958 by Bantam Books. The book was an outgrowth of "TV Key," Scheuer's nationally syndicated column offering capsule reviews of network shows. By 1958, "TV Key" grew with television itself and was the most widely syndicated feature in the U.S., read by 15 million readers of nearly 100 newspapers, including the *New York Daily Mirror, New York Journal-American, Chicago Tribune, Detroit Times, Kansas City Star, Baltimore Sun, Philadelphia Bulletin, Los Angeles Herald-Express,* and *Tulsa Tribune.* Scheuer coordinated reviews from a five-man staff, and *Time* claimed that a favorable evaluation from "TV Key" could boost a show's Trendex rating by as many as nine points.

TV Movie Almanac & Ratings arrived the year after Arthur Knight's *The Liveliest Art,* and in the same year as *Agee on Film,* during the timely revival on TV of Hollywood feature films from the 1940s and earlier. In a 1972 perspective, Stanley Kauffmann emphasized that 1958 was the key year in film criticism and film appreciation. This was partially due to the Agee book, as well as Manny Farber's writings about bygone Hollywood directors and the concurrent release of old studio films on TV. The studios didn't stop worrying about competition from TV, but they certainly learned to love its ancillary market.

Scheuer capitalized on that. The 5,000-some entries in Scheuer's shrewdly packaged book carried a star rating, release year, several actors, and brief synopses and evaluations. The grandfather of the mass-marketed capsule-review form, Scheuer's book was intermittently updated and reprinted. It prefigured by more than a decade Leonard Maltin's *TV Movies* (1969), the first edition in a similar and more renowned volume of capsule reviews, from Signet Books.

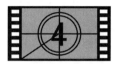

THE FILM GENERATION: THE 1960s

Hollywood in the 1960s continued manufacturing wide-screen epics, star-laden gambols, and youth-culture genre items from the threadbare fringe while the bitter aftertaste of film noir was still alive in the land. Clumsy attempts to push the boundaries of sexual mores were encouraged by the unfettered affairs seen in "exotic" releases from France, Italy, and Sweden. Some critics deemed foreign films superior to the Hollywood product when, as critic Andrew Sarris later pointed out, the imports were, in fact, merely just uninhibited and sexier.

Hollywood's older B-pictures and selected genre items and their makers preoccupied such renegade film critics as Robert Warshow, Manny Farber, and Andrew Sarris. A strain of subdued English films dealing with the working classes arrived on these shores. Epitomizing this "kitchen-sink" genre were the films of director Tony Richardson, including his adaptations of John Osborne's plays *Look Back in Anger* (1959) and *The Entertainer* (1960), as well as *The Loneliness of the Long Distance Runner* (1962) and the adaptation of Henry Fielding's picaresque novel, *Tom Jones* (1963), which won the Academy Award for best picture.

One critic who didn't take automatically to the Brits' "kitchen-sink" strain of gritty melodramas was the extremely uneasy-to-please Dwight Macdonald, who was film critic of *Esquire* from 1960 to 1966. "If directors may be compared to horses, without offense to either party," Macdonald wrote, "I see Antonioni as a thoroughbred flat-racer, Truffaut as a steeplechase jumper soaring lightly over obstacles, Renoir as a Percheron who puts his great hooves down with delicacy, and Kazan as a show horse who turns out to be broken-winded (Bergman is Black Beauty).

"Tony Richardson I see as a hackney, by which I mean 'hack,' for he is ambitious and serious, but merely the dictionary definition: 'a horse for ordinary driving and riding.'. . . His new film, *The Loneliness of the Long Distance Runner*, is not bad. It has realism, pathos . . . a cinematic liveliness rare in British films about working-class life. Mr. Richardson appears to have been stimulated by the *Nouvelle Vague* into an unwontedly spirited gait. But he remains a hackney and his film offers simply trans-portation. A virtue—most movies don't get you anywhere—but a modest one."

Macdonald was a critic who other critics read regularly. He was admired for the surety and precision of his writing and the strength of his opinions, which were often based on par-ticularly high standards. As one of the great commentators on American culture and politics during the American midcentury, Macdonald still did more than dabbling in film criticism. His book, *Dwight Macdonald on Movies*, a packaging of his *Esquire* reviews with other essays, remains among the dozen great collec-tions of film criticism.

Macdonald's leads were often succinct. "This film estab-lishes Joseph Losey," he wrote about *King & Country* (1964), "as a versatile director who commands a wide range of styles for wrecking a movie." The critic could fix his attention on a primary component—photography or a performance—that is essential and transcendent to a film's impact, yet one that oth-ers ignored. Sifting the extraordinary acting in Stanley Kubrick's *Dr. Strangelove Or: How I Learned to Stop Worrying and Love the Bomb* (1964)—particularly by Peter Sellers and George C.

Scott—Macdonald wrote that the least showy performance was the key to his overall reaction: "The great grotesque is Sterling Hayden as the loony general who launches the attack. He is a certifiable madman . . . I have never thought much of Mr. Hayden's acting, but he is very good here, so good as to be more than a grotesque: he is mad but human; one never knows quite what to expect next, so one has a certain empathy. This suggests one of my two criticisms: There are no overtones. All the characters, except Mr. Hayden, roll smoothly along their predestined satirical tracks."

Macdonald was a legend in New York journalism. "Billing Dwight Macdonald as 'Author and Critic' is rather like describing Niagara Falls as a steady drip," wrote Ruth Biemiller in the *New York Herald-Tribune*. "Macdonald was practically a living history of American magazines," Carol Polsgrove wrote. "He had been a writer at *Fortune* magazine in the thirties, an editor at *The Partisan Review* in the late thirties and early forties, then editor of his own magazine, *Politics*, from 1944 to 1949. He had been on the staff of *The New Yorker* since 1951 and film critic at *Esquire* since 1960. He was a smart, pugnacious writer, whose political sympathies veered, by his own account, from liberal to radical to Communist sympathizer to anti-Stalinist to conservative anarchist." Macdonald summarized his politics in *Memoirs of a Revolutionist*, a 1957 volume that was reexamined during the youth-culture revolution of the late 1960s, when he claimed no political affiliation, calling himself a mugwump.

Born in 1906, and raised in New York City with boyhood summers spent on the New Jersey coast, Macdonald was forced by circumstances as a teen to work to support the once-affluent family after his lawyer father's death. He eventually attended Phillips Exeter Academy in New Hampshire, where his intellectual curiosity was ignited, and Yale University, where he was editor-in-chief of the *Yale Record*, managing editor of the *Yale Literary Magazine*, and a columnist for the *Yale News*. With three friends, Macdonald edited a 600-circulation movie magazine called *The Miscellany* from 1929 to 1931. In one of his early involvements with film culture, Macdonald was remembered at board meetings organized by Lincoln Kirstein to create a New York film society in October 1932. At that point, Macdonald supported Harry Alan Potamkin's insistence that the society exhibit only communist films. Meanwhile, Macdonald earned a living on staff at Henry Luce's business magazine, *Fortune*, becoming great friends with fellow staffer James Agee. Macdonald resigned in 1936 after he claimed editors stripped the guts from his fourth and final installment of an exposé on United States Steel Corporation.

Macdonald helped revive the *Partisan Review* in 1937, and freelanced widely: *The Nation*, *The New Yorker*, *Harper's*, etc. He condemned the United States' involvement in World War II, disagreeing with *Partisan Review* principals Philip Rahv and William Phillips over the issue, and founded *Politics*. His second wife, Nancy Rodman, had been business manager of the *Partisan Review*, then of *Politics*, until it folded in 1949. He wrote the biography, *Henry Wallace: The Man and the Myth* (1948), wickedly debunking the public face of the former secretary of agriculture, vice president under Franklin D. Roosevelt, and *New Republic* editor.

In 1951, Macdonald joined the staff of *The New Yorker*. He wrote a series for the magazine that became a book, *The Ford Foundation: The Men and the Millions* (1956), the subject of which he described as "a large body of money completely surrounded by people who want some." In the central essay to his most admired book, *Against the American Grain* (1962), Macdonald writes in "Masscult and Midcult" on a subject that has preoccupied film critics from the National Board of Review in the 1920s to members of the National Society of Film Critics in the 21st century: the mass production and mass marketing of movies for the masses. Macdonald was dismayed by mass culture, which is easily influenced by marketing and usually not by aesthetics. He also complained that middlebrow culture, which respected high culture, tended to parody it as well. Parody of high culture, he felt, worked to adversely influence and undercut the efforts of aspirants to high culture.

Macdonald's view of America's mass culture audience as greatly susceptible was ahead of its time, and fairly snobby, as well as only tangentially aware of the economics and planning necessary to sway the hoi polloi. Movie publicists, who have propagandized the wares since the early silent days, streamlined their techniques after *Jaws* (1975). Macdonald, who died in 1982, foreshadowed saturation marketing and the notion of the lemmings drawn to the multiplex. But perhaps his mistrust of the big pre-sold movie was an idiosyncratic prejudice, a throwback to his radical days. Joseph McBride considered Macdonald's well-established ideas on mass culture, and made this conclusion about his film criticism: "This nagging idea, that if the masses go for it there is something fishy, gives brusqueness to the best of Macdonald's work and a paradoxically philistine shortsightedness to his worst."

As his politics shifted through the years, Macdonald's standards for quality in films held firm. His minority opinion of the great William Wyler, a three-time winner of the Academy Award for best director, is illustrative of his tastes. After looking over Wyler's credits, Macdonald wrote that he found "many pretentious middlebrow duds, like *Wuthering Heights*, *Dead End*, *The Best Years of Our Lives*, *The Children's Hour*, and many films like *Ben-Hur* and *Friendly Persuasion*, that are unpretentious lowbrow duds." Of Wyler's biblical epic and Academy Award-winning best picture, *Ben-Hur* (1959), Macdonald wrote, "Watching it was like waiting at a railroad crossing while an interminable freight train lumbers past, often stopping completely for a while."

Once Macdonald's standards were in place, his thorough search for merit was consistent with any any-brow picture. "Macdonald in his drive for quality sometimes sets superhuman standards," wrote F. Anthony Macklin in *Film Heritage*. "Some consider him smug or snide, but his criticism is frank, direct, but, most of all knowledgeable. He substantiates his criticism, and seldom is his criticism out of context. Criticism is hard work. Macdonald worked at it. Macdonald was one of criticism's fiercest spirits, and also one of its most careful proponents."

Despite the high expectations, Macdonald never was high-toned. Accessibility was always in his mission as a writer. John Simon, in an essay entitled "Let Us Now Praise Dwight Macdonald," cited the critic's virtues as being threefold: "breadth of vision . . . his style, or perhaps more properly, his tone . . . [and] his sense of humor." An opinion couched in such virtues can become exponentially forceful. For instance, director George Stevens met his Golgotha, sans resurrection, with his all-star gamble on the Christ story, *The Greatest Story Ever Told* (1965). Most critics felt it an especially bloated kind of cinema purgatory, and Macdonald amplified its pretenses, considering the casting of stars such as John Wayne and Sidney Poitier in small roles "like some nutty relative bursting in dressed up as Napoleon. There was also that 'Woman of No Name' who pushes through the crowd as Jesus is healing the sick and, after he has grappled with her, cries out in purest Bronx, 'Oi'm cured! Oi'm cured!,' and turns around to run toward the camera with arms waving in triumph—and damned if it isn't Shelley Winters. A shock like that can suspend belief for quite a while."

In 1967, Joseph McBride assessed the criticism of Pauline Kael, Stanley Kauffmann, and Macdonald, calling them the best in the business, citing Macdonald as "the most brilliant of the three, the strongest theoretician and the best writer." McBride wrote that Macdonald's criticism is especially useful "when he discusses the very best films—those of Fellini, Antonioni, Truffaut, Resnais, Bergman, Kurosawa—the most important, complex works. . . . When he reviews inferior work, such as *The Sound of Music* and *The Greatest Story Ever Told*, he uses the opportunity to unload his satirical arsenal, and somewhat obscures one of the critic's supplementary tasks: to change the opinion of the reader who happens to like the work in question."

Macdonald's analyses could cover difficult terrain with style and toughness. He wrote a dissenting review of one of the most highly regarded American films of the 1960s, Sidney Lumet's *The Pawnbroker* (1965). He built his case by writing about his ideas of the "good bad movie"—primarily genre items of the 1930s and 1940s—and the "bad good movie," which he identified as a contemporary strain having "serious intentions and pretensions that turns its back haughtily on the box-office in order to make a Meaningful Statement." Among his examples of the latter were Serge Bourguignon's *Sundays and Cybele* (1962), Lindsay Anderson's *This Sporting Life* (1963), Orson Welles's *The Trial* (1963), and Arthur Penn's *Mickey One* (1965). Macdonald called Lumet's film "the good bad film that has everything: alienation, anomie, neurosis, inability to love or communicate, the inhumanity of the metropolis, and the two great traumatic experiences of our age, the Jewish and the Negro, Harlem and the Nazi death camps. These are expressed with the most advanced technique: camera angles, extreme close-ups, jump-cutting, subliminal flashbacks, bleakly sophisticated photography by Boris Kaufman (Vigo's cameraman in the thirties), art direction by the accomplished Richard Sylbert, and the lead played by Rod Steiger . . . well-suited to the catatonic character he was required to play here. Yet *The Pawnbroker* seems to me a bore and a phony, a vulgarization of a serious theme, an exploitation of cinematic 'effects' used without taste or intelligence." Macdonald blamed the story, the music, and the seemingly heaped-on scenes of alienation. In the end, he blamed the director: "Mr. Lumet is a director who leaves no stone unturned, no bet unhedged."

Macdonald had no established criteria for judging movies. But he "put some guidelines down on paper," which were printed in 1969 in both *Esquire* and *Dwight Macdonald on Movies*. Roger Ebert wrote decades later that as a young critic he reviewed this five-part code about once a month:

(1) Are the characters consistent and in fact are they characters at all?
(2) Is it true to life?
(3) Is the photography cliché or is it adapted to the particular film and therefore original?

(4) Do the parts go together, do they add up to something; is there a rhythm established so that there is form, shape, climax, building up tension and exploding it?

(5) Is there a mind behind it; is there a feeling that a single intelligence has imposed his own view on the material?

Another time, Macdonald wrote, "It comes down, ultimately, to value judgments ('taste,' 'opinion') which can never be settled as conclusively as the freshness of an egg. Which is not to say that one man's opinion is as good as the next one's. Before the ultimate is reached, a critic goes through a process of defining, describing, reasoning, and persuading which is drawn from his own special experience and knowledge and which may or may not persuade his readers that his judgment is more accurate—'true' or 'right' would be claiming too much—than other judgments, according to their experience and knowledge. Readers have their own ideas, too, if they're worth writing for."

Macdonald became one of the esteemed targets sighted by Pauline Kael in her beginnings as film criticism's grand agent provocateur and mistress of verbal mayhem. "I always read [Macdonald] in *Esquire*, although I don't think he's a great film critic or even a really good one (although he's great fun on Biblical spectacles)," Kael wrote. "I think he's a great human being, and first things first."

This cheerfully couched slam was printed in a 1964 state-of-the-art examination of film criticism in the *Saturday Review*. A year later, in his review of Kael's first book, *I Lost It at the Movies* (1965), Macdonald started out like a gentleman, generally discussing the craft. "The trouble with most film criticism today is that it isn't criticism," he wrote. "It is, rather, appreciation, celebration, information, and it is written by intellectuals who have become 'insiders' in the sense that they are able to discourse learnedly about almost any movie without thinking much about whether it's any good—the very question must strike them as a little naive, and irrelevant—because they see it as a greater, or lesser, manifestation of the mystery, the godhead of Cinema." Macdonald continued, appreciating Kael's talent, even though she judged both him and Stanley Kauffmann as "squares." In the book review, Macdonald figured that Kael was not an exponent of this "insider" school of criticism, and that she also covered his definition of the critic's threefold job:

(1) to judge the quality of the film;
(2) to state precisely, with examples, just why one thinks it is good, bad or indifferent; and
(3) to relate it to other films and the history of art.

Macdonald mentioned that he at first approached the book with measures of respect and admiration. But at the close of his book review, he quotes her, "Movies are, happily, a popular medium (which makes it difficult to understand why Dwight Macdonald with his dedication to high art sacrifices his time to them)." His courtliness eroded on the page: "Considering that I have been writing about the movies as the most interesting 'high art' of our century since the early thirties . . . this is a bit much. Nor has it ever bothered me that Griffith—or Dickens—were popular. Maybe *I Lost It at the Movies* isn't as good a book as I thought it was when I began this review," he snapped, "And the hell with that 'respect and admiration.'"

Kael, whom Macdonald labeled, "The cat that walks by herself," was on the prowl, in search of very large prey. Siegfried Kracauer roamed into her view. He was a theorist who, like Parker Tyler in the 1940s, refused to think that the movies were art. He had written a classic history of the German film, *From Caligari to Hitler* (1947), via a Guggenheim Fellowship. His dogmatic views on film were culled into his magnum opus, *Theory of Film: The Redemption of Physical Reality* (1960).

To him, art was absent in movies because, "In order to make us experience physical reality, films must show what they picture. This requirement is so little self-evident that it raises the issue of the medium's relation to the traditional arts." Kracauer seemed to discount the work and nuances of actors and the people who design the meaning of what happens in the frame. To him, some readers inferred, a movie was like looking out (or in) a window, not at the realization of a concept.

Kracauer's book, from Oxford University Press, was welcomed down intelligentsia's red carpet by Richard Griffith, the curator of the Museum of Modern Art's Film Library, who said, "Dr. Kracauer's work supersedes all previous aesthetic theories of the film." Historian Paul Rotha, who wrote the influential *The Film Till Now* in 1930, and upgraded it with Griffith's help in 1949, called Kracauer's book, "The most important work to date in the English language on the theory and aesthetic of film. It will make a deep impact in all places where cinema is regarded as an art." One place it made an impact was inside Pauline Kael's ever-percolating mind.

In 1962, beginning a lifelong hunt to slaughter the fat and sacred cows, she mounted a drive against Kracauer entitled "Is There a Cure for Film Criticism?" in the British-based *Sight & Sound*. This 8,000-word analysis was hammered home in her obliterative style.

"After 300 pages Kracauer triumphantly reaches 'the Redemption of Physical Reality'"—interpreted here three paragraphs back—"and when he finally presents the proof of the pudding, it turns out to be—a pudding," Kael wrote. ". . . And so on into the night. We've covered all that heavily trod old ground, from Nietzsche to Comte to Whitehead, and Spengler and Toynbee and Durkheim. Kracauer must think we read books on the movies to get our knowledge of history and philosophy. . . .

"Films are not made by cameras, though many of them look as though they were, just as a lot of dialogue sounds as if it were written by typewriters," Kael pressed on. "Art is the greatest game, the supreme entertainment, because you discover the game as you play it. There is only one rule . . . Astonish us! In all art we look and listen for what we have not experienced quite that way before. . . . Why should pedants be allowed to spoil the game? There are men whose concept of love is so boring that you decide if that's what love is, you don't want it, you want something else." It was one of her first major allegorical treatments of the movies in sexual terms. "That's how I feel about Kracauer's 'cinema,' I want something else," she concluded.

She would get a lot more else—attention like no one else on the critical landscape. And she would dish it out like no one else before or since. Every few years for two decades, she came out with a fairly savage or polemical mega-essay, bloodying some corpulent or pretentious target. These ambushes were always full of her trademark sass and sexual innuendo, and they invariably altered the critical landscape. Any rules were usually heaved over her shoulder as she left the scorched earth for the next horizon. With each new ravaging, Kael added more confidence and ballast, preached a more egalitarian and for-the-moment common-sense homily than old Hollywood or the old guard wanted to hear. Whichever exponent of either was unlucky enough to be dead center in her sights was ground up in her literary shredder.

Between the grand events, Kael chewed up the everyday big shots. Three 1967 westerns—Andrew V. McLaglen's *The Way West*, Burt Kennedy's *The War Wagon*, and Howard Hawks's *El Dorado*—contained star pairings out of the trio of John Wayne, Robert Mitchum, and Kirk Douglas. Kael saw these films as symptomatic of a genre drained of ideas, and using big names to counterfeit the content void. "The heroes nobody believes in—except as movie stars—are the result of a corrupted art form," she wrote. "Going to a western these days for simplicity or heroism or grandeur or meaning is about like trying to mate with an ox."

Rounding up 1960s epics, including David Lean's *Doctor Zhivago* (1965), Kael wrote that she couldn't abide the director's precision: "What makes a David Lean spectacle uninteresting finally is that it's in such goddamn good taste. It's all so ploddingly intelligent and controlled, so 'distinguished.' The hero may stick his arm in blood up to the elbow but you can be assured that the composition will be academically, impeccably composed." She turned a review of director-producer Stanley Kramer's *Ship of Fools* (1965) into a career indictment of the man, concluding: "Kramer asks for congratulations on the size and importance of his unrealized aspirations. In politics a candidate can hope to be judged on what he intends to do, but in art we judge what is done. Stanley Kramer runs for office in the arts."

Kael's intensely personal reviews were distantly reminiscent of the responses of Otis Ferguson and James Agee. But where Ferguson or Agee bemoaned a dud, Kael ratcheted up the provocation levels, wantonly throttling individuals in print. Aside from "Is There a Cure for Film Criticism?" Kael's broad, benchmark compositions include: "Circles and Squares" in *Film Quarterly* in 1963, in which she blithely shot Andrew Sarris, the American messenger of the French auteur theory, figuratively in the kneecaps with a scattershot pen; a glowing watershed review of Arthur Penn's *Bonnie and Clyde* (1967) in *The New Yorker*, certainly one of the single most important film assessments in history; and "Trash, Art, and the Movies" in *Harper's* in 1969, which stands as her essential manifesto on the movies and reviewing.

Kael was born in Petaluma, California, in 1919 and raised on a farm. Her parents were Jewish Polish immigrants. She wrote that her father was adulterous, agnostic, a moviegoer, Republican, and "democratic in a way that Easterners still don't understand." She attended the University of California at Berkeley from 1936 to 1940 and began freelance writing in 1953. The piece of lore that traveled from those early days into career coverage of her was that, in her first review, of Charlie Chaplin's *Limelight* (1952), for San Francisco's *City Lights*, she referred to the picture as "Slimelight."

She broadcast reviews over KPFA radio in Berkeley and managed two theatres there from 1955 to 1960. Her creative programming for the Berkeley Cinema Guild theatres included revivals of films featuring W.C. Fields, the Marx Brothers, and Mae West, as well as Busby Berkeley musicals. Her one-paragraph program notes showed some of the spirited prose to come. After moving to New York, she contributed essays to *Film*

Quarterly, The Massachusetts Review, Kulchur, and other small magazines as well as Great Britain's esteemed *Sight & Sound.* Those provocative pieces led to gigs as a film critic for *Life* in 1965, *McCall's* from 1965 to 1966, *The New Republic* in 1967, and a permanent home in 1968 at *The New Yorker.*

She was fired from *McCall's* for her negative reviews, including of Robert Wise's *The Sound of Music* (1965). She called it "the big lie, the sugarcoated lie that people seem to want to eat." The musical, an Academy Award-winning best picture, didn't smack of genuine family life for her. "Wasn't there perhaps one little Von Trapp who didn't want to sing his head off," she wrote, "or who screamed that he wouldn't act out little glockenspiel routines for Papa's party guests, or who got nervous and threw up if he had to get out on a stage?" Her reviews "became less and less appropriate for a mass-audience magazine," claimed *McCall's* editor, Robert Stein. "From the beginning I thought I was the wrong person for their readers," Kael said. "But they were willing to take the risk. I had realized that I would sock the ladies right between the ears, but what the hell is the point of writing if you're writing banality."

"She went to movies, not films, and she scorned abstract theory as a barrier between the moviegoer and the actual experience of losing it at the movies," wrote Roger Ebert after her death, using a wordplay reference to the first collection of her criticism, *I Lost It at the Movies.* Atlantic Monthly-Little Brown published the book in 1965, and it was a best seller. In retrospect, it was the most important collection of film writing published since two posthumous volumes that eventually accrued classical status: *Agee on Film* (1958) and Robert Warshow's *The Immediate Experience* (1962). In *The New York Times Book Review,* Richard Schickel, then film critic of *Life,* welcomed Kael's book and called her "the sanest, saltiest, most resourceful and least attitudinizing movie critic currently in practice in the United States."

Richard Corliss once described Kael's modus operandi in her pre-*New Yorker* period: "She couldn't have been further out of the loop—the double helix, really, that embraced Hollywood movies and Manhattan media—so she devised a piquant strategy for being heard. She would go to a movie and review the audience. Sometimes, she would review the reviewers, a tactic that led to slams on *The New York Times'* Bosley Crowther and epochal tussles over the auteur theory with *The Village Voice's* Andrew Sarris. Not until Kael joined the *New Yorker* in 1968 did she move to the front line and have to concentrate pretty much on reviewing the damn movies."

Kael preferred the earthiness in films, was at the forefront of espousing liberal sexuality on the American screen, and wanted to release moviegoers from following traditional Hollywood mores. She was all for a more sensual experience at the movies and her sword cut both ways. When she didn't get what she thought she should from a movie, she still could portray it in sexual terms. She felt that Richard Lester's *A Funny Thing Happened on the Way to the Forum* (1966) was "like coitus interruptus going on forever." Her style carried impact, and analyses of it were occasionally as probing as her own reviews. Joseph McBride likened her to an ethnologist more than a critic for her pronounced interest in social traditions. He surveyed some of the themes in her work, such as nostalgia for the films of Preston Sturges and Ernst Lubitsch, but a cold shoulder to Federico Fellini and Ingmar Bergman, her obsessive sexual similes, and a noticeably thin regard for the aesthetics of movies.

"In spite of her severe limitations, which often make her work infuriatingly perverse, she is original, provocative, and, most important, the best American critic currently practicing," McBride wrote. ". . . Most of Miss Kael's work is about equally criticism and polemic; her inclinations, it seems, favor the latter; she has the candor to call the last section of her *I Lost It at the Movies*, 'Polemics.'" Kael's greatest diatribe was against the auteur theory, igniting the longest-lasting major debate on the American critical landscape. The theory was launched in America from the small magazine, *Film Culture*. This was a now legendary 68-page piece, "Notes on the Auteur Theory in 1962," written by the magazine's associate editor, Andrew Sarris, who eventually became film critic for *The Village Voice* and, decades later, the *New York Observer*.

Sarris espoused opinions appearing in the Paris-based *Cahiers du cinéma* that expressed the notion that, since a film is a work of art, it carries the imprint of a creator, and that creator is the director, who guides any film during its production. Despite all the people involved in the making of a movie, including the writer who conceived it and the stars whose personalities can reshape the original writer's vision, the director is the one who can claim its authorship. The theory, as Sarris reaffirmed it later in his controversial 1968 book-length ranking of directors, *The American Cinema: Directors and Directions, 1929–1968*, was one of film history and not prophecy, meaning historically bad directors can make good films, and bad films can come from generally good directors.

In the book, Sarris identified the great directors as being in "The Pantheon." They are Charlie Chaplin, Robert J. Flaherty, John Ford, D.W. Griffith, Howard Hawks, Alfred Hitchcock, Buster Keaton, Fritz Lang, Ernst Lubitsch, F.W. Murnau, Max Ophüls, Jean Renoir, Josef von Sternberg, and Orson Welles. The critic created 11 descending categories. Down in category five, "Less Than Meets the Eye," are such storied greats as John Huston, Elia Kazan, David Lean, Carol Reed, Billy Wilder, Joseph L. Mankiewicz, William Wyler, and Fred Zinnemann. The firestorm touched off by the magazine piece, then the book, continues to smolder to this day, like the eternal embers in that coal mine beneath Pennsylvania, vented by Kael, who hauled off at the typewriter keys for her famous bash, "Circles and Squares."

"If his [Sarris's] aesthetic is based on expediency, then it may be expedient to point out that it takes extraordinary intelligence and discrimination and taste to *use* any theory in the arts, and that without those qualities a theory becomes a rigid formula (which indeed is what is happing among auteur critics)," Kael wrote. "The greatness of critics like Bazin in France and Agee in America may have something to do with their using their full range of their intelligence and intuition, rather than relying on formulas. Criticism is an art, not a science, and a critic who follows rules will fail in one of his most important functions: perceiving what is original and important in *new* work and helping others to see," she wrote.

These beginnings of the auteur theory controversy have been resurrected from time to time throughout film criticism history, over which a few of the longer-lasting exponents have taken a certain proprietary care, including Richard Schickel. "She was even then a devastating polemicist, with a special gift for making anyone who disagreed with her look not just wrong but foolish," Schickel wrote decades later. "The portrait of Andy that emerged from her piece was a sort of *idiot savant* desperately hammering together a theoretical structure—in my mind's eye (or maybe hers) it looked something like the *Our Gang* clubhouse—to shelter what she implicitly identified as an arrested passion for old Hollywood crap."

When Kael wrote the piece, she was amid an extended period of bashing other critics. Dwight Macdonald, Bosley Crowther, and Stanley Kauffmann all took multiple jabs from her stinging quill. She often quoted them in denigrating ways in her reviews as a method to set up her own opinions. McBride, who appreciated her talent but was ambivalent on her methods, specified her unfairness to Sarris. "In one 24-page essay (in *I Lost It at the Movies*) she blasts Andrew Sarris and the auteur theory by using his most extreme statements, often taken out of context, to make him look like a moron," McBride wrote. "Only about half her essay hits the mark because the other half is grossly unfair to Sarris; like every other critic who can construct a sentence, he is used as a springboard for Miss Kael's criticism."

Sarris responded, too: "As often happens, the attack on the theory received more publicity than the theory itself. Unfortunately, the American attacks on the auteur theory only confirmed the backward provincialism of American film criticism. Not that the auteur theory is beyond criticism. Far from it. What is beyond criticism is the historical curiosity required to discuss any critical theory on film."

Decades later in *Film Comment*, Sarris wrote: "Nothing had prepared me for the polemical fury of Pauline Kael, who denounced me and my ilk as a bunch of closet queens with a passion for Howard Hawks action movies with barechested heroes—much as if we were all auditioning for the Sal Mineo role in *Rebel Without a Cause*. . . . I was magnified as a menace to all that was enjoyable and worthwhile in movies. The estimable Dwight Macdonald went so far in that epoch to describe me as a Godzilla clambering from the depths. (I am gratified to say we later made up in print—something I cannot say about Pauline Kael and me)."

But before that was written, Sarris shot back and the fur flew with "Notes on the Auteur Theory in 1970," which was published in his book *The Primal Screen: Essays on Film and Related Topics* (1973). As can happen with long, bitter arguments, things got personal. Citing Kael's "misapplied feminist zeal," Sarris wrote, "Whereas Miss Kael believes that Barbra Streisand's cavortings in trashy musicals are worth thousands of words of gushy Kaeleidoscopic prose, I believe that movies like *Point Blank*, *Gunn*, *Madigan* and *Once Upon a Time in the West* are infinitely more interesting than any of Barbra's barbarities. And that is about all that can be said on the subject short of the Me Jane, you Tarzan fulminations Miss Kael originally invoked to add a new dimension to her *ad hominem* arguments."

The last sentence might assume the case was closed, but Sarris continued: "Unlike the great Garbo in *Ninotchka*, Miss K has always made too much of an issue of her womanhood. . . . Even Miss K's most fervent admirers do not hold her to the humdrum standards of coherence and consistency to which the rest of us are accountable. Her critical apparatus has more in common with a wind machine than a searchlight, and when all the papers and ticket stubs stop blowing around, it is difficult for the more orderly readers to find their bearings.

"Miss K is more an entertainer than an enlightener, and she is singularly ungenerous (at least in print) to her colleagues." Sarris wrote that Kael disdained good manners, lacked kindness, and was scornful. "Indeed, the increasingly perverse otherness of film criticism seems to cause her genuine distress despite all the success and recognition she received," Sarris continued. "Her toleration of dissent is comparable in degree to Spiro Agnew's, and her capacity to communicate with any critic she hasn't spiritually castrated is virtually nil. Consequently, there is no point in arguing with Miss K; the most anyone can do is co-exist in the same sphere of influence without succumbing to the Perils of Pauline, a tagline I invented seven years ago and still find timely," Sarris wrote.

Sarris was right about there being no point in arguing with Kael. She never returned for any Round Two. She was all about closing the case at the outset and walking away, concluded with the issue, the earth trod and scarred. She never felt the need to return to allow the impugned their day in court. She wasn't about debate. In the coming decade, this arrogance left at least one major issue hanging when she bushwhacked Orson Welles with "Raising Kane" in *The New Yorker* (see Chapter Five).

Corliss summed up the meaning of the Kael-Sarris jousting to film criticism: "They raised the musty level of film criticism to a volcanic, love-hate art. Their wrangles over the auteur theory had excitement and politics and sport. The intensity of their debate lured people to see new films, and to see old (especially old Hollywood) movies in a new way. They opened eyes, awakened curiosity, aroused intelligence.

"They made film criticism sexy. Pictures were things that mattered; ideas were worth fighting over. Forget Tracy-Hepburn. Sarris and Kael were more like Ali-Frazier. Film criticism was the main event, and these two were the champs." This battle royal only worked to draw attention to, and enhance, the reputation of the profession.

A new era of film criticism found 6,000 words to stand on, an essay that remains one of the most important pieces of film writing. "The audience is alive to it," Kael wrote about *Bonnie and Clyde* in *The New Yorker*, tapping into the film's visceral, amoral immediacy, a spin ripe for a generation changing in fast

and violent modes due to Vietnam, civil rights, political assassi-
nations and the drug culture—a generation searching for touchstones.

"Our experience as we watch it has some connection
with the way we reacted to movies in childhood: how we came
to love them and feel they were ours—not an art that we learned
over the years to appreciate but simply and immediately ours."
Kael enthused. ". . . The whole point of *Bonnie and Clyde* is to
rub our noses in it, to make us pay our dues for laughing. The
dirty reality of death—not suggestions but blood and holes—is
necessary. . . . Suddenly, in the last few years, our view of the
world has gone beyond 'good taste.' Tasteful suggestions of violence would at this point be a more grotesque form of comedy
than *Bonnie and Clyde* attempts. *Bonnie and Clyde* needs violence; violence is its meaning."

Joe Morgenstern of *Newsweek* dismissed the film as
a "squalid shoot-'em-up for the moron trade" on August 21,
1967. But he was convinced to take a second look at the picture and then did something unheard of up to that time in film
criticism: he reversed his opinion. And he wrote about that—the
very next week. "I am sorry to say I consider that [first] review
grossly unfair and regrettably inaccurate," Morgenstern wrote.
"I am sorrier to say I wrote it." The second time around, Morgenstern wrote that he witnessed "scene after scene of dazzling
artistry." *Bonnie and Clyde* served as the galvanizing point for
the generation of young, outsider filmmakers who came through
Hollywood's front door in the next decade. The film pushed the
envelope with its culminating slow-motion massacre of the title
duo. The pinnacle of Penn's directorial career, the film created
new stars in Faye Dunaway and Gene Hackman and affirmed
Warren Beatty's place as a top talent and box-office draw.

Finally ensconced at *The New Yorker* in 1968, Kael socked
away. "She anointed herself the liberator of American film criticism, freeing it from snooty academics who treated movies as
weightless *divertissements*," wrote Neal Gabler. "Pauline Kael
taught us to stop worrying and love movies." She stirred up the

juices of cineastes as several editions of *Film Heritage* produced different considerations of her style and influence—one editorial condemning her university lecture-circuit penchant for bashing formal education.

But by 1968 she came to mainstream attention, earning profiles in both *Time* and *Newsweek*, profiled by Nora Ephron at the *New York Post* and straying onto the radar of Eliot Fremont-Smith at *The New York Times*, who wrote, "Miss Kael is the most quotable critic writing, but what is important and bracing is that she relates movies to other experience, to ideas and attitudes, to ambition, books, money, other movies, to politics and the evolving culture, to moods of the audience, to our sense of our-selves—to what movies do to us, the acute and self-scrutinizing awareness of which is always at the core of her judgment."

The books packaging Kael's reviews became best sellers. No film critic before her captured the media's fascination the way Pauline Kael did in the late 1960s. Other critics in later decades would become multimedia darlings through their own commands of television forums, primarily Roger Ebert and Leonard Maltin, both of whom were first and foremost writers, and have had perennial success as authors. But Kael came upon the 1960s critical scene like a gunslinger, proved her mettle early and damned the consequences, and made a great deal of sense to a generation of moviegoers who were also looking for something new and exciting on the screen. For her calamity, she was offered a premium job in the media capital. *New Yorker* editor William Shawn gave her carte blanche on editorial space. She began by alternating half-years on film criticism coverage, writing the fall through late spring reviews, while British novelist and screen-writer Penelope Gilliatt handled the balance. Originally the ulti-mate outsider, she in time became the ultimate insider.

Kael's primary career manifesto was published in the 1969 *Harper's* essay, "Trash, Art, and the Movies." John Pow-ers, writing decades later in *LA Weekly*, went so far as to say that this piece, which was republished in her collection, *Going Steady* (1969), "gave the pop sensibility its credo, almost explicitly." She verified many of her previously espoused notions, which had been scattered piecemeal throughout her reviews and essays—insistence that movies were to be enjoyed and not studied like other art forms. "Rather than argue that movies should be elevated to the status of art, and therefore taken seriously, she insisted that pop culture has a worth all its own," Powers interpreted. "It can touch us as deeply as art, or simply excite us with its wit, grace and excitement—qualities every bit as valuable as high-mindedness. In one of her most moving passages, Pauline saw that what was at stake in all this was an idea of community."

That passage began: "An actor's scowl, a small subversive gesture, a dirty remark that someone tosses off with a mock-innocent face, and the world makes a little bit of sense. Sitting there alone or painfully alone because those with you do not react as you do, you know there must be others perhaps in this theater or in this city, surely in other theaters in other cities, now, in the past or future, who react as you do. And because movies are the most total and encompassing art form we have, these reactions can seem the most personal and, maybe the most important, imaginable. The romance of movies is not just in those stories and those people on the screen but in the adolescent dream of meeting others who feel as you do about what you've seen. You do meet them, of course, and you do know each other at once because you talk less about good movies than about what you love in bad movies."

"Trash, Art, and the Movies" was often re-read by Kael's minions, and referenced as an essential parchment for novices coming into the field. Richard Schickel, who wrote a column for *Harper's* during the time the manifesto was published, judged from a 2006 perspective that the essay "was a typical Kael production: 42 seemingly endless pages of dither and blither, good ideas and half-baked ones all mixed up in her characteristic edge-of-hysteria manner."

Kael's idea that the movies bring a sense of community to cineastes has some connection to views of the audience expressed by Hugo Münsterberg in the 1910s, Gilbert Seldes in the 1920s,

Parker Tyler in the 1940s, and her old nemesis, Dwight Mac-donald, in the 1950s and 1960s. "The cat that walks by herself" found that fellow moviegoers shared in the ideas of "bad good movies" and "good bad movies," maybe not in the same ways as Macdonald or even Andrew Sarris did, but shared just the same. Her position in the catbird's seat of film criticism—where she roosted as if it were an eagle's nest—did not last long enough for her to analyze the moviegoer's brand of sharing in the 1990s, which, in the most jaundiced view, occurred among multiplex hordes after TV reports of boffo box-office weekends.

It's easy in hindsight to point out shortcomings and pin-point errors, and it's particularly easy to see Kael's rabble-rousing for what it was. It is, however, much easier to see her brilliant writing for what it remains, her razor-sharp opinions for what they were, and her legacy for what it truly is: she was the great-est film critic to practice in America. The virtues of her work are self-evident, as are her mistakes and sheer meanness to filmmak-ers and fellow film critics, a meanness to rival her contemporary, John Simon. She loved movies, thought they should be better, never expected them to be better, but kept going to the theatre anyway, for that glimmer of hope or those aspects that she could love in bad movies.

In the 1960s, the decade that film criticism became *de rigueur* on campuses, in newspapers and mass-market periodi-cals, and began on television, Pauline Kael was at the spiritual center of the new fascination for movies—and she was just get-ting started. What's rarely pointed out about Kael is her seem-ingly incipient need to create a commotion every few years to make it clear that she was out there doing the pioneering of the trade. Kael would continue inciting temblors on film criticism's landscape in the coming decade by fatuously and foolishly im-pugning Orson Welles regarding his screenplay for *Citizen Kane* (1941), rapturously extolling Bernardo Bertolucci's *Last Tango in Paris* (1973), and raving over Robert Altman's *Nashville* (1975) months before its release, earning the ire of Paramount Pictures, for whom she then went to work in a script-consulting capacity, a post attained through the agency of Warren Beatty. But she returned shortly thereafter to the pages of *The New Yorker* to reign supreme as the top film critic through the 1980s.

She was clearly at the top of the field, even if many of the practitioners standing on the lower slopes glared upward with a baleful eye. To remain on top requires real staying power, which requires planning ahead, which requires a keen cultural radar, and a ruthlessness to keep the engines hot. In her own way, Kael kept the engines stoked to remain facile for new readers, not unlike, in other fields, the difficult yet powerfully enduring courses charted by Franklin D. Roosevelt, or even Frank Sinatra or Willie Mays. She was practically peerless among women as the roundly regarded No. 1 in her particular specialty. In a way, her career was akin to the great undiminished mistresses of the screen, Katharine Hepburn and Bette Davis, even if the memory of her tiny, meanly uncompromising specter might translate to those souls who crossed her path without a clean getaway to appear more like one of Mercedes McCambridge's hard-bitten harridans.

While Kael's story continues later on in these pages as her status among the cognoscenti remained at the head of the table, another assertive female film critic rose to greater prominence among the hoi polloi through the decade. Judith Crist began reviewing movies first on New York's ABC-TV affiliate in 1962, then nationally on NBC's *The Today Show* in 1963, and concurrently in the last years of her newspaper, the *New York Herald-Tribune*, which folded in 1966 with several other Big Apple dailies after a prolonged union strike. She also reviewed movies airing on television for *TV Guide*, beginning in 1966. Crist was the first nationally known film critic and the first multimedia celebrity of film criticism.

Kael's and Crist's shared traits included tough opinions and intolerance for Hollywood schmaltz, concurrent arrivals on the critical landscape in middle age, Eastern European Jewish heritage, and the choppy monosyllabic surnames ripe for confusion. The fact is that they were confused with each other or fused as one in some contemporary as well as historically distant reporting.

Crist was a celebrity in the early 1960s to the general public, which hardly knew of Kael until later in the decade after the publishing of *I Lost It at the Movies*. Even after that, Kael became well known only among the intelligentsia, and remained elusive to the public at large until *Time* and *Newsweek* wrote about her in 1968, when *The New Yorker* appointed her film critic. Kael's profile rose even further in the coming years as Crist's faded. Today, Crist is largely forgotten while Kael is considered the greatest film critic of them all. Then again, Crist never demonstrated the writing style, the impassioned crusader's approach to film criticism, or the vast knowledge of movies and the arts that Kael did by rote. Yet, the two of them have been confused, as late as the 1990s and by no less than *The New York Times*.

Crist, a product of the newspaper business, came to film criticism at age 40. She was born in New York City on May 22, 1922, and attended Hunter College and then Columbia University. She taught at the State College of Washington in Pullman (now Washington State University) and joined the staff of the *Herald-Tribune* in 1945 as a reporter. She was associate drama critic from 1957 to 1963, working, as she wrote, "as handmaiden to God," or second string to the great theatre critic, Walter Kerr. Crist was arts editor on the *Herald-Tribune* from 1960 to 1963, and film critic from 1963 to 1966. For eight months into 1967, she was film critic on the short-lived *New York World Journal Tribune*, a merger of three newspapers that occurred after the catastrophic citywide newspaper union strike of 1966.

The Private Eye, the Cowboy and the Very Naked Girl, the 1967 collection of Crist's reviews and essays from Holt, Rinehart and Winston, mostly contained her writings from the *Herald-Tribune*. "I am a journalistic critic with no pretensions to esoterica," Crist wrote in the introduction. "I speak for the movie-lover rather than the cineaste, for the audience rather than the industry." She was like Kael in that she was tough to please. But unlike her, Crist had no sociological bent, espoused no polemics, and had little interest in trotting out autobiographical details. She wrote in lucid, direct terms exactly what she thought, without allegory or ambiguity. "I have subscribed to the James Agee premise that film criticism is a conversation between moviegoers," Crist wrote. "I relish agreement but I think quite frankly that my immediate goal is to keep the conversation going, to stimulate my listener into a response, whether it involves a reappraisal of his own opinions or an affirmation of his disagreement. Ours is the age of the expert, where we sit and wait to get the word from on high, to operate on a consensus of what the ephemeral 'they' think. If I can prod a person or two into just thinking for himself, let alone organizing his thought into opinion form, let alone even articulating that opinion— critical mission practically accomplished."

Crist's mission hit a minefield after a few months on the beat for the *Herald-Tribune*. Writer-director-producer Delmer Daves's *Spencer's Mountain* (1963) was a studio-touted family film photographed in glorious color by Charles Lawton, Jr., amid the splendor of Wyoming's Teton Range. The film starred Henry Fonda and Maureen O'Hara in charge of a homogenized brood of the type that later became popular on TV. Crist witnessed the juxtaposed scenes of church hymn singing with the sex education of the eldest teen, the rather unworldly Clayboy (James MacArthur), which included barnyard observations and the unchecked predations of the local boarding-school teen girl, Claris (Mimsy Farmer), home for the summer with hormones in overdrive. Crist wrote that the girl raped the boy offscreen, after scenes of heavy petting. Crist was not unconcerned with the depiction of sex, but more concerned with the alternation of what she called scenes of piety with vulgarity.

Crist wrote, "For sheer prurience and perverted morality disguised as piety," the film "makes the nudie shows at the Rialto look like Walt Disney productions." Crist wrote that the venue, Radio City Music Hall, one of New York City's major tourism draws, especially during student vacations, colluded with Warner Bros. in exposing youth to a film that was "outstanding for its smirking sexuality, its glorification of the vulgar, its patronizing tone toward the humble, its mealymouthed piety." She blamed Daves for his skewed idea of "wholesome," and called the "deplorable" result the product of the "trite aspirations of vulgarians."

Warner Bros. and Radio City Music Hall did then collude. They jointly pulled advertising from the venerable *Herald-Tribune*, a 400,000-circulation daily. Newspapers before and since have been threatened by film distributors and exhibitors when their critics panned pictures. And reviewers have often been told by newspaper advertising departments to soft-peddle any real criticisms of certain films, because the bills were being paid by the studios' advertising dollars.

But this was suddenly a big stage for such an epic rug-pulling. Crist was a celebrity in New York prior to becoming the *Herald-Tribune*'s critic, mostly by virtue of her TV exposure throughout the previous year during the newspaper strike of 1962, when she was a regular twice a day on Channel 7, WABC-TV. Also, the *Herald-Tribune* wasn't about to compromise its editorial content for an advertiser, which paid for the privilege of being on its pages, or to be pushed around by anyone in Hollywood. The timeliness of the issue also figured into its cause célèbre status. Film criticism was part of a growing cultural phenomenon that was later dubbed the "Film Generation." The Crist affair happened at a high point in the rush to assess movies as a vital part of the general social discourse as an art form.

The New York media covered this imbroglio in an era when news coverage rarely had anything to do with developments in entertainment or developments in the media itself. This lack of news coverage for entertainment and media might seem practically prehistoric to today's studio publicists and Internet film critics, or to a general public that has been raised on attention paid to the film and TV businesses through *Entertainment Tonight* and *People*. In 1963, there was miniscule entertainment reporting outside of the trade papers, *Daily/Weekly Variety*, and its smaller rival, *The Hollywood Reporter*. Yet the treatment of

Crist and the *Herald-Tribune* received widespread general coverage, even outside New York.

On June 5, 1963, the *Herald-Tribune* published an editorial that stated, "A newspaper whose comments and critiques can be controlled by advertisers cheats its readers and ceases to be an honest newspaper. . . . We feel sorry for film producers who consider themselves above criticism. . . . They injure their own reputations, and hurt the critic not at all. Mrs. Crist is one of journalism's most competent critics. The *Herald-Tribune* is proud of her talent and integrity. We are also proud of journalistic standards which leave no room for such inane pressure tactics."

"The editorial was brilliant," Crist later told author Barbara Belford. "It had never happened before in the history of newspaper criticism, and it changed the way editors throughout the country viewed their movie critics." Part of that change included a popularization of the job. During this time, and in relatively few years, judging movies shifted from a sidelight as something in the columns next to the funny papers and the crossword puzzle to a place of respect. It kept evolving as a position for which to strive, a cultural profession of knowledge and ideas.

After the *World Journal Tribune* shut down, Crist found new venues, reviewing for *TV Guide, New York* magazine, and NBC's *The Today Show.* A star name in journalism, Crist made the public aware that film criticism was a specialty and something on which to spend a lifetime. While other critics had hopped on and off the film beat at other career venues—William K. Zinsser at the *Herald-Tribune* and John McCarten at *The New Yorker* for instance—Crist was one of the most notable film critics to transfer her vocation to different venues and across media barriers. Other film critics changed outlets in the 1960s, including John Simon and Rex Reed. Richard Schickel moved from one Henry Luce-owned magazine, *Life*, to another, *Time*. But Crist instilled the idea that once a film critic, always a film critic.

The new understanding of film criticism was part of the new respect for movies. This translated as part of the paradigm shift in the thinking of writers, directors, actors, and technicians who quit flying out to Hollywood on a piecemeal basis in the postwar era to make the occasional film "for the money," only to return to Broadway, where eastern theatrical snobbery dictated where the "real work" was done. Television production moved practically wholesale to Hollywood by 1962. The talent settled under the sun as regular Angelenos, and made their entire livings in the movie and TV businesses. Simultaneously, attention to Hollywood and its product became more keenly focused in newspapers and magazines. Many people in Middle America who had never considered film criticism started finding it in their periodicals. Judith Crist soon became synonymous with film criticism after she went on national airwaves on NBC-TV's *The Today Show* in 1963. Crist's opinions on the latest films became a regular portion of the morning ritual with coffee and anchorman Hugh Downs.

Crist's levelheaded look at Hollywood had no tolerance for bloated extravagance like Joseph L. Mankiewicz's *Cleopatra* (1963), the most expensive movie made up to that time, costing $40 million, and released by Twentieth Century-Fox. It was brought out by Darryl F. Zanuck's studio with fanfare, the way standard bearers might have announced and borne the Queen of the Nile herself on a chaise longue. Starring Elizabeth Taylor, with Rex Harrison as Julius Caesar and Richard Burton as Marc Antony, *Cleopatra* was filled with gaudy spectacle. Crist couldn't believe for one minute that she was transported by the film anywhere near Egypt, as she described Taylor's work more like "carrying on in one of Miami Beach's more exotic resorts," and the actress's epic arguments with Burton's Antony as akin to "having it out in the Egyptian wing of the Metropolitan Museum." The critic concluded: "All is monumental—but the people are not. The mountain of notoriety has produced a mouse."

Twentieth Century-Fox couldn't abide the fact that its enormous spectacle, six years in the making, was being compared to a tiny rodent. Zanuck's studio barred Crist from future screenings, and one of that studio's publicists labeled her "a snide, supercilious, sour bitch." Battle-hardened by a career as a female reporter during the war, when there weren't that many women in the trade, Crist blithely concocted a shortening of this label. Nicknamed the "Triple-S" rating, it became a badge of honor she offered to journalists covering her exploits.

Reviewers have been barred before and since from screenings arranged by certain studios, told to stay out of specific prearranged press previews after panning the company's previous picture(s); that has been an ongoing fact of film criticism. But Fox's barring of Crist lasted only a short time. The general press picked up on her exploits, and editorials again supported freedom of the press. Roger Ebert in particular had a long memory for the *Cleopatra* incident.

"The single most influential event in the history of modern newspaper film reviewing took place as recently as 1963," Ebert wrote in the 1990s in *Film Comment*, "when 20th Century Fox banned Judith Crist from its screenings after she attacked *Cleopatra* in the *New York Herald-Tribune*. This development so tickled the public fancy that it became necessary for the trendier papers to import or create their own hard-to-please reviewers. Before 1963, with the exception of a handful of papers in New York, Los Angeles, Washington, and a few other cities, newspaper criticism existed on a fan-magazine level, if at all. . . . Movie reviews were ghosted by various staff writers under a house byline (Mae Tinee—get it?—in the *Chicago Tribune*). But by the middle years of the decade, any self-respecting paper had its own local critic, and every one of them had studied Kael's *I Lost It at the Movies* and [in 1968 in book form] Andrew Sarris's *The American Cinema*," Ebert explained.

Ebert himself began reviewing films in the late 1960s for the *Chicago Sun-Times*. He represented a new breed of newspaper film critic, one who carried on the daily-deadline tradition while also recognizing the new trend of public awareness about movies. One of the new newspaper critics in the decade, Ebert was the opposite of the gentlemen-critic holdovers from another generation who upheld a moral center in film storytelling and seemed squeamish on issues of more prevalent sex and violence. At the head of this table was the longtime anchor of *The New York Times*'s film coverage, Bosley Crowther, while spiritual disciples included Philip K. Scheuer at the *Los Angeles Times*, Archer Winsten at the *New York Post*, and Harold V. Cohen at the *Pittsburgh Post-Gazette*.

The gradual youth movement that began in film criticism in the 1960s was a push that had to have a shove on the other end. Because of his position as the lead man at both the paper of record and the New York Film Critics Circle, Bosley Crowther had calcified over time into something of a monumental institution. He became the target of other critics, particularly Pauline Kael, who bashed Crowther's opinions in print any chance she could. His ideas seemed not only arcane and didactic to her, but they also expressly misplaced the public's trust in him by misrepresenting the films and characters in them through his own moral compass. An interpretation of his judgment, in retrospect, worked like an extension of the pervasive social responsibility, ethical unassailability, and honor implicit in the steady rudder behind *The New York Times*. If other critics were the eye-level social workers of the trade, Crowther maintained aspects of the stern and unwavering Monsignor.

Kael attributed to Crowther "barbarous language" for running down playwright John Osborne's conceptions of the lead characters in Tony Richardson's films *Look Back in Anger* (1958) and *The Entertainer* (1960). Not reviewing the film or going back to the source play, Crowther's writing telescoped back all the way to Osborne's very conception of putting these characters on paper. Crowther wrote that Laurence Olivier's Archie Rice in the latter film was "a hollow, hypocritical heel . . . too shallow and cheap to be worth very much consideration." The character was disreputable, Crowther said, so forget about considering going to the movies to see him, the great actor whose mastery made him so unforgettable, or Richardson's film, which had the temerity to present such a self-involved cad to the public at large.

In his review of Martin Ritt's *Hud* (1963), Crowther wrote that Hud Bannon's (Paul Newman) affair with another man's wife pointed to "one of the sure, unmistakable tokens of a dangerous social predator." Irked by this, Kael went so far as to reference her own family, citing her "generous and kind" father's extramarital rovings in print. Her attacks on Crowther became occasionally completely dismissive. Beginning an essay on Stanley Kubrick's *Lolita* (1962), she sideswiped the *Times*'s man early in the goings—"Bosley Crowther, who can always be counted on to miss the point . . ."—and went on to actually review the film.

Kael's campaign pointed at certain truths. In a time in which the growing youth and counterculture movements were alive in the land, upholding the status quo of an outmoded generation wasn't going to last. Crowther made the attacks on him very easy by veering frequently into his stuffy, bourgeois, New York-centric, eastern-elite, condescendingly beneficent viewpoints. They were occasionally very difficult to accept. In his assessment of Satyajit Ray's *Pather Panchali* (1955), Crowther wrote, "Chief among the delicate revelations that emerge from its loosely formed account of the pathetic little joys and sorrows of a poor little Indian family in Bengal is the touching indication that poverty does not nullify love and that even the most afflicted people can find some modest pleasures in their worlds."

If other critics weren't on the attack the way Kael was, they at least considered Crowther's opinions irrelevant, even though—or especially because—they issued from the greatest paper in the land. Crowther's place at the head of the table as the main critic of *The New York Times* also made other critics particularly envious of him. The prevailing wisdom was that the greatest paper sorely lacked anything near the best critic. Newspapermen of the midcentury tended to hold onto their hard-won posts, and management tended to let them do it while the younger and perhaps more intellectually facile heir apparents—film buffs in this case, on and off the *Times*—dropped aspirations and moved on. But Hollis Alpert of the *Saturday Review*, Joe Morgenstern of *Newsweek*, Judith Crist, and Andrew Sarris all felt that Crowther had outlasted his time on the changing critical landscape. Joseph McBride wrote in *Film Heritage* that Crowther was a "dashingly incompetent blurb-writer." Crowther's smugly elder-statesman brand of commentary only prodded cavalier asides in print from the respectfully distant likes of Dwight Macdonald and Stanley Kauffmann. And only then did they cite Crowther because his widely read words demanded attention as the view of the *Times*'s man—and certainly not because they were especially prescient or adroit.

It was only a matter of time before forces inside the *Times* who recognized Crowther as an archaic liability succeeded in forcing him to step down from his high perch. Actually, he was shot down by *Bonnie and Clyde*, perhaps the most influential film in the history of film criticism. Arthur Gelb, who was in charge of the *Times*'s cultural coverage at the time, re-created in his autobiography, *City Room*, the conversation with Turner Catledge, the executive editor, about the fate of the paper's movie criticism. On Catledge's desk were Crowther's rave review of the bloated *Cleopatra* and the critic's excessive bash of *Bonnie and Clyde*. Gelb wrote that Catledge did not believe rumors that Crowther protected the big studios by going easy on or even praising such overproduced clinkers as Twentieth Century-Fox's *Cleopatra*. "I think he's just simply tired after doing the same thing all these years," Catledge told Gelb. "He's sixty-three, you know. Times are changing and we have to change, too."

Crowther's offensive review of director Arthur Penn's movie concerning the bank-robbing Clyde Barrow gang of the 1930s, read, in part: "It's a cheap piece of bald-faced slapstick comedy that treats the hideous depredations of that sleazy, moronic pair as though they were as full of fun and frolic as the jazz-age cut-ups in *Thoroughly Modern Millie*." The reference point Crowther makes is to George Roy Hill's *Thoroughly Modern Millie* (1967), a frothy period musical starring the scrubbed Julie Andrews. Crowther's annoyance with *Bonnie and Clyde* was acute: "This blending of farce with brutal killings is as pointless as it is lacking in taste, since it makes no valid commentary on the already travestied truth. And it leaves an astonished critic wondering just what purpose Mr. Penn and Mr. [producer/star Warren] Beatty think they serve with this strangely antique, sentimental claptrap."

An active prejudice against Crowther's mien that had been alive for a decade or more in critical circles crystallized in a rally not exactly for *Bonnie and Clyde*, but certainly against Crowther. Kael's epic piece in *The New Yorker* and Morgenstern's rewriting of his own opinion in *Newsweek* were only two manifestations of this. "Perhaps fearing that the Crowther review would slaughter the box-office chances of *Bonnie and Clyde*, several critics avidly quoted by Warner Bros. went literally overboard in their defense of the film," Hollis Alpert wrote, mentioning Crist, Sarris, and Penelope Gilliatt, who soon would share *The New Yorker* beat with Kael. Sarris accused Crowther of a crusade against the film "that makes the Hundred Years War look like a border incident." Alpert pointed out that Crowther's insistent call for moral values in films was "to put it bluntly . . . old-fashioned in critical circles."

The *Times* decided that their critic was the strangely antique one. His dismissal, while a long time coming, ranks as the most controversial in film criticism. "It was [Crowther's] just-don't-get-it 1967 review of *Bonnie and Clyde* that dug his grave, but his crankiness and irrelevance had emerged much earlier," film critic Molly Haskell wrote in 2001. "As a self-appointed upholder of public morals, he proved to be tone-deaf to the interestingly bleak mood and seat-of-the-pants spontaneity of the *Nouvelle Vague* and the whole sweeping challenge of Sixties cinema." Occasionally, the Crowther dismissal is referenced in articles about other film-criticism snits. Writing in 1997 in *Vanity Fair*, James Wolcott perceived Crowther's influence as pervasive in his time, and the critic's end at the *Times* also the end of something more epochal in the trade, which he called "the gentleman-hack approach to film crit [sic] in the weeklies that had prevailed since the deaths of Agee and Ferguson."

Renata Adler was announced in June 1967 as Crowther's

replacement, officially beginning on January 1, 1968, initiating the second controversy regarding the paper's film critic post in as many years. A native of Milan, Italy, who grew up in Danbury, Connecticut, Adler was educated at Bryn Mawr, the Sorbonne, and Harvard, and joined *The New Yorker* as a book critic. Disdaining the New Journalism literary movement and seeking accuracy, she filed stories from the roughly and ostensibly desegregating American South, and on such topics as group therapy and pop music. She wasn't yet 30 when she accepted the unexpected *Times*'s offer to replace Crowther. Harry Truman sliding up to fill in for the deceased Franklin D. Roosevelt is an easy analogy. Truman's enemies and dissenters were everywhere. Adler's critics were everywhere, too, even inside her own building, where her copy was not sacrosanct.

"Being film critic of *The New York Times* . . . was for me a particular kind of adventure," Adler wrote, "with time, with tones of voice, with movies, with editing, with the peculiar experience it always is to write in one's own name something that is never exactly what one would have wanted to say. . . . The idea at the *Times* is that reviews are not edited at all, but the reality was a continual leaning on sentences, cracking rhythms, removing or explaining jokes, questioning or crazily amplifying metaphors and allusions, on pieces that were not that good in the first place."

She reprised her reviews of that time—without the heavy *Times* staff editing that she said had stifled her voice—in the book, *A Year in the Dark: Journal of a Film Critic 1968–1969*. During her short, adventurous tenure, Adler also attracted the adversarial editing of her several editors. *Variety* kept a running log of her errors. A full-page ad in her own newspaper pointed out that she wasn't making the grade. Senator Strom Thurmond of South Carolina denounced the *Times* in Congress and read Adler's pan of John Wayne and Ray Kellogg's hawkish *The Green Berets* (1968) into the Congressional Record. Adler's lead paragraph referred to Wayne's Vietnam War movie as "so unspeakable, so stupid, so rotten and false in every detail . . . vile and insane. . . . On top of all that, it is dull." Despite the fact that she expressed a majority critical opinion and Senator Thurmond's act was interpreted as him sticking up for the U.S. Army Special Forces, which were the subject of Wayne's film, the incident was one more overt criticism.

Twentieth Century-Fox studio boss Darryl F. Zanuck fired off letters to *Times* editor Clifton Daniel over the critic's dismissal of Robert Wise's *Star!* (1968), featuring Julie Andrews portraying Gertrude Lawrence, in Adler's words, "as a kind of monster, with none of the crispness or glamour or wit that would give her ambition style." Adler had left the screening early due to illness, which had been reported to Zanuck, who seized on the issue to denigrate her work.

At any rate, after a year and two months of battling, Adler was moved aside for her backup, Vincent Canby. Richard Schickel, writing in *Harper's*, recalled, "Renata Adler jumped, fell, or was pushed from the job as movie critic of *The New York Times*, ending a serio-comic cultural crisis that had been simmering through the last years of Bosley Crowther's twenty-seven-year tenure in the post and which boiled up still more furiously during her fourteen months as his replacement." Canby filled the role very quietly, competently avoiding contretemps.

But Adler had, in effect, been the martyr of an experiment by the *Times* that provoked backlash within and without the paper of record. With so-called women's liberation and the ad hoc youth movement joined at the hip in America as both relevant social issues and chic radical causes at the height of their media notoriety in 1968, trying a young woman in the post made some sense as both a sound move and a placating gesture. And with Crist en vogue on TV and Kael admired by the cognoscenti, and especially with the grinding criticisms the *Times* endured through Crowther's final years on the beat still fresh in mind, hiring a young woman showed flexibility and a willingness to change with the times. It gave the paper of record some street credibility and appeal to the growing youth market.

Thus, the under-30 Adler was assigned the top film criticism job in America. Whatever the interpretations of her inside battles with editors were—arguments that never produce a concrete verdict—the envy and chauvinism that were generated by her hiring were de rigueur for the era. The fact that the changing of the *Times*'s film critic created such a brouhaha on the cultural landscape was only testimony to the popularity of movies and the esteem for the judgment of them.

Adler's aptly titled *A Year in the Dark* joined paperback copies of *Agee on Film*, Robert Warshow's *The Immediate Experience*, Kael's *Kiss Kiss Bang Bang*, Stanley Kauffmann's *A World on Film*, Joseph McBride's *Persistence of Vision*, and other film-criticism collections that were becoming ubiquitous on campuses into the 1970s. These heady times for film appreciation and reappreciation led to an outpouring of literature about the movies. Sarris in particular packaged his thoughts on the auteur theory regarding individual Hollywood directors in *The American Cinema: Directors and Directions 1929–1968*. He and other critics pointed toward new ways of looking at old pictures. Revival houses sprang up in major cities and college towns. Universities and even some small colleges developed some level of cinema curricula, while ad hoc film clubs and societies flourished on campuses.

The spiritual resurrection of Humphrey Bogart, who died in 1957, as a new cult figure was a result of this rush to reappreciate old films. The lisping tough-guy actor with the small frame and big talent was the object of underground appreciation at Harvard years after his death, prodding Peter Bogdanovich to write a 1964 essay in *Esquire* capturing Bogie's appeal. Books about filmmakers were finding a ready audience. Bogdanovich wrote monographs published by the Museum of Modern Art on Alfred Hitchcock, Howard Hawks, and Orson Welles; produced an important book-length interview with John Ford; and authored other volumes on Fritz Lang and Allan Dwan. Film critics John Simon, Andrew Sarris, and Hollis Alpert all wrote books reprising their reviews and describing their profession. While the 1970s would contain the considerable resulting waves, or fallout, or mainstream culmination of the cultural upheavals of the 1960s, so, too, would the Film Generation of the 1960s see the most productivity and results of a growing awareness of film culture in the coming decade. The film criticism explosion began in the 1960s, but the golden age arrived in earnest in the 1970s.

Both mainstream magazines and small esoteric journals were bringing film criticism to wider audiences. *Film Culture* began publishing in 1955 and, by the time Sarris planted the auteur theory in it in 1962, had grown to a circulation of 6,000. *Film Comment*, published by the Film Society of Lincoln Center, appeared in 1962, as did the movie buff's bible, *Classic Images*. Also starting up in the 1960s was *Action!*, the first magazine of the Directors Guild of America. *Cineaste* and *Film Heritage* came into being, the latter capturing many interviews with directors of the 1930s and 1940s, and essays about critics, too. The December 26, 1964, edition of the *Saturday Review* carried the special report "The Movies and the Critics," which dissected the critic's function. Both of the magazine's critics, Hollis Alpert and Arthur Knight, participated, as did filmmakers Otto Preminger and John Frankenheimer, who wrote that a film critic should be aware of the filmmaker's intentions, encourage public love of film, and help create an atmosphere conducive to better films.

With the newsweeklies and daily newspapers more attentive to reviewing new releases, some of their critics started doing double duty as interviewers, writing advance pieces and conducting star interviews. The "film beat" at these papers didn't separate its critics from those who wrote news and trend coverage. Ebert's reportage on his studio-arranged time spent with John Wayne, Robert Mitchum, Lee Marvin, and others became classics of a type. Occasionally, periodicals such as *The New York Times* would send reporters other than critics to interview filmmakers, reasoning that the practice eliminated any conflict of interest that might arise for a critic interviewing an actor in a film that he or she later would review favorably. Ebert and many other critics who were the sole reporters on film at their respective newspapers understood their objectivity as newsmen up front, and vowed that actors or filmmakers could not and did not sway them into giving certain movies supportive reviews.

Moreover, film critics' interviews with actors and directors helped readers understand the process of filmmaking and the transference of on-set techniques to onscreen effects. And people started knowing more about the movies that was apart from fandom. Historical knowledge also started to enter the mainstream through the film-beat coverage of astute newspapermen. Knowing how many films and which ones James Stewart starred in for director Anthony Mann, or how many Randolph Scott made for director Budd Boetticher, became a cineaste's knowledge. A genre as disreputably escapist as the western, typified in the times by the glut of horse operas on all three TV networks, returned scholars to the vaults for further film study. Kael's early work as an exhibition manager in Berkeley was a part of the national re-inauguration of interest in the comic actors who formerly had invigorated the cinema, primarily the Marx Brothers and W.C. Fields, an interest that blossomed into the 1970s.

Efforts to re-circulate the films of Alfred Hitchcock, John Huston, Howard Hawks, and others for another look became an active practice of art-house schedulers and even some local television programmers. Even if she couldn't cotton to the auteur theory, and she espoused the notion that most movies were trash, Kael contributed to the same new national film awareness in which the writing of Andrew Sarris and Manny Farber returned moviegoers to the work of such Hollywood masters as Leo McCarey, John Ford, and William A. Wellman. People began seeing movies as something much more than two hours of sheer escapism in the dark.

Films were being talked of in terms of art. Movies in the immediate postwar era and through the 1960s were directly linked to the long-evolving technological command in Hollywood and elsewhere by directors as well as their minions—cinematographers, actors, set designers, etc.—to infuse in them elements of style and meaning. The central document in these times describing the general conversation extending outside high culture that linked Hollywood movies and other films to the arts in general was written in 1966 by Stanley Kauffmann in *The New Republic*, called "The Film Generation."

"There exists a Film Generation," Kauffmann wrote, "the first generation that has matured in a culture in which the film has been of accepted serious relevance, however that seriousness is defined." Kauffmann presented five reasons for the rise of the Film Generation, which included those born since 1935 or after a generation that only saw movies in terms of escapism. The critic contended that:

(1) In a technological age, "film art flowers out of technology."
(2) The inherent documentary technique of pictorially recording items, what Kauffmann refers to as the "world of surfaces and physical details," can give "great vitality to a film by a gifted artist."
(3) Film can "externalize psychical matters," such as "inner states of tension, or of doubt or apathy" better, he says, than the novel or the theatre.
(4) "Film is the only art besides music that is available to the whole world at once, exactly as it was made."
(5) "Film has one great benefit by accident: its youth, which means not only vigor but the reach of possibility."

Of course, Kauffmann wrote this at a time when his No. 4 was nearly always true. Fulminations by directors over studio-dictated final cuts, represented by Sam Peckinpah's fight with Columbia Pictures over its truncating of *Major Dundee* (1965), were still isolated incidents. And "director's cuts" were still a generation away from being co-opted into an ancillary market by video salesmen. Kauffmann's directly stated and cleanly broken down essay was written in his characteristically precise and quietly professorial style. "The Film Generation" supplied historical context and reasonable definition for film culture. And it looked optimistically toward the future, despite a downside that Kauffmann saw in indulgent and trite "underground" films, which he called susceptible to radicalization for no larger purpose.

Kauffmann came to his conclusions after nearly a decade of writing film criticism for *The New Republic* and experience in both the theatre and publishing. Born in New York City on April 24, 1916, the son of a dentist, Kauffmann was educated at New York University. He joined the Washington Square Players in 1931, and functioned as a stage manager as well as an actor through the Depression. After World War II, he joined Bantam Books, then became editor-in-chief of Ballantine Books from 1952 to 1956. He was an editor at Alfred A. Knopf from 1959 to 1960. Kauffmann's most celebrated acquisition as a book editor was for Knopf, Walker Percy's *The Moviegoer*, which won the National Book Award for 1962. Kauffmann's novels include *The King of Proxy Street* (1941), *The Hidden Hero* (1949), *The Tightrope* (1952), *A Change of Climate* (1954), and *Man of the World* (1956). Most of Kauffmann's plays, some of them for children, have been published by Samuel French.

Kauffmann has interchangeably reviewed fiction, theatre, and movies, but mostly movies, for half a century. In 1958, he was appointed film critic of *The New Republic*. His stints on theatre coverage included *The New York Times* in 1966, *The New Republic* from 1969 to 1979, and *Saturday Review* from 1979 to 1985. It was his stepping aside to cover theatre for the *Times* that allowed Kael her brief stint at *The New Republic* before she was offered a post at *The New Yorker*. Kauffmann has taught at Adelphi, Yale, Hunter College, and York College of the City University of New York. He was one of the first notable film critics on TV, presiding over interviews, reviews and discussions on *The Art of Film*, broadcast from 1963 through 1967 on WNDT-TV in Newark, New Jersey.

Having stayed the course off and on for a half-century in film criticism, Kauffmann maintained his standards and his faith in movies. His writing was professorial in tone, often referenced with examples in other arts. He was respectful of the filmmaking process, but possessed a strong detector for artifice and sham. His humor has been, as Joseph McBride pointed out, more wry than pronounced. "Sometimes I am more relieved than at other times that I am not a Christian," Kauffmann wrote about George Stevens's *The Greatest Story Ever Told* (1965). "These occasions include the experience of most films about Jesus." During his first full decade as a film critic, Kauffmann became one of the profession's most admired writers for the directness of his spare prose. His initial collection of film reviews, *A World on Film*, remains one of the best. He wasted little time in getting to the point. Of an Irvin Kershner film, his lead read, "*The Luck of Ginger Coffey* . . . is the sort of work that is vastly over-praised simply because it is not phony."

Among Kauffmann's major distinctions from other film critics was a preoccupation with actors. Having been an actor himself, he was sensitive to performers while other film critics treated them tangentially, if at all, even if they were icons on the order of Cary Grant or Marilyn Monroe, who had the screen power to shape the force and nature of their films. Kauffmann was the antithesis of those critics who believed that "serious" film criticism had everything to do with theory, genre, politics, auteurism, or other theme-couching considerations—while they parenthetically deigned to cite a lead actor. To word-shoveling spiritual rhapsodists descendent of Parker Tyler in the Kael era, Burt Lancaster might as well have been Arnold Stang.

Kauffmann was at his liveliest discussing performers. "Two concurrent films present the happy task of discussing Paul Newman," he blithely jotted for an October 1961 lead on a dual review of Robert Rossen's *The Hustler* and Martin Ritt's *Paris Blues*. Of Brenda de Banzie's performance in *The Entertainer* (1960), he wrote, "Her drunk scene is one to which all Studio actors should be taken and held fast by the nape the neck until they have seen it a dozen times."

Kauffmann's three-paragraph review of *The Apartment*

(1960), Billy Wilder's Academy Award-winning best picture, is completely a reaction to the actors, beginning, "Jack Lemmon is the kind of problem American films need. He is a vigorous, highly talented, and technically equipped actor with a wide emotional range. Can Hollywood supply him with material that is good enough for him?" Kauffmann could also be stingy, even to the time-honored greats. Of Ralph Richardson's performance as the faded matinee idol James Tyrone in Sidney Lumet's film of Eugene O'Neill's *Long Day's Journey Into Night* (1962), Kauffmann wrote that the actor "provides a sound performance, instead of the affected distortion that he often palms off as originality. One cannot quite believe that his face ever set feminine hearts aflutter or that he is more than occasionally Irish (when he remembers the brogue); but he drives hard and honestly for the center of this warped, grandiloquent man."

Kauffmann was not without his detractors, and most of the complaints coalesce in the notion that he was too distant in print. Kael, not surprisingly, was one of his critics. She had paired him with Dwight Macdonald, calling them "squares," and later linked him with Brendan Gill of *The New Yorker* as critics who don't crusade for films, who are too impersonal in their reviews to make others want to see the movies they like. This general sense of Kauffmann's dispassionate writing, especially for so exacting a critic, was shared by Joan Didion and Jack Richardson in separate reviews of Kauffmann's books in *The New York Times Book Review*. Didion wrote that Kauffmann was so temperamentally at odds with movies that his "nasty disclosure about the circus is to reveal that the aerialist is up there to get our attention."

Kauffmann and Kael were allied on one front. They were among the magazine critics who convened in 1966 to create the National Society of Film Critics. Ostensibly, the group formed because the New York Film Critics Circle excluded magazine critics. Chaired by Bosley Crowther since 1951, the NYFCC confined itself to reviewers for the city's daily newspapers. Crowther's lordly dominance of the circle provided those on the outside with another reason to consider him contemptible. However, there was a general feeling within the Film Generation, and the intelligentsia in general, that a need existed to elevate the discussion on movies. The impetus to form the NSFC ran toward a deeper responsibility to film culture.

"As charter members of the National Society of Film Critics, Sarris, Kael, and others created an association to counter the middlebrow sensibility of the New York Film Critics Circle, whose tastes were deemed too similar to those of the Academy and its Oscar Awards," film critic Emanuel Levy wrote. Joining the new group, which had its first meeting in Hollis Alpert's New York apartment, were Alpert and Arthur Knight, both of *Saturday Review*; stage director Harold Clurman, who had just begun reviewing for *The Nation*; Philip T. Hartung of *Commonweal*; Stefan Kanfer and Richard Schickel of *Time*; Joe Morgenstern of *Newsweek*; Andrew Sarris of *The Village Voice*; historian and political analyst Arthur M. Schlesinger, Jr., who had reviewed films for *Show*, then *Vogue*; Wilfrid Sheed of *Esquire*; Penelope Gilliatt of *The New Yorker*; and John Simon of *The New Leader*.

While the best picture Oscar and the NYFCC best picture award of 1966 went to Fred Zinnemann's *A Man for All Seasons*, the National Society chose Michelangelo Antonioni's British mystery, *Blowup*. The group's maverick identity was reinforced when Ingmar Bergman's Swedish films *Persona* (1967) and *Shame* (1968) were selected as the best pictures of their years. In 1969, Costa-Gavras's French-Algerian production about Greece, *Z*, was chosen as best picture. These selections made the National Society appear entirely international in collective taste.

In an arrangement with Simon & Schuster, the National Society began putting out an annual anthology of reviews by its member critics. The first volume, *The National Society of Film Critics Write on Film 67/68*, was edited by Simon and Schickel. Alpert's reviews of Mike Nichols's *The Graduate* (1967) and Peter Yates's *Bullitt* (1968), Sheed's of Gene Saks's *The Odd Couple* (1968), and Schlesinger's of Anthony Harvey's *The Lion in Winter* (1968) were packaged with dozens of others to raise awareness of the group and offer filmgoers a taste of ostensibly premium American movie criticism.

A measure of natural elitism was alive in the National Society from the start. After all, any group forming to provide a higher plane of critical thought above the generally accepted notions of middlebrow culture fostered by the New York Film Critics Circle and the Academy of Motion Picture Arts and Sciences was bound to have its share of not only severely opinionated egos, but also righteously severely opinionated egos. Charter member Richard Schickel, in 1999, recalled the salad days of the society in terms of Andrew Sarris's membership in it.

"[Sarris] had observed . . . that most of the people who had previously made names for themselves in this field were widely perceived much the way most of the National Society's membership perceived themselves, that is to say, as 'being too good to be reviewing movies,'" Schickel wrote. "In contrast, people coming out of the little film journals, as he had, 'were not considered much good for anything else.' This was fine with him. And liberating."

The prickly John Simon, who will be discussed later on, wrote his observations about the early years of the National Society in 1976: "There was some vestigial notion of merit connected with membership: not every magazine critic was voted in, whereas every working newspaper film reviewer was ex officio admitted to the [New York Film Critics] Circle. . . . The society always voted on whom to admit to membership, and these elections were often hotly debated. Frequently, they made no sense at all. Someone might be kept out year after year simply because most members disapproved of his sexual preference. Someone else might be voted in just because his publication had 'clout,' which struck me as equally nonsensical.

"A well-known novelist then writing film criticism that seemed to me quite amateurish was admitted because, as one member put it, 'He would be an ornament to the society,'" remembered the occasionally ultra-acerbic Simon. "('In that case,' I said, 'let's hang him from the chandelier.') A member I genuinely esteemed explained to me why he kept voting for people I thought he could have no use for; looking around our table, he said, he saw so many incompetents that he could find no grounds on which to exclude others no worse than they. My answer was that a plurality of nonentities seemed to me preferable to a majority of them."

Like other members of the National Society, Simon, who had been excluded from the NYFCC because he wasn't a newspaperman, was eventually invited into the group along with other magazine critics after the great newspaper strike of 1966 eventually killed off several dailies, including the *New York Herald-Tribune*, the *World-Telegram & Sun*, and the *New York Journal-American*. "As newspapers began to bite the dust all around, the circle . . . started to admit society members, provided they wrote for mass-circulation magazines," Simon recalled. "To be sure, there were some funny goings-on. For example, when one eminent magazine critic was considered for membership, the Circle's chairman inquired about the number of copies his publication printed. 'One hundred fifteen thousand,' someone said. 'In that case,' decreed the chairman, 'let's make one hundred and fifteen thousand the cut-off line.' A couple of society members turned down the Circle, one of them declaring he had nothing in common with most of 'those people.' But many accepted this dual citizenship, one of them shamefacedly muttering something about 'power.' In the end, there was precious little difference between the groups, and the overlapping membership inevitably spelled little difference between their respective awards."

The changes in newspaper history had other effects on film criticism history in the 1960s, particularly in California. Crowther was shown the door in New York, but out on the other coast, fissures formed under traditions that had been fixed for generations at the Chandler family's *Los Angeles Times*. The main newspaper in Hollywood's backyard was being swept clean by family scion Otis Chandler. Through the midcentury, the *Times* was more than occasionally superciliously arcane, windbag-written, and union-bustingly corrupt—an eyesore of American journalism. It was slanted steeply to the right, and its political power broker, Kyle Palmer, was instrumental in the rise of homegrown boy Richard Nixon to national prominence.

"It is a dynasty . . . surviving the dual contemporary onslaught of modern inherence inheritance taxes and normally thinning genes," wrote David Halberstam in 1979. "Its power and reach and role in Southern California are beyond the comprehension of Easterners. . . . [The Chandlers] did not so much foster the growth of Southern California as, more simply, invent it. There is water because they went and stole water. . . . Who is to say that the history of the West and the history of California would be better if Harry Chandler had been someone who thought the law applied to him . . . ? Los Angeles is the major city in America most resistant to the power of labor unions, not because it evolved naturally that way but because first General Harrison Gray Otis and then Harry Chandler fought the unions in a constant ongoing struggle that was nothing short of war, mobilizing all other businessmen under their wing, tearing the entire city apart with a bitterness that lasted some 60 years."

The portraits of corruption under the fictional umbrella that became the buzz term "L.A. noir" by the end of the 20th century—the portrayal of the city's nightscapes by pulp and celluloid as brutal terrain for criminals and fringe dwellers, graft, and avarice—had bases in fact. One of the main bases for this was a brand of citywide journalism that took its cue from the *Times*, especially when it came to covering and judging the entertainment product in the industry's own town. Some cities across the country spawned their own formidable film critics and movie coverage, but nowhere outside of the cultural pulse of New York had the writing about movies been more scrutinized than in Los Angeles. Actually, some would say that it was more controlled in L.A. than anywhere else.

Otis Chandler changed all that. Beginning in 1960 when he was named publisher, the *Times* underwent a complete transformation into one of the nation's bastions of daily journalism. Its film coverage, like that of most of the city's papers in the 1950s—the *Los Angeles Herald and Express, Los Angeles Examiner, Los Angeles Mirror,* and *Hollywood Citizen-News*— often amounted to running multiple promotion stills from a new movie in a de facto extension of studio marketing. But the *Times*'s cultural coverage changed with the rest of the product under Otis Chandler's watch.

Edwin Schallert and then Philip K. Scheuer were known for fairness in the industry's hometown and had guided the entertainment coverage of the *Times* from the silent era until the latter's retirement in 1967. In his last decade, Scheuer entrusted a copy boy to do some stringing on movie reviews, beginning in 1962. This allowance started Kevin Thomas, a second-generation *Times* employee, on a career odyssey that continued into the 21st century, making him the longest-serving film critic on the same daily newspaper in American journalism history. "I like pictures that bear a personal stamp to them," Thomas told *Action!,* the first magazine of the Directors Guild of America, in 1969. "I like criticism that is personal. I write primarily for myself, because I am not really sure who is reading me. . . . It is ultimately the personality of the director coming through. . . . *Planet of the Apes* (1968) was a picture that I enjoyed enormously. . . . I have seen Frank Schaffner's films and I think they are all marked by a certain kind of intelligence. . . . I don't think you can separate form and content, but I do think there is something above either of these: style. That is what interests me."

Scheuer's replacement as the guiding force of the *Los Angeles Times*'s arts coverage was Charles Davenport Champlin, a former *Time* magazine correspondent who became the principal film editor and critic, and took charge of the paper's overall arts and entertainment coverage. Hallmarks of Champlin's and Thomas's reviews were clarity and fairness, which dovetailed with Otis Chandler's vision of a journalistically sound *Los Angeles Times.* The dream factory's main sheet established two names, Champlin and Thomas, to front for its film criticism that would appear on it pages for more than four decades between them— just as Scheuer had served for 40 years before them.

Champlin provided bedrock integrity to the *Times*'s movie coverage and, in the words of screenwriter Clancy Sigal, "helped keep nervous readers loyal when the paper broke with its stuffy, provincial past and transformed itself into a major national daily." Born on March 23, 1926, in Hammondsport, New York, in the Finger Lakes region, Champlin lived a small-town boyhood under the influence of a particularly benevolent stepfather, times that he recorded vividly in the memoir, *Back There Where the Past Was*. He served in the infantry as a corporal during World War II and collected a Purple Heart for injuries sustained on the eve of V-E Day near Remagen, Germany. After the war, he married and graduated *cum laude* from Harvard. While raising six children, Champlin worked as a correspondent for *Life* magazine in Chicago, Denver, and New York through the 1950s, and for its sister publication, *Time*, in Los Angeles and London from 1959 to 1965, before he was hired by the *Los Angeles Times*. He became the paper's leading film critic when Scheuer retired, and remained in the top post until 1980, writing the syndicated column "Critic at Large."

In a town of well-known entertainment columnists of the midcentury—from Hedda Hopper, Louella O. Parsons, and Sheilah Graham to James Bacon at the *Los Angeles Herald-Examiner* and Sidney Skolsky at the *New York Post*—Champlin evolved into a voice of atypical common sense on the Tinseltown landscape, especially during the cultural transformations of the 1960s and 1970s. His simultaneous role as the city's leading film critic carried with it a sense of values that never came across as preachy. Writing from a 21st-century perspective, Clancy Sigal imparted: "In the nicest possible way, Champlin is a gee-whiz reporter, seeking out the personal and colorful while refusing to dwell on the dark and negative. The style is the man. Unfashionably, he seems to have been, for most of his life, optimistic, happy, and eminently reasonable."

Champlin's ascent as Los Angeles's leading film critic during the rise of the Film Generation was not accidental or insignificant. He was the right person at the right time for Otis

Chandler's mission. And the influence of the right man in the top job in the midst of the dream factory's spin doctors had a way of making itself felt by rote. Champlin's writing and opinions issued in Los Angeles became the acceptable and accepted stabilizing force on the big paper. He had his imitators and radical competition, those who wanted nothing more than to approach film coverage differently than he did. This was because Hollywood evolved into a magnet for film enthusiasts whose writing would influence film coverage and film criticism.

Some of these writers were thrown the title of "film critic" and it stuck, whether it was truly applicable or not. In some cases, assumptions were made. Peter Bogdanovich had written essays on film for *Esquire* during Dwight Macdonald's tenure as the magazine's film critic. After Bogdanovich became a filmmaker, writing and directing *Targets* (1968) and the marvelous *The Last Picture Show* (1971), his book-length studies of directors such as John Ford and Allan Dwan kept accruing recognition, and he became part of the Film Generation's rush to reappraise Hollywood's past. So, Bogdanovich's name was tossed into the "film critic" hopper by the undiscerning or the unconcerned, to whom the label was an easy identifier.

Film historian Joseph McBride, whose writing on Hollywood began in the 1960s, and who would go on to write seminal histories on the lives and careers of Orson Welles, Howard Hawks, Frank Capra, Steven Spielberg, and John Ford, worked as a film critic during two separate stints for *Daily Variety* in the coming decades. His legacy is as a historian; his identity is as a film critic. The label got slapped onto others in a similar fashion. Rex Reed, who was a film critic for various publications, had the greater identity as a celebrity interviewer who wisecracked on TV talk shows. His celeb-dish patter became identifiable as that of a "film critic" to the Middle America watching shows hosted by Merv Griffin and Mike Douglas. In some cases, once one is stamped with that identity, it becomes as irremovable as a biker's tattoo. In the end result of the 21st century, "film critic" could mean anything from academic masters forging theoretical theses to dweeb bloggers with two lines of profanity-laced snark-speak or fave rave on the latest CGI-constructed superhero flick.

By the end of the 1960s and into the 1970s, several relatively young film critics were beginning stints on publications the longevities of which they never could have predicted. The astute Richard Schickel mastered the succinct *Time* magazine format of constricting brevity. Roger Ebert was firmly established on the *Chicago Sun-Times*, Gene Siskel was his crosstown counterpart on the *Chicago Tribune*, and Vincent Canby was chief film critic of *The New York Times*. And the youngest member of the Film Generation was just getting started. In 1969, Leonard Maltin's first edition of his paperback compilation, *TV Movies*, was published.

Maltin's prolific career as a film historian—and occasionally as a film critic for the syndicated *Entertainment Tonight* TV program in the 1980s—began at age 15 in his home in Teaneck, New Jersey, when he took over the publication of the previously Vancouver, Canada-based *Film Fan Monthly*, a 2,000-circulation film buffs' favorite. Maltin published it using carbon paper, then hectograph, then mimeograph, in his parents' garage. In 1968, at age 17, he was introduced by one of his high school teachers to an editor at New American Library, who asked Maltin to assess the annual *Movies on TV*, edited by Steven H. Scheuer. That guide had been updated and published by Bantam Books intermittently since 1958.

"I said I would include more of the cast, the character actors; director; running time; whether it was color or black and white," Maltin remembered. "Well, he didn't have the nerve to sign a contract with a 17-year-old high school student, so we wrote the contract through *Film Fan Monthly*."

THE GOLDEN AGE: THE 1970s

The 1970s marked the last great period of artistic expression in Hollywood. The scores of filmmakers who came to prominence as the Film Generation matured included Francis Ford Coppola, who directed *The Godfather* (1972), *The Godfather Part II* (1974), *The Conversation* (1974), and *Apocalypse Now* (1979). Other directors who emerged as creative forces included Martin Scorsese, Steven Spielberg, Robert Altman, Woody Allen, George Lucas, Milos Forman, Hal Ashby, Bob Rafelson, William Friedkin, and Peter Bogdanovich.

The new vitality in Hollywood corresponded to fast and furious changes in American values and attitudes, and the embracing of the movies by both youth culture and high culture, meeting in the moment in the theatre for Altman's *M*A*S*H* (1970), Rafelson's *Five Easy Pieces* (1970), Bogdanovich's *The Last Picture Show* (1971), and Ashby's *The Last Detail* (1973). "It had something to do with the counterculture," explained Pauline Kael from a 2000 perspective. "The anger about the Vietnam War and the chaos of American society in that period helped produce some good movies. Directors had something to be against. It stirred their juices, and it gave their movies a sense of social criticism."

Film criticism and film culture in general became more

formalized in the 1970s. Even outlying universities established courses on film aesthetics and theory. There was an explosion in books published about the movies—biographies and autobiographies, but also popular and scholarly works, and those about offbeat filmmakers, such as Nicholas Garnham's *Samuel Fuller* (1971), Stuart M. Kaminsky's *Don Siegel: Director* (1974), and Jeanine Basinger's *Anthony Mann* (1979).

Many critics packaged their reviews, interviews, and essays into books, including Pauline Kael, Stanley Kauffmann, and John Simon—each with a new anthology every few years—along with Manny Farber, Andrew Sarris, Wilfrid Sheed, Vernon Young, Judith Crist, Rex Reed, Penelope Gilliatt, Charles Champlin, Joseph McBride, and Richard Schickel. The National Society of Film Critics continued annual anthologies until *The National Society of Film Critics Write on Film 73/74*.

More critics tried the television and radio airwaves as Judith Crist, Rex Reed, John Simon, Pauline Kael, Gene Shalit, and the Chicago duo of Roger Ebert and Gene Siskel became recognized personalities. More awards were doled out from more critical organizations, including the upstart Los Angeles Film Critics Association in 1975. More esteem was accorded the profession as it became hip to judge movies and understand the prevailing fortunes of the Hollywood zeitgeist.

Magazines embracing film history, filmmakers, and film criticism included *Film Comment* (published by the Film Society of Lincoln Center, and edited by Richard Corliss from 1970 to 1990), and *American Film* (published by the American Film Institute from 1976 to 1992 and edited from 1975 to 1981 by Hollis Alpert). Smaller and more esoteric periodicals, in the tradition of the continuing *Film Quarterly* (1945) and *Film Culture* (1954), thrived in the atmosphere of the 1970s' film appreciation, including *Cineaste*, founded in 1967 and edited by Gary Crowdus, and *Velvet Light Trap*, founded by Russell Campbell in 1971 and edited by graduate students at the University of Wisconsin-Madison.

The first time a film critic was awarded the National

Book Award occurred when Pauline Kael won in the Arts and Letters category in 1974 for *Deeper into Movies*. The concerted efforts of the National Book Foundation to recognize writing on the movies included a nomination for John Simon's *Movies into Film: Film Criticism, 1967–1970* in 1972, and three nominees in 1973: Leo Braudy's *Jean Renoir: The World of His Films*, Arlene Croce's *The Fred Astaire & Ginger Rogers Book*, and Vernon Young's *On Film: Unpopular Essays on a Popular Art*.

Kael's win was for her third collection of film-related pieces, written between September 1969 and March 1972, including reviews of Bogdanovich's *The Last Picture Show*, and Altman's *M*A*S*H* and *McCabe & Mrs. Miller* (1971).

"Movies are a hybrid, all-encompassing art and I suppose that what I've devised for dealing with them is a mongrel form of criticism," Kael said in her acceptance speech. "But systematic criticism seems to me a violation of the very qualities that make movies such a powerful art form. It's an attempt to impose order on a medium which incorporates the appeal of the circus, the wild-west show, the penny dreadful, of theatre, opera, and the novel, a medium that bites off chunks of anthropology, journalism, and politics, and a medium that is always, of course, the domain of eros. Movies can take in so much from the other arts, and so much from the world, that the job of the critic is to not close himself off."

The first time a film critic was awarded the Pulitzer Prize occurred when Roger Ebert won in 1975 for his reviews and essays in the *Chicago Sun-Times*. The citation specified Ebert's win "for his film criticism during 1974." It would be more than a quarter of a century before another film critic won the same honor (Stephen Hunter of *The Washington Post* in 2003). Ebert's win occurred the same year that he and his crosstown rival, Gene Siskel of the *Chicago Tribune*, began their TV series about contemporary films, a show that took film criticism in a new and popular direction and touched off intermittent grumbling inside the profession among champions of the written word.

Film criticism itself received academic and literary attention, with attempts to put the profession in perspective. Stanley Kauffmann and Bruce Henstell's anthology, *American Film Criticism: From the Beginnings to Citizen Kane* (1972), collected the work of the first film critics for a new generation. Myron O. Lounsbury's *The Origins of American Film Criticism, 1909–1939* (1973) celebrated the magazine critics of the same era. Joseph D. Blades, Jr.'s *A Comparative Study of Selected American Film Critics, 1958–1974* (1974) provided studies on contemporary critics John Simon, Pauline Kael, Stanley Kauffmann, Andrew Sarris, Judith Crist, and Vincent Canby. Edward Murray's *Nine American Film Critics* (1975) studied most of those writers and resuscitated the memories of such distinctive voices as James Agee and Robert Warshow.

"Some may argue with [Murray's] preference for James Agee, Dwight Macdonald, Vernon Young, and Stanley Kauffmann over Robert Warshow, Andrew Sarris, Parker Tyler, John Simon, and Pauline Kael," wrote Marshall Deutelbaum on *Nine American Film Critics* in *Library Journal*. "But Murray's analysis of their work demonstrates the generally low level of critical achievement which results when reviewing, writing for the moment, is accepted as criticism, even though it lacks the reflection normally associated with the latter."

Revisionist criticism, prodded in part by the auteur theory and the writing of Andrew Sarris and Manny Farber, started an investigation through Hollywood's past, concentrating in part on genre masters, purveyors of westerns and crime films. Movies such as John Ford's *The Searchers* (1956) and *The Man Who Shot Liberty Valance* (1962), Jacques Tourneur's *Out of the Past* (1947), Nicholas Ray's *Johnny Guitar* (1954), and Charles Laughton's *The Night of the Hunter* (1955) were given art-house lives along with dozens more and upgraded to classical status.

Sarris's *The American Cinema: Directors and Directions, 1929–1968* (1968) and Farber's *Negative Space* (1971) became archaeological touchstones of Hollywood's rich past. In the homes of cineastes, they joined such quick-glance treasure troves as Leonard Maltin's *TV Movies* (1969) and Steven H. Scheuer's

Movies on TV. The four were a set for any two-hour couch potato session with "the late show," vernacular for the local vintage film program forums after the 11 PM news in many of the metropolitan television markets.

The venerable Richard Schickel took the revisionist movement completely to heart with *Second Sight: Notes on Some Movies, 1965–1970* (1972), which reprinted his *Life* reviews along with his second thoughts. "I over-praised this movie," Schickel wrote of Bud Yorkin's *Divorce American Style* (1967). "It seemed pretty thin the second time around." Schickel began reviewing for *Time* in 1972. He has said he mulls films for a week before writing. "It gives you a chance to change your mind," he told his *Life* editor, "which I do constantly."

Other critics don't recall ever reversing themselves. One of the most influential film critics of the 1970s, Vincent Canby of *The New York Times*, claimed, "I don't think I've ever changed my mind after having written a review." He told film critic Stephen Farber, "I may have overstated either the positive or the negative qualities of a film. Sometimes I'll see a review months later and feel I went a little too far."

Despite the battlefields already behind Pauline Kael, the 1970s marked her preeminent decade, when she settled in at *The New Yorker*, becoming the major voice of the maturing Film Generation and boosting the national prominence of her parochial publication. "Her hyperactive intelligence wanted movies to speak up, move fast, go crazy, make her swoon," characterized Richard Corliss in *Time* three years after her 1991 retirement. "She needed pictures to do for her what her reviews did for her readers." She believed that her conversational tone brought her readers into a closer relationship with movies.

David Ehrenstein, writing in the *Los Angeles Times Book Review* in 1994, suggested that perhaps her readership "simply came to realize that Kael wasn't just giving them her straight-from-the-gut unvarnished opinion, she was virtually demanding that they respond in kind: immerse themselves in film as fully and passionately as she did, and talk about what they saw once they surfaced."

Kael's place as the great provocateur of film criticism came fraught with controversies both on the page and in cineaste circles. She held court with other film critic devotees, whom Corliss dubbed "Paulettes," a moniker of pejorative clubbiness, which her acolytes despised and which stuck hard and fast. Richard Schickel described Kael as "this almost demonically possessed little woman" to whom he deferred until "the meanness, hysteria, and power-tripping took over completely." Schickel called the Paulettes "that little cell of not entirely secret agents." When Warren Beatty spotted Kael and her Paulettes at a screening, the man who played Clyde Barrow quipped, "Ma Barker and her gang."

Peter Biskind, in his opus *Easy Riders, Raging Bulls: How the Sex-Drugs-and-Rock 'N' Roll Generation Saved Hollywood*, described Kael in the 1970s as "a tiny, birdlike woman who looked like she might have been the registrar at a small New England college for women. Her unremarkable appearance belied a passion for disputation and a veritable genius for invective. Her writing fairly crackled with electricity, love of movies, and the excitement of discovery. Emerging in middle age from the shadows of Berkeley art houses, where she wrote mimeographed program notes for a coterie of whey-faced devotees, Kael blinked in the glare of the New York media world, then went to work.

"She shunned politics, but something of a New Left agenda nevertheless found its way into her reviews," Biskind continued. "Her version of the antiwar movement's hatred of the 'system' was a deep mistrust of the studios and a well-developed sense of Us versus Them. She wrote about the collision between the directors and the executives with the passion of Marx writing about class conflict." This particular aspect of Kael's writing helped ingrain the notion of her friends Robert Altman and Sam Peckinpah as rebels of the filmmaking cause. Peckinpah referred to Kael as "fun to drink with."

Phillip Lopate saw that Kael contained the attributes of both a film scholar and a no-nonsense communicator. "Since

Americans dislike the idea of being lectured to or (God forbid) taught about movies by specialists, the field continued to promote witty amateurs—often accomplished writers in other fields, such as political maven Dwight Macdonald, theatre critic John Simon and novelists Brendan Gill and Penelope Gilliatt," Lopate wrote in 2008. "The gentleman critic who was not taken in by arty nonsense, and therefore would protect his or her middle-class readership from their insecurities about the difficulties of new cinema, settled in for a long run. Pauline Kael, probably the most influential film critic of her day, reconciled the two tendencies by being both a bona fide movie expert and a champion of populist anti-snobbery."

Cultural critic and longtime *Rolling Stone* rock critic Greil Marcus credits Kael as a pathfinder. "She showed us what critics could be, what the possibilities were in terms of writing about popular culture," Marcus said. Mark Feeney of the *Boston Globe*, a cultural critic who won the 2008 Pulitzer Prize for criticism, felt that Kael's influence went beyond film criticism, claiming she "revolutionized how people see movies and how people write about movies—how people write, period."

Kael became the pivotal film critic in the 1970s, but she was unwittingly at the center of a media transformation as far as the profession was concerned. Following on Judith Crist's battles with studios over her pans of certain films in the 1960s as the film critic for the *New York Herald-Tribune*—as well as those studios' barring of her for those untoward reviews—and the cataclysmic changeover at *The New York Times* from Bosley Crowther to Renata Adler to Vincent Canby, film critics incrementally started filling voids on newspapers, which eventually deployed them to the forefront of review and general trend and interview coverage, and relegated syndicated columnists and other Hollywood wire copy to backup filler.

A film critic was a hip thing to have for newspaper entertainment departments. Newspaper drama critics, who had been the main voices on their sheets regarding everything—theatre, music, movies—started paying more attention to films. Emerging as local forces in the late 1960s or the 1970s as movie critics were Roger Ebert at the *Chicago Sun-Times*, Gary Arnold at *The Washington Post*, Gene Siskel at the *Chicago Tribune*, George Anderson at the *Pittsburgh Post-Gazette*, Edward L. Blank at the *The Pittsburgh Press*, Harper Barnes at the *St. Louis Post-Dispatch*, David Elliott at the *San Diego Union*, John Hartl at the *Seattle Times*, Malcolm Johnson on the *Hartford Courant*, and others.

"Those who started out in film criticism in the late sixties and early seventies—everyone, not just Pauline Kael's friends— slowly realized that they had stumbled into a happy moment," David Denby wrote in *The New Yorker* in 2003. "After years of the Vietnam War, the culture had attained a degree of bitter self-knowledge, a mood more conducive to good popular work than the shocked rage and frenzy of the sixties, which yielded movies that were, too often, pushy, and consciously Zeitgeisty—*Easy Rider* careering out of control.

"Things were settling down aesthetically," Denby continued. "Suddenly, art was possible—the audience, sometimes in sizeable numbers, was up for it. . . . We were just a bunch of journalists, not revolutionaries, but, still, there was a spirit of insurgency in the air, and we were part of it. Like the boldest of the rock critics, Pauline was sure that American mass culture at its best was plugged into the country's most vital instincts—anti-authoritarian, subversive of cant and lies and genteel feelings, individualistic but yearning for community."

"It was a very exciting time," recalled Dave Kehr, who developed his film sensibility at the University of Chicago, poring over Hollywood genre films as a habitué of the Documentary Film Group (or "Doc Films"), a campus haven for cineastes. "Every week seemed to introduce fascinating new figures," he wrote, including Allan Dwan, Raoul Walsh, Frank Borzage, Gregory La Cava, and others "whose films had long been ignored or dismissed by the official American critical establishment.

"These were the days when you could provoke a passionate argument at a party," Kehr wrote, "over whether a so-called hack like Hitchcock was worthy of even being mentioned in the same breath with an obvious, transcendent genius of the form like Fred Zinnemann or George Stevens (though I have come back to respect Stevens's early films since then)—or, much less, vaunted European masters like Ingmar Bergman or Federico Fellini, both of whom in my adolescent hubris I found to be bloated and basically worthless (an opinion I will stand by today, with a few carefully chosen exceptions)."

That "very exciting time" was shared by the vanguard of film critics who were students in the late 1960s and early 1970s, and were beginning to write film criticism. Pauline Kael became a public and private provocateur, according to those whom she chose to argue movies with as well as those with whom she picked fights. She concocted brouhaha-instigating broadsides in *The New Yorker*.

In the February 1971 essay, "Raising Kane," which appeared in two consecutive issues of *The New Yorker*, she clobbered the legend of Orson Welles. The critic called Welles's masterpiece, indeed America's masterpiece, *Citizen Kane* (1941)—which was loosely inspired by the life of publishing tycoon William Randolph Hearst—"a comic strip about Hearst." The Kane pieces were published between hard covers the same year with the Mankiewicz/Welles screenplay as *The Citizen Kane Book* from Atlantic Monthly-Little, Brown.

The upshot of this epic—a "50,000 word digression," according to Kael's old nemesis, Andrew Sarris—was that Herman J. Mankiewicz, who shared the screenplay credit for *Citizen Kane* with Welles, was the great, unsung creative force behind the film, which was produced and directed by Welles, who also starred as Kane. Kael goes so far as to say that Mankiewicz wrote almost the entire script with only perhaps minor alterations by Welles, and that Welles actively tried to deny Mankiewicz on-screen credit and take it all for himself, then Mankiewicz was "blackmailed into sharing credit with Welles."

Mankiewicz, a veteran of credit battles from the silent movies, took his case to the Screen Writers Guild and, according to Kael, "raised so much hell that Welles was forced to split the credit and take second place in the listing." Points made by Kael were that Mankiewicz was an acquaintance of William Randolph Hearst, the model for Charles Foster Kane, and Welles was not, and that Mankiewicz had lost a prized conveyance in childhood, a bicycle, converted in the movie to a snow sled (the mysterious "Rosebud"), and Welles had not.

The Kael piece was an obvious extension of her attack on the auteur theory in 1963, when she lambasted Sarris in the essay "Circles and Squares" in *Film Quarterly*. "Raising Kane" was composed with the base argument that a screenwriter had as much claim to film authorship, even of the great *Citizen Kane*, as the director did. Her partiality for Mankiewicz, who died in 1953, included his former status as a staffer on her magazine, *The New Yorker*. It was obvious that she thoroughly investigated and analyzed his career prior to *Citizen Kane*.

She did nothing of the sort concerning Welles's career to create a comparison. She also never spoke to Welles, which any journalist would have tried to do in the name of fairness. She relied instead on conversations with Mankiewicz's family, old RKO Radio Pictures head George Schaefer, and Welles's old partner, John Houseman, who denied that Welles had written anything, even though Houseman's personal papers, housed at UCLA, say otherwise, according to Welles biographer Barbara Leaming.

Kael also related an anecdote attributed to screenwriter Nunnally Johnson that contended Welles tried through a third party to pay off Mankiewicz with a $10,000 bribe if the financially strapped writer would leave his name off the screenplay credits. An ancillary thrust of Kael's analysis was that cinematographer Gregg Toland had displayed some of the camera techniques—which were thought to be groundbreaking on *Citizen Kane*—as far back as Karl Freund's *Mad Love* (1935).

Welles was a large and easy target in his raconteur years as the boy-genius-gone-outsized-celeb on the talk-show circuit, commiserating with Merv Griffin about religion. His seemingly rudderless career had him poking around as a filmmaker with the unfinished (still, today) movie about movies, *The Other Side of the Wind*, and settling as an actor for third-wheel loitering in George Peppard and George Segal movies, well on his way to appearing in Paul Masson wine commercials on TV.

Kael had mined deeply into the Houseman contention that Welles was an egomaniac beyond pall, who loved to believe that every project with which he was involved deserved his sole credit. As Mordecai Richler wrote in *The New York Times Book Review* about *The Citizen Kane Book*, Kael achieved success at "cutting Orson Welles down to size, denying his needlessly grandiose claim to having been solely responsible for everything that went into *Kane*."

Richler was only one member of the mainstream press who applauded Kael's persuasive yet unsubstantiated and reckless attack. Part of that acceptance of Kael's opinion had to do with her growing reputation as the best film critic in the land. The book-trade reviews were mixed on *The Citizen Kane Book* as new gospel. "['Raising Kane'] is probably the best thing Kael has written, a mixture of journalism, biography, autobiography, gossip, and criticism, carried along by a style so exhilarating that one seems to be reading a new, loose kind of critical biography," wrote J.A. Avant in *Library Journal*. But Ken Russell in *Books and Bookmen* called the treatise "Hedda Hopperish and Louella Parsonish."

Kael had become a success by wielding a brash style in the 1960s, and was continuing in that vein. Outside of perhaps a sage scribe at *The New York Times* or maybe one of the major newsweeklies, if any other critic would have launched such an oddball tirade at the roundly regarded greatest film of all time, it probably would have raised few eyebrows, but been deemed unworthy of rebuttal. But this was the mercurial Kael firing at the solar plexus of American film art.

Kael bashed film scholars in the process, including Welles biographer Joseph McBride, for the underestimation of Mankiewicz. "Aside from cackling at another film scholar for the benefit of the philistines, Miss Kael creates the impression that

McBride and his ilk never had the foggiest notion that Herman J. Mankiewicz had written the screenplay," Andrew Sarris wrote. "McBride's greatest sin [is] apparently his willingness to consider *Citizen Kane* as a work of art rather than in Miss Kael's terms as 'kitsch redeemed,' a culturally defensive attitude for readers and editors who would be shocked to have any movie taken too seriously."

Return volleys issued from McBride in *Film Heritage* in 1971 and Jonathan Rosenbaum in *Film Comment* in 1972. "Not that Mankiewicz doesn't deserve appreciation," McBride wrote, "But it's an infuriating shame that to resurrect his name Miss Kael had tried to bury Orson Welles in the process. . . . Miss Kael is not accredited as a probate attorney, and *The New Yorker* is not a court of law, and *Citizen Kane* is not a script or even a book. She herself acknowledges that the greatness of the film is in the direction. Her 'criticism' is even less enlightening than her gossip. She has so many preoccupations that she not only can't see the forest for the trees, she can't even see the trees. . . . At one point she refers to a crane shot as a 'vertical pan.' That kind of sloppiness wouldn't be tolerated in any critical discipline outside the movies."

In Great Britain, George Coulouris, who acted in *Kane*, and Bernard Herrmann, who wrote its score, rebutted Kael's piece in *Sight & Sound* interviews. Welles and his old pal, Peter Bogdanovich, assembled a point-by-point refutation under Bogdanovich's byline, "The Kane Mutiny," published in the October 1972 edition of *Esquire*. Bogdanovich tracked down Charles Lederer, a screenwriter who was a great friend of Mankiewicz as well as being Marion Davies's nephew (film star Davies was Hearst's mistress for more than 30 years).

Lederer underscored Welles's involvement in the scriptwriting. "Manky was always complaining and sighing about Orson's changes," Lederer said. "And I heard from Benny [Hecht] too, that Manky was terribly upset." Mankiewicz asked Lederer, as a Davies relative and confidant, to read the script to gauge the Hearst camp's possible reaction. Kael claims at that point,

Hearst lawyers were called in.

"That is 100% whole-cloth lying," Lederer told Bogdanovich. "I gave it *back* to him. He asked me if I thought Marion would be offended, and I said I didn't think so." Lederer also said that much of the film's base information wasn't derived from Hearst's life, but that of Harold F. McCormick of the *Chicago Tribune*, who divorced his first wife, Edith Rockefeller, to marry Gauma Walska, underwriting the latter's attempt at opera stardom. Bogdanovich also collected ample testimony supporting Welles as an active writer on *Citizen Kane* and not just an overseer. Included was a 1941 affidavit from RKO President Richard Baer, which states, "The revisions made by Welles were not limited to mere general suggestions, but included the actual rewriting of words, dialogue, changing of sequences, ideas and characterizations, and also the elimination and addition of certain scenes."

The time between "Raising Kane" and the rebuttals was many months. The 13-page *Esquire* piece arrived 20 months after Kael's first essay of "Raising Kane" appeared in *The New Yorker*. There was plenty of time for Kael's grandstanding trash to calcify as fact. "So the appearance of research behind 'Raising Kane' was misleading," wrote David Thomson in *Rosebud: The Story of Orson Welles* (1997). "Yet it helped give substance to the belligerent tone and the air of exposure. . . .

"The bias in Kael's approach blinded her to the ample evidence (later detailed by Bogdanovich and others) of how much Welles had contributed to the scenario," Thomson continued. "More important than that, Kael the screen hound seemed to have set aside her acute response to the sniff and excitement of [cinema] itself and to the roots of authorship that rested in how the whole thing was done in terms of light, space, movement, sound and atmosphere.

"'Raising Kane' was not generous to that broad area of genius and control, and it did not pay much attention to how modestly Mankiewicz and Gregg Toland had fared without Welles. The essay seemed calculated and mean-spirited, as well as less than thorough or completely accurate. . . . So in large as well as small respects, the essay was misguided."

"Raising Kane" remains the most agregious transgression of Kael's otherwise generally wisely calculated career. After the fulminations it caused, and the defenses of Welles that it inspired, after its wrongheadedness was either accepted or rejected or forgotten, after the damage was done, no follow-up occurred from the Kael camp for 25 years, or until the celebratory republishing of "Raising Kane" twice again in 1996 without alterations, in *For Keeps*, the collation of Kael's major works, from Plume, and in *Raising Kane and Other Essays*, from Marion Boyars. Copies of the original *Citizen Kane Book* also rest in libraries so that Welles can be defamed forever by this coffee-table-sized compilation of balderdash.

Arranging new ways to shake up the film scene was more important to Kael than any rubble left in her wake. She had made a great impact in the 1960s with her review of *Bonnie and Clyde* and she succeeded in writing an assessment of similar impact in the 1970s. Roger Ebert deemed Kael's review of Bernardo Bertolucci's *Last Tango in Paris* (1973) as "the most famous movie review ever published." The film starred Marlon Brando in perhaps his greatest performance as an American in the title city despairing in middle age after the death of his wife, leading to his no-questions-asked extended sexual liaison with a young Parisian woman. The film was famous for its explicit, varied sexual couplings, and for Brando's astonishingly risky and revealing performance.

"The movie breakthrough has finally come," Kael wrote, in *The New Yorker*. "Bertolucci and Brando have altered the face of an art form." The date of the premiere, Kael said, would become a landmark in movie history comparable to the night in 1913 when Stravinsky's *The Rite of Spring* was first performed, marking modern music's debut. "This is a movie people will be arguing about for as long as there are movies," Kael declared. The early review was reprinted in its entirety by United Artists as a double-page ad in the Sunday *New York Times*. In retrospect, the review's prediction didn't come to pass, but the review itself, its treatment by Hollywood, its reverberation in film culture—all illustrated the newfound esteem in which Kael and the profession were held.

Kael infamously wrote a review of Robert Altman's *Nashville* (1975), published in *The New Yorker* four months before the film's release, based on a six-hour rough cut, calling it "an orgy for film lovers." Kael wrote, "I sat there smiling at the screen, in complete happiness," as well as, "I've never before seen a movie I loved in quite this way."

This pre-review, her "greatest breach of professionalism," according to Alan Vanneman in *Bright Lights Film Journal*, caused as much a stir as the film did. Vincent Canby suggested in *The New York Times* that Kael might next dispense with the movie entirely and review the shooting script. "It was a typical Kael move," Peter Biskind wrote in 1998, "calculated to prevent Paramount from re-cutting the movie and to goad the studio into putting some marketing muscle behind it. Her piece was full of the excitement of discovering a great work." It was a brash attempt of film criticism to alter Hollywood, to embrace the film artists, and it was also full of praise in favor of her friend, Altman.

As a formless slice of life in country music's capital, *Nashville* was nevertheless an evocative series of vignettes, hung on the vague notion that the musicians, drifters, everyday barmaids, wives, wannabes, and other disaffected characters somehow formed a snapshot of American ambitions at the crossroads of the 1970s. Familiar faces—Keith Carradine, Barbara Harris, Lily Tomlin—peopled the cast. "Its failure to perform at the box office, despite the blitz of good press, was not only another indication that the passions that animated the first half of the decade were on the wane, it also underlined the limits of Kael's power," Biskind wrote. "When Altman was asked why it hadn't done better, he said, 'Because we didn't have King Kong or a shark.'"

Kael played a gunslinger's role in the National Society of Film Critics' private Algonquin Hotel chats with filmmakers. Kael would wait until the guests were sufficiently softened up and then go for the jugular, according to one witness. "Sooner or later she would, under the guise of free and open discussion, launch into a vicious assault on our guest," Schickel recalled. "We were used to it, of course—we had all, at one time or another, been the victims of these near sociopathic outbursts—but they shocked people who had come expecting a polite exchange of ideas. David Lean was so distressed by his evening with the critics that he would claim (with considerable melodramatic license) that it prevented him from making a film for fourteen years. John Frankenheimer, bless his heart, gave back as good as he got. Others fell somewhat befuddled between both these extremes, but the tone Kael kept setting subverted the purpose of these gatherings and we soon abandoned them."

On the pages of *The New Yorker*, Kael championed the little guy, ordaining, among others, Martin Scorsese, calling *Mean Streets* (1973) "a true original of our period, a triumph of personal filmmaking." She called the youthful Steven Spielberg "perhaps the new generation's Howard Hawks" after the release of his first (and still underrated) feature, *The Sugarland Express* (1974). She recognized these greats of the immediate future while the mainstream guard waited a year to join the bandwagons with Scorsese's *Alice Doesn't Live Here Anymore* (1974) and Spielberg's industry-altering *Jaws* (1975). Kael was at the core of the critical notion that raw, outsider cinema with fresh ways of expression and new talent boldly testing the status quo had to have more heart than anything green-lighted and cranked out by the studio fogies' assembly line. It wasn't a new idea; it just crystallized as part of her reputation.

Still, her put-downs and exacting comparisons are among the well-remembered things about her writing. She called Lean's *Ryan's Daughter* (1970) "gush made respectable by millions of dollars tastefully wasted." Of Bresson's *Four Nights of a Dreamer* (1971), she wrote, "Robert Bresson used to postpone emotion deliberately; here he postpones it indefinitely." Her one-time protégé, Paul Schrader, didn't escape her purview with his pornography-world drama *Hardcore* (1979): "The father feels no temptation, so there's no contest; he's above sex, and he hates porno the way John Wayne hates rustlers and Commies." Joseph L. Mankiewicz's *Sleuth* (1972), a showcase for Laurence Olivier and Michael Caine, was tired stuff to her: "It's Olivier in the kind of material he outgrew more than thirty years ago—it's Olivier in a George Sanders role."

Warren Beatty asked Kael to join Paramount Pictures in 1979 as a script consultant, and she lasted through a five-month contract, after which she got back to the calling that made her famous. "I find that with picture projects, so much is at stake that anybody getting involved in a picture wants to talk over the same issues endlessly," Kael told journalist Jane Garcia. "Day after day, they'll talk over the same little points, and I would go crazy. . . . I'm rather quick in temperament, and I just don't have the disposition to chew over the same subject. They're terribly anxious about each thing they do, and it's understandable. Their careers are really at stake all the time. But it doesn't mean much to me."

After her studio tenure, Kael explained that the finer points of studio finance were at odds with making good films in "Why Are Movies So Bad?" a practices-and-trends piece in *The New Yorker* in 1980 that was the epitomic blast at the suits and the deals—a 10-point definition for the uninitiated on the anti-art evil of the studio empire.

Meanwhile, her influence as the key figure of the Film Generation on its progeny was enormous. "If thousands of students devoted themselves to investigative journalism because of the example set by Bob Woodward and Carl Bernstein's Watergate dispatches, it's likely that an equal number of film curates pursued periodical-based parishes to spread the movie-love gospel that Kael preached from the high church pulpit of the *New Yorker*," Ken Tucker wrote in *Entertainment Weekly*.

Established in both the New York media and film criticism worlds by the time of Kael's rise in the 1960s was John Simon, an occasional nemesis. Simon was the theatre critic of *The Hudson Review* in 1960, of *Commonweal* in 1967 and 1968, and *New York* magazine from 1968 to 2005, when he was fired three days shy of his 80th birthday after dismissing a production of Tennessee Williams's *A Streetcar Named Desire* as "degrading, detestable," and warning of "rotary earthquakes" near the grave of Marlon Brando. Simon was also film critic of *The New Leader* from 1963 to 1973, then *New York* magazine beginning in 1975, *Esquire* from 1973 to 1975, and later *The National Review*. To some, Simon was the most admired film critic of the 1960s and 1970s.

"John Simon is the most informative critic writing in these two areas [film and drama criticism] today," claimed a 1967 editorial in *Film Heritage*, the magazine edited by F. Anthony Macklin. ". . . Simon loves meaning; and he must be infuriated when critics and artists sneer at it as something superfluous. He works as a critic; one can see the labor in his essays. The sheer amount of examples and quotations shows a tremendous keenness toward the work, and Simon has a respect for the idea of art, the labor, detail and vision behind it. . . . John Simon is a fair critic (fairness is a commodity missing from the bright, militant parades flourishing over most of the pages of contemporary criticism)."

Poet W.H. Auden was a Simon fan. "As a critic, Mr. Simon is lucid, learned, witty, and even when he is most savage, just and in good taste," Auden wrote. Some would argue about Auden's "good taste" contention, especially as Simon's career continued and his poison-pen brand of personal criticism emerged. His background was unlike any other critic's, arriving as he did from war-torn Europe into the intelligentsia.

John Ivan Simon was born on May 12, 1925, in Subotica, Yugoslavia, and immigrated to the United States in 1941 to join his businessman father. John Simon served in the U.S. Air Force in 1944 and 1945, then taught at Harvard, the University of Washington, Massachusetts Institute of Technology, and Bard College. He edited for the Mid-Century Book Society and Appleton-Century-Crofts, both in New York, while his criticism career got underway. Simon was the first of three film critics to have been conferred the George Polk Memorial Award for criticism, in 1968 (the others were Pauline Kael in 1970, and Stanley Kauffmann in 1982). Simon also won the George Jean Nathan Award for Dramatic Criticism for his work in 1969 and 1970. For someone not born into the language, Simon became a watchdog of English, and eventually published *Paradigms Lost: Reflections on Literacy and Its Decline* (1980).

In the preface to an anthology of his film reviews, *Reverse Angle: A Decade of American Films* (1981), Simon explained himself as a critic in comparison to Pauline Kael, who, he notes, "by way of supreme praise, applies the epithet 'liberating' to a movie." Movies, he said, were aimed at adolescent and "less speculative minds" as a means of escapism from "adulthood, reality, truth."

His was an atypical case, Simon wrote. He was transplanted as a teenager to America from Europe, and he saw Hollywood films as the escapism they were, but also looked at the arriving postwar European films as "full of steamy sex, adultery, betrayal, failure, often unheroic destruction and waste—the Lost Paradise of realism: of being honest, strong, and imbued with the tragic sense of life. In some strange way, these contradictory biases canceled each other out, leaving me to look at films with a different set of idiosyncrasies, predilections, fallibilities."

Whether the absence of appreciation for lowbrow comedy was one of Simon's fallibilities is a matter of taste. "No mention of *Blazing Saddles* can be brief enough," Simon huffed about the hit 1974 comic western by the major spoof-meister of the times. "Mel Brooks's film, like his previous *The Producers* and *The Twelve Chairs*, is a model of how not to make a comedy. It is like playing tennis not only without a net but also without a court, and with twenty balls simultaneously. All kinds of gags—chiefly anachronisms, irrelevancies, reverse ethnic jokes, and out-and-out vulgarities—are thrown together pell-mell, batted about insanely in all directions, and usually beaten into the ground."

A former Harvard and MIT teacher, Simon admired Terrence Malick as a "former Harvard man, Rhodes scholar, and

MIT philosophy lecturer turned filmmaker with remarkable perception and quiet bravura" in his review of *Badlands* (1973), which he said "bears superficial resemblance to *The Sugarland Express* and *Thieves Like Us*," concurrent films from Steven Spielberg and Robert Altman. "But [*Badlands*] is immeasurably finer than both those films rolled, or unrolled into one. It is, in fact the next-to-last word about the virulent alienation youth has been going through, a subject on which the last word can probably never be spoken. Wisely, Malick refrains from even trying."

Like Kael, Simon occasionally reviewed the reviewers. Andrew Sarris, Kael, and Vincent Canby were targets. "I tend to disagree with Andrew Sarris's taste in movies and to despair of his stylistic insufficiencies as a writer," was one opening salvo. After taking a few bites from Simon in print, Sarris fought back on the pages of *The New York Times*, calling Simon "the Count Dracula of critics."

Simon was in the minority when Peter Bogdanovich's *The Last Picture Show* (1971) arrived. The writer-director, Simon wrote, "is America's answer to the *Cahiers* phenomenon of film critic turned film-maker; yet behind every answer there is a question. In this case, how good was he as a critic in the first place? The answer is that he was never a serious critic, only an *auteurist* hero-worshipper." In fact, Bogdanovich was an essayist, regularly for *Esquire*, who also wrote monographs on Welles, John Ford, Fritz Lang, and other directors.

"And how is he as a film-maker?" Simon asked rhetorically. "His first film, *Targets*, handled a valid subject in a trashy way; his new one, *The Last Picture Show*, is a great hit with the reviewers, so too with the audiences, and strikes me as not bad by current standards. . . . Above all, Bogdanovich's direction is sheer derivativeness. To put it bluntly, it is cinematheque direction. A John Ford shot is followed by a George Stevens one; a Welles shot by one out of Raoul Walsh. Even if every sequence is not as patently copied as the funeral is from *Shane*, the feeling is unmistakable that one is watching a film directed by not a young director in 1971 but by a conclave of the bigger Hollywood directors circa 1941. . . . *The Last Picture Show* rises to the heights of pastiche."

In his review of Kael's book, *Deeper into Movies*, Simon wrote: "What emerges from collating these bits of over-praise or pathetic true confessions is that the shoddy films Miss Kael extols all possess one or more of the following characteristics: They are reminiscent of the kind of movies that she uncritically devoured in her early years; they exalt so-called healthy vulgarity as a way of life or filmmaking; they undermine the middle-class values from which Miss Kael sometimes (though not consistently) wishes to feel liberated; and they feature a homely or butch heroine who nevertheless achieves romantic fulfillment."

Some evidence of a Kael-Simon parlor feud made it into *The New Yorker*, recounted by David Denby in 2003. "If they took [Kael] on, they got knocked off their feet, more often than not, by a lightning comeback," Denby wrote. "'John, you're too old to be writing like a punk,' she informed the elaborately educated Europhile slasher John Simon at a meeting of the National Society of Film Critics. Some of the men walked away, muttering, 'Ball-breaker.'"

Openly priggish and eager with poison-pen hostility, Simon apparently adhered to rigorous standards. Richard Schickel was one of the critics who wondered in print whether Simon might be the only film critic without a passion for the movies. James Wolcott wrote, "*New York*'s John Simon cast aspersions in print and spittle in person; the mere mention of Barbra Streisand sent him orbital." In his review of *Up the Sandbox* (1972), Simon mercilessly and infamously ground his literary heel into Streisand for the unalterable sin of her genetic features.

"Quite aside from her persona, however, I find Miss Streisand's looks repellent," Simon confessed. "Perhaps this is my limitation, but I cannot accept a romantic heroine who is both knock-kneed and ankle-less (maybe one of those things, but not both!), short-legged and shapeless, scrag-toothed and with a horse-face centering on a nose that looks like Brancusi's Rooster cast in liverwurst." Simon compared Liza Minnelli to a beagle,

Kathleen Turner to a "braying mantis," and never let up on his mission against Streisand, once writing that her nose "cleaves the giant screen from east to west, bisects it from north to south. It zigzags across our horizon like a bolt of fleshy lightning."

In one of the more memorable reactions of a performer who had been upset by a critic, the actress Sylvia Miles spotted Simon in a New York restaurant in 1973, and unceremoniously dumped a bowl of pasta on his head. Unusually headstrong in some reactions, he apparently in this case inspired the same in another.

Simon walked out on the National Society of Film Critics and joined the New York Film Critics Circle, like a politician exiting the U.S. Senate for a city council seat. This was in the early 1970s when Charles Champlin was one of 10 critics considered for National Society membership. "Ten new names were proposed for membership. . . . Since I did not believe that there were ten people in the entire country—in and out of the society—who lived up to the rigorous demands of film criticism, the very quantity seemed ludicrous," Simon said.

"I remember Hollis Alpert arguing on behalf of Charles Champlin of the *Los Angeles Times* that, though he lived right there in L.A., Champlin, admirably, was not 'bought by the industry,'" Simon wrote. "'Of course not,' I said, 'Why should they pay for something they can have for free?' Champlin was elected, and I resigned—which I would have done over other candidates as well, but Champlin preceded them alphabetically," Simon contended. Champlin had graduated *cum laude* from Harvard University in 1947, the year between Simon's undergraduate and master's degrees at the same school.

Simon, like Kael, was as blunt as anyone in the business, but he cornered the market on mordancy. In the history of film criticism, no one as prominent wrote more scathingly more often than he did. Even giving Simon the benefit of any doubt for his high standards and posture of superiority, the sheer hostility in his prose belied a proficient meanness that took criticism to the level of personal insult. Streisand wasn't just plain; she was hideous. John Cassavetes wasn't just a bad screenwriter; he was mentally deficient, as the following Simon-ized lead would attest, in a bash at the darling of other critics.

"The films of John Cassavetes are, by and large, sterile actors' exercises," begins Simon's review of Cassavetes's *The Killing of a Chinese Bookie* (1976), starring Ben Gazzara. "They are not even for all kinds of actors, but mostly for friends of Cassavetes and amateurs like his family and his wife's family. They are doggedly pretentious and often of enormous duration; unless you are an actor or a friend, or a relative of the director's, you should find them quintessentially trivial and boring. Cassavetes, who is quite a good actor but a bad director and worse writer, has insisted . . . his films are 'scripted,' though they seem to be taped and transcribed improvisations. . . . If Cassavetes is telling the truth and really writes this trash that postures as plot characterization, and dialogue, he must be an even bigger simpleton than I take him to be."

In his review of Simon's *Private Screenings: Views of the Cinema of the Sixties* (1967) in *The New York Times Book Review*, Andrew Sinclair saw the critic as a Jekyll-and-Hyde-like dual personality. "The good John Simon claims to be the best film critic now writing on either side of the Atlantic. He is learned, dedicated, witty, and determined to raise the level of the cinema by the quality of his criticism. Yet the moment that the good John Simon has his readers in a state of stimulated gratitude, the bad John Simon leaps onto the page in an explosion of squibs and graffiti. Like Marlowe's Faustus, he exchanges the search after truth and enlightenment for the puerile satisfaction of lighting bangers under the tails of the great. Inside the good John Simon the imp is always larking about. . . . He is as absolute and arrogant in his judgments as any dictator of culture, a rigidity that is his great strength and weakness."

The same anthology was reviewed by Peter Bogdanovich. "Unable to discuss film on its own terms, [Simon] usually seeks refuge in a fancy comparative literature phrase," Bogdanovich wrote in *Book World*. "So D.W. Griffith is compared to Achilles

Tailus, Richard Lester to John Bunyan, Truffaut's *The Soft Skin* to Pound's *Cantos*. . . . [Reviewing Truffaut's *Fahrenheit 451*] Simon spends most of his space on books vs. movie stuff, then admires 'an impressive device'—'closing in with tiny jump-cuts,' he inaccurately describes it—not knowing it was first used in Hitchcock's *The Birds*. . . . Film is not literature, comparative or otherwise, and it deserves to be criticized with as much specialized attention and knowledge as any other art. . . . A critic who just hears the words or sees only the most obvious of cinematic 'devices' is about as much help as a legless man teaching running."

Simon vs. Bogdanovich was another skirmish on the film criticism battlefield, which was expanding on the pop-culture landscape. The National Society burgeoned, too, and by the early 1970s included not only Champlin, but also Gary Arnold of *The Washington Post*, Bruce Williamson of *Playboy*, David Denby of *The Atlantic Monthly*, Molly Haskell of *The Village Voice*, Robert Hatch of *The Nation*, Paul D. Zimmerman of *Newsweek*, Jacob Brackman of *Esquire*, Vincent Canby of *The New York Times*, and *Time/Life* colleagues of charter NSFC member Richard Schickel, including future Martin Scorsese collaborator Jay Cocks; veteran Brad Darrach, who had been reviewing since 1951; and the first *Time* critic to get a byline on a movie review, Stefan Kanfer.

The hotbed of so many issues other than movies, the nation's capital joined the film discussion through Gary Arnold's radical approach on publisher Katherine Graham's *Post*. "In 1969 Gary Arnold was signed on as the chief movie critic and he quickly proved to be highly controversial," wrote Chalmers M. Roberts in *The Washington Post: The First 100 Years*. "In a column on the ten best films of 1969 he wrote that 'at the moment I think the abrasive pictures, the ones that are concerned or worked up—often to the point of confusion—about contemporary life are more important to see and encourage.' His power as the critic of the city's leading paper to make or break new films has been enormous."

Arnold thought that George Roy Hill's *Butch Cassidy and*

the Sundance Kid (1969) was "shallow . . . overdressed . . . alien-ating." Franklin J. Schaffner's Academy Award-winning best pic-ture, *Patton* (1970), was for Arnold "oddly evasive. . . . Is it left, right, confused, or nonexistent?" Of Arthur Hiller's hit weeper, *Love Story* (1970), Arnold wrote, "It's a smug tear-jerker, worth resisting on principle, because it's been so deliberately designed as a mass-culture bromide, a reactionary bridge over political and artistic troubled waters of the last few years."

One of Arnold's tougher reviews covered Alan J. Pakula's *All the President's Men* (1976), the adaptation of the best seller on the Watergate scandal written by *Washington Post* reporters Carl Bernstein and Bob Woodward. "Of all the reviews, mostly raves, none was more critical than the paper's own Gary Arnold's," Chalmers M. Roberts wrote. Pakula and his crew recreated Ar-nold's own workspace, the *Post* newsroom, for the film. Arnold found the film "engrossing and enjoyable" but with a "restrictive framework" that omitted many scenes from the book.

Criticizing a movie about your own newsroom was one thing, but Charles Champlin was criticized *in* his own news-room and by his own newspaper for his film criticism. *Los An-geles Times* media critic David Shaw quoted a source to the ef-fect that Champlin was like Will Rogers, he "never met a film he didn't like." Hundreds of examples exist to the contrary, but that blast was a stinger. "When that appeared in the paper, I was mad," said Jean Sharley Taylor, who oversaw the "soft news" operation at the *Times* in the 1970s. "I called Bill Thomas and I said, 'Why are we doing things like this?'" Thomas, the *Times*'s editor-in-chief, and publisher Otis Chandler had hired Shaw for the same reason they hired Champlin in 1965, to ensure that the *Times* had a clean bill of journalistic health. Chandler and Thomas backed Shaw.

"Courtly in demeanor, he possesses an arsenal of envi-able attributes including swift understanding, a literate nature and an anecdotal turn of mind," wrote Marshall Berges about Champlin in *The Life and Times of Los Angeles: A Newspaper, a Family, and a City*. "A kind and generous state of mind frames his own window on the world."

Champlin was well aware of the position he held as the lead film critic for the biggest paper on the West Coast—right in Hollywood's backyard. "If you are a film critic and you work for the *Times*, you are conspicuous," Champlin told Berges. "You have a certain amount of power and responsibility. It sounds pretentious but the *Times* gives you an influential voice and you become a kind of synapse, a junction point for producers and distributors. They want to show their films, and mostly as a favor you will go to see them. Or a local distributor may be debating whether to run a film, and he invites you over. So you spend an awful lot of afternoons schlepping out to see the latest Balkan masterpiece. . . . And then the big commercial Hollywood studio screenings tend to be in the evening at eight-thirty. So the day begins early at the typewriter, and ends quite late as the lights come on after the film."

Champlin grew up in a small town in upstate New York during the Great Depression. "Neither then nor at any time since have I found any effective substitute for hard work," he said. Of the David Shaw controversy, Champlin said, "Given the choice, I would rather be fair than colorful. It's awfully easy to be scathing. . . . Destruction is kind of a mug's game." He received a note that he has kept from director Joseph Losey after one of the filmmaker's films was panned by the majority of critics, including him. "Chuck," it read, "at least you tried to see it as a movie and not a crime against civilization." "I rather cherished that," Champlin said, "because I had tried to be fair." Often tougher than fairness can be the task of communicating the attributes of a great film.

As Janet Maslin of *The New York Times* once said, "It's very hard to write a rave." Yet Champlin did just that with economy, his own syncopated tone, and an even-handed mixture of individual praise, useful description, and the couching of craft insight. "*The Conversation* is a movie which seems to me to work at every level," wrote Champlin in the *Los Angeles Times* in 1974 of Francis Ford Coppola's film, "as a message picture dramatizing the nightmare possibilities of privacy breached; as an intricate and suspenseful plot; as an engrossing character study of a man become the captive of his own dark skills; as a social document fascinatingly detailed in its look at the techniques of electronic eavesdropping."

In another 1974 review, Champlin wrote, "In its total recapturing of a past, in its plot, its vivid characterizations, its carefully calculated and accelerated pace, its whole demonstration of a medium mastered, *Chinatown* reminds you again—and thrillingly—that motion pictures are larger, not smaller than life; they are not processed at drugstores and they are not television. They are, at their best, events calculated to transport us out of ourselves, as *Chinatown* does."

The notion existed that the *Los Angeles Times* was always conscious of its role as the major paper in the industry's hometown, while the *Los Angeles Herald-Examiner* seemed to never care about that. At the *Herald-Examiner*, Michael Sragow was film critic from 1977 to 1980. Perhaps his decimations of major studio films wouldn't have been as conspicuous to the studio suits if he were in Iowa, but Sragow pulled no punches in the heart of Hollywood.

When the mighty stumbled and fell, as Steve McQueen did in George Schaefer's *An Enemy of the People* (1977), Sragow understood the severity. "Think of Clark Gable as the tragic Parnell, or Gregory Peck playing Ahab as if he were Abraham Lincoln," Sragow wrote. "Recall Elizabeth Taylor as if she were the Cleopatra of Great Neck. Then add to this list of big-star follies the typical, lean, tight-lipped action hero Steve McQueen. Here, he's plump, bearded, and avuncular, a bit like Kris Kringle. For McQueen to play Ibsen's volatile, idealistic intellectual Dr. Stockman is as unusual as it would be for Dr. Carl Sagan to try and play Darth Vadar."

Michael Schultz's *Sgt. Pepper's Lonely Hearts Club Band* (1978) was as much an insipid mess as critics said it was, including Sragow, but Universal Pictures pulled its advertising from the *Herald-Examiner* anyway. Then Twentieth Century-Fox followed suit when Sragow panned such costly, obviously prestige pictures as Franklin J. Schaffner's *The Boys from Brazil* (1978) and Richard Attenborough's *Magic* (1978). *Herald-Examiner* editor James Bellows and publisher Frank Dale stood by Sragow, staving off the loss of thousands of dollars in lost advertising revenue.

Wise to Hollywood's tricks, Sragow appreciated the good studio film when he saw it. *The Stunt Man* (1980) was a "popular work of modernist art," he wrote, and "Richard Rush's whirligig virtuosity has created an alternate reality bigger and better than life."

Another savvy veteran, but from an older school, was Robert Hatch, who had been reviewing since 1954, straight through appointments to various editorships at *The Nation*, and he was one of the steadiest voices of reason in film criticism for three decades. An early member of the National Society of Film Critics, Hatch retired from *The Nation* in 1978 after a dozen years as executive editor, but continued to review films. He died in 1994 at the age of 83.

He didn't think Federico Fellini was a good choice to direct *The Clowns* (1971), a documentary probe into the world of circus clowns that also pokes fun at documentaries. Made for Italian television, *The Clowns* was released theatrically in America.

"They are fragile; Fellini is dominating," Hatch wrote in *The Nation*. "They are finished; he is in his prime. Fellini making a picture about clowns is something quite different from a Fellini picture about clowns. I doubt that—so late—he could have made the latter; I am not glad that he went ahead with the former. There are instants of flashing and cheeky good humor in the film, but overall, it has a vaultlike chill."

Hatch provided a continuity of smoothly honed writing and acute perceptions through the Bosley Crowther-dominated years of foreign films and widescreen American product into the creatively explosive 1970s and beyond. Meanwhile, at Crowther's old paper, *The New York Times*, Vincent Canby was hired away from *Variety* in 1965, and replaced Renata Adler as the lead film critic for the *Times* in 1969. Canby's reviews exhibited the direct descriptive strength and deft layering of opinions that fit the succinct *Times* style and advanced the notion that he was film-scene savvy the way Crowther was not. Canby combined the continuity of the Crowther years with an accumulating notion that understood the prevailing winds, and could decipher the trends and meaning on the cinema landscape.

In his review of Sam Peckinpah's *The Wild Bunch* (1969), Canby predicted that the picture's violence would be controversial. "The movie . . . is very beautiful and the first truly interesting American-made western in years. It's also full of violence—of an intensity that can hardly be supported by the story—that it's going to prompt a lot of people who do not know the real effect of movie violence (as I do not) to write automatic condemnations of it. . . . Peckinpah also has a way of employing Hollywood life to dramatize his legend. After years of giving bored performances in boring movies, [William] Holden comes back gallantly in *The Wild Bunch*. He looks older and tired, but he has style, both as a man and a movie character who persists in doing what he always has done, not because he really wants the money but because there's simply nothing else to do."

Canby found Michelangelo Antonioni's *Zabriskie Point* (1970) lacking in substance. "Because of the fundamental emptiness of his American vision, all sorts of flaws that one might overlook in better Antonioni films become apparent," Canby wrote in *The New York Times*. "The two young leads, who never acted before, are beautiful (he, I'm afraid, has the edge), but they move and talk with all the conviction of the life-sized mannequins who perform in a Sunny Dunes television commercial within the film. Only Rod Taylor, a real actor, seems human. Various Antonioni mannerisms—the blank screen suddenly filled with a face, the endless tracking shots, the pregnant pauses between unfinished thoughts—are finally only tolerable because you remember the times when they were better used. In *Zabriskie Point*, Antonioni, like Mark and Daria, succumbs to the hostile terrain."

After alternating reviews for the *Times* with Nora Sayre from 1973 to 1975, Canby was teamed on the film review beat with another woman in 1977, former *Boston Phoenix* and *Rolling Stone* critic Janet Maslin, for perhaps the greatest one-two set of critics in the history of film reviewing. She had reviewed films for *Newsweek* in the early 1970s, creating at mid-decade a daily mainstream tandem that was widely regarded as the best and most astute in the country. Canby championed the films of Woody Allen, particularly *Annie Hall* (1977) and *Manhattan* (1979). For all intents and purposes, and despite his denial of his power, Canby inherited the mantle and influence of the legendary Bosley Crowther.

Richard Schickel called Canby "a wry and civilized man who took the job seriously but didn't take himself too seriously." Canby espoused a "balance in his view of movies that was particularly useful for a critic appearing before the public on an almost daily basis," Schickel added. He was also funny. He called John Boorman's *Deliverance* (1972) "an action melodrama that doesn't trust its action to speak louder than words on the order of 'sometimes you gotta lose yourself to find something.' If anybody said that to me—seriously—in the course of a canoe trip, I think I'd get out and wade." Of Ann-Margret's performance in Ken Russell's *Tommy* (1975), he wrote that the actress/sex symbol "sings and dances as if the fate of Western civilization depends upon it."

Canby was born in Chicago, Illinois, in 1924. He served in the navy during World War II and studied English literature at Dartmouth College, earning a bachelor's degree in 1947. After writing for the *Chicago Journal of Commerce* and working in public relations in New York, he joined the staff of *Variety*. In his *New York Times* columns in the 1970s, he created a sometime companion, Stanley, a "producer friend" of excess, to lampoon the film business. Canby felt that the film critic's great problem was the same one that forced Alexander Bakshy to quit as film critic of the *New Republic* in the early 1930s, and that dogged Kenneth Turan of the *Los Angeles Times* in the 1990s: Critics see too many movies, especially too many mediocre movies. And, like Roger Ebert later wishing occasionally that he could point a sideways thumb, Canby said the vast majority of films are "neither very good nor very bad, and as writers, there is a problem with trying to make that interesting to read."

Canby was shrewd and plain-spoken on the page. "Not since *The Great Gatsby* two years ago, has any film come into town more absurdly oversold than *Rocky*," he wrote. He exposed imposters: "Although *The Turning Point* is set in the somewhat rare world of ballet, it's essentially an old-fashioned backstage musical that contains every backstage cliché I can think of." Canby did not have a high opinion of the Academy Awards. "We are drawn to our television sets each April the way we are drawn to the scene of an accident," he said.

Through most of the 1970s, Canby followed the groove of a crumbling tradition that carried the last vestiges of Bosley Crowther's influence over the world of film criticism. Films in those days opened on Wednesdays, not Fridays, as they do today to blitzkrieg the all-important weekend trade. The trade papers *Daily Variety* and *The Hollywood Reporter* were the only periodicals in the 1970s that were allowed by the studios in a code-of-honor way to run reviews before the daily newspapers. The newsweeklies, *Time* and *Newsweek*, were on newsstands on Monday and never ran reviews of the previous week's releases prior to then, especially without the studio's express consent. Crowther, as the head man at *The New York Times*, was adamant that the dailies have the first crack at new pictures, and the *Times*, as Stuart Byron wrote in *New York* magazine, "was, as always, first among equals."

"So prestigious was Crowther that for 21 straight years, from 1941 to 1961, no movie won a best picture Oscar unless it had appeared on his list of ten best films of the year," Byron stated. "And few foreign films succeeded at all without Crowther's imprimatur. A press agent had hell to pay if anybody scooped Bosley."

But after Bosley, or since 1968, foreign films such as *The*

Garden of the Finzi-Continis (1971) or *Dona Flor and Her Two Husbands* (1978) were successful even if they were panned by Canby, who acknowledged that his and his paper's influence over films, especially foreign and independent films, was gradually lessening as the film criticism ranks expanded. More critics meant more studio press management and more ways to get the word out about films to columnists, television critics, and news services. The competitive nature of journalism seeped into film criticism and a scoop mentality developed.

Jay Cocks of *Time* reviewed *The Wild Bunch* (1969) a week ahead of time, and Cocks and Judith Crist of *New York* magazine reviewed Stanley Kubrick's *A Clockwork Orange* (1971) two weeks early. Other early reviews through the decade were posted by Canby in the guise of a column in the Sunday *Times* on Francis Ford Coppola's *The Godfather* (1972), Pauline Kael in *The New Yorker* on Robert Altman's *Thieves Like Us* (1974) as well as the previously discussed *Nashville*, Archer Winsten in the *New York Post* on Jack Clayton's *The Great Gatsby* (1974), Rex Reed for the Chicago Tribune Syndicate on John Guillermin's *King Kong* (1976), and Frank Rich in *Time* on Steven Spielberg's *Close Encounters of the Third Kind* (1977). The Advertising-Publicity Committee of the Motion Picture Association of America decided to issue a policy that all movies from mid-1978 on would be reviewed on opening day, and administrations of the three New York dailies—*Times*, *Daily News*, and *Post*—agreed. The *Times* even ran a "To Our Readers" announcement.

"When you review a film first, you set the terms of the discussion," said Joseph Gelmis of *Newsday*. "With *Nashville*, for example, everybody else either became a footnote to Pauline or reacted to her. The person who reviews a film first, even when a studio has had nothing to do with it, becomes part of the opening apparatus."

Byron recalled that Crowther was the one instigating the discussion for a quarter of a century. "The current system, or lack of one, at least allows a broader spectrum of critics to become famous," he wrote, "if only for fifteen minutes."

Others lasted longer. Carrying on tradition with strength of vision and a masterly style was Stanley Kauffmann, one of the great reliables, an institution at *The New Republic*. He scoffed at auteurism. "It was directed by Don Siegel," he wrote of *Charley Varrick* (1973), "a great favorite of the auteur critics, and it proves yet again that there's nothing wrong with an auteur director that a good script can't cure" (Howard Rodman and Dean Riesner adapted John Reese's novel, *The Looters*). On this issue, Kauffmann had a kindred spirit in John Frankenheimer, who once cracked, "I'm one of the few people who can pronounce the word 'auteur,' and I think it's bullshit." Kauffmann also saw the wisdom of the director's casting. In his critique of Frankenheimer's version of *The Iceman Cometh* (1973), Kauffmann praised the performance of Lee Marvin, a portrayal that many other critics felt let the production down, especially in comparison to Jason Robards's legendary stage rendition.

"And to crown the work there is Lee Marvin, as Hickey, the salesman-apostle," Kauffmann wrote. "To put it simply: Marvin was born to play Hickey. He has the perfect understanding of the man and perfect equipment to deal with it. . . . Marvin understands the bumps and sags, and he lifts it all adroitly with gesture, with vaudevillian's *esprit*, to present both the man who was and who is. Then comes the payoff, the great last act. Marvin is wonderful. I have seen James Barton, the first Hickey, and Jason Robards (along with others), and though they were both unforgettably good, Marvin goes past them—so powerfully that he makes the crux of the play clearer than I have ever found it before, on stage or page."

Kauffman's strengths as a critic "are said by both admirers and detractors," wrote Janny Scott in *The New York Times*, "to consist of a literate, cultivated approach; a deep knowledge of theater and a strong feeling for acting; an economical writing style, and a refusal to conform to anyone else's doctrine." He dismissed the French influence of *Nouvelle Vague* in the 1960s and gave short shrift to Kael's admirers, the "Paulettes," who raved over pop-culture flicks.

But Kauffmann's love for the movies was sublime. In the 1974 essay, "Why I'm Not Bored," he wrote that a film may be boring, but the idea of going to it isn't. Boredom is incompatible with hope, he averred, and hope is more of a constant in film than in any other art. "No matter how much I know about a film's makers or its subject before I go, I never *really* know what it's going to do to me," he wrote. "Depress me with its vileness, or just roll past, or change my life in some degree, or some combination of all three, or affect me in some new way that I cannot imagine."

An upstart among the news magazines was *New Times*, which operated from 1973 to 1979, taking the pulse of government and social and cultural trends between Watergate and Reaganomics. Its film critic in its first three years was Frank Rich, a Harvard University graduate who had been co-editor of the *Richmond Mercury* in Virginia. *New Times* was a steppingstone for Rich, who then became film critic of the *New York Post* from 1975 to 1977, where he alternated reviews with Archer Winsten, who had begun critiquing movies for the paper in the 1930s. Rich advanced to film and TV critic for *Time* from 1977 to 1980, trading the beat with Richard Schickel. Rich was replaced by Richard Corliss when *The New York Times* hired him as chief drama critic. Rich became an op-ed columnist in 1994, and, in 2008, a consultant for HBO.

Rich's voice of reason couched an intelligence that couldn't abide certain lapses in common sense. For Rich, Michael Winner's *Death Wish* (1974), starring Charles Bronson roaming New York City as an anti-crime vigilante, was "a work of honest to God idiocy." The politics beneath Alan J. Pakula's *All the President's Men* (1976) were at the surface of Rich's stylish review in the *Post*: "It works as a detective thriller (even though everyone knows the ending), as a credible (if occasionally romanticized) primer on the prosaic fundamentals of big league investigative journalism, and best of all, as a chilling tone poem that conveys the texture of the terror in our nation's capital during that long night when an aspiring fascist regime held our democracy under siege."

Rich reviewed from a big-picture point of view, and seemed to look past the films—especially big films that announced their own importance—to see where they came from and, occasionally, where they might be going. "There's really only one motivation for this movie, and that's the desire to make money," Rich wrote of John Frankenheimer's *Black Sunday* (1977). "Why else would anyone make an ostensibly anti-terrorist film that in actuality could end up promoting terrorism."

Vitality in film reviewing in the 1970s was found in sometimes raw, as well as refined, versions in the alternative weekly newspapers that cropped up in cities. These were mostly arts-oriented tabloids that were distributed free throughout their respective metropolitan areas on Wednesday, Thursday, or Friday to prepare city dwellers for weekend activities. Their pioneering parent was the famous *The Village Voice*, founded in 1955 and expanded through half a century into an empire of 17 alternative weeklies under the banner of Village Voice Media. The chain was sold in 2005 to its main competition, New Times Media, which then adopted the brand name of Village Voice Media.

A literary tradition was established by *The Village Voice*, founded in a two-bedroom apartment in Greenwich Village by Ed Fancher, Norman Mailer, and Dan Wolf. The paper's roster of literati included Ezra Pound, Henry Miller, Katherine Anne Porter, Allen Ginsberg, Lorraine Hansberry, Nat Hentoff, and James Baldwin. A watchdog for New York City politics, *The Village Voice* became a must-read for younger generations in the 1960s and 1970s. Underground filmmaker Jonas Mekas wrote the "Film Journal" column, and the film critics included auteur theory purveyor Andrew Sarris and his eventual wife, the film critic and feminist writer Molly Haskell, and, later, J. Hoberman, Tom Allen, Tom Carson, Amy Taubin, Manohla Dargis, Michael Atkinson, and Dennis Lim.

The *Village Voice* model was found to work in other cities, where the alternative weeklies, which thrived on classified, entertainment-oriented, and, later, adult services advertising, included *The Boston Phoenix* (1965, initially *Boston After Dark*), *San Francisco Bay Guardian* (1966), *Philadelphia Weekly* (1971), *Chicago Reader* (1971), *Seattle Weekly* (1976), *Baltimore City Paper* (1977), *LA Weekly* (1978), and others. Rowdy in their coverage of politics and the arts—usually from a ragged-edge, liberal perspective—alt-weeklies ran long take-out cover pieces that occasionally rattled the status quo.

Reading these alternative weeklies became a ritual for all strata of city life, from the terminally hip to anyone of any age who enjoyed vibrant coverage of politics, restaurants, theatre, galleries, music, and movies. Their success unwittingly spawned alternatives to themselves, such as *The Real Paper* (1972) in Boston and *Los Angeles Reader* (1978), and, later, *SF Weekly* (1985), *New York Observer* (1987), and *New York Press* (1988). Creating competition for the established big dailies for advertising dollars in their respective cities, the weeklies carved a new niche.

The alternative weeklies built pugnacious identities and flourished as business ventures as well as news outlets. They developed exciting new writers and critics who were often allowed the leeway and space for epic essays. The editorial direction continued in the heritage of the underground press, the independent, rabble-rousing publications that sought radical political and social change, such as the *L.A. Free Press* (1964), *East Village Other* (1965) in New York, *Fifth Estate* (1965) in Detroit, and various irregularly published sheets. The alternative weeklies embraced the New Journalism identified by Tom Wolfe in his 1973 namesake anthology, which used fiction techniques to tell nonfiction stories, through scene-setting, dialogues, and impressionistic description—characteristic of writers such as Wolfe, Norman Mailer, Truman Capote, Hunter S. Thompson, Joan Didion, and others. The weeklies also borrowed a page from *Rolling Stone*, founded in San Francisco in 1967 by Jann Wenner, in that they generally were hip to the zeitgeist, flaunted street lingo, and reached deep into issues with passion and literary flair. *Rolling Stone* rock critics Greil Marcus and Lester Bangs were models for the latitude and longitude of arts coverage in the weeklies.

Prisoners weren't taken, historical context mattered, and dexterous stylists were welcome.

Joan Micklin Silver's *Between the Lines* (1977), written by Fred Barron, starred Lindsay Crouse, John Heard, Jeff Goldblum, Bruno Kirby, Joe Morton, and other future familiar faces in the story of a Boston alternative underground paper, loosely based on both *The Boston Phoenix* and *The Real Paper*. "*Between the Lines* is more interesting for what it is than for what it is about, which is to say that it is a pleasant showcase for half a dozen talented performers rather than an overwhelming overview of the underground press or a compelling study of '70s disenchantment in '60s radicals," wrote the greatest film critic of the alternative press, Andrew Sarris of *The Village Voice*.

With the battle royal of the auteur theory behind him, along with two decades of writing about film, and his *The American Cinema: Directors and Directions, 1929–1968* gathering more meaning (and/or exasperation) among cineastes as the 1970s advanced, Sarris was already conferred by rote with a certain deference and admiration after the accumulation of hard knocks. Like Kael, he was an inspiration to a generation of younger film critics who admired—as Manny Farber might have noted—his termite-art-like steadiness at *The Village Voice*.

"Having been wary of Sarris for some time, I must now confess that he has made a convert of me," Richard Schickel wrote in *Harper's* about Sarris's *Confessions of a Cultist* (1970), the collection of his 1960s *Film Culture* and *Village Voice* reviews. "He is undoubtedly one of our best and most serious critics, a writer whose general soundness and catholicity of taste will have to be reckoned with if anyone should undertake to write an intellectual history of this fevered period in films. . . . As the books about movies threaten to flood the market, Sarris's collection of criticism strikes me as one of the few indispensible items the torrent has yet churned up." Stuart Byron went another step, writing in *The New York Times* that the book "is for me the best book of film criticism this country has yet produced." Filmmaker Robert Benton remarked, "Reading Sarris was like listening to Radio Free Europe."

Andrew Sarris was born on October 31, 1928, in Brooklyn, New York, into a Greek-American household whose patriarch's real estate business went bankrupt during the Great Depression. After a decade of little or no employment, his father died of leukemia when Andrew was 15. The boy had grown up consistently underweight, partially deaf, and requiring two mastoid operations.

Out of the army and attending Columbia University on the G.I. Bill in 1954, he met Jonas Mekas and began writing for *Film Culture*. Sarris lived with his mother in a small apartment, working odd jobs. "He was still living in poverty, and had been almost since he could remember," wrote Kevin Michael McAuliffe in *The Great American Newspaper: The Rise and Fall of the Village Voice*. Sarris was asked by *Voice* movie columnist Mekas to fill in while he went on vacation in 1960. Up for review that week was Alfred Hitchcock's *Psycho*.

"Hitchcock is the most daring avant garde film-maker in America today," Sarris wrote. Further, he maintained, "besides making previous horror films look like variations on *Pollyanna*, *Psycho* is overlaid with a richly symbolic commentary on the modern world as a public swamp in which human feelings and passions are flushed down the drain." By 1963, Sarris and Mekas were splitting the beat, with Mekas preferring to measure the more offbeat product and underground films while Sarris covered the Hollywood output.

Despite the leftist nature of the *Voice*, Sarris was his own voice of measured pragmatism as a Kennedy Democrat. Because of the paper's ragged-fringe reputation in New York media circles, Sarris was marginalized in the early 1960s, McAuliffe wrote, as a "screwball" living down the reputation of an "underground rag." Sarris was certainly tough on the mainstream product.

The big musicals of the 1960s didn't impress him. "I don't like any of Lionel Bart's songs or any of the singers," Sarris wrote in the *Voice* of Carol Reed's *Oliver!* (1968), which won the best picture Academy Award. "And I don't appreciate a rather disquieting spectacle of a horde of pint-sized chorus boys doing Jerome Robbins imitations in the midst of fustian melodramatics. As for Ron Moody's fey Fagin, his school-of-hard-knocks song spiels remind me of nothing so much as Zorba the Fiddler from La Mancha, that all-purpose monster of middle-class, middle-aged, middle-brow metaphysics." Of George Cukor's *My Fair Lady* (1964), another Oscar winner for best picture, Sarris remarked, "The property has been not so much adapted as elegantly embalmed."

Often alone in his opinions, yet faithful to those reactions, Sarris claimed that Howard Hawks's *El Dorado* (1967) was the best picture of the year, in complete contrast to Pauline Kael's contention that it was a tired dud in a waning genre. Sarris called the John Wayne-Robert Mitchum reconstitution of *Rio Bravo* (1959) "a poetic fantasy . . . tinged with melancholy." To Sarris, the aging stars contributed to the film's greatness. Wayne's "oldness has become spiritually resurgent," Sarris wrote. "His infirmities ennoble rather than enfeeble him, and every wrinkle on his skin has come to terms with his endless quest."

Sarris's ragged reputation gradually reversed itself as the *Voice* and alternative weeklies gained acceptance among the youth culture. He began teaching at Yale University and New York University, eventually joining the faculty of Columbia University in 1969, the same year he married Molly Haskell, whom he met in the French Film Office in New York, and who also began reviewing for the *Voice*.

Sarris's staying power at the *Voice* became recognized as the levelheadedness of his reviews established consistency and the publication's reputation solidified. The reputation of his books grew. He served a stint as chairman of the National Society of Film Critics. He was lionized within film criticism circles, and in 1984 became the second film critic, after Manny Farber in 1981, to be conferred with the Los Angeles Film Critics Association's special award for film scholarship.

Don Siegel's *Charley Varrick* (1973) ran toward Sarris's predilection for sharp and smart action dramas served up by one of the crime genre's most efficient auteurists. "The narrative line is clean and direct," Sarris wrote, "the characterizations economical and functional, and the triumph of intelligence gloriously satisfying." Sarris pegged Richard Fleischer's *Incredible Sarah* (1976), a biopic of French actress Sarah Bernhardt, starring Glenda Jackson, "an incredibly old-fashioned movie full of the most unforgettable moments you have ever tried to forget." Sarris had a knack for the serviceably clever pithy truth that never got quoted, because it often was not positive. Then again, Sarris called Woody Allen's *Manhattan* (1979) "a masterpiece that has become a film for the ages by not seeking to be a film of the moment."

Brian De Palma's *Obsession* (1976), a Hitchcockian thriller starring Genevieve Bujold, was deemed by Sarris "merely a mannered cerebral exercise without any emotional underpinning or unconscious feeling of its own." Of Federico Fellini's *And the Ship Sailed On* (1983), Sarris wrote, "Too much a work of the pure imagination with the result that the audience is cast adrift on a Styrofoam sea without a lifeline to any kind of recognizable reality."

While she freelanced film-related pieces for *The New York Times*, *Saturday Review*, and other periodicals, and later would become film critic of *Vogue*, Haskell also broadcast reviews on WNET-TV in New York and on National Public Radio's *All Things Considered*. Haskell profiled Sarris's automobile-driving dexterity in "He Drives Me Crazy," a 1989 humor piece in *The New York Times*, and related his near-fatal, six-month bout with an encephalitic virus in *Love and Other Infectious Diseases* (1990), published by Morrow. Haskell's major contribution to film studies was the 1973 book *From Reverence to Rape: The Treatment of Women in the Movies*. She traced Hollywood's ideas and ideals of womanhood and marriage by decade, discussing Bogart and Bacall, and Tracy and Hepburn, and many pairings before and since. The 1987 edition from the University of Chicago Press included an added chapter, "1984–1987: The Age of Ambivalence," stressing that the promise of more, better, and diverse roles for women in the 1970s had gone unfulfilled.

"The trickle of feminist-inspired movies of the 1970s—
A Woman Under the Influence, Alice Doesn't Live Here Anymore,
and *An Unmarried Woman*—had led us to anticipate, if not a
revolution, at least a gaggle of films that would chart our evolution as emerging feminists," Haskell wrote in the 1987 edition.
"Instead, women virtually disappeared from the screen, as sex
objects or anything else, for over a decade. Our oratory of protest and hope was greeted with a yawn of indifference, as the
multinational executives and 'deal packagers' of the New Hollywood panted after the youth market, abandoning—and being
abandoned by—the adult audience in the process."

Les Keyser, writing in *Hollywood in the Seventies* (1981)
about *From Reverence to Rape*, averred, "Many of the finest female
performers in seventies films tried to cope with aging by seeking
more realistic roles, characterizations outside the panorama of
stereotypes Molly Haskell lamented in her well-written survey.
Hollywood's concept of what 'little girls' were made of in the sixties and early seventies, Haskell observed, included a demeaning
collection of warped personalities: 'Whores, quasi-whores, jilted
mistresses, emotional cripples, drunks, daffy ingenues, Lolitas,
kooks, sex-starved spinsters, psychotics, icebergs, zombies and
ballbreakers.'" Keyser disagreed with Haskell's ultimate assessment that Hollywood had abandoned feminist roles. "Powerful
Hollywood women like Shirley MacLaine, Anne Bancroft, Ellen
Burstyn, Faye Dunaway, and Jane Fonda were to change all this,
as they labored to raise the consciousness of all America," Keyser
claimed.

Outside of New York in the 1970s, the three alt-weekly
hotbeds of development as far as film critics were concerned
were in Boston, Chicago, and Los Angeles.

In the mid-1970s, David Ansen was the lead film critic
at *The Real Paper* in Boston, while Janet Maslin held the same
position at the crosstown *Boston Phoenix*. In 1976, when Maslin
left the *Phoenix* to become a film critic for *Newsweek*, she stayed
only a few months before *The New York Times* called and hired

her away to alternate film reviews with Vincent Canby. She remained as the *Times* film critic until 1999. Ansen followed her into the vacated *Newsweek* post, where he stayed for 30 years. Replacing Maslin at the *Phoenix* was David Denby, who remained film critic of *The Atlantic Monthly*.

Denby left the *Phoenix* in 1978 to become film critic of *New York* magazine, and Stephen Schiff, who had been the backup reviewer to Ansen at *The Real Paper* and then to Maslin on the *Phoenix*, took over as head film critic of the latter. Schiff also reviewed for *Glamour*, then *The Atlantic Monthly*, during his stint into the 1980s on the *Phoenix*. In 1975, he became the first film critic after Roger Ebert to be associated with the Pulitzer Prize. Schiff was named runner-up for the prestigious honor in 1983 to the winner, general arts writer Manuela Hoelterhoff of *The Wall Street Journal*. Schiff was cited for his criticism written at the *Phoenix* in the same year he was hired as film critic of the reconstituted *Vanity Fair*. As he once explained the *Vanity Fair* situation, Gore Vidal was hired as the film critic for the retooled magazine, but didn't want to leave Italy, where he then resided, so Schiff got the post by default.

Fred Schepisi's *The Chant of Jimmie Blacksmith* (1980) is the story of a racially motivated murder spree by a frustrated Aboriginal who has been marginalized in Australia by whites and blacks. "[Schepisi's] images are spare and clean and imbued with a quiet, sorrowing fatalism," Schiff wrote in *The Boston Phoenix*. "Things move forward calmly, and at an unemphatic pace suitable to legend. The measured gait, the assurance and quietude, create an almost Brechtian distance, and yet the story Schepisi tells is so frightening that it knocks the wind out of you. I don't think I've seen anything quite as powerful since *The Deer Hunter*, and I can't recall another film that conveys so much of the passions that brew when two races share the same ground."

Schiff thought that memories of actual youth in the 1950s had been replaced by the posturing pop-culture characters of *Grease* and Henry Winkler in the sitcom *Happy Days*. "In fact, I had despaired of ever seeing the decade afresh until

I watched a tender, breathtakingly honest new comedy called *Diner*—which turned out to be the most wonderful surprise I've had at the movies in ages," he wrote in the *Phoenix*.

Columbia University graduate Denby was film critic of *New York* magazine for 20 years, until 1998. By that time, he had started writing for *The New Yorker* and shared the film criticism beat there with Anthony Lane into the 21st century. Like Richard Schickel and Stanley Kauffmann, Denby had been attentive to the history and state of film criticism. He edited the 1972–1973 edition of the National Society of Film Critics anthology and then compiled *Awake in the Dark: An Anthology of American Film Criticism, 1915 to the Present* (1977), from Vintage. Included were James Agee's essay on D.W. Griffith, William Troy's review of Fritz Lang's *M* (1931), Andrew Sarris on Costa-Gavras's *State of Siege* (1973)—44 pieces in all, including those by Harry Alan Potamkin, Gilbert Seldes, Otis Ferguson, Manny Farber, Dwight Macdonald, Pauline Kael, Molly Haskell, Susan Sontag, Penelope Gilliatt, Richard Corliss, and others. "The book crackles with intellectual energy and thought-provoking insights," wrote the reviewer for *Publishers Weekly*.

"Almost every minute of *M*A*S*H* is filled with detailed invention," Denby wrote in *The Atlantic Monthly* about Robert Altman's 1970 Korean War comedy during, as the critic pointed out, the age of Vietnam. "The movie has a prodigal throwaway quality that may remind some viewers of a vintage thirties comedy like Howard Hawks's *Bringing Up Baby*. I wouldn't be surprised if it became a college-film-society classic and was loved by generations of students."

Denby's foresight was close enough—the film was adapted into a TV series that was loved by a generation. Denby questioned what he perceived as director Arthur Penn's tack through *Little Big Man* (1970) of "altering the tone of the movie according to who is being slaughtered," and also draws a Vietnam comparison: "What starts as an elegy for lost values winds up as an exercise in white self-hatred, and although it may seem incongruous to say so, I can't help feeling that Penn's movie is another victim of the war in Vietnam."

Myron Meisel was the first film critic for the *Chicago Reader*, in 1971, and the first lead critic for *Los Angeles Reader*. Between gigs, he left the University of Chicago for Harvard Law School, and became an entertainment lawyer as well as a critic and filmmaker. Meisel cowrote David Helpern's documentary *I'm a Stranger Here Myself* (1975); cowrote, coproduced, and co-directed the documentary on Orson Welles's ill-fated 1942 Brazilian adventure and namesake RKO documentary, *It's All True* (1993); and was a crew member on pictures directed by Paul Bartel and Barbet Schroeder. *It's All True* won special citations from the National Society of Film Critics and the Los Angeles Film Critics Association.

"The keynote is involvement, not identification, and Cassavetes understands the way to accomplish this is to implicate the audience in the feelings of the characters," Meisel wrote about *A Woman Under the Influence* (1974) in his essay on John Cassavetes in Jean-Pierre Coursodon and Pierre Sauvage's anthology, *American Directors* (1983), from McGraw-Hill. "This is why Cassavetes' great expressive talent resides in the cumulative power of his images of actors. The first principle in a Cassavetes film is acting—not the actor, but acting itself—and his preoccupation with human behavior as performance. [Gena] Rowlands uses her considerable technical skills as an actress to make a nigh unbelievable connection between her lexicon of personal psychological experience on the one hand and the emotional circumstances of the dramatic moment on the other. She is not alone. Everyone in the film *performs*."

Dave Kehr, one of Meisel's successors at the *Chicago Reader*, was another University of Chicago alumnus who consistently venerated the university's student-run film society, the Documentary Film Group (or "Doc Films" for short). Other prominent film critics, including Jonathan Rosenbaum and Henry Sheehan, have been grateful to Doc Films as a virtual training ground. The group sponsored 10 to 12 screenings a week, drawing on a huge library of 16mm prints. This, of course, predated the videocassette recorder (VCR) as a mass-market essential, before cable went huge, when true cinephiles would mark calendar dates for opportunities to see vintage or foreign films at the one or two "art houses" in town or at a venue like Doc Films, or set the alarm for 1 AM, when a scratchy TV print of a film directed by Nicholas Ray, Anthony Mann, Sam Fuller, or Phil Karlson would air, and could finally be sat through and scratched from the must-see list.

Kehr's encyclopedic memory and intelligent point-counterpoint comparisons to other films have often caused his reviews to resonate deeply with cinephiles. The themes from John Cassavetes's films *Husbands* (1970) and *A Woman Under the Influence* (1974) are distilled in *Love Streams* (1984). "The synthesis produces a masterwork, a film that brings together the insights and innovations of an entire career and allows them to cross-breed and flower," Kehr wrote in the *Chicago Reader* in September 1984. "*Love Streams* is by far the best American film of 1984; as the culmination of Cassavetes's personal aesthetic, it will probably prove to be one of the best American films, period." At the close of his *Chicago Tribune* review of John Singleton's *Boyz N the Hood* (1991), Kehr wrote that the movie "wants to be *The Learning Tree* and *Superfly* at once, an ambition that doesn't seem quite honest."

The audience had to keep up, understand that Gordon Parks's *The Learning Tree* (1969) was an African-American coming-of-age film, and accept the contention that *Love Streams*, which was barely released in a few cities, was the best picture of the year. Kehr compared Albert Brooks's *Lost in America* (1985) to the "most formally aggressive works of Jean-Marie Straub and Danièle Huillet—it's that radical." German filmmakers who had adapted Franz Kafka's *Amerika* into *Class Relations*, Straub and Huillet's film and *Lost in America* are both about "uprooted naifs, trying to make their way across an alien landscape" but also have a "striking similarity in the design of the brutally stripped-down images and a shared taste for impossibly protracted long takes." Kehr estimated that "it isn't likely that Brooks has ever seen a

Straub-Huillet film—or an Ackerman, a Bresson, or a Godard. Yet, working on his own (and from a very different set of premises), Brooks has arrived at much the same point they have; he's one of the leading modernist filmmakers."

Kehr was one of the alternative weeklies' strongest critics and one who moved on to bigger papers, eventually to home-viewing columnist for *The New York Times*. When the *LA Weekly* launched, its main film critic was Michael Ventura, who has become a cultural essayist, screenwriter, and novelist. Manohla Dargis, who reviewed for the *LA Weekly* before she became film critic of the *Los Angeles Times* and, later, *The New York Times*, characterized Ventura as "one of the great unknowns of American film criticism," treating him in the tradition of "outsider critics" such as Otis Ferguson, James Agee, Andrew Sarris, and Pauline Kael, who refused not to take movies seriously.

"As good as he was—and sometimes he was brilliant, astonishing, really—he could also be sloppy, windy, and an alarming overwriter," Dargis wrote from a 1997 perspective. "F.X. Feeney, who started writing for [*LA Weekly*] soon after it was launched, jokingly and fondly compares Ventura to Lawrence of Arabia, as a man who would 'dynamite the train and dance on the wreck.' Given that image, it isn't surprising that, as has often been the case in the alternative publishing world, Ventura could also be solipsistic to the point of self-parody."

"And here was Ventura, coming to terms with his own complex reaction to Cimino's film," wrote Scott Foundas, *LA Weekly* film editor since 2005, about the paper's first film review, of Michael Cimino's eventual Academy Award-winning best picture, *The Deer Hunter* (1978), "at once exalting it for its aesthetic triumphs and deriding it for its moral shortcomings." Ventura's review carried this passage: "When I walked out of the theatre I was so swept away with the excellence of this movie that it took me a day to start getting angry at how I'd been lied to." He concluded, after several thousand words of persuasion, that "the infuriating trait of American movies—from D.W. Griffith to John Ford, from *Rebel Without a Cause* to *The Deer Hunter*—is that you find greatness nearly always side by side with what's shame-lessly self-serving. But then, that is also the infuriating trait of America."

On the total ragged fringe to the left of the lefties of film criticism were the appreciators of underground film. *Film Culture* and other periodicals continued to keep tabs on under-ground film, the independently made, creatively diverse movies of varying lengths, often concerning still socially taboo subject matter, occasional sexual variety or unorthodox violence. The counterculture fringe of independent cinema, especially in New York and San Francisco, carried on the avant-garde tradition, which was encouraged in early film criticism by Harry Alan Potamkin, Lewis Jacobs, and, later, Manny Farber.

Parker Tyler resurfaced as a prolific author with such books as *Sex, Psyche, Etcetera in the Film* (1970), *Underground Film: A Critical History* (1970), and *The Shadow of an Airplane Climbs the Empire State Building: A World Theory of Film* (1973). Tyler's assessments of most underground films were largely neg-ative. "Since the underground aims at exploring new ways of seeing and communicating unfettered by any pre-established artistic criteria, one wonders if Tyler's rather rigid historical standards are entirely appropriate," wrote J.W. Palmer in *Library Journal*. ". . . The writing, however, is frequently obscure and laden with esoteric references so that non-specialists will find it difficult reading."

Vernon Young agreed with Stanley Kauffmann, who generally disliked the avant-garde, seeing the movement as a trend and drift. "Jonas Mekas tells us that the avant garde artists 'are trying to bring some beauty into a world of horror,'" Young wrote in the *Hudson Review*. "His own films and those of such fellow travelers as Carl Linder, Jack Smith, Kenneth Anger, and the Kuchar brothers would appear, rather, to be bringing more horror into a world of beauty."

Men's magazines found a voice of wisdom in Bruce Wil-liamson, who was the film critic for *Playboy* from 1968 to 1998 after brief stints at *Time* and *Life*. He also interviewed actors for the magazine and, as if to counterbalance the perceived chauvinism of his flagship forum, wrote a movie column in the 1980s and 1990s for *New Woman* magazine. His pieces were succinct, his voice sensible and intelligent. Of John Schlesinger's *Sunday Bloody Sunday* (1971), he wrote, "Much can be read between the lines of acrid dialogue penned by English author and film critic Penelope Gilliatt, whose brisk scenario devotes a lot of footage to the telephone—as if those miles of cable and eager hearts just missing each other through an answering service were a fair measure of the quality of human communication most of us achieve." Gilliatt, of course, shared *The New Yorker* film review beat with Pauline Kael, and shared her life with Vincent Canby as his longtime companion.

The idea that passing judgment on pictures qualified critics to concoct screenplays gained some favor. Peter Bogdanovich came out of film journalism; he had written Hollywood profiles for *Esquire* and groundbreaking monographs on Orson Welles, Howard Hawks, Fritz Lang, Allan Dwan, and John Ford. The Ford monograph is especially a bona fide classic. Leonard Maltin, who updates the most frequently used, unwittingly plagiarized, and usually dog-eared annual source of them all, *Leonard Maltin's Movie & Video Guide*, said he was struck by how often he has used Bogdanovich's slim interview book, *John Ford* (1968), from the University of California Press, for source information.

Bogdanovich worked as a screenwriter and director while his books hit the shelves. *Allan Dwan: The Last Pioneer*, from Praeger, was released the same year as Bogdanovich's breakthrough film as a director, *The Last Picture Show* (1971). As Richard Schickel did with the documentary films and companion book, *The Men Who Made the Movies* (1973), Bogdanovich was able to record conversations with Ford, Dwan, Welles, and the others about their methods during the making of their great (and not-so-great) pictures. The filmmakers were mostly in old age in the 1960s and 1970s and were pleased to sit down and recall not just the good old days, but bad ones as well, and leave their stories for posterity.

Dwan wrote and directed 250 mostly one-reel westerns between 1911 and 1913, worked with D.W. Griffith, refined the dolly shot using a Ford Motor Company car, directed John Wayne in *Sands of Iwo Jima* (1949), as well as hundreds of stars in other movies, all the way through his last assignment, *The Most Dangerous Man Alive* (1961). "[This book] is derived from prolonged, taped interviews, taking the director through his career chronologically, at once prompting his memory and exciting his comment with intelligent questioning," wrote Roger Manvell in *Encounter* of Bogdanovich's *Allan Dwan: The Last Pioneer*. "As a result Dwan relives his past experience; simple fact and opinion are recorded idiomatically, but in addition his invaluable first-hand technical comment recalls studio practices in the past. Dwan is revealed as a man of quick intelligence, humanity, humor, and complete professionalism."

Bogdanovich and Joseph McBride had both written books on Orson Welles by the time they acted in the writer-director's infamously unfinished film, *The Other Side of the Wind* (1972), starring John Huston as an aging film director hoping to make a comeback by making a film exploiting sex and violence. The film was begun in 1970 and was never released. Featuring Dennis Hopper, Oja Kodar, Edmond O'Brien, Lilli Palmer, and Susan Strasberg, the film also included cameos by directors Claude Chabrol, Paul Mazursky, Henry Jaglom, Curtis Harrington, and Norman Foster. The film's cinematographer, Welles scholar Gary Graver, plays a role. While the film was mulled over, shot, and discussed, McBride had moved from a reporter on the *Wisconsin State Journal* to a position at the *Riverside Press-Enterprise* in Riverside, California, and was a reporter and film critic at *Daily Variety* from 1974 through 1977. Bogdanovich and McBride were among the film critics getting into the act, so to speak.

McBride became a full-time screenwriter in 1977 and continued as a part-time actor. He wrote the low-budget pictures *Blood & Guts* (1978) and *Rock 'n' Roll High School* (1979), acting in them both as well as in *Cannonball* (1976), *Hollywood*

Boulevard (1976), and *Olly, Olly, Oxen Free* (1978). Like critics Frank E. Woods, Frank S. Nugent, and James Agee decades ago, and Ebert and McBride in the 1970s, other film critics dabbled in screenplays. Peter Rainer, who was soon to become the lead film critic of the *Los Angeles Herald-Examiner*, cowrote *Joyride* (1977) with its director, Joseph Ruben. *LA Weekly* critic Michael Ventura wrote the screenplays for Alan Rudolph's *Roadie* (1980) and Robert Dornhelm's *Echo Park* (1985). Former *Time* film critic Paul D. Zimmerman wrote *The King of Comedy* (1983), directed by Martin Scorsese. The same magazine's other film critic, Jay Cocks, a Scorsese friend, rewrote the director's *The Last Temptation of Christ* (1988), and later shared screenplay credit with the director on *The Age of Innocence* (1993).

Scorsese was used to raiding the critics' corps for his collaborators. Paul Schrader, who had been editor of *Cinema,* and before that had reviewed movies for the *L.A. Free Press* after Pauline Kael had put a good word in for him, wrote the screenplay for the director's *Taxi Driver* (1976), and cowrote *Raging Bull* (1980) with Mardik Martin. This was prior to Schrader's quirky career as a writer-director. (A factoid that has followed Schrader was that he was fired by the radical *L.A. Free Press* for panning Dennis Hopper's *Easy Rider* [1969].) Schrader's contribution to film scholarship was *Transcendental Style in Film: Ozu, Bresson, Dreyer* (1972), from the University of California Press.

Coziness with filmmakers has and has not been involved in these collaborations. "Once you've passed your scripts around to enough people, it becomes, 'Am I watching a movie by the company or the director I submitted my screenplay to?'" Zimmerman told Sharon Edelson of *Premiere* in 1989. "At that point, you are no longer reviewing a movie, you are reviewing your own career."

Ventura met Alan Rudolph during an interview, and the director complimented him on his review of the filmmaker's *Remember My Name* (1978). "If you're in the film-critic business, you make contacts," Ventura said, alluding to the fact that most film-beat journalists interview stars and filmmakers as well as review films. "But if you're trying to curry favor, you're not going to be respected. I don't think anybody has ever accused me of fawning." Ventura once backed out of reviewing films from Columbia Pictures, for which he wrote screenplays. "Frankly, I did it because I didn't want to shoot myself in the foot," Ventura told Edelson. "Columbia, like all studios, puts out a lot of shit."

Maintaining the coziest of relationships with filmmakers was Pauline Kael. It's curious that after *The Citizen Kane Book*, clearly an offshoot of her assault against the auteur theory, Kael took to ordaining filmmakers who were primarily known as directors. What happened to championing the screenwriters? She took particular interest in boosting hyphenates, those who both wrote and directed their films: Altman (*M*A*S*H, McCabe & Mrs. Miller, Nashville*), Peckinpah (*The Wild Bunch, Straw Dogs, Bring Me the Head of Alfredo Garcia*), Philip Kaufman (1978 remake of *Invasion of the Body Snatchers, The Right Stuff*), Brian De Palma (*Carrie, The Untouchables*), Paul Schrader (*American Gigolo*, the 1982 remake of *Cat People*), and journeyman Irvin Kershner (*The Luck of Ginger Coffey, Eyes of Laura Mars, The Empire Strikes Back*).

Literary interest in the movies extended, of course, way beyond the review anthologies. The stars, of course, were the subjects of mass-market books—new biographies on Humphrey Bogart, John Wayne, Marilyn Monroe, Laurence Olivier, and others. The *Pyramid Illustrated History of the Movies* was a series on stars and genres, with individual titles written by Leonard Maltin, Joseph McBride, Howard Thompson, Gerald Peary, Foster Hirsch, Tony Thomas, Jeanine Basinger, Jerry Vermilye, Alan G. Barbour, Alvin H. Marill, John Belton, and others. It was a time when historians such as Anthony Slide and James Robert Parish became cottage industries unto themselves as prolific writers and editors of movie books, and would continue as such for generations, crossing the century mark each in volumes written or edited.

Specializing in film studies were Praeger Publishers, Frederick Ungar Publishing, Arno Press in New York, and Twayne

Publishers in Boston, as well as collegiate presses, such as the University of California Press and University of Indiana Press.

The most industrious contributor to bookshelves among American critics in the 1970s was Maltin, as an author, credited editor, and editor of book series. His own name was on the spine on volumes about comedy stars, character actors, Carole Lombard, and short films. Richard Schickel compiled the classic testimony from directors, *The Men Who Made the Movies*, from his filmed conversations with King Vidor, Howard Hawks, William A. Wellman, Raoul Walsh, and other filmmakers. Schickel wrote other volumes on Walt Disney and Douglas Fairbanks. Books were issued from Parker Tyler, William S. Pechter, Richard Corliss, Joseph Gelmis, Molly Haskell, Todd McCarthy, Jonathan Rosenbaum, Judith Crist, and David Thomson, whose first edition of the film connoisseur's standard, *The Biographical Dictionary of Film*, was published in 1975.

The reassessment of old films also brought about the academic reassessment of old film critics, as individual anthologies were published containing the reviews of Robert E. Sherwood, Otis Ferguson, and Harry Alan Potamkin. Packaging pieces from their bygone days as film critics were Pare Lorentz and Bosley Crowther, who also became one of the first film critics after James Agee to receive his own book-length analysis, *Bosley Crowther: Social Critic of Film, 1940–1967* (1974) by Frank E. Beaver from University of Michigan Press.

THE TELEVISION AGE

The caricature of the generic critic in American culture has been the imperious character of Sheridan Whiteside, created by George S. Kaufman and Moss Hart for the 1939 play, *The Man Who Came to Dinner*. The wheelchair-bound know-it-all was based upon their friend, Alexander Woollcott, a legendary arbiter of the Algonquin Round Table and a prolific book and drama critic for *The New York Times* and *The New Yorker*. Woollcott died at age 56 in 1943, after his CBS Radio broadcast, "Is Germany Incurable?" on *The People's Platform*.

Despite the many critics, including movie critics, through the mid-20th century, the public image of them would always be tainted by a priggish loftiness ingrained into the culture by Whiteside. The snobbery on the public face of criticism was also alive inside the realm of criticism, where film and television critics were outsiders extolling upstart media, let alone art. Movie criticism in the early and mid-20th century was often looked down upon by drama critics and other art-form critics from under lofty brows, an attitude epitomized by the great drama critic George Jean Nathan, who consistently denigrated film as art in print.

Nathan considered movies the "physic of the proletariat," providing "anesthesias" for the masses. Even toward the end, in his midcentury columns in the *New York Journal-American*,

Nathan impugned the art form in which Lillian Gish became one of the first superstars. More than half a century after his 1958 death, it's only speculation to suspect that attitude had anything to do with Gish's steadfast decade of rebuffing Nathan's overtures of marriage.

The personal warmth and good will for cinema history expressed by later, television-age critics, such as Leonard Maltin and Robert Osborne, couldn't wipe out the Whiteside traits. When the animated show *The Critic* aired from 1994 to 1995 (from the creative camp that supplied *The Simpsons*), the character of film critic Jay Sherman, voiced by Jon Lovitz in 23 half-hour episodes, retained the cranky, arrogant, and fussy characteristics of Whiteside.

Television began as an orphan on the cultural landscape, looking for acceptance and knowledge. In its experimental years, John Mason Brown became the first critic to anchor a regular network program, *Critic at Large*, on ABC in 1948 and 1949. Brown had been the drama critic for the *New York Evening Post* prior to World War II, and wrote the "Seeing Things" column for the *Saturday Review* after the war and until his death in 1969 at age 68. The popular column was packaged into three books by McGraw-Hill: *Seeing Things*, *Seeing More Things*, and *Still Seeing Things*. The man responsible for the statement, "Some television programs are so much chewing gum for the eyes," Brown was the in-studio host of the half-hour *Critic at Large*, featuring such guests in its short run as impresario Billy Rose, humorist and publisher Bennett Cerf, and *New York Times* film critic Bosley Crowther.

The establishment of Alistair Cooke as a TV host on CBS was based on the tendency to appreciate critics, supplemented by the general American midcentury cultural acceptance of British performers as being more schooled and skilled than native-grown talent. The film critic of the BBC from 1934, Cooke had also been a consummate freelancer as the London correspondent for NBC Radio, a columnist for the *Manchester Guardian*, and a foreign correspondent for *The Times* of London.

Cooke's early projects included the editing of British and American reviews into the first book-length anthology of film criticism, *Garbo and the Night Watchmen*, published in London by Jonathan Cape in 1937. British by birth, but American by choice, Cooke married a great-grandniece of Ralph Waldo Emerson and became a naturalized American citizen on December 1, 1941, six days before the Japanese attacked Pearl Harbor. Cooke was the first American with a film criticism background to become a TV personality. He was named host of the first American TV network cultural arts program, *Omnibus*, which debuted on CBS in 1952. The show was picked up by ABC from 1956 to 1957, and aired on NBC from 1957 to 1959.

As the host through a weekly 90-minute forum dedicated to drama, dance, and other performance and fine arts, Cooke came off as pleasant, knowledgeable, charming, and refreshingly absent of the prevalent ego of other TV personalities. The viewer's consummate guide, he perfected similar duties a generation later as the silver-haired host of PBS's drama anthology, *Masterpiece Theatre*, which imported British programs through affiliate WGBH-TV in Boston. Cooke was so iconographic by the 1970s that *Saturday Night Live*, *The Carol Burnett Show*, and even *Sesame Street* satirized his urbanity and smooth delivery.

After *Omnibus* moved to ABC, CBS replaced it with a similar, ambitious, but short-lived cultural arts program, *The Seven Lively Arts*. This show was named for CBS programming head Gilbert Seldes's famous 1924 book about American popular culture. John Crosby, TV critic for the *New York Herald-Tribune*, was the host. The film coordinator for *Omnibus*, *The Seven Lively Arts*, and the network's children's arts program, *Odyssey*, was Arthur Knight, who had already begun his distinguished career as film critic of the *Saturday Review*. His seminal study of movie history, *The Liveliest Art: A Panoramic History of the Movies*, was published by Macmillan in 1957 during the run of CBS's *The Seven Lively Arts*.

Some newspaper critics established presences on local TV stations in the 1950s and 1960s. Drama and film critic W.

Ward Marsh of the *Cleveland Plain Dealer* wrote and produced a local TV quiz show on the movies, called *Lights, Camera, Question*. Drama and film critic Harold V. Cohen of the *Pittsburgh Post-Gazette* introduced films in a Sunday afternoon format on the CBS affiliate, KDKA-TV, and later, after CBS's telecasts of the National Football League took precedence on Sundays, on the Steel City's ABC affiliate, WTAE-TV.

Critics were appreciated on TV as intellectuals and taste-makers, and were hired for emphasis. For instance, when *Play of the Week* aired Sidney Lumet's two-part adaptation of Eugene O'Neill's *The Iceman Cometh* in 1960 on WNDT-TV in Newark, it was characterized as a crucial event in the maturation of TV drama. Brooks Atkinson, the longtime drama critic and entertainment editor of *The New York Times*, was called upon for the introduction, and he set a sober tone. In an era when theatre criticism was greatly prized, Atkinson's preamble to an outstanding production faithful to the playwright, starring Jason Robards and Robert Redford, received the most ecstatic reviews of any TV program up to that time.

The first TV stardom for an American film critic as a film critic resulted, ironically, from contention in the newspaper business. The fray was the 114-day New York newspaper strike of 1962 and 1963. ABC News chief James C. Hagerty, who had been President Dwight Eisenhower's press secretary, offered *New York Herald-Tribune* drama critic Judith Crist the opportunity to critique plays and movies on New York's ABC affiliate, WABC-TV, Channel 7. She presented strong opinions in plain, accessible, and occasionally slangy language.

Her WABC moonlighting made an impact at her paper. After the strike, on April 1, 1963, Crist was named the *Herald-Tribune*'s movie critic by arts editor Herb Kupferberg. She had been a city desk reporter since World War II on the *Herald-Tribune*, and was the paper's drama critic from 1958 to 1963. She kept her base at the *Herald-Tribune* until it folded in 1966, along with several other New York dailies, after another, and ultimately devastating, labor strike. In the meantime, Crist impressed Al Morgan, the producer of *The Today Show* on rival NBC-TV.

Judith Crist soon became synonymous with film criticism for millions of Americans after she went on the national airwaves in 1964 on *The Today Show*. As the regular reviewer through 1973, Crist's opinions on the latest films became a morning ritual with coffee and anchorman Hugh Downs. She also began reviewing movies airing on television for *TV Guide* in 1966, a circumstance that led to the capsule-review book *Judith Crist's TV Guide to the Movies* (1974).

Crist was the first nationally known film critic and the first multimedia celebrity of film criticism, notoriety that resulted from her appearance on TV. She was brought to TV because she was a proven journalist, someone with lengthy experience as an avowedly tough reporter. This was still a TV era when established print journalists were occasionally hired by CBS as on-air personalities, in the manner of columnists Ed Sullivan of the *New York Daily News* in the 1940s and Dorothy Kilgallen of the *New York Journal-American* in the 1950s.

As a talking head on TV, Crist was pleasant and not unattractive, no matter what her opinions happened to be. She commanded the attention of even the great filmmakers. Billy Wilder's indelible quip on Crist was: "Inviting her to review your movies is like inviting the Boston strangler to massage your neck." When asked if Crist was too blunt in her assessments, Alfred Hitchcock was said to have remarked, "Not blunt, sir, but very sharp." Crist left a pie chart on film criticism for posterity. "To be a critic," she said, "you have to have maybe three percent education, five percent intelligence, two percent style, and ninety percent gall and egomania in equal parts." She also said, "Critics who love are the severe ones. . . . We know our relationship must be based on honesty." The notion remains that Crist's pithy, across-the-table style was perfect for morning TV in her time, as well as for *TV Guide*'s pages later.

She could dismiss pictures in a minimum of harsh words like few other critics. The *TV Guide* column gave her a chance to do that with a frequency and sameness that brought the column in line with weekly rituals, like mowing the grass or moving the trash to the curb. While Crist's recommendations were strong and detailed, her disapprovals came week after week in similar Crist code. She adopted a shorthand with her readers in the 1960s. Threadbare productions were "cheapjack," and, as a matter of routine, a lot of pictures were "routine," and often "a disaster." And the depiction of violence, for her, had better have a very clear purpose.

This is where Clint Eastwood's early career clearly made an impression on her. Of Sergio Leone's *The Good, the Bad and the Ugly* (1966), she wrote, "This 161-minute mess is strictly for viewers with a lust for gory garbage." Don Siegel's *Coogan's Bluff* (1968) was a "spew of sex and slaughter," and Siegel's *The Beguiled* (1971) was "a must for sadists and woman-haters." Brian G. Hutton's *Kelly's Heroes* (1970) "is a dumb-dumb immoral movie made for no possible reason than a chance to use the Yugoslav army at cut rates." The Eastwood-directed *Play Misty for Me* (1971) was "woodenly routine . . . a schlock shocker."

Crist's standards of taste and morality often came into play, and her economy with the put-down cut straight to the chase: King Vidor's *Ruby Gentry* (1952) was "pure lard"; David Swift's *Under the Yum Yum Tree* (1963) a "nauseating bottom-of-the-barrel dud"; Edward Dmytryk's *The Carpetbaggers* (1964) "incoherent, vulgar, and tedious"; Jack Smight's *Harper* (1966) amounted to "stale succotash"; Otto Preminger's *Hurry Sundown* (1967) was a "brew of slickness, soap and slobbery [that] ranks with the worst films of all time"; and J. Lee Thompson's *Eye of the Devil* (1967) was "so dreary a horror it can give black magic nonsense a bad name."

"Crist ranks as a good, gutsy critic, a self-styled 'preacher' with a tendency to moralize," wrote Richard R. Lingeman about her review anthology, *The Private Eye, the Cowboy and the Very Naked Girl* (1968), in *The New York Times Book Review*. "Her thinking is grooved down the middle of the intellectual road. . . . I enjoyed most of her deflationary reviews . . . of *Spencer's Moun-*

tain [and] *Hurry Sundown* (hilarious) . . . but these are, after all, big flabby targets.

"With harder cases, such as *Persona*, *8½*, or *Blowup*, she is somewhat less satisfying," Lingeman contended, "tending to give the esthetic complexities involved a superficial dusting and then put them on the shelf among the other objets d'art."

The gentleman who became Crist's counterpart on NBC, Gene Shalit, conformed to the NBC system—as much as anyone could with an enormous Afro-like hairdo and big moustache in a rather bushed-out visual version of Bob Hope entourage regular Jerry Colonna, replete with an ingratiating twinkling of the eyes. Shalit's trademark was a multicolored bowtie collection.

Shalit also expressed a consistent penchant for puns, alliteration, and other wordplays and repetitions that for decades wouldn't, and didn't, abate. In reviewing Adrian Lyne's *Fatal Attraction* (1987), Shalit offered that the picture was "filled with suspense, surprise, secrets . . . it's sexy, it's scary, it's some kind of movie!" When the words were read back to him, Shalit replied, "That was my Swinburne moment for the year." Shalit was dubbed the "Ayatollah of Alliteration" in the *Los Angeles Times*, and the "King of Schmaltz" in *Brill's Content*.

"Peppard chases Sarrazin . . . Sarrazin chases Peppard . . . Peppard chases Sarrazin . . ." was his sing-song description of Lamont Johnson's high-tech thriller *The Groundstar Conspiracy* (1972). Making wordplays on the titles was a Shalit constant. "Bring me the head of the studio that released this one," he said of Sam Peckinpah's *Bring Me the Head of Alfredo Garcia* (1974).

Shalit began at WNBC-TV in 1967 and by 1969 was occasionally reviewing movies concurrent with Crist on the parent network's *Today*. By 1974, Shalit was a *Today* regular, reviewing motion pictures, plays, and books, while also reviewing simultaneously on radio and in major magazines for 37 years. His film reviews were a regular feature in *Look* magazine, and he wrote the "What's Happening" page for the *Ladies' Home Journal* for 12 years. For a dozen years, he wrote and broadcast a daily essay as the *Man about Anything* on the NBC Radio Network, which was carried on more stations than was any other NBC radio feature. Shalit was also a regular panelist on *What's My Line?* and *To Tell The Truth*, and has written for *Cosmopolitan*, *TV Guide*, *Seventeen*, *Glamour*, *McCall's*, and *The New York Times*.

"Many people will leave the theater with tears of joy on their cheek," Shalit said of Tom Shadyac's *Patch Adams* (1998), starring Robin Williams. "In my case, both cheeks. . . . If you don't feel wonderful after seeing this, perhaps you need to make an appointment with Dr. Patch Adams."

While Crist was becoming established in the early 1960s in New York on Channel 7, a more erudite brand of film criticism was brought to public TV. Stanley Kauffmann was one of the first film critics to use television as a means of consistently investigating film culture. Kauffmann was the host of *The Art of Film* on the old WNDT-TV, based in Newark, New Jersey, from 1963 to 1967. WNDT merged with the National Educational Network (NET) in 1970, when the Public Broadcasting System was formed, and became PBS's New York affiliate, WNET-TV, Channel 13.

Kauffmann conducted discussions on *The Art of Film* regarding the techniques, processes, and artistry of filmmaking with guests who included directors, producers, screenwriters, and actors. Film clips were interspersed to illustrate points in a documentary-like manner rather than used as they mostly were in later years, as free advertising by studios trying to plug their newest releases.

In 1964, WNDT-TV and the producer of *The Art of Film*, Edith Zornow, won a local New York-area Emmy Award for the program's general excellence. *The Art of Film* helped establish Kauffmann's reputation as a critic of perception and power in New York during the mid-1960s—as much as his reviews in *The New Republic* and the books that anthologized them.

Charles Champlin also got his start in front of the cameras on public TV. The main film critic and entertainment columnist for the *Los Angeles Times* became host for two limited-run programs on PBS, *Homewood* and *Film Odyssey*. The former presented Champlin introducing musical performances and the latter saw him introducing foreign film classics with remarks on their directors. Champlin presented such classics as Jean Renoir's *The Rules of the Game* (1939), Akira Kurosawa's *The Seven Samurai* (1954), and François Truffaut's *Jules et Jim* (1962).

For six years, Champlin was also a host of the public affairs program, *Citywatchers*, a multifaceted look at Los Angeles aired by the city's PBS affiliate, KCET-TV. When cable arrived, Champlin sustained his onscreen relationship with the medium as the host of *On the Film Scene* on the Los Angeles-based The Z Channel, then with *Champlin on Film* on Bravo. He interviewed hundreds of stars and filmmakers over the years on these two forums, from Robert Mitchum and Gene Hackman to Barbara Hershey and Jodie Foster. Champlin approached these interviews mostly as cordial visits, and always managed to steer the discussions around why and how certain films were made and their effects were achieved.

Among the critics of the 1960s and 1970s who became semi-regulars on the talk show circuit was John Simon, an extremely discerning critic with an exceptionally literate style and a great understanding of the arts and culture in America and Europe. Like Kauffmann, Simon was also one of the few film critics to have won the George Jean Nathan Award for theatrical criticism, in 1969–1970. Simon was one of the first critics to have his collected reviews published in book form after James Agee's posthumously assembled *Agee on Film* (1958) and before Pauline Kael's first volume, *I Lost It at the Movies* (1965). Simon's *Acid Test* (1963) was published by Stein & Day, with an introduction by Dwight Macdonald.

Simon tested New York cultural arts discussion shows, then network talk shows, and proved himself to be as erudite and unwavering in person as his writing was on the page. While he exhibited the civilized traits of a distinguished man of letters, there was the notion about his TV appearances that he might break out into a Sheridan Whiteside rant at any moment. *Film Heritage* noted that, on a TV show, "Simon came close to hu-

miliating Moira Walsh (the film critic for [the Catholic maga-
zine] *America*), and it was mostly due to the fact that Miss Walsh
found herself in the untenable position of defending Catholic
censorship."

Simon was involved in a near-skirmish with agitated actor Robert Blake over his role as a film critic on an installment of
The Dick Cavett Show in 1970. "Have you ever been an actor?"
Simon was asked on the air by Blake, whose career was renewed
when he starred as a manipulative murderer in Richard Brooks's
In Cold Blood (1967). Cavett looked on as Blake pursued a rhe-
torical line of insistent questions. "Have you ever directed anything? What do you know about it? What allows you to sit here
saying this is good, and this is bad? *Who are you?*" Stephen Koch
recounted the incident in the *Saturday Review*, writing, "The
audience started to cheer. Blake twitched angrily in his chair and
Simon looked for a moment as if he had just been hit with a flying brick. Lamely, defensively, he began to recover."

Richard Schickel, who moved as the resident film critic
of *Life* to its sister publication *Time* in 1972, wrote in *Harper's*
that too many critics were becoming celebrities. "The problem is
this: people who don't know the first thing about the principles
or functions of criticism are suddenly reading the stuff with new
interest, because it is now more widely available than ever and
because it is being written about as a subject that everybody
knows something about and which is widely fashionable—the
movies," Schickel wrote.

On the fringes of culture, everyone knew about the movies, but film criticism was seen as something like an exotic creature, not yet fully comprehended. John Simon's bearing, erudition, and deep intonation ran toward the Sheridan Whiteside
cliché. Even more problematic was Rex Reed.

While Judith Crist and Gene Shalit promulgated the notion of themselves as critics by actually reviewing on TV in the
early 1970s, the greatest notoriety for being a film critic during
that time came, like the attention accorded Simon, not by practicing film criticism, but by being identified as a film critic on

TV talk shows. Reed's frequent television exposure as a gadfly convinced Middle America—whose familiarity with film critics was either incrementally growing because of Crist and Shalit or was otherwise practically nil—that perhaps the major distinctions of "film critics" were too much eyeliner and glib snipes about the celebrities of the week.

When Crist, Shalit, Simon, Reed, and Champlin were beginning on TV in the 1960s and 1970s, cable was another decade away as a national phenomenon, and only the three commercial national networks—ABC, CBS, and NBC—were on the air, along with PBS. Rex Reed seemed to be ubiquitous—on *The Mike Douglas Show*, *The Merv Griffin Show*, *The Dick Cavett Show*, *Dinah* starring Dinah Shore, and at least 16 occasions from 1970 through 1973 on *The Tonight Show Starring Johnny Carson*. Reed sometimes talked about new studio releases in these gab sessions, occasionally touching on ancillary film critics' job topics, such as screenings. But his celeb-trawling adventures received the most attention.

While Reed earned his living as a writer, his appearances on TV drove his fame into national attention. Well short of a phenomenon, he nevertheless became the most famous film critic in America through his pervasive TV exposure, boosted by the obvious approval of hosts such as Carson and Cavett. One of America's biggest stars, Carson occasionally acted like an authentic fan when he interviewed various movie stars. And he couldn't hide his enjoyment of Reed's catty snipes, priggish assessments, and juicy tidbits. Reed, a wiry gentleman whose vocal manner often carried airs of insinuation, was a crafty and cocky speaker. Occasionally funny, and expert at suggesting something naughty, he courted audience approval.

"In many a culturally underprivileged American home he has become the archetype of the critic," Simon wrote about Reed. "In superficially bright circles he passes for a fearlessly outspoken wit." Moreover, average American families came to identify film critics as Rex Reed types. Although he reviewed movies at various times for many outlets—*Women's Wear Daily*,

Vogue, Status, New York Daily News, Gentleman's Quarterly, Cosmopolitan, Holiday, New York Post—Reed was more famous for his celebrity interviews.

Reed's reports became characterized as episodes in which the stars were stripped of their glamour. It was the trendy way in the 1960s to sell a pitch to a magazine, and at the same time conduct business as usual through studio public relations departments and press agents. The studio sold pictures at the time of their release through star interview stories, by "allowing" press access to the "talent"—the same way it was done in Errol Flynn's era and later in Mel Gibson's day.

By 1965, Reed's celebrity interviews ran in *The New York Times* and *New York* magazine. *Esquire* and *Cosmopolitan* followed suit as his mini-empire grew and TV underscored his own star status. Reed also wrote articles for *Playboy, Ladies' Home Journal,* and *Harper's Bazaar,* and he was a columnist for the Chicago Tribune Syndicate and, years later, for the *New York Observer.*

Reticent and normally press-evasive stars such as Paul Newman, Walter Matthau and Geraldine Page talked to Reed. Somehow, the notion was promulgated that it was a badge of honor to have survived a supposedly blistering Reed interview. Enduring "the Rex Reed treatment," according to Henry Flowers in *The New York Times Book Review*, became one of the measures of success for an actor or director. While he could be as cozy as any other celeb interviewer, Reed became known as the "hatchet man" of show business journalism, an identity he exploited—even as he was introduced, each time, as "film critic Rex Reed."

"There is panic and fearful insecurity behind this frantic compulsion to mix with the famous and sniff the hem of power," wrote John Lahr in *The New York Times Book Review*. "But Rex sees neither the humor nor the mediocrity in a system that elevates his brand of witless ballyhoo to stardom." Reed's personality features were repackaged in several books with the provocative titles of *Conversations in the Raw, Do You Sleep in the Nude?,*

People Are Crazy Here, and *Valentines and Vitriol.* The notion of Reed as the TV generation's second-division Oscar Wilde flamed and extinguished in the early 1970s, leaving an acrid odor. The face of the critical profession had been altered to that of a cocktail circuit wag with an Olivier-like fascination for the makeup tray. Reed occasionally looked positively waxy on camera.

Stephen Koch lumped Reed and Simon together after inventorying a laundry list of critics in 1970. "Then there are the writers who neither think deeply nor give good advice, but who play an entirely different game," Koch wrote in the *Saturday Review.* "The Rex Reeds and John Simons of this world (along with a few hundred thousand chintz TV 'personalities') . . . are simply performers themselves, putting on their own sometimes entertaining but usually self-serving little show." Koch obviously hadn't read much of Simon's precise and cogent criticism.

Koch wrote that Judith Crist was at least a competent journalist, but "Rex Reed, on the other hand, does remain rather amusing. He is as competent a journalist as Mrs. Crist, but has somewhat more staying power. What bewilders me is: a) that he is mistaken for a critic on any level, or of any description (obviously, he is totally uninterested in movies; he *is* interested in Fame, a very different subject); and b) that he has been touted as a 'tough' interviewer. On the contrary," Koch contended, "he is an amazing sucker for the movie star's song and dance."

As a prolific writer of features and reviews, Reed achieved some distinction. A Reed piece on Ava Gardner was included by Tom Wolfe in the 1973 anthology, *The New Journalism.* Wolfe maintained that Reed "raised the celebrity interview to a new level through his frankness and his eye for social detail. He has also been a master at capturing a story line in the interview situation itself."

Despite Wolfe's praise and Reed's wide identification as a "film critic," the latter's reviews are less known than his interviews. His emphases in reviews often were outlandish point-counterpoint comparisons or contrasts, and his opinions were often directly related to stars and filmmakers. As with his interviews, Reed concentrated on the personalities of the people in front of him. He converted his reviews into commentaries on the stars and filmmakers in the manner of his profiles.

In the MacMillan anthology of Reed's reviews, *Big Screen, Little Screen* (1971), are reviews of three 1968 releases: Joseph Losey's *Secret Ceremony*, Roger Vadim's *Barbarella*, and John Frankenheimer's *The Fixer*. Reed makes these respective observations: "That's about all there is to the movie, except that Robert Mitchum (in the worst bit of miscasting since Doris Day played a pregnant housewife shot through the stomach by the Ku Klux Klan in *Storm Warning*) shows up with a hippie beard and invites some flap about whether or not he raped his own step-daughter. . . . I find [Vadim's] manipulation of Jane Fonda increasingly more indigestible with each successive film. In this smoker version of an intergalactic *Candy*, she is required to do nothing more than coordinate a certain toss of her mane with a certain toss of her mammary glands. Miss Fonda, I am happy to report, is in excellent physical shape for the assignment. . . . A terrible misfortune from start to finish, this monstrosity John Frankenheimer has made from Bernard Malamud's novel shows what can happen when an anti-Establishment director sets out to have his cake and eat it, too, not realizing it was only, after all, a moldy bagel."

Born in Fort Worth, Texas, on October 2, 1938, Rex Taylor Reed earned a bachelor of arts degree at Louisiana State University. The enduring factoid of his pre-New York years is that, while at LSU's campus newspaper, he wrote an editorial entitled "The Prince of Prejudice," for which he was burned in effigy by Baton Rouge's white supremacists. An aspiring actor in his early years, Reed critiqued music as well as movies and made ends meet as a diner cook, among other things.

After his features began being collected between hard covers, Reed's books were like the successful movies he disdained—they flourished despite the preponderance of nearly blanket bad reviews. *Valentines and Vitriol*, Reed's 1977 collection of interviews, "is superficial even in its shallowness," John

Lahr wrote. "Rex calls himself a 'critic,' as much a misnomer as 'sanitary engineer.'"

Book critic A.J. Kraul wrote, "Few critics have bestowed upon his work the respect and dignity [Reed] hopes to earn. His notoriety and celebrity status may have prompted professional jealousies that found their way into the snide and caustic assessments of his writing." John Simon wrote an essay entitled "Why Reed Can't Write," which was a fuel-drenched and match-lit diatribe on Rex Reed in a volume that also singed film critics Vincent Canby of *The New York Times* and Andrew Sarris of *The Village Voice*, as well as Gore Vidal, David Halberstam, Barbara Walters, John Gregory Dunne, and dance critic Clive Barnes.

"Rex Reed is the most read, seen, and heard film and theater reviewer in this country," Simon began. "Millions read (or, at any rate, have access to) his column, which is distributed by the Chicago Tribune-New York News Syndicate; further, millions of nonreaders can catch him on *The Tonight Show*, where he is one of the regulars, and *The Gong Show*, or on his spots on CBS radio; and tens of thousands of select women and homosexuals can enjoy him also in the pages of *Vogue*." Simon then pointed out a dozen of Reed's transgressions of English usage. One is a description of a Dorothy McGuire role: she enacts an "old maid with hidden feelings of observation and understanding so full of pride and kindness." Simon wrote, "I never knew that observation and understanding were feelings; still less that they could be simultaneously filled with the sin of pride and the virtue of kindness.

"That, I suppose, is what they call mixed feelings," Simon wrote. "I could go on quoting forever, but must conclude with an excerpt from Reed's review of *Providence*, where this 'often . . . confusing to comprehend [sic]' work is declared Resnais' 'most coherent and moving film. Pay attention to detail and allow it to wash over you like a warm surf and you'll be rewarded.' It takes singular obtuseness not to recognize that paying attention to detail is the exact opposite of letting something wash over you like warm surf, but at least there can be little doubt about which of these two approaches Reed takes in his criticism."

Dubbed "King Weed" by Andrew Sarris (precisely, "King Weed and Gene Shallow," in a tangential sideswipe at the TV critics), Reed bears much of the responsibility for blurring film critic with Hollywood gadfly or celebrity schmoozer—the traditional domain of columnists Louella O. Parsons, Hedda Hopper, Sheilah Graham, James Bacon, and Sidney Skolsky. While other film critics were writing criticism and celeb interviews as equal responsibilities of film-beat coverage—Roger Ebert and Gene Siskel in Chicago, William Wolf of *Cue*, Gary Arnold of *The Washington Post*, and many others—Reed did it more visibly, more egocentrically, and certainly more aggressively than as a practical matter of beat coverage.

Reed also acted, with Mae West, Raquel Welch, and a momentarily rudderless John Huston in Michael Sarne's *Myra Breckinridge* (1970), the atrocious adaptation of Gore Vidal's novel about a transsexual, and a candidate for the most critically reviled movie of all time (the novel, incidentally, mentioned film critic Parker Tyler several times and was instrumental in revitalizing his career). "This is a horrifying movie, but not because it's dirty," wrote Joe Morgenstern in *Newsweek*. "It's horrifying because it's an entirely incompetent, impotent attempt at exploitation by an industry that knew once, at the very least, how to make a dishonest buck." Despite that quip, the industry remembered in the 1980s.

Warner Books published *Rex Reed's Guide to Movies on TV and Video* in 1992, which arrived late in the capsule-review trend, and was issued presumably based on the fact that Reed was back on TV. When Roger Ebert and Gene Siskel moved their movie-review show from PBS to commercial TV in 1986, public TV kept *At the Movies* on the air, replacing the Chicago-based pioneers with Reed and Bill Harris. A diminutive and bespectacled gentleman with a paintbrush moustache, Harris had been a gossip reporter on *Entertainment Tonight*, and later worked behind the scenes on documentaries on the Arts & Entertainment Network. Reed and Harris lasted as a tandem until

1988, when Harris was replaced by Dixie Whatley, an entertainment reporter at local TV stations in Los Angeles and Boston. She had also been a host and reporter on *Entertainment Tonight* in the early 1980s.

For the four years that *At the Movies* stayed on the air with Reed, it floundered in the shallows, lacking not only in the forceful personalities that Ebert and Siskel evolved on the air, but also the significant and insightful observations that the Chicago duo brought to the balcony. Identifying Reed as "a veritable fright mask of foppish mannerisms" who was "spoofing himself near 20 years ago in the film *Myra Breckinridge*," Patrick Goldstein also wrote in the *Los Angeles Times* that, "Reed and his *At the Movies* partner Bill Harris certainly don't seem to expend much brainpower on their quickie reviews. With their chirpy, used-car-lot smiles and high-decibel plot descriptions, they seem more intent on promoting the product than making any sense of what they've seen on the screen."

Reed, who roamed onto such programs as *The Gong Show* and *You Don't Say*, appeared (as did Bill Harris) on *The New Hollywood Squares* in the late 1980s, reaching his nadir as another half-remembered face of TV whose notoriety had long before crossed into the public consciousness where synapses of recognition fire off the vague memory of even foggier memories. Reed became another Pat Carroll or Wink Martindale or Slappy White, one of Koch's "chintz TV personalities," another quasi-famous person still somehow famous for previously being famous.

TV critics were recognized as the equals of their print siblings when the Los Angeles Film Critics Association was organized in 1975, and its members included TV critics. That had not been the case, of course, when the New York Film Critics Circle was formed in 1935, or when the National Society of Film Critics organized in 1966.

Ruth Batchelor, a songwriter who had written for Elvis Presley and penned TV specials—and put out an album of feminist songs entitled *Reviving a Dream*—also wrote film criticism for the *L.A. Free Press* and broadcasted it on National Public Radio. Batchelor conceived the LAFCA and became its president and executive director. Founding members included Charles Champlin, Kevin Thomas, and Linda Gross of the *Los Angeles Times*; Richard Cuskelly and Ray Loynd of the *Los Angeles Herald-Examiner*; Arthur Knight and Todd McCarthy of *The Hollywood Reporter*; and Joseph McBride and A.D. "Art" Murphy of *Daily Variety*.

TV personalities who also reviewed movies were charter members as well, including Rona Barrett of ABC-TV and David Sheehan of KNXT-TV, which at the time was the CBS affiliate in Los Angeles. The omnium-gatherum membership included two of the most ubiquitous talk- and game-show hosts of all time, Robert Q. Lewis, then of KRLA Radio, and Regis Philbin, then of KABC-TV. Lewis was one of the bona fide pioneer hosts of the medium, a multifaceted living-room presence whose experience rivaled that of Bud Collyer, Bill Cullen, and Dennis James. Lewis had been host on such network shows as *The Show Goes On* (1950–1952) on CBS, *The Name's the Same* (1951–1952) on ABC, *The Robert Q. Lewis Show* (1954–1956) on CBS, *Make Me Laugh* (1959) on ABC, *Play Your Hunch* (1962–1963) on NBC, and others. The host of three TV series in the year he became a founding member of LAFCA, Philbin was celebrated on August 20, 2004, for breaking the *Guinness Book's* world record for most hours on camera, 15,188, not many of those hours having to do with film criticism.

LAFCA's television involvement became one of the group's formative imbroglios. Through the years, the L.A. group would face quirky controversies that became an almost comfortable tradition, kick-started at the first meeting when Bridget Byrne of the *Herald-Examiner*, after only moments as a member, walked out during the talks because she didn't feel that any group should give out "instant awards" without defining its function. Among those awards, announced at a February 1976 press conference, were two citations for best picture of 1975, for Milos Forman's *One Flew Over the Cuckoo's Nest* and Sidney

Lumet's *Dog Day Afternoon.*

Two more best pictures were named the following year, Lumet's *Network* and John G. Avildsen's *Rocky*, but the group settled on one "best" selection for the remainder of the decade: *Star Wars* (1977), *Coming Home* (1978), and *Kramer vs. Kramer* (1979). Both the 1978 and 1979 awards ceremonies were taped and televised as installments of the Metromedia-syndicated *The Merv Griffin Show*, with Griffin as emcee. The TV exposure for the upstart group rankled some members, and it would continue into the next decade to be a sticking point. Some felt that the show was too gaudy a forum for the purposes of a critics group.

When the renewal of the TV awards show came up for LAFCA board discussion in 1982, the *Los Angeles Times* contingent—Charles Champlin, Kevin Thomas, and Sheila Benson—threatened to walk out on the organization.

The glitz of a TV awards show put LAFCA's shindigs with Merv Griffin in the same class as Golden Globes telecasts, some members felt. A TV show, the prevailing wisdom went, amounted to a tacky thing for critics to be doing. So, when LAFCA veered back to the more subdued track of awarding filmmakers at a Tuesday hotel luncheon, Champlin, Thomas, and Benson stayed in the group, and Batchelor, who quipped, "This has taken three months out of my life," never again attended a meeting of the group that she instigated. Meanwhile, the Hollywood Foreign Press Association's Golden Globes were all about gaining fame and money.

The Golden Globes, which are awarded to TV shows and stars as well as movie folks, became another annual part of the TV year rather than a strict monitor of film and TV artistry. The HFPA's first telecasting of the Golden Globes in 1964 was arranged through connections with *The Andy Williams Show* on NBC. Since then, the Golden Globes have been on and off the air (but mostly on) and considerations of their importance have vacillated through the years from harbingers of Oscars to doorstops, their significance to many nominees merely a reason for a well-advertised banquet party and another chance to be on TV.

The usual informal feel to the annual affair, with its table hopping and relaxed schmoozing often caught by the TV cameras was/is usually helped along by the free flow of champagne.

The hazard presented to film critics by the Golden Globes was that members of the HFPA were known as "film critics," as well. The HFPA members were invited to screenings as regulars on the studios' press lists, and they voted for best-of-the-year honors to nominate and award the Golden Globes. Some of them even wrote reviews for notable periodicals.

"After years of being ridiculed as a bunch of part-time journalists and full-time freeloaders who would sell their votes for a vodka tonic and cross the Alps for a hot dog, the association has become respectable," wrote former *New York Times* Hollywood correspondent Aljean Harmetz in 2000 in the *Los Angeles Times*. "The television contract it signed with NBC in 1996 enabled it to pay 2.1 million in cash last August for an office building in West Hollywood. Long derided as a comic opera of quarrelsome waiters and shoe store clerks who occasionally wrote for obscure publications in Lithuania or Bangladesh, the Hollywood Foreign Press Assn. has survived into a world tailormade for it, a world where celebrity beats fame to the finish line every time and a history of cutting corners is not shameful if you put on a good party."

Even in reports that consider the HFPA a slipshod front for freeloaders, the group usually ends up being identified as film critics. Roger Friedman's lead on a 2008 FOXNews.com piece on the HFPA's 2007 taxes began, "That crazy group known as the Hollywood Foreign Press is back in the news again." By paragraph nine, the HFPA was referred to as a "bunch of movie critics."

Among the imbroglios smoothed over by the somehow always buoyant HFPA was the bestowal of the 1981 Best New Star of the Year Award to petite prefab starlet Pia Zadora at the Golden Globes. Zadora starred in Matt Cimber's *Butterfly* (1982), which had not yet been released. Later, it was learned that Zadora's tycoon husband, Meshulam Riklis, had treated all

80-some members of the HFPA to a few days of frolic in Las Vegas at his Riviera hotel and casino. The Federal Communications Commission took the Globes award show off the air for this influence peddling, and the association promised to police its ranks and beef up policies. When HFPA members received luxury watches from Sharon Stone, stumping for her performance in Albert Brooks's *The Muse* (1999), they were ordered to return them.

The HFPA has policed its ranks since then. It suspended member Nick Douglas in 2005 for selling a photograph of Tom Selleck to a tabloid newspaper, and then lying about it, drawing attention to the HFPA during the all-important, year-end awards season. The suspension cut off Douglas's access to press junkets, screenings, and celebrity interviews. His editor, Barry O'Kane, at *Big Buzz*, an entertainment magazine in Northern Ireland, canceled Douglas's column, which became toothless without his access to screenings and stars. Despondent at his inability to find journalistic work, Douglas hanged himself on December 8 in a charity retail shop in Belfast. O'Kane linked the death to the HFPA suspension. Sharon Waxman, writing in *The New York Times*, described the suspension as "disciplinary procedures to protect a lucrative show that has become an important part of the Hollywood awards game."

"We've had many people suspended for actions we deemed harmful to Hollywood Foreign Press—we're trying to protect our image," HFPA president Philip Berk told *The New York Times*. "Certainly, none ended up in suicide. If Nick did take his life, which seems apparent, I don't think you can say there's a causal relationship between the two."

The HFPA canceled the Golden Globes TV show in 2008 because of the Writers Guild of America strike, and shaved back its charitable donations from more than a $1 million to about $750,000, citing the "lost revenue" of $6 million that it had expected to earn from NBC for the TV show. The HFPA's 2007 tax return reported that the group had assets of $18 million.

No matter how often the HFPA is battered in the press

as a collection of Hollywood hangers-on, it manages to survive on the name recognition of the Golden Globes—the annual industry party that is one of the most watched of the televised awards shows. It's usually in the top three, ratings-wise, along with the Oscars telecast and the Grammy Awards. The HFPA has incrementally been propped up by the studios, which benefit from the nominations and awards. "[The Golden Globes] are coveted in the entertainment industry as a promotional tool and have become a closely watched indicator of prospects in the annual Oscar race," Waxman wrote.

Some HFPA ambassadors are or have been film critics. Philip Berk, the main apologist, introduced himself at junkets in the 1990s as "from South Africa" when other journalists would name themselves and their media outlets to interviewees for round-table sessions. Berk served as secretary of the Los Angeles Film Critics Association in the early 1990s, when he was the film critic of the *B'nai B'rith Messenger*, a Jewish newspaper that ceased publication in 1995. Another crossover member from LAFCA, Jorge Camara, has been president of both groups. He has reviewed for the main Spanish-language newspaper in Los Angeles, *La Opinión*, and been an on-camera reviewer and correspondent for Univision and KMEX-TV, Channel 34, in Los Angeles. The HFPA functions as a private club, accepting as many as five applicants per year for membership, and usually choosing less.

The profile of film criticism on the TV landscape into the 1970s had mostly consisted of the notoriety of Crist and Shalit on NBC, and the talk-show hopping of Rex Reed and John Simon. Local stations evolved criticism into entertainment reporting during this time, so that on-air personalities became known for their reviews: Regis Philbin and David Sheehan in Los Angeles, for instance.

The public face of film criticism received its biggest lift when the Chicago-based team of Roger Ebert of the *Chicago Sun-Times* and Gene Siskel of the *Chicago Tribune* went national on PBS in 1978 with their half-hour film-review program. The waiting audience caught PBS and the country off guard; *Sneak Previews* became the highest rated show in PBS history.

For a half hour once a week, the Siskel and Ebert show—even through all of its essentially unvaried transformations—retained the same basic format through three decades: two guys giving their opinions on four or five films. Each man spoke his mind between film clips of the week's releases. The other critic was allotted time for a rebuttal opinion if one was called for, and an agreement, disagreement, or argument ensued. Sometimes the arguments pitched toward vociferous loggerheads. Weekly features were added and subtracted through the years, but the format remained constant, as did the interspersing of film clips.

The thumbs-up or thumbs-down visual that accompanied the opinions of each critic quickly entered popular culture. For better or for worse, the opposable digits, pointing north or south, became the marketing key for the Chicago pair. The adage "all thumbs" took on a new meaning. The film criticism fraternity reacted in differing ways. There was some pride in the notion that film criticism was in the bright spotlight as the familiar "Gene and Roger" became true TV stars.

But envy also developed over the fact that the Chicago duo got to be the most recognizable film critics—and critics, period—in America. And there was the creeping notion that their TV success was not only taking precedence over written criticism, but also eroding critical standards—as if there were any—by reducing intellectual discourse to the rustic level of thumbs-up or thumbs-down.

"Who's left out of this cozy new marketing equation—TV Critic Blurbs + Film Clips = Free Advertising?" Patrick Goldstein asked rhetorically in the *Los Angeles Times* in 1988, before providing an answer: "Today's print critic, who finds himself with less space—and less clout—than ever before. Is it any wonder that print critics seem to have a love-hate relationship with their TV counterparts. That is—they'd love to have their jobs, but they hate to admit it."

In one way, Siskel and Ebert played right into studio

marketing hands. They showed teasers of the new movies, donating the studios airtime. The viewing public could see a piece of a new release, which might entice them to want to see more of that film, and they heard an informed discussion on the film that might sway them to see it or not. From a studio marketing point of view, the Siskel and Ebert forum was an automatic victory, because the studio would get its product shown to millions of viewers.

The adage that any publicity is good publicity was enjoyed by Warner Bros., Twentieth Century-Fox, Paramount Pictures, and the other big and small studios whose wares were shown in snippets on the Siskel and Ebert show. If the subject matter or the star in the clip was to the viewer's liking, the opinions of the Chicago boys didn't matter a bit. The clip drew that viewer into committing his dollar to the next Eddie Murphy comedy or Julia Roberts romance. Siskel and Ebert supplied informed and serious film criticism through their personable home-viewing-friendly deliveries, but the fact of the matter was, they also supplied free advertising.

Ebert, however, was adamant about his show with Siskel having the same effect as print reviews, and the timing of his and Siskel's broadcast opinions on new releases was similar to newspapers' treatments of studio releases. "It's not advertising because it's not paid for by the studio, and frequently, of course, we get negative effects," Ebert told the *Los Angeles Times*. ". . . When a newspaper film critic reviews a movie, isn't that advertisement for a movie? Have you ever noticed that interviews with famous stars [appear] in newspapers just at the time the movie is coming out? Why do *you* time it like that? Why don't *you* give free publicity when their movie is coming out? It's [just] more useful to review a film when it's in release."

Ebert also saw the show as much better than normal TV fare. "What do you think is better to have on TV—movie criticism or *Wheel of Fortune*?" he rhetorically asked a reporter in 1988. "I think I try to be as fair and accurate and evocative to what a movie is about as it is possible for me to be."

Hand in hand with success was a power unprecedented in film criticism. "Siskel and Ebert go, 'Horrible picture,' and I'm telling you, [they] can definitely kill a movie," Eddie Murphy said in 1987. Conversely, the duo is credited with "saving" small films that were lagging at the box office. Their positive reviews turned the fortunes around for such films as Jozu Itami's *Tampopo* (1985), Jonathan Demme's *Something Wild* (1986), and Carl Franklin's *One False Move* (1992). Tom Sherak, a top executive at Twentieth Century-Fox, once called a thumbs-up from Siskel and Ebert "the Good Housekeeping Seal of Approval for movies."

The sustained popularity of the show for more than a quarter century outlasted Siskel's death from a brain tumor and then Ebert's battle with cancer. The show became even bigger than the namesake stars. It started in 1975, when WTTW-TV, the PBS station in Chicago, teamed Siskel and Ebert for a show about new movies, called *Opening Soon at a Theater Near You.*

Both crosstown rivals expressed reservations about working with the competition, but only revealed them years later. An early problem was the master visual. The rangy Siskel towered over the portly Ebert, who tended to slump in his theatre seat. "The two, as old Channel 11 hands recall, were a cameraman's dismay," wrote Jon Anderson in the *Chicago Tribune* in 1985. ". . . Ebert was too low-key. Siskel was too hard-edged." Thea Flaum, the WTTW-TV producer who paired them up, said, "With Roger, most of the work was to let the day-to-day Roger, the ebullient Roger we knew, come across on the screen." Because they fought so much behind the scenes, they learned to harness that onscreen. They fought over billing and stolen scoops. All messages brought into the taping studio in this era prior to cellular telephones were brought sealed to Siskel and Ebert to ensure privacy.

"Making this rivalry even worse was the tension of our early tapings," Ebert remembered. "It would take eight hours to get one show in the can, with breaks for lunch, dinner, and fights. I would break down, or he would break down, or one of us would do something different and throw the other off, or the accumulating angst would make our exchanges seem simply bizarre. There are many witnesses to the terror of those days. Only when we threw away our clipboards and 3x5 cards did we get anything done; we finally started ad-libbing and the show began to work. We found we could tape a show in under an hour."

The weekly local presentation entertained Windy City filmgoers, and caught the attention of PBS officials, who repackaged it as a national show. *Sneak Previews*, which was aired nationally by PBS beginning in 1978, found a waiting audience beyond Chicago, on KQED-TV in San Francisco, KCET-TV in Los Angeles, WQED-TV in Pittsburgh, WNET-TV in New York, and public television affiliates across America. It didn't take long for "Gene and Roger" to become regular living room favorites, reasons for weekly rendezvous and cocktail parties.

The critics' early navigation of the TV waters was tempered by concessions to their effect. They told journalist Mary Beth Logas that they "questioned the wisdom of attacking films that might thrive on controversy." This apprehension largely evaporated when public protest was added to the duo's shared hate of Meir Zarchi's *I Spit on Your Grave* (1978), which played in a major Chicago theatre in 1980. The film contained an extended gang-rape sequence. Ebert wrote in the *Sun-Times* that the film was a "vile bag of garbage." The film was withdrawn from the theatre, and Siskel and Ebert both picked it on the show as the worst film of 1980.

In 1982, the Chicago duo went to commercial television, signing a deal with Tribune Entertainment, and airing their largely unchanged review show under a new title, *At the Movies*. This program transformed into *Siskel & Ebert & the Movies* in 1986 when the pair signed a deal with Buena Vista Television. Between eight and eleven million viewers a week were tuning in to their opinions. While they were a hit, they weren't altogether a critical hit, something of which they were well aware. Tom Shales, the Pulitzer Prize-winning TV critic of *The Washington Post* referred to the duo as "Jolly Roger and

Tweedle Gene, the Film Flam Men."

The pop-culture landscape became their turf. Aside from the general consumer and film buffs, some Americans who cared nothing for film criticism tuned in weekly to see if Gene and Roger were going to argue. Toward the decade's close, they were national celebrities, doling out opinions and trading barbs on *The Tonight Show* to the delight of Johnny Carson.

Their antagonistic banter became shtick, not exactly Laurel and Hardy or Hope and Crosby, but entertainment all the same. Siskel told Ebert never to wear a brown sweater on the show, because he could be mistaken for "a mud slide." A favorite Ebert retort was, "One of the little known things about Gene is that from the height of an astronaut circling the Earth, the only objects visible are the Great Wall of China and his forehead." The portly Ebert's barbs concentrated on Siskel's thinning hair, suggesting Gene comb his eyebrows north, and: "He has the only receding hairline so spacious that it has applied for its own ZIP Code."

The rivalry belied the fact that, in Siskel's estimation, the pair agreed about 70 percent of the time. Ebert had a theory as to why the public maintained the notion that they argued a lot. "There's hardly any disagreement or any real conversation on television," he said. "In the early days of television, there were open-ended talk shows with people like David Susskind, Irv Kupcinet, and others on which people who disagreed with each other came on the air and fought. Then, for a long time, all that disappeared and there was all this blandness. Now you have some confrontational stuff on TV, especially on some of the cable stations. But still, it's very rare for anyone on a polite show to express disagreement." This state of affairs changed when a new breed of talk shows began airing on cable in the 1990s, hosted by such provocateurs as former Cincinnati mayor Jerry Springer.

The prevailing opinion of Siskel and Ebert in their first decade together (or up until 1985) was that Siskel took less of a forgiving approach, was wont to be spikier and defensive, and held fast to his initial reaction. Ebert seemed more in love with the movies and more willing to appreciate a film's meaning to the movies and its genre. But he, too, could be intolerant, especially of gratuitous violence. And he could brace himself back against his theatre seat to return a heated volley at Siskel. Actually, they both ridiculed requisite, unnecessary car chases in action and violent horror films, especially those using hand-held cameras as if the frame were a stalker's vision. Both deplored the trend of colorizing vintage black-and-white movies.

After showing clips of new releases, each critic stated his pithy piece. *Sneak Previews*, with its simple format and the critics comfortably seated in movie-theatre-like surroundings—and with the studio-friendly use of clips—allowed both critics' personalities to spill into living rooms. Neither critic allowed the other to know his opinion until the taping started, which offered each other and the audience the freshness of the "first take" as they say. The only time they re-taped was if one or the other stumbled over their words. "We're not actors saying the same lines over and over," Siskel told *People* magazine in 1984.

However, they were rivals through and through, as newspapermen, TV personalities, and friends by circumstance through the years. Ebert had an imperious streak, which Siskel cited as often as people would ask him. "For some reason, Roger has a need to prove himself, and maybe to the rest of the world, that he is better than me in every facet of life, not only as a film critic, but as a human being," Siskel told journalist Lawrence Grobel. Ebert confirmed that: "What Gene can't figure out is that, despite all his efforts, I always seem to wind up on top. I'm smarter, funnier, I'm a better writer, I'm a better talker, I'm better on television. It's just astonishing."

There appeared to be no TV "handling" of these personalities, no repackaging of the simple, raw nature of two guys talking, no concessions for going national, no knocking the wind out of the Windy City boys. "The duo's half hour became one of PBS' highest-rated shows—in no small part because, like that other halcyon PBS hero, chef Julia Child, Ebert and Siskel were unusual but natural TV personalities," judged TV critic Ken Tucker in *Entertainment Weekly.* "Their genuine Chicago-newspaper competitiveness came through the screen." Ebert has said that when the two were engaged in a heated argument, they usually ignored signals from the stage manager to cut short the ragged discussion.

The Siskel-and-Ebert dynamic translated as opposites forced by the nature of the show into a working relationship, in which the differing opinions and outright arguments have a natural place to exist without the artificiality of a point-counterpoint prearrangement, as with debaters on CBS's *60 Minutes.* "They are two men who never would have chosen each other for friends," said Thea Flaum. "They have no natural affinity for each other. But TV has forced them to find a way to work together. What makes their show work is that, despite their differences, each regards the other as a worthy combatant."

Their points of reference were widely dissimilar, film critic Bob Strauss contended in the *Los Angeles Daily News* in 1989. "Ebert's enthusiasm is piqued by the technical aspects of film and analytical criticism, while Siskel seems to look at things in more philosophical, emotionally informed terms," Strauss wrote.

They both eventually conceded in Grobel's 1991 interviews that they were friends. "He knows me better than anybody outside of my family, and, in certain areas, better than anybody else in the world," Siskel said of Ebert. "Whatever else I might think of Roger, I do think highly of him and his mind. He can be a very good person, and an exceedingly good friend." Ebert said of Siskel, "I do admire him and like him a good deal more than you might think."

On the 10-year anniversary of Siskel's death in 2009, Ebert recalled that neither of them ever thought about splitting up. "We were linked beyond all disputing," Ebert wrote. "'You may be an asshole,' Gene would say, 'But you're my asshole.' If we were fighting—get out of the room. But if we were teamed up against a common target, we were fatal. The first time we were on his show, Howard Stern never knew what hit him. He picked on one of us, and we were both at his throat."

Roger Joseph Ebert was born on June 18, 1942, in Urbana, Illinois. The precocious only child of an electrician at the University of Illinois and a bookkeeper, Ebert has said that the first film he ever saw was Sam Wood's *A Day at the Races* (1937), starring the Marx Brothers, on a bill with cartoons at the Princess Theatre in Urbana. He was president of his high school's senior class, and a member of the swim team. At the University of Illinois, where he edited the student newspaper, *The Daily Illini*, he also authored the history, *An Illini Century*, for the University of Illinois Press. He graduated in 1964 with a bachelor's degree in journalism, and became a staff writer for the Champaign-Urbana *News-Gazette*, to which he had been contributing sports and other stories since 1958, when he was 15. He won an Associated Press sports writing competition for the state of Illinois in 1960.

Ebert was hired by the *Chicago Sun-Times* in 1966, and in 1967, discontinued postgraduate studies at the University of Chicago, after having spent a year abroad at the University of Capetown, in South Africa. The move to full-time work as the film critic of the *Sun-Times* forced him to discontinue a doctoral dissertation on critics Dwight Macdonald, Edmund Wilson, and Paul Goodman.

"Papers wanted young film critics," Ebert said, "because films such as *Blowup*, *The Graduate*, *Easy Rider*, and *Bonnie and Clyde* were very important and they were for young audiences." Ebert's steady stream of reviews, features, and essays for the *Sun-Times* showed a film critic of intellectual dexterity, liberal convictions, and sometimes tenacious opinions. In 1975, the year he went on the air opposite Siskel on *Opening Soon at a Theater Near You*, the 33-year-old Ebert was awarded the Pulitzer Prize for criticism, and was the first film critic to win that honor. Ebert's coworker among the *Sun-Times* entertainment writers, Ron Powers, won the Pulitzer in criticism two years prior to Ebert's win, for opinions of television.

Eugene Kal Siskel was born in Chicago on January 26, 1946, the youngest of three children whose parents helped found the first synagogue in the North Shore area, between Chicago proper and the Wisconsin state line. Both died by the time Siskel was 10, and he admits not believing at first that his mother was dead. The Siskel siblings grew up in the household of an aunt and uncle and three cousins. Siskel attended prep school at Culver Military Academy in northern Indiana. Planning to be a trial lawyer, he attended Yale University and studied philosophy. Siskel won a public affairs fellowship, and spent time in California on a political campaign. He graduated from Yale in 1967 with an M.A. in philosophy.

Siskel became interested in journalism while he was in the Army Reserve and joined the *Chicago Tribune* in 1969 as a news reporter at the age of 23. He was later named film critic of the *Tribune* and was hired by WBBM-TV, Chicago's CBS affiliate, as a film reviewer in 1974. A year later, he was asked to join Ebert on the PBS review show, *Opening Soon at a Theatre Near You.*

An inveterate sports fan with courtside seats for Chicago Bulls games, Siskel occasionally manned a microphone for Chicago TV telecasts from the Bulls' home court, Chicago Stadium. Siskel was never the one-man band achiever that Ebert became. While Ebert wrote books, syndicated his reviews, wrote later for the Internet, ran or attended film festivals, presided at seminars, and acquired hosting duties and guest spots on TV apart from Siskel, the latter led the quieter life. "I have a family that lives in Chicago," Siskel told Bob Strauss, "and I define myself by that."

Siskel's review efforts for the *Tribune* were scaled back to capsule assessments and two columns a week in 1986, which were nationally distributed by Tribune Media Services. Siskel was replaced on the day-to-day movie beat. The first-string film critic at the *Tribune* was Dave Kehr from 1986 to 1992. When Kehr left to become film critic for the *New York Daily News* (from 1992 to 1998), Michael Wilmington arrived from the *Los Angeles Times* to take over reviewing, and stayed with the *Tribune* through 2007, when Michael Phillips replaced him.

Ebert usually pointed out this scaling back of Gene's duties thereafter in any discussions of the show and the rivalry.
"They said he was overextended," Ebert told Jerry Buck of the
Associated Press. "During the four years we were with Tribune
Entertainment, they never said he was overworked." Meanwhile,
Ebert soldiered on in all directions, the books piling up behind
him after his first anthology of interview features, *A Kiss Is Still
a Kiss* (1984), was published by the Kansas City house of Andrews, McMeel & Parker.

"Siskbert," as the Chicago duo became known—to the
chagrin of Ebert, which amused Siskel—changed TV film criticism from the one-talking-head mode used by Gene Shalit, Judith Crist, David Sheehan, and a few other TV personalities, to
a weekly exchange of ideas between two distinct and increasingly
familiar, if unpredictable, personalities. They would surprise the
audience and each other with certain takes on specific films. The
arm-waving and even bellowing occasionally portended a tangle.
At their best, Siskel and Ebert's lively talks were marked by the
immediacy, drama, comedy, intelligence, and surprise of live
theatre.

"I don't think we would have been on the air as long as
we have been if people were convinced it was a fraud of some
sort," Siskel said. "When people ask me, 'What is your friendship like?' the best answer I can give is, it's what you see. If you
see a little bit of dislike, there's probably a lot going on." After
the duo had been on the air for 14 years, and copycat pairs of
critics had emerged on TV, Ebert said, "Other people doing this
format tend to be too polite to each other: 'Well, maybe you
have a point there,' or 'maybe we can agree on this.' Gene and I
never want to agree on anything. This edge in our relationship is
good for the show. The bottom line is—both of us can't wait for
the other guy to shut up so he can start talking."

Ebert judged that on most shows they agreed and liked
each other's opinions. However, "Sometimes during a show
something will be said that will make the hairs on the back of
the neck curl," he said. "Anybody can see when that happens

and when it doesn't happen. That's not manufactured. . . . If Gene disagrees with me, I take it personally, and vice versa. We are still very competitive. We know how to push each other's buttons in such a way that there is a real feeling of risk when we're taping. For both of us. . . . I have more innate confidence in the fact that I am right. I just assume I'm right, partially out of conviction and partially as a pose, because it drives Gene up the wall." Siskel found an explanation for the tangles of these two type-A personalities: "The best definition I've seen of our relationship is that it's a sibling rivalry and we both think that we're the smarter, older brother."

Ebert attributed this spot analysis to a 1977 talk show on which they appeared with Charles "Buddy" Rogers, who had been one of Mary Pickford's husbands as well as the star of the very first Academy Award winner for best picture, William A. Wellman's silent World War I epic, *Wings* (1927). "He said, you guys have a sibling rivalry, but you both think you're the older brother," Ebert remembered. Ebert also said that he and Siskel both thought the same things were funny. "That might be the best sign of intellectual communion," Ebert wrote from a 2008 point of view.

Both sorted issues alive in individual movies and talked about them at length—a performance, the portrayal of children, the cinematography—and, despite their thumbs-up or thumbs-down decisions, weighed a picture's complexity and minor merits before making their final decisions. They took the latitude afforded for wide and complex opinions allotted by their newspapers and applied that as best they could to the TV format. They couldn't do that every time, but they squeezed as much nuance and detail into 30 minutes as they possibly could.

They did theme shows on such topics as colorization of black-and-white films and the letterboxing of films originally shot in wide-screen formats. The duo reached a nadir of sorts when, for showmanship's sake, they brought in trained critters to introduce the dog or the stinker of the week. "If I look back on the tapes of the early shows," Ebert said, "I find it startling that Gene and I agreed to work with a trained dog. And I find it even more startling that we later agreed to work with a trained skunk. . . . And even at that time, Gene and I used to ask each other, 'do you think Pauline Kael would appear on television with a trained animal?'"

The thumbs took some getting used to. "One of the things that get[s] me is that we're usually quoted as 'two thumbs up!'" Ebert griped in 1991. "I liked it better before we had the thumbs. Then, at least, you were allowed to have an opinion, like 'I enjoyed this movie' or 'a hilarious film.' It's almost like the two of us are little jack-in-the-boxes and all we can say is 'two thumbs up!—Siskel and Ebert.' We have plenty of reviews that are somewhere around the middle. You just have to jump one way or the other because of this idiotic business of being able to vote only thumbs up or thumbs down. I'd like to give a sideways thumb occasionally."

The debate that television critics were ruining traditional film criticism hit the fan in a big way in 1990, when Richard Corliss and Ebert battled on the pages of *Film Comment*, the national magazine that had become an outpost of good, informed, intelligent film criticism. Corliss was stepping down as the magazine's editor, making way for Richard T. Jameson. In his valedictory essay "All Thumbs: Or, Is There a Future for Film Criticism?" Corliss wrote that Jeffrey Lyons, an ubiquitous film critic in the 1980s and 1990s for various ABC and NBC affiliates, "isn't a film critic, but he plays one on TV. The resident movie sage on PBS's *Sneak Previews* and superstation WPIX, Lyons has no thoughts, no wit, no perspective worth sharing with his audience. To anyone knowledgeable about pictures, he is a figure of sour mirth.

"In today's movie criticism, less is more," Corliss continued. "Shorter is sweeter. Today's busy consumers want just the clips, ma'am. And an opinion that can be codified in numbers, letters, or thumbs. . . . On *Siskel and Ebert and the Movies*, the critics play Roman emperors and award a thumbs-down condemnation or a thumbs-up reprieve. . . . The print guys will quote with approval the observation of ABC-TV's Joel Siegel, who told *Theater Week* magazine, 'Frank Rich [theatre critic of *The New York Times*] got hired because he could write. I got hired because I can read.' They will surely scoff at Lyons's prickly pretensions when he accuses his print brethren of jealousy: 'They resent our money and exposure. They look down their noses at us. And that's the reason I make a point of being called a critic as opposed to a reviewer. It's my way of saying I'm doing exactly what they're doing.'"

Corliss emphasized, "The long view of cinema aesthetics is irrelevant to a moviegoer for whom history began with *Star Wars*. . . . Movie criticism of the elevated sort, as practiced over the past half-century by James Agee, and Manny Farber, Andrew Sarris and Pauline Kael, J. Hoberman and Dave Kehr—in the mainstream press and in magazines like *Film Comment*—is an endangered species. . . . Soon it may perish, to be replaced by a consumer service that is no brains and all thumbs."

Corliss had crystallized a notion that had been at large for some time in film criticism circles, that the TV critics, particularly Siskel and Ebert, were dumbing down the profession. By the 1990s, Siskel and Ebert were institutions, more known than many of stars they interviewed. They and their TV-show style were memorialized by satirists on *Saturday Night Live* and *In Living Color*. Cartoonist Mort Drucker paid them tribute in *Mad* magazine with "Sissy and Ebore at the Movies." Their format and styles were lampooned in three 1987 movies: Robert Townsend's *Hollywood Shuffle*, Lyndall Hobbs's *Back to the Beach*, and Carl Reiner's *Summer School*.

Both critics realized the place they had attained in popular culture, but also admitted that they were flabbergasted when TV legends Bob Hope and Danny Thomas satirized them on one of Hope's NBC specials. Siskel and Ebert were cohosts on *Saturday Night Live* and did the talk-show circuit, appearing alongside Johnny Carson, Jay Leno, Oprah Winfrey, David Letterman, and others. Both critics agreed to avoid film roles and commercials, which were frequently offered. "We don't feel it's proper, as long as we're film critics," Ebert said. They maintained ethical standards in a profession that they led across the straddling of media, standards that were elsewhere eroded.

Ebert didn't need to rebut Corliss in *Film Comment*, a 40,000-circulation, New York-based magazine run by and written for cinephiles—an oracle that for all intents and purposes functioned as the keeper of film-criticism tradition in America. But Ebert is, as Jonathan Rosenbaum writes, "a hard-core film buff," part of that tradition, central to it, a keeper of it, unlike many self-styled "critics." And he's tenacious, as Siskel readily testified. Ebert wasn't about to take a shot from the central bunker of the serious film criticism camp without firing back.

The Chicago icon responded with "All Stars: Or, Is There a Cure for Criticism of Film Criticism?," which *Film Comment* published in the 1990 edition following Corliss's blistering attack. Ebert agreed that the quick-info thumbs and star ratings had taken over, but added, "What Corliss does not realize is that this is an improvement, not a deterioration, of the situation as we both found it in the mid-Sixties when we started in the business of writing about films. That was a time when there was no regular film criticism on local or national TV. Film magazines did not appear on the newsstands; although *Film Quarterly* and *Film Comment* were being published, few outside academia and the film industry knew about them. . . .

"Yet what about film criticism in these dark ages?" Ebert asked rhetorically. "It is thriving. There is more of it than ever before. Corliss can be forgiven, I think, for the elegiac tone of his farewell article; he is saying goodbye to *Film Comment* after many productive and valuable years. . . . But at least part of his discontent is a textbook case of mid-career crisis. . . . What strikes me as slightly disingenuous is his lament for serious film criticism. . . . Corliss' apocalyptic vision notwithstanding, good film criticism is commonplace these days. *Film Comment* itself is healthier and more widely distributed than ever. *Film Quarterly* is, too. . . . At the top of the circulation pyramid is the glossy *Premiere*, rich with ads and filled with knowledgeable articles that are not all just puff pieces about the stars."

Ebert surveyed the landscape and found it rich with critics. "Kael, our paradigm, continues at *The New Yorker*," he wrote. "Kauffmann gets more sense into less space than any other critic alive, at *The New Republic*. Denby is at *New York*, Rosenbaum at the *Chicago Reader*, Hoberman at *The Village Voice*, Mark Crispin Miller just had a cover story in the *Atlantic*. . . . The weekly *Reader* in Chicago [and *Village Voice* before it], born in 1969, has spawned a new kind of national newspaper, the give-away lifestyle weekly, and each of these papers—*The* [*Boston*] *Phoenix*, *LA Weekly*, etc.— has its own resident auteurist or deconstructionist.

"Daily newspaper film criticism at the national level is better and deeper than it was in Corliss' golden age," Ebert contended. "Corliss mentions the invaluable Dave Kehr of the *Chicago Tribune*. Has he read Michael Sragow in San Francisco, Sheila Benson and Peter Rainer in Los Angeles, Jay Scott in Toronto, Howie Movshovitz and Bob Denerstein in Denver, Jay Carr in Boston, Jeff Millar in Houston, Philip Wuntch in Dallas?"

Ebert, in a footnote, corrected Corliss on the latter's assumption that TV reviews are always shorter than print reviews. Ron Shelton's *Blaze* (1989) was discussed in 755 words on *Siskel and Ebert* and with only 324 words in Corliss's reviewing venue, *Time*; Kathryn Bigelow's *Blue Steel* (1990) received 864 words on the show, while *Time* handled it in 267 words. Ebert agreed that his TV format didn't allow for in-depth criticism, but chided Corliss for cavalierly treating his and Siskel's show, and pointed out that it had aired segments or whole shows on colorization, letterboxing, Spike Lee, black-and-white cinematography, laserdiscs, product placement, and the Motion Picture Association of America's rating system.

Ebert urged Corliss to look at another problem: "I submit to Richard Corliss that he missed the real source of distemper in today's American film market, and that is the ascendency of the marketing campaign, and the use of stars as bait to orchestrate such campaigns," Ebert wrote. ". . . Hollywood has never been more star-driven than at this moment, and publishers and producers have never been more eager to get their piece of the star of the week. . . . The sad fact is that film criticism, serious or popular, good or bad, printed or on TV, has precious little power in the face of a national publicity juggernaut for a clever mass-market entertainment."

If not on the lasting and legendary scale of Pauline Kael vs. Andrew Sarris in the 1960s, Corliss vs. Ebert shook out the main issues of the day. Corliss added a kicker to what he called this "civilized debate" that was appended to Ebert's response. "Devising copy for the publicity machine need not be a despicable craft (I still treasure *USA Today*'s critic Mike Clark's appraisal of some forgettable actioner: 'makes Rambo look like Rambeau'), but it's not what I'd put first on my job application. For Roger Ebert, that function is even more confining. Ads usually yoke him to Siskel, Siamese-twin style, and quote him not with an adjective but with a thumb. I'll bet that sometimes," Corliss concluded, "he'd like it to be a finger."

Ebert appreciated the fracas with Corliss, and eventually included it in his anthology, *Awake in the Dark: The Best of Roger Ebert; Forty Years of Reviews, Essays, and Interviews* (2006) from the University of Chicago Press.

In a lesser print fracas, Ebert defended his TV work apart from Siskel. The *Sun-Times* legend became the centerpiece of criticism in the *Los Angeles Times* in 1994 concerning the perceptions of a critic's duties—what one should and shouldn't do on TV. Pulitzer Prize-winning *Times* TV critic Howard Rosenberg lambasted Ebert in print after the Academy Awards. On Oscar day, Ebert hosted a locally televised pre-show gab-a-thon, and the TV critic questioned whether the film critic was behaving appropriately. The headline on Rosenberg's March 23 column read: "The Eberts: The New Awards for Fawning," with the subhead: "The film critic thumbs his nose at objectivity hosting KABC's pre-Oscar schmoozefest—a job he seems born for."

Rosenberg thought Ebert's casual turn at celeb-yakking was a job reserved for happy softball-toss personalities such as

Regis Philbin. Of course, Ebert has never been one to take any journalistic assault lying down. Ebert's April 4 "Counterpunch" piece in the *Times* chided Rosenberg for lacking a sense of humor in a general defense. Ebert said he "had a jolly good time," and "I never have any difficulty in telling the truth about a movie, even if I've interviewed one of its participants." He also said he paid his own way when attending junkets. Ebert's capper both revealed his own sense of humor and underscored his critical power.

"Writing truthful reviews is what a critic does," Ebert wrote, defining his job; he then defined himself: "But I am not only a film critic. I am also an interviewer, a raconteur, a friend, a fan, a gossip, a teller of jokes, a teacher of classes, a writer of books, a sketcher of pictures, a host of pre-Oscar telecasts. I am even online. I am large, Mr. Rosenberg. I contain multitudes."

As it appeared that Siskel and Ebert were about to enter the new century still yoked together, as Corliss put it, fate took a turn. Early in 1998, Ebert began to notice that Siskel would sometimes get things out of order, then that the latter needed consistent private briefing during a benefit gala that they both hosted. Later, Siskel said he had severe headaches before a Jay Leno telecast during which the Chicago critics were to judge Leno lookalikes. "My headache is too bad to focus on it," Ebert remembered Siskel saying. "You do it, and I'll agree with everything you say. You can look amazed. We can make it a shtick."

Soon after, Siskel underwent brain surgery to remove a tumor at Memorial Sloan-Kettering Cancer Center in New York City. Tom Shales, who had panned the show in *The Washington Post*, agreed to fill in for Gene. That summer, Siskel came back to the *Tribune*, back to regular screenings and the show for the remainder of 1998 and into 1999. For his final shows, Ebert wrote, the set was cleared so Siskel's nephew could walk him to his theatre seat. "His pain must have been unimaginable," Ebert wrote. "But he continued to do his job, and I never admired him more.

"Our eyes would meet, unspoken words were between us, but we never spoke openly about his problems or his prognosis," Ebert remembered. "That's how he wanted it, and that was his right." Ebert said he and Siskel once discussed a sitcom project with Disney and CBS that would mirror their lives and professions, called *Best Enemies*. "Maybe the problem was that no one else could possibly understand how meaningless was the hate, how deep was the love," Ebert wrote.

"I'm in a hurry to get well because I don't want Roger to get more screen time than I," Siskel wrote in the February 3, 1999, edition of the *Chicago Tribune*, announcing a leave of absence. On February 20, he died in Evanston Hospital, near Chicago, of complications from the original operation. He was 53. He is survived by his wife, Marlene, and three children.

"I will miss Siskel as the friend who entered my home every Sunday night beside his partner, Roger Ebert, with whom he shared a platform that made them the most influential movie critics ever," wrote Howard Rosenberg in the *Los Angeles Times*. "And with whom he shared the fruits of a vast movie-reviewing franchise that made them more famous than most of the actors they critiqued, and made superstars of their thumbs. Their *thumbs*. Talk about marketing genius."

Since the death of Siskel in 1999, Ebert plugged along with his half-hour syndicated review program and as the most recognized film critic in the land. He temporarily offered Siskel's old seat to a variety of critics, including Shales, Todd McCarthy of *Daily Variety*, and a committee of Chicago-based scribes including the *Chicago Tribune*'s Michael Wilmington and the *Chicago Reader*'s Jonathan Rosenbaum. But in the fall of 2000, Richard Roeper, a columnist and sometime film reviewer from Ebert's own *Chicago Sun-Times*, became a full-fledged partner, and the show was renamed *Ebert & Roeper & the Movies*.

The reception for the youthful looking Roeper was partially rude. "His huffs aren't as tough as Siskel's were," wrote Ken Tucker in *Entertainment Weekly*. "Roeper's slender thumb doesn't carry the authority of a man, who, at the very least, had sat through more movies in one year, good and bad, than most of us will see in a lifetime. There's a lot to be said for having a basis for comparison, and Roeper's judgments so far—'there's nobody else like Danny DeVito,' he enthused recently—don't fill me with confidence even as consumer guidance."

By the summer of 2008, Ebert had been off the program that bore his name for two years, fighting cancer of the jaw, unable to speak. It had been nearly a decade since his original TV partner, Gene Siskel, died of a brain tumor in 1999. *Ebert & Roeper & the Movies* officially ended in August 2008. Richard Roeper also left the air in a contract dispute. Ebert continued at his base of operations, writing reviews and features for the *Sun-Times* and his blog at the paper's Web site. Roeper, a columnist at the paper, also continued writing.

Meanwhile, Disney-ABC Domestic Television continued the dual-critics show with a pair of third-generation entertainment scions. Ben Lyons, 26, Jeffrey's son, was the third in the Lyons lineage on the entertainment beat, and the first TV film critic son of another TV film critic. Both Jeffrey and Ben Lyons invariably used the moniker "Lyons Den" for their entertainment beat reporting, Jeffrey on WCBS Radio from 1975 to 1993, and Ben for a blog on E! Online. Known as the "movie dude" on E! Entertainment Television, Lyons, who also critiqued movies on MTV, got his start by joining his father and British host Alison Bailes to present *Reel Talk*, a short-lived 2005 NBC talk show about movies.

Lyons received a rude reception in 2008 when he joined Ben Mankiewicz, 41, a frequent host on Turner Classic Movies on the Walt Disney Company's retooling of *At the Movies*. The basic format of two guys reviewing between clips of the new releases was retained. The vitriol expressed would have surprised Rex Reed, or even the elder Lyons. Relatively young movie-show hosts John Burke on AMC and Richard Roeper received rude receptions when they stepped into the shoes of longtime favorites, but the blanket ire Lyons received was special.

"With his meat-and-potatoes good looks, frat-boy bonhomie, and straight-down-the-pike delivery—more reminiscent of a *SportsCenter* commentator than an erudite cultural arbiter—

Lyons is certainly not your father's movie reviewer," wrote Chris Lee in the *Los Angeles Times*. "But it's his way of shrinking a sweeping critical pronouncement down to glossy sound-bite size that seems to most affront Lyons' detractors. Especially," Lee added, "when held up to his predecessors' standards." Lyons "crystallizes everything that's wrong with American pop culture right now," said Scott Johnson, who operates StopBen Lyons.com.

The cry of nepotism that is peripherally cited as the reason Lyons got the *At the Movies* job wasn't leveled at Mankiewicz, the grandson of screenwriter Herman J. Mankiewicz, who wrote *Citizen Kane* (1941) with Orson Welles, and the nephew of Academy Award winner Joseph L. Mankiewicz, who wrote and directed *A Letter to Three Wives* (1949), *All About Eve* (1950), and others. The Disney-ABC show went on without the thumbs. The trademark for thumbs-up and thumbs-down is owned by Siskel's widow, Marlene Iglitzen, and Ebert.

"Ben and Ben could well prove the critics wrong," wrote Christopher Borrelli, former film critic of the *Toledo Blade*, in the *Chicago Tribune*. "I hope they do. But what chills the blood is that film criticism has been so diminished in recent years that Disney-ABC didn't even attempt to replace reputation with reputation, or continue what Gene Siskel and Roger Ebert started. It's like replacing Peter Jennings and Tom Brokaw with Star Jones and Ryan Seacrest."

Ebert's endurance on the film criticism landscape has been mirrored across generations in all media by Leonard Maltin. The author and organizing editor of the *TV Movies* film-capsule annual as well as the author of *The Great Movie Comedians*, *The Disney Films*, and many other books, Maltin used a 1982 guest appearance on *The Today Show* as a springboard to a television career.

"I was on *The Today Show*, plugging one of my books, being interviewed by Gene Shalit," Maltin remembered. "He was in a lively mood, and we really had a great interview. Someone from Paramount Television saw me, and they interviewed me for *Entertainment Tonight*, and that's the whole story." The bearded and bespectacled Maltin functioned as a film critic, historian, interviewer, and feature reporter for the venerable *Entertainment Tonight* while maintaining his multimedia writing career.

Born in New York City, Maltin grew up in Teaneck, New Jersey, the son of an immigration law judge and a former nightclub singer. He became enamored of the *Our Gang* series, Laurel and Hardy and other comics, and Walt Disney's Sunday night TV show. Considering a career in cartooning in his early teens, Maltin was a proactive sort of precocious, finding Rube Goldberg's name in the Manhattan telephone book and setting up an interview, writing to Charles M. Schulz and Jay Ward and getting positive responses. He began writing articles for the Vancouver, Canada-based *Film Fan Monthly* and eventually took over its publication at age 16. He was editor and publisher of the monthly through 1974 while he took journalism courses at New York University. He had already been approached to do the first version of the variously titled home-viewing bible, first known as *TV Movies*, which was published in 1969.

Because of his affable nature, which was amplified by TV, Maltin was occasionally pegged for a lightweight critic early on, but as a hardcore film aficionado, he can draw on an encyclopedic memory of the movies. Maltin has taken special pleasure in elucidating specific performances in the careers of such character actors as Nigel Bruce, Frank Cady, or Blanche Yurka, and, in fact, edited three books on character actors. As historian George Rehauer wrote in *Cinema Booklist* about Maltin's book *The Great Movie Shorts* (1972), "the author has researched his work with such diligence that he establishes a standard that will be difficult for most writers to meet."

The great care with which Maltin composed his books was transferred to his TV career, and he struck a balance that could satisfy both the novice and the buff, and spoke to adults as well as kids without homogenization or condescension. His skill as a TV communicator was more polished than, say, Ebert's. "Maltin has a unique ability to create film-knowledge excitement in the average person without being too technical or condescending," said George Feltenstein, former director of video programming for Metro-Goldwyn-Mayer. "He has a way of making the historical aspect of film interesting to anyone. I think that's his real gift."

Both Maltin and Ebert relied on their film expertise to expand their influences and transcend media like no other critics. Both became cottage industries unto themselves. A.O. Scott, film critic of *The New York Times*, used A.J. Liebling's self-assessment to describe Ebert: "Nobody who writes faster can write better, and nobody better is faster." A similar statement might be applied to Maltin.

Ebert always saw himself first and foremost as a newspaperman. The introduction to his PBS-era shows with Siskel had both of them grabbing editions of newspapers as if to signify their print bases. Ebert's role as critic of the *Chicago Sun-Times* has been his vocational center. The TV show, other TV work, the syndication of his reviews to other newspapers, and his books, including the annual *Roger Ebert's Video Companion*, organically grew out of his *Sun-Times* notoriety. "I'm not a performer; I'm a writer, and I'd just as soon not be recognized," Ebert told *Editor & Publisher* in 1987. "The question from most people that gets me the most is, 'Where's Gene?' My answer usually is, 'Who Cares?' Believe it or not, I was a movie critic before the TV show, and I'm still a movie critic."

Maltin maintained that *Entertainment Tonight* was the engine driving his own mini-empire. "*E.T.* is priority one," he said in 1990. "It's my soapbox, my job center. Here, I have the ability to reach 10 to 20 million people. I've been able to introduce aspects of film history that couldn't or wouldn't get shown anywhere else. I've done segments here on Erich von Stroheim, Fritz Lang, and Michael Powell. I seek to do unusual and offbeat stuff. When I do my spots, I feel that I may introduce someone to some aspect of film history that will enlighten or inform them on something that he or she may not have been exposed to before. That makes me feel good—doing missionary work for movie history."

Maltin has stayed the course and enjoyed more than a quarter of a century on the same show. He has also been a regular on the Starz cable network, and has hosted the syndicated radio program *Leonard Maltin on Video* and the syndicated TV show *Hot Ticket* with Boston film critic Joyce Kulhawik. He was hosting the show *Secret's Out* on ReelzChannel as this book went to press. Maltin has been president of the Los Angeles Film Critics Association, and taught at the New School for Social Research in New York City and the University of Southern California. In his twenties, Maltin edited a series of cinema history books for Popular Library.

Not to lump together Ebert with Maltin more than either critic should be with the other—especially after the Chicago icon hated so much to be consistently joined at the hip with Siskel—but both portly, bespectacled TV successes have also been front-rank educators, arbiters, and writers about film as art for several generations, with more than two dozen books apiece. "It is this print corpus that will sustain Mr. Ebert's reputation as one of the few authentic giants in a field in which self-importance frequently overshadows accomplishment," A.O. Scott wrote.

It is also the understanding by viewers that Maltin, as well as Ebert, was thoroughly steeped in film aesthetics, historical context, styles of individual directors, genre developments, knowledge of criticism, film history in other countries, and changes on the cinema landscape made by technology and economics. The viewers who grasp the rudimentary frameworks of those same subjects detect a thorough understanding in Ebert and Maltin, recognizing the expertise in their TV work. Both men built trust by rote in the shorthand world of TV.

While Ebert and Maltin followed through on missions to be astute and informative, other pundits began peopling local newscasts with the desire to become famous. Viewers could be informed by them even as their opinions often came dispensed in glib gab and via the clip-and-clap trade. These TV critics prompted Patrick Goldstein to write in the *Los Angeles Times*,

"Making a sale—as a performer—is what separates TV critics from their print peers."

Gary Franklin was a particularly bombastic case. A German-born radio news reporter for 25 years in Virginia and then Los Angeles, Franklin was hired as a full-time film critic on KNXT-TV, the forerunner of KCBS-TV, in Los Angeles in 1981, replacing David Sheehan as entertainment editor, before moving to KABC-TV in 1986, where he remained through 1991. From 1992 through 1995, Franklin was an entertainment reporter at KCOP-TV in Los Angeles. Franklin became known beyond his Southern California audience for his method of rating movies.

"On a scale of one to 10," he traditionally intoned in a staccato-like delivery, "10 being best, So-and-So is a . . . seven!" Franklin's shtick became water-cooler and schoolyard fodder. He was satirized onscreen, in Steve Sharon's screenplay for Clint Eastwood's fifth and final turn as Dirty Harry Callahan in Buddy Van Horn's *The Dead Pool* (1988). Dirty Harry's serial-killer investigation includes the tongue-in-cheek treatment of the murder of San Francisco's most visible TV film critic, who used a method and phrasing similar to Franklin's. Franklin, who relished all the attention, tooled around L.A. in a car whose license plate read: "ONE 2 TEN."

"The problem is that many critics find it hard to differentiate recognition from influence," Goldstein wrote in the *Times*. "Give Gary Franklin credit—he recently acknowledged, 'the day I lose my job, nobody will give me a screening anymore.'" There was the notion among Franklin watchers that his flamboyance and enthusiasm got the better of his levelheadedness. Franklin declared that John D. Hancock's prison drama, *Weeds* (1987), "will stand for a long time as a great American film classic long after you and I are dead." Franklin passed away in October 2007 at the age of 79 and his claim about *Weeds* has yet to come to pass.

"Bobbing his bald, conical head vigorously, he rates films with the arch, over-enunciated manner of a schoolmarm lecturing a sixth-grade science class," Goldstein wrote in 1983, noting that it was difficult to take a critic seriously who "scores movies as if they were earthquakes."

Franklin detested sex and violence in movies. "I have always let my social conscience influence my criticism," he said. "People should be speaking out about the effects of movie violence, brutality and sexuality in the world, and I'm glad I've had the chance to make a tiny impact. . . . That's how I'd like to be remembered. And perhaps for having saved [my viewers] a few bucks here and there."

Alek Keshishian's documentary on Madonna, *Madonna: Truth or Dare* (1991), earned a "minus five" from Franklin. Oliver Stone's *Natural Born Killers* (1994), which Franklin deemed a "cultural crime," earned, on a scale of one to 10, a "minus five." Conversely, Franklin's enthusiasm for certain films helped them succeed. Independent theatre chain owner Bob Laemmle said that Franklin's continual mention of *Runaway Train* (1985) as a picture to see helped save it from oblivion.

Franklin's competition on the local Los Angeles TV airwaves was David Sheehan. "Watching KNBC's Channel 4 critic David Sheehan is like viewing a TV image doubling back on itself," Goldstein wrote. "With his arched eyebrows and vague air of superiority, Sheehan most closely resembles the reviewer character that Bill Murray used to play on *Saturday Night Live*. He's not a critic. He's a parody of a parody of a critic."

"All stories are two to three minutes long," said Sheehan, a former actor. "Even on the biggest national news story, you're limited in terms of your segment time. In the two or three minutes that I have, I try to give the viewer as comprehensive an idea as possible . . . of the overall feeling of any particular film . . . so that a viewer almost can make up his or her own mind. If I do my job right, you might like a movie for the very reasons that I don't," Sheehan said in 1988.

Sheehan has said that he is supplied with three to eight clips per film to choose from by studio marketing departments, and "most of the time they give you exactly what is needed to describe the story and to give the character definitions. Most of the studios are pretty good." But studios occasionally supply clips that sell the movie more than inform the viewer. "Not more than once a month, I'll get a batch of clips that are not what I want." Whether the clips pertain to the aspects Sheehan wanted to concentrate on or not, the clips selected for airing usually do what the studio marketers want, which is sell the movie.

"The one advantage we have over other media is that we can show scenes from the movie," Franklin told the *Los Angeles Times* in 1988. "You [the *Times*] can't do that. Only we can do that, which in the final analysis is probably the most important part of our review. I let the scenes often speak for themselves."

PBS continued to air *Sneak Previews* after Siskel and Ebert departed for greener pastures with Tribune Entertainment in 1982. Taking over initially as hosts were Neal Gabler and Jeffrey Lyons. Gabler, the film critic for *Monthly Detroit*, stayed on the show for three years. Michael Medved replaced him in 1984 and stayed on with Lyons for nearly 12 years.

The bespectacled Lyons was the son of celebrated *New York Post* columnist Leonard Lyons, who wrote the syndicated "Lyons Den" from 1934 to 1974 as a contemporary of such Broadway beat columnists as Walter Winchell, Sam Zolotow, and Ed Sullivan. Jeffrey Lyons was a cohost on *Sneak Previews* from 1982 to 1996. A survivor in the TV film criticism trade, Lyons also was film critic for *WNBC Today* in New York from 1992 to 1993; for WPIX-TV in New York and WABC-TV *World News Now* in Washington, D.C., from 1994 to 1996; for WFSB-TV in Hartford, Connecticut; and for WMAR-TV in Baltimore.

"Jeffrey Lyons is big on S-words," wrote Patrick Goldstein in 1988 in the *Los Angeles Times*. "In recent months, he's touted *Planes, Trains and Automobiles* as "SEARINGLY FUNNY!," *Wall Street* as "STUNNING!," *Dirty Dancing* as "SENSATIONAL!," *No Way Out* as "SEARING!," *Baby Boom* as "SASSY!," and *Stakeout* as "A SIZZLER!"

Lyons's *Sneak Preview* partners were interested in aspects of popular culture that propelled them in different directions. The Chicago-born Gabler graduated from the University of Michigan with degrees in film and American culture and he taught at Michigan and Penn State before he was selected from a field of 300 candidates as one of PBS's replacements for Siskel and Ebert. A prolific freelance writer, Gabler contributed articles to *Esquire*, *Playboy*, *Brill's Content*, *The New York Times*, *The New Republic*, *American Heritage*, and other periodicals, and the PBS notoriety led to his appearances as a guest or analyst on *The Today Show*, *The CBS Morning News*, *The News Hour with Jim Lehrer*, *Entertainment Tonight*, and *Good Morning America*. When American Movie Classics used multiple hosts in the early 2000s, Gabler introduced movies on weekends and on *Director's Showcase* on Wednesday nights. Until February 2008, Gabler was also a panelist on *Fox News Watch*.

Gabler's largest contributions on the cultural landscape were certainly his distinguished books. *An Empire of Their Own: How the Jews Invented Hollywood* (1989) won the Los Angeles Times Book Prize for history. Gabler's *Winchell: Gossip, Power, and the Culture of Celebrity* (1995), which was adapted into *Winchell* (1998), the Emmy Award-winning HBO movie directed by Paul Mazursky, was named the nonfiction book of the year by *Time*. Gabler's third big book was his bulkiest and most cerebral, *Life: The Movie; How Entertainment Conquered Reality* (1999). The book traces American entertainment history, noting its affinity for the lowbrow, covering territory previously examined by Gilbert Seldes, Dwight Macdonald, and Pauline Kael. "Trash was deliberate," Gabler said. "Americans were literate. They chose trash because it was a glorification of the democratic impulse."

Michael Medved was born in Philadelphia in 1948, and raised in San Diego, California. He graduated from Yale University and began reviewing movies for CNN after a screenwriting stint in Hollywood. He was chief film critic for the *New York Post* from 1993 to 1998, giving up the job when he became a nationally syndicated radio talk show host for station KVI-570 in Seattle, eventually deciding on conservative social commentary over film criticism.

The Michael Medved Show aired on the Salem Radio Network after Medved guest-hosted Rush Limbaugh's nationally syndicated program. Medved's show is the result of an evolutionary politicizing of popular culture. He wrote *The Shadow Presidents: The Secret History of the Chief Executives and Their Top Aides* (1979), which led to his friendship with President Gerald Ford's chief of staff and future vice president, Dick Cheney. Medved wrote the best seller *What Ever Happened to the Class of '65*, with classmate David Wallechinsky about their high school class, and has written four books on bad movies with his kid brother, Harry Medved, who became the publicist for the Screen Actors Guild: *The Fifty Worst Films of All Time* (1978), *The Golden Turkey Awards* (1980), *The Hollywood Hall of Shame* (1984), and *The Son of Golden Turkey Awards* (1986).

The biggest-impact Medved book was *Hollywood vs. America* (1992), about what he considered to be the damaging impact of popular culture on America and especially on its youth and families. Medved married the author and clinical psychologist Diane Elvenstar, who had condemned the Medved brothers' *The Golden Turkey Awards* in a *Los Angeles Times* review. Michael Medved's Web site includes two untoward judgments on *Hollywood vs. America*, by filmmaker Michael Winner ("My worst read of the decade.") and David Denby ("This is the stupidest book about popular culture that I have ever read through to its conclusion.").

"A lot of reviewing is moralizing, making gross judgments," Richard Schickel told *Movieline* in 1993. "I used to be far more judgmental. Michael Medved is probably the prime example of that approach today. But moral judgments are the easiest to make, and they will not hold up over the years."

TV critics began sprouting up everywhere after the success of Siskel and Ebert. Although Joel Siegel became a critic for WABC-TV in New York in 1976, he reached a national audience in 1981 when he became the regular film critic for the parent network on *Good Morning America*. Born in Los Angeles and an alumnus of UCLA, Siegel became an advertising copy-writer who sold articles to *Rolling Stone, Los Angeles Times*, and other periodicals. He worked for Dr. Martin Luther King, Jr.'s Southern Christian Leadership Conference in Macon, Georgia, in 1965, and wrote jokes for Robert F. Kennedy's 1968 presidential campaign. Siegel was a news anchor for KMET-FM Radio in Los Angeles, then a correspondent for WCBS-TV in New York from 1972 to 1976, when he joined WABC-TV.

For his review of Richard Attenborough's *Magic* (1978), starring Anthony Hopkins as a ventriloquist, Siegel exploited the visual medium. "So I went and got a ventriloquist dummy and did the review, with me saying I liked the movie, and the dummy saying how he hated it," Siegel said. "So I got to do another review the next day. And I've kept that in mind, that every day is really an on-air audition." Siegel's endurance for 25 years on ABC was a testament to his mastery of the medium, where quick and catchy soundbites meant much more than supporting arguments for an opinion. During his career, Siegel won five New York-market Emmy Awards.

Siegel seemingly effortlessly skimmed credibility problems. He designated Andrew Bergman's *Striptease* (1996) "One of the summer's best!" on WABC-TV. The *Los Angeles Times* ran a graphic prominently carrying that quote to illustrate its story on critics who chronically offer up rave reviews, "The Movies' 'Riveting!' Blurb Mill," on March 24, 1997, directly beside a story announcing, "Demi Moore, *Striptease* Win 6 Razzies for Hollywood's Worst."

Siegel was diagnosed with colon cancer in 1997, and died in 2007 at the age of 63. Siegel cofounded the nonprofit Gilda's Club with actor Gene Wilder and others to offer emotional support for cancer sufferers and their families. "When Joel came into your office to talk about something, it was going to be interesting and you were going to learn something," said Charles Gibson, the ABC News anchor who had been host of *Good Morning America*. "He had an inexhaustible supply of stories—most funny, many poignant, all with a point or punch line."

While Siegel was a leading voice quoted in blurbs on movie posters, the studios began relying to a great degree on TV publicity in all its forms in the 1980s. As cable expanded the talk-show circuit beyond the usual forums of Johnny Carson, Tom Snyder, Merv Griffin, Dick Cavett, and Mike Douglas, others such as Charlie Rose, Oprah Winfrey, and Larry King became established.

Talkative stars, and occasionally directors, sat the circuit on the eves of their new films' releases. The cable explosion also brought about several services that offered something more for film buffs, film critics, and filmmakers. In greater Los Angeles, the Z Channel was more than an alternative; it became a showcase, and made room for the great unknown films and talents.

Begun in 1974 in cable's dark ages, the Z Channel evolved into a film lover's virtual heaven, especially after Jerry Harvey became head of programming in 1981. "A legitimate case can be made that the director's-cut craze on DVDs today can be traced back to Harvey's insistence on running complete cuts of films that had been butchered by studios," wrote G. Allen Johnson in the *San Francisco Chronicle*. These restored director's cuts included versions of such celebrated films as Sam Peckinpah's *The Wild Bunch* (1969), Michael Cimino's *Heaven's Gate* (1980) and Sergio Leone's *Once Upon a Time in America* (1984).

The channel's original programming included *On the Film Scene*, on which host Charles Champlin interviewed filmmakers and stars. Because the Z Channel reached so many movie industry homes in Los Angeles, it became influential in the Academy Awards races by repeatedly showing certain films in the year-end and year-beginning months, when members of the Academy of Motion Picture Arts and Sciences voted for the Oscar nominations and then the winners. Producer Charles Joffe credits the Z Channel's saturation playing of Woody Allen's *Annie Hall* (1977) during the voting season for its best picture Oscar. James Woods said that the Z Channel's repeats of Oliver Stone's *Salvador* (1986), in which he starred, helped him and Stone receive nominations for best actor and screenplay, respectively.

As HBO and other cable companies grew, the Z Channel became strapped for cash, and Harvey sold it to a Seattle outfit, which changed its format. Born in Bakersfield, California, and educated at UCLA, Harvey lived his life as a mostly functional alcoholic. Harvey's personal tragedies included the suicides of two elder sisters and one of his girlfriends. On April 9, 1988, after a night out with friends, Harvey shot and killed his wife, Deri Rudolph, then killed himself. The handgun was reportedly given to him by Peckinpah, who died in 1984.

The stories of Harvey and the Z Channel are twined in Xan Cassavetes's documentary, *Z Channel: A Magnificent Obsession* (2004), which featured commentary by film critics Champlin and Kevin Thomas of the *Los Angeles Times*, and film critic F.X. Feeney of the *LA Weekly*. Feeney, who had been Harvey's friend and chief programmer of the Z Channel, was a coproducer of the documentary.

Other cable networks showing offbeat films and innovative programming came to prominence, such as the Arts & Entertainment Network and Bravo, which debuted *Inside the Actors Studio* in 1994, hosted by James Lipton in a theatre filled with theatre and film students at the New School for Social Research in New York City. Interminably professorial, Lipton evoked the Sheridan Whiteside characteristics, relying on avowedly exhaustive notes on index cards for his interviews with film and TV actors. No one went Whiteside like Lipton, not even "Professor" Richard Brown during his New York University seminars aired on American Movie Classics.

While not technically a film critic, and never referred to as such, Lipton ingratiated his way into film scholarship by reciting an endless litany of awards and nominations received by a particular guest from all the critical groups in front of the honoree, with both the toadying of a valet and the gaudy intonation of Robert Goulet practicing *King Lear* in the mirror. Lipton's ripeness for parody wasn't lost on Will Ferrell, who created an even more over-the-top version than the original on *Saturday Night Live*. A former soap opera writer who acted for a decade on *The*

Guiding Light, Lipton married and divorced actress Nina Foch, wrote the Broadway musical *Sherry!* (1967), the novel *Mirrors* (1983), and was on the production team for Bob Hope TV specials. Perhaps it's not coincidental that Lipton adapted *Sherry!* from Kaufman and Hart's *The Man Who Came to Dinner*.

Lipton's shtick usually hasn't interfered with guests' often thoughtful and surprising answers and their communion with the New School upstarts. "What makes Bravo's *Inside the Actors Studio* interviews so fascinating aren't Lipton's hilariously arch questions, it's that performers (and sometimes directors) are talking to aspiring performers and directors," wrote film critic Jeff Simon in the *Buffalo News*. "They are telling them seriously in a way they simply can't when they're talking to Letterman, Leno, and Regis." However, Lipton's ritual of asking each guest his or her favorite curse word has remained part of the show's continuity.

While Lipton continued on his rapturous way as *Inside the Actors Studio* became an institution, intended film critic parodies became mainstays on TV. John Bloom, the film critic of the *Dallas Times-Herald*, created an alter ego in 1982, Joe Bob Briggs, whose reviews of lowbrow fare were channeled into the column "Joe Bob Goes to the Drive-In," which, as David Chute wrote in *American Film*, "siphoned off schlock items like *Bloodsucking Freaks* and *The Naked Cage*—films that John Bloom, 'serious film critic,' secretly enjoyed but found unreviewable." By 1984, the column was syndicated to 57 newspapers nationwide.

Joe Bob Briggs's unapologetically redneck, chauvinistic style was infused into descriptions of usually sleazy, violent, or low-budget (or all of these) movies, and end with tallies, often words with the suffix "-fu" to describe fights, and the usual kicker, "Joe Bob says, 'Check it out.'" Gory movies would be rated on the "vomit-meter." Sexual intercourse was euphemized as "aardvarking." Dead bodies were always counted. A typical Joe Bob review concluded, "No dead bodies, 117 breasts, multiple aardvarking, lap-dancing, cage dancing, convenience store dancing, blindfold aardvarking, blind-man aardvarking, lesbofu, pool-cue-fu, Drive-In Academy Award nomination for Tane McClure. Joe Bob says, 'Check it out.'"

The column, which created as many protests as it did ardent fans, was canceled by the *Times-Herald* management in 1986 when Joe Bob lampooned the celeb-filled fundraiser rock song and video of the USA-for-Africa cause, "We Are the World" as "We Are the Weird." The newspaper apologized on its front page, and the Los Angeles Times Syndicate canceled distribution of the column, after which the Universal Press Syndicate picked it up. Bloom resigned.

"The premise of ['We Are the Weird'] was that all the drive-in stars—Charles Bronson, Sybil Danning, Leatherface— are gathering in a recording studio in Grapevine, Texas, to do *their* idea of a benefit song for world hunger," Bloom recalled. "So you have that framework and you have Joe Bob's interpretation of what the event means, and then you have the song. So it's like the song is refracted through two different twisted lenses. The main thing about it was that it was a parody of African relief efforts, not a parody of starving Africans."

Bloom decided to take Joe Bob off the page and onto the stage, a first step, it turned out, toward television. *An Evening with Joe Bob Briggs*, a one-man show starring Bloom as Joe Bob, debuted in Cleveland in 1985. Later re-titled *Joe Bob Dead in Concert*, the show played more than 50 venues across America, including Caroline's in New York City and the Great American Music Hall in San Francisco. In 1986, Bloom signed on with The Movie Channel for Joe Bob to host *Drive-In Theater*, a late-night B-movie showcase that was renamed *Joe Bob's Drive-In Theater* and ran for a decade. Chris Aable, an actor and Los Angeles TV personality, was the sidekick, whose main job was to recline with a bevy of beautiful girls to make Joe Bob envious. The show received two CableACE Award nominations.

The Briggs shtick was transferred to TNT in 1996 sans Aable. This was *Monstervision*, featuring Joe Bob in a lawn chair near a pickup truck surrounded by junkyard ephemera, roasting hot dogs, with beer can and flyswatter in close reach. *Monstervi-*

sion lasted until 2000. All through his heyday as a lowbrow anti-dote to generally accepted film criticism, Bloom appeared on the talk-show circuit and was host of "God Stuff," a regular segment on the first two years (1996 to 1998) of *The Daily Show*, covering religion. Bloom has appeared in more than a dozen films, including Martin Scorsese's *Casino* (1995) and John Woo's *Face/ Off* (1997), and has written seven books as Joe Bob, including *A Guide to Western Civilization, or My Story* (1988), *The Cosmic Wisdom of Joe Bob Briggs* (1990), and *Profoundly Disturbing: Shocking Movies That Changed History!* (2003).

Like Joe Bob Briggs, *Mystery Science Theater 3000* took off from the vestiges of film criticism's world, and then became a phenomenon on its own, a cult favorite that was smartly written and performed. *MST3K*, as it came to be known, originated in 1988 at KTMA-TV in Hopkins, Minnesota, serving the Twin Cities, and ran on the Comedy Channel (later Comedy Central) from 1989 to 1996, and was picked up by the Sci Fi Channel from 1997 to 1999. A spin-off movie, *Mystery Science Theater 3000: The Movie* (1996), was issued by Gramercy Pictures.

The basic premise found a human space traveler and three robots stranded on an asteroid and forced by an evil scientist to watch terrible movies. That they did, in a theatre-like situation so that they were seated, silhouetted, with backs to the viewer at the bottom of the analog frame as the home viewer and the TV characters together watched abysmal films. However, the astronaut, Joel Robinson, played by the show's creator, Joel Hodgson, and his three sardonic robot pals, Crow T. Robot, Tom Servo, and Gypsy, kept up a running commentary on the film at hand, often a sci-fi entry or exploitation number. The gashouse humor, in-jokes, buffoonery, film-buff nuggets, camaraderie, and general, lively commentaries often coalesced into a hilarious whole. Among the nearly 200 films shown on *MST3K* were *Jungle Goddess* (1948), *The Saga of the Viking Women and Their Voyage to the Waters of the Great Sea Serpent* (1957), *First Spaceship on Venus* (1962), *The Robot vs. the Aztec Mummy* (1959), *Santa Claus Conquers the Martians* (1964), and *The Million Eyes of Sumuru*

(1967).

Bestowed with a Peabody Award in 1993 as "an ingenious eclectic series," *MST3K* was nominated for Emmy Awards for its writing in 1994 and 1995, and for CableACE Awards from 1992 through 1997. Leonard Maltin joined the good-natured ribbing on an *MST3K* episode during the ninth season to retract his positive review of *Gorgo* (1961). For his endurance as a film critic in the public consciousness for more than a generation, Maltin became, like Roger Ebert and Gene Siskel, ripe for the flattery of satire. Maltin was also discussed on *The Simpsons* and portrayed on *South Park*, helping rid the world of Barbra Streisand, who had morphed into an outsized monster-robot.

Showing classic movies and communicating information on films from Hollywood's past have received rather conventional presentations, with expert commentary by sage and learned ambassadors on the cable networks American Movie Classics and Turner Classic Movies.

On October 1, 1984, American Movie Classics was launched. The Jericho, New York-based cable network began broadcasting movies from throughout Hollywood history. However, after its first decade, AMC began to air more movies from the 1970s and later decades. The movies were hosted mainly by Bob Dorian, an owlish, schoolmasterly actor whose post-film wrap-ups were often followed by his brusque repeat commands leading to documentary shorts, "Now watch this!" as if there might be consequences if the viewer channel-surfed. Dorian's research was studious, and his historical perspective adequately framed the viewing experience. But his rigid authority lacked the scholarly depth or the earned trust of a Maltin. Dorian concentrated on star appeal and standard production and casting stories.

Dorian's work was supplemented by the suave and understated Nick Clooney, who was often the daytime host. Clooney had been a daytime host on WLWC-TV in Columbus, Ohio, then WCPO-TV, and later WKRC-TV in Cincinnati, and worked as newscaster for KNBC-TV in Los Angeles and as a columnist for the *Cincinnati Post* until it closed in 2008. The

Kentucky-born brother of singer-actress Rosemary Clooney, Nick Clooney made an unsuccessful run as the 2004 Democratic candidate for a U.S. House of Representatives seat in Kentucky. Clooney's greatest contribution to entertainment was his son, actor-director George Clooney.

AMC telecast New York University professor Richard Brown's interviews under two umbrella titles, *Reflections on the Silver Screen*, with such greats as Audrey Hepburn, Katharine Hepburn, James Stewart, and Robert Mitchum, and *Movies 101 on AMC*, with such contemporary personalities as Martin Scorsese, Jennifer Aniston, George Clooney, Meryl Streep, and Kevin Kline. Film critics made a few appearances on AMC to introduce favorite or neglected classics. Peter Rainer, for instance, introduced William A. Wellman's classic western about lynch injustice, *The Ox-Bow Incident* (1943), starring Henry Fonda and Dana Andrews.

AMC's youth movement arrived in 2001, when the young, chiseled, twinkle-eyed John Burke completely replaced the alternating old-school hosts, Dorian and Clooney. Many of Burke's introductory and closing commentaries came in vanilla and without toppings. "I'm sorry, but when this guy John Burke starts telling me how crucial John Ford was to cinema history, I snort, 'Ahh, you couldn't pick out Walter Brennan from Ward Bond in a lineup, ya punk!'" TV critic Ken Tucker wrote in *Entertainment Weekly*.

As if to compensate, the network also added Neal Gabler in 2001 as an on-air host. Engaging and informed, with epic books behind him on Walter Winchell and Jewish moguls who invented Hollywood, as well as an op-ed-page profile on big newspapers, Gabler gave the network more integrity in hosting than it ever had. But AMC underwent other changes in the new century, adding commercials, original programming, and movie-star introductions—Laurence Fishburne and Vince Vaughn hosting *Tough Guys*, for instance. Sharon Stone, Alec Baldwin, Renée Zellwegger, and Shirley Jones became semi-regular AMC hosts.

Washington Post TV critic Tom Shales called AMC "sloppier with its movies" than its growing competition, Turner Classic Movies, which began operating in 1994 with a viewing base of 1.1 million. TCM's subscribers eventually reached more than 50 million after the turn of the century, while AMC's reached more than 75 million. Shales hated AMC's addition of commercials in 2000. "It was a dirty trick to play on loyal viewers," he griped. "They haven't been the same since they banished Bob Dorian, anyway. Apparently they're trying to lower their demographic profile—partly by lowering the standards of the movies they show."

Conversely, TCM "has cultivated a loyal fan base of movie mavens without having to drastically change its simple, straightforward format," wrote Josh Chetwynd in 2001 in *USA Today*. "Every month, it shows about 300 classic movies. . . . Its primetime host, the encyclopedic Robert Osborne, has been with TCM since the beginning; and the network runs no commercials."

Robert Jolin Osborne was born in Colfax, Washington, on May 3, 1932. Osborne graduated from the University of Washington with a degree in journalism, and tried an acting career, securing a contract with Lucille Ball's Desilu Studios. The rangy Osborne had a small role as an assistant bank manager in the pilot of Desilu's *The Beverly Hillbillies*. As an actor, he appeared in commercials, but never flirted with thespian fame. Osborne joined *The Hollywood Reporter* in 1977 and has written the "Rambling Reporter" column since 1982. He was also a regular entertainment reporter on Los Angeles's KTTV-TV's 10 PM newscasts.

His book, *80 Years of the Oscar: The Official History of the Academy Awards*, has been updated periodically under other titles, lastly in 2008. Osborne served as president of the Los Angeles Film Critics Association from 1981 to 1983, and introduced films on The Movie Channel before TCM hired him in 1994.

Like Siskel and Ebert, Osborne wasn't a personality chosen, adapted, and tweaked by TV executives to form a composite that appealed to a wide demographic. A longtime Hollywood insider who had paid his dues, he made a difference to the discerning movie fan. Osborne's knowledge of movies, capacity for trivia, innate affability, and enthusiasm for his well-researched lore combined to make him a distinguished, knowledgeable, and trusted host. "You feel like it's not just a guy up there reading copy that people prepared for him to read," Richard Schickel told *The Washington Post*. "That's a good quality and increasingly rare in the television climate of our times. He's something a lot more than just a talking head."

Osborne, whom TV critic Shales called "ultra-erudite," continued to be the nearly exclusive host on TCM, as the network has made very few changes since its inception. TCM consistently programmed genre blocks of films, director blocks, star blocks, and displayed a laudable tendency to air little-seen films from the 1930s, and even a Sunday-night tradition of showing classic and often rare silent movies. TCM has remained noncommercial, straightforward, informative, and unpretentious—a resource, and occasionally a forum, for critics. Ted Turner bought the 1,700-film MGM film library in 1986 for $1.2 billion, and TCM owns the rights to all Warner Bros. films before 1950 in addition to the RKO Radio Pictures library.

On the Osborne-hosted *The Essentials*, classic films selected by one critic, filmmaker, or actor are shown with that person's introductory and closing remarks with Osborne. Film critic Molly Haskell found a bigger constituency in 2006 on TCM than she ever enjoyed on the page, talking with Osborne about Robert Rossen's *The Hustler* (1961), John Frankenheimer's *The Manchurian Candidate* (1962), and other favorites. *The Essentials* also brought out Peter Bogdanovich for one of his returns to film scholarship. Other guests on *The Essentials* have included Rob Reiner, Sydney Pollack, Carrie Fisher, Rose McGowan, and Alec Baldwin.

On *Private Screenings*, Osborne has interviewed dozens of stars, who seem enthusiastic to schmooze with him. Like Charles Champlin, Osborne has an easy, living-room style, and it's tailored to a cable service with many older viewers. Yet Osborne's interviews are not softballs and sugar. His interviewees have included Leslie Caron, Jane Fonda, James Garner, Sidney Lumet, and the tandems of Robert Mitchum and Jane Russell, and Jack Lemmon and Walter Matthau.

In 2008, TCM aired *Elvis Mitchell: Under the Influence*, featuring the former *Fort Worth Star-Telegram* (1998 to 2000) and *New York Times* (2000 to 2004) film critic and National Public Radio commentator doing one-on-one studio interviews with such guests as Bill Murray, Quentin Tarantino, Sydney Pollack, Joan Allen, Laurence Fishburne, and Edward Norton.

"It isn't, by the way, that Mitchell asks remarkably astute questions during those [Sydney] Pollack and [Bill] Murray interviews," film critic Jeff Simon wrote in the *Buffalo News*. "It is just as valuable, if not more so, to present an interview subject with someone they actually want to give an intelligent and candid answer to. That's why Mitchell is a great TV interviewer about movies and these people know it. He truly understands whatever they are going to say."

The growing number of TV, radio, and online Internet critics were represented by the Broadcast Film Critics Association, which was founded in 1995 by Rod Lurie and Joey Berlin and grew into the largest film critics organization in the United States and Canada, representing nearly 200 individuals by 2009. "Our collective membership is the primary source of information for today's entertainment consumers," the BFCA Web site says. "The very first opinion a moviegoer hears about new releases at the multiplex or the art house usually comes from one of our members."

A declaration of standards is also posted on the Web site: "All film reviews represent the unique and honest opinion of the authoring member. Any attempt to influence a review beyond providing information is a violation of BFCA standards. 'Quotes' may only be provided from reviews that have been, will be or are intended to be broadcast or printed, and cannot be altered in any way without the expressed permission of the reviewer." The criteria for membership is that a potential member provide a large television, radio or Internet audience with subjective assessments of the quality of motion pictures being released theatrically.

Among the TV members in the 21st century were several print-electronic media crossover critics, such as Duane Dudek of WTMJ-TV and the *Milwaukee Journal Sentinel* and Jack Garner of Gannett Newspapers, the *Rochester Democrat and Chronicle* and WHAM-TV, as well as Rod Gustafson of CFCN-TV in Calgary, Terry Hunter of KGMB-TV in Honolulu, Jake Hamilton of KHOU-TV in Houston, Sandy Kenyon of WABC-TV in New York, Shep Morgan of KCAL-TV in Los Angeles, Jim O'Brien of WEWS-TV in Cleveland, George Pennacchio of KABC-TV in Los Angeles, David Ramsay of KPHO-TV in Phoenix, Sam Rubin of KTLA-TV in Los Angeles, Rachel Smith of KVVU-TV in Las Vegas, Lee Thomas of WJBK-TV in Detroit, Sara Voorhees of KOB-TV in Albuquerque, Max Weiss of WBAL-TV in Baltimore, and Bill Zwecker of WBBM-TV in Chicago.

Film critics on TV enjoyed their season of prominence in the 1980s and 1990s. And the studios got the greatest promotional play from the medium in those decades as film clips, some masquerading as behind-the-scenes documentaries, were supplied to syndicated daily entertainment news shows, such as *Entertainment Tonight*, *Access Hollywood*, and *Inside Edition*. These shows became staples of programming on network affiliates as cable networks, such as E!, MTV, and VH-1, were also voracious for Hollywood dish.

"We live in a complete media culture now," said Mark Crispin Miller, head of the media studies program at Johns Hopkins University in 1990. "By which I mean the culture's central concern seems to *be* media. Movies have become ubiquitous. We live in Dick Tracy for two months; we live in Batman for months. You can't escape it, it's all around you. And it's because we live in a culture of TV. Through TV, the season's blockbusters become inescapable."

TV film critics, like newspaper film critics, began having their jobs squeezed back to entertainment reporters covering all media. With more and more promotional clips streaming on the Internet and reviewer blogs proliferating, cyberspace was now the venue to not only view teaser clips but also to gauge reviewers' reactions. And several sites, such as Rotten Tomatoes, carried many critics' quotes about the same film, so consensus critical judgments could be gauged.

A great segment of the American public felt it didn't need to read or listen to critics anymore. They would see saturation advertising, be cognizant of the last weekend's box-office numbers, and listen to what John Travolta or Neve Campbell had to say on the talk shows. By then, the public would be glutted with information on which to decide the film to see that weekend.

It was one thing to give up the vocation of film critic for a job in the industry, as Frank E. Woods and George Terwilliger did in the silent era, and Quinn Martin, Frank S. Nugent, as well as Rod Lurie, who was the film critic for *Los Angeles* magazine and a talk radio host in Los Angeles on KMPC and KABC, did more in recent times. But it was quite another to keep the job of film critic and still be a prolific and consistent filmmaker. That's what Richard Schickel has done in the documentary field as a writer, director, and producer of TV productions almost exclusively about the movies. In a behind-the-scenes capacity, Schickel has been one of the greatest film critics on TV.

Schickel's total body of work is one of the major, dynamic, one-man collections to have resulted from the investigation of film culture. While Schickel made his share of TV appearances and commentaries as a film critic and historian on shows and in others' documentaries, no one intrinsic to film criticism has written, directed, and/or produced as many documentary films about the movies. His filmmaking output is remarkable in light of his reviewing job for *Time* and his sideline career of writing books (more than 20, including those on D.W. Griffith, Douglas Fairbanks, Walt Disney, Gary Cooper, Marlon Brando, and Clint Eastwood), not to mention his freelance articles. Schickel has written and directed at least 30 documentaries, including the pioneering interview studies of eight directors, encompassing Raoul Walsh and William A. Wellman, under the umbrella title of *The Men Who Made the Movies* (1973) on PBS. Schickel also produced most of those 30, and appeared onscreen in nearly 50 others.

Schickel discussed his friendship with writer-director Richard Brooks in the critic's book of essays, *Matinee Idylls: Reflections on the Movies* (1999). Brooks, whose films include *Cat on a Hot Tin Roof* (1958), *Elmer Gantry* (1960), *The Professionals* (1966), and *In Cold Blood* (1967), imparted a manifesto of sorts that makes sense when tallying, let alone assessing, Schickel's work. "In the course of this friendship he taught me a valuable lesson," Schickel wrote, "that it does not really make that much difference whether the work you do is finally judged to be 'great,' particularly if 'greatness' is decreed by critics who know nothing—not in their bones, anyway—of the confusions, improvisations and compromises that go into the making of the most communal of expressions, a movie. What really matters is what greatness of spirit—that compound of honor, passion, decent impulse, and, yes, eccentricity and awareness of your own flaws—you bring to that work, that process, that mess."

Schickel's documentaries include examinations of James Cagney, Cary Grant, Gary Cooper, Myrna Loy, Barbara Stanwyck, Elia Kazan, Clint Eastwood, Arthur Penn, Robert Wise, and Stanley Donen, among others. The titles include *The Movie Crazy Years* (1971) on PBS, *Life Goes to the Movies* (1976) on NBC's *The Big Event*, *Hollywood on Hollywood* (1993) on AMC, and *Beyond the Law* (1998) for the American Film Institute.

"Schickel . . . is able to piece together smooth, appealing, middle-brow TV pieces, his latest being this somewhat airless proof of his thesis that 'the idea of Hollywood is the most original idea Hollywood ever had,'" wrote Lisa Schwarzbaum in *Entertainment Weekly*. "The best chunk of *Hollywood on Hollywood* is the segment about the on-screen image of Hollywood after the war. In the 1950s, as Schickel puts it, 'the industry that congratulated itself on winning the war lost the peace and underwent a fascinating, bitter, cleansing period of self-hatred.'" The films cited include Robert Aldrich's *The Big Knife* (1955) and John Cromwell's *The Goddess* (1958).

For all his filmmaking skills and lifelong attention to his profession, Schickel never got around to producing a documentary about film critics. That finally arrived in 2009. Gerald Peary, film critic of the *Boston Phoenix* and contributor to *Film Comment* and other publications, as well as a longtime instructor of film studies at Rutgers, Boston University, Tufts, and elsewhere, wrote, directed, and produced a Valentine to film criticism, the feature documentary *For the Love of Movies: The Story of American Film Criticism* (2009), featuring onscreen interviews with Roger Ebert, Owen Gleiberman, Stanley Kauffmann, Harry Knowles, Elvis Mitchell, Wesley Morris, Rex Reed, Andrew Sarris, Lisa Schwarzbaum, A.O. Scott, Kenneth Turan, and Scott Weinberg.

"As a film critic, I see myself as a kind of social worker," Peary said. "I'm not really interested in writing about the big Hollywood movies—other people can do that. I am interested always in finding little documentaries and strange independent films that nobody has heard of and writing about them in a way that gets people to see them." If *For the Love of Movies* turns out to be in Peary's vein of marginalized films, no one who has ever written film criticism will be surprised. And, of course, some who have, like Peary, might even get around to extolling it.

THE MALAISE: THE 1980s and 1990s

Movies eased into a formulaic decade after the creative explosion of the 1970s as commercial cloning drove the business with hit sequels distinguished by nothing, vehicles for Sylvester Stallone, Arnold Schwarzenegger, and Bruce Willis in the action-and-gadget genres, and franchises in belch-and-leer comedy.

"People have been complaining about the movies since 1914," Andrew Sarris said in 1999. "In the 1950s, they thought the movies had been much better in the '30s. In the '60s, they talked about the '40s. Now we talk about the '70s. People say movies are bad now. But movies have always been bad. Most of everything is always bad. Most plays are bad. Most paintings are bad. But I find there are always enough movies every year—20 or 30 or 40 of them—that I can mention fondly at the end of the year."

Some opinions by the pundits in the 1990s left no room for Sarris's brand of optimism. "I wish somebody could convince me that the movies are not just about over," wrote Mark Crispin Miller in *The Atlantic Monthly*. "They're so sensationalistic, they're so empty, they're so cruel, they're so fast paced. The only thing that convinces me I've been to the movies is that I'm sick to my stomach."

The cutting-edge filmmaking by novices that was under-written by the risk-taking studio heads in the 1970s was marginalized into the outlands as the Sundance Film Festival and other festivals at Park City, Utah, and Toronto and elsewhere became the places to show and see original and daring movies. Developing into distinct stylists in the 1980s were Oliver Stone, David Lynch, Spike Lee, Jim Jarmusch, and John Sayles. Cineastes anticipated their films as antidotes to the studio assembly lines.

The studio marketing departments worked overtime to streamline their procedures and avoid bad notices. They took advantage of the growing number of film critics, a situation that in and of itself reduced the effectiveness of each critic. If the pundit down the block has the opposite opinion, what good is yours? With more reviewers weighing in with sometimes instantaneous opinions and zero analysis, the critics who used to matter in defining the artistic trends alive in the cinema became less potent, less known. Studio marketing departments expanded screening privileges across the media landscape in the 1980s to rake in 10,000-watt radio stations and weekly throwaway circulars, cultivating "blurbmeisters" and exploiting these minor reviewers' words in advertising. This was nothing new either, but the practice became institutionalized to the consternation of critics who felt that it reduced their value to mainstream audiences.

A desirable profession and hip position to have on a publication, from both periodical managements' and the critics' points of view, "film critic" naturally became ripe in the 1980s for lampooning, as the hoi polloi surmised that the know-it-alls knew nothing after all. Cartoonist Matt Groening provided a 1985 broadside in his weekly "Life in Hell" feature in the alternative press with a nine-box scribble entitled "How to Be a Clever Film Critic." Among the sections were: "How to Pad Out a Clever Film Review When You Don't Have Anything to Say," including "Write about yourself"; "For Advanced Clever Film Critics Only! . . . Can you use 'mise-en-scene' in a review that anyone will finish reading?"; and "Clever Words to Use in Reviews So as to Ensure You Will Be Quoted in Film Ads: . . .

Column A, Adverbs: Richly, Marvelously, Wonderfully, Oddly, Provocatively, Refreshingly, Stunningly . . . Column B, Adjectives: Haunting, Touching, Absorbing, Evocative, Compelling, Elegant, Original . . . and don't forget these handy phrases: 'I loved it!' . . . 'It sizzles!' . . . 'Great fun' . . ." and, of course, "'A masterpiece.'"

By the late 1980s, press junkets were standard affairs and integral parts of studio marketing campaigns. Studios flew entertainment writers—who often doubled as critics—to Los Angeles, New York, or points more exotic to see new releases and chat up the stars and directors for feature stories or items to be used as soundbites and in columns. Sometimes these were quick one-on-one interviews, but mostly they were at round-table discussions with the stars and filmmakers leapfrogging from table to table of eight or ten journalists apiece; they functioned for the studios as sets of small press conferences, yet were cozy enough for a handshake. Junkets weren't new; but their use increased.

A home media explosion changed movie-viewing habits in the 1980s as cable television channels and VCRs proliferated. Cable and video became large, established, ancillary markets for studio product. For a lot of couples, a night at the movie theatre became a quick trip to the video emporium and a comfortable night on the couch. Most older, one-screen community theatres became antiques and went the way of drive-ins, as multiplexes offering a dozen or more choices in strategically located malls became the viewing venues of the masses.

The established critics who thrived in the 1970s were having less fun. Peter Biskind recalled a mid-1980s moment at a critics meeting, when Pauline Kael leaned over to Richard Schickel and whispered, "It isn't any fun anymore." When Schickel asked why, she answered, "Remember how it was in the '60s and '70s, when movies were hot, when we were hot? Movies seemed to matter."

The box office now mattered more than ever, as Monday media reports broadcast what used to be the hip Hollywood discussion: that weekend's box-office hits. As the money discussion became the hip discussion in Middle America, the lemming syndrome took over, with the pull being the wish to see the movie that everyone else is seeing.

The New York Times was still perceived as a particular throne of film criticism, having "a huge impact on the fate of specialty film," wrote film business reporter Anne Thompson in 1988. "Many out-of-town exhibitors won't book a film until it has the imprimatur of a positive *Times* review. This sets distributors and publicists to second-guessing the veteran [Vincent] Canby and Janet Maslin. According to conventional wisdom, Canby is an Anglophile, has a soft spot for slapstick, leans toward off-beat American stories, tends to praise Woody Allen and Jean-Luc Godard, and just *hates* Alan Rudolph. The younger Maslin likes rock music and tends to be less harsh, although she has gained a stronger voice over the years. One producer-distributor even rejected a director candidate because Canby supposedly didn't like him.

"To Canby's irritation, some distributors have been known to schedule New York openings around his vacation plans," Thompson wrote. She found that David Denby in *New York* magazine could have clout as an antidote to a *Times* rejection. "*Mona Lisa*, *She's Gotta Have It*, and *River's Edge* were saved from mediocre runs by Denby raves," Thompson reported. "National exhibitors want New York quotations on their ads, plus national reviews from the likes of *Time* and *Newsweek*. . . . Los Angeles is a backwater when it comes to national media."

"One of the funniest, most unsettling, most imaginative, and most surprisingly affecting movies of its very odd kind I've ever seen," was Canby's assessment of Robert Altman's *Secret Honor* (1985), starring Philip Baker Hall in the adaptation of a one-man play about Richard M. Nixon boozing and ranting alone in the Oval Office. "Mr. Altman recoups his reputation with *Secret Honor*, a most unlikely work—a one-character movie, set entirely within a single set. . . . The result is something of a cinematic tour de force, both for Mr. Altman and for the previously unknown Philip Baker Hall, whose contribution is a legitimate, bravura performance, not a *Saturday Night Live* impersonation. . . . An extremely skillful, witty, dramatic work with an extraordinary character at its center. Mr. Altman serves it beautifully. He never undercuts the material or Mr. Hall's immense performance, which is astonishing and risky—for the chances the actor takes and survives."

Supporting both "art house" fare such as *Secret Honor*, Charles Burnett's *To Sleep with Anger* (1990), and Peter Masterson's *Convicts* (1991), as well as the deserving big Hollywood product, Canby mixed his reportorial skills with clear evaluative terms. "Oliver Stone has made what is, in effect, a bitter, seething postscript to his Oscar-winning *Platoon*," Canby wrote about *Born on the Fourth of July* (1989), based on the life of Vietnam War veteran Ron Kovic. "It is a film of enormous visceral power with, in the central role, a performance by Tom Cruise that defines everything that is best about the movie. . . . Watching the evolution of Ron Kovic . . . is both harrowing and inspiring."

The first-string critic at the *Times* since 1969, Canby weathered one of the roughest cases of high-profile critic-bashing outside of Pauline Kael's and John Simon's literary thrashings. Raymond Carney, a fellow of the Stanford Humanities Center who wrote *American Dreaming: The Films of John Cassavetes and the American Experience*, sharpened his pen for "A Critic in the Dark: The Corrupting Influence of Vincent Canby and *The New York Times*," an eight-page ambush in the June 30, 1986, edition of *The New Republic*. The piece swung wide to nick the bigger names of the critical establishment, and might have been dedicated in the name of John Simon if it weren't for the fact that Carney had such high regard for Cassavetes.

"The bourgeois repressiveness and reactionary values implicit in Canby's writing are, alas, typical of so many other film critics' writing today," Carney wrote. "Canby is popular in part because his attitudes are so much of a piece with the premises of most filmgoers and film reviewers, especially his admiration for genre or escapist garbage, and his pride in that admiration, as if it represented a kind of aesthetic radicalism and not simply another form of conservatism. Genre critics of Canby's stripe are legion—from television commentators like Neal Gabler, Leonard Maltin and Gene Shalit, to journalistic reviewers like Richard Corliss, Richard Schickel, and Pauline Kael, to many of the academics. . . .

"The real tragedy of Vincent Canby's 16 years at the *Times* is not that he sends thousands to the likes of *Porky's, Tootsie, Private Benjamin, Raiders* [*of the Lost Ark*], *Nashville, Dressed to Kill, Blow Out* or *Manhattan*," Carney wrote. "These films probably would have audiences in any case. It is that the vulgarity of his criticism—his taste for the glitzy, the tame, the trashy, the escapist, the entertaining, the safely bourgeois morality play—has misrepresented or failed to appreciate almost every one of the two or three dozen genuine works of greatness that have appeared in the movies during his tenure at the *Times*." Among Carney's examples of greatness are Cassavetes's *Minnie and Moskowitz* (1971).

One critic's tragedy is another's victory, although most critics agreed on sending moviegoers to *Tootsie* or *Manhattan* and skipping *Porky's*. Throughout nearly a quarter century as the lead reviewer for America's greatest newspaper, Canby was a voice of reason without ostentation; a sharp, clear writer with facility for expressing his directly written opinions based on films' aesthetic charms and emotional and intellectual power. While the politics and sociological impacts of such films also received his comment, he never judged the pictures from the pulpit or schoolmaster's chair. He was the corrective conscience of Bosley Crowther at *The New York Times*, something that was palpable in his early years as a critic. He was a logical and trusted critic for a generation of moviegoers. He would never, however, allow that he had much power.

"Confronted with . . . a description of his critical clout, Canby vehemently denies it," Carney wrote. "First, he argues, that certain films are almost guaranteed to find bookings and make money no matter what is said about them; the association of a particular star or director with a project (say Barbra

Streisand, Clint Eastwood, or Steven Spielberg), or the presence of certain trendy themes, combined with the commitment of a major studio to a saturation advertising campaign, can make a specific movie practically critic-proof. Still, these guaranteed blockbusters are few and far between (as investors learn to their sorrow). Indeed, as the exceptions, they only prove the rule of Canby's power in the vast majority of other instances."

Canby's dismissal of Ivan Passer's *Cutter and Bone* (1981) became a bone of contention. "It was withdrawn in three days because . . . Canby wrote that the movie was incomprehensible," Passer said. "And then all of the other critics, when their reviews came out . . . were very positive, practically all of them. So there was some kind of discussion at United Artists about this. And then some critics attacked Vincent Canby. They called him noodle-headed and all of that." UA renamed the film *Cutter's Way* in re-release and it found a small audience. Still, Canby refused to believe he was to blame. "I didn't close *Cutter's Way*," he said, "the distributor did."

Canby abided as a force in the film criticism world until 1993, the same year as the death of his longtime companion, novelist and film critic Penelope Gilliatt. She had retired in 1979 as the critic sharing the film beat at *The New Yorker* with Pauline Kael. Canby switched to theatre criticism when Frank Rich moved off the stage beat to become an op-ed columnist. Canby died of cancer in 2000.

Canby's film-reviewing partner from 1977 to 1993, Janet Maslin, wrote in his *Times* obituary that Canby was more true to his school than most. "A Dartmouth grad," she labeled him, "who forever dressed the part in tweed jacket, oxford shirt with button-down collar, gray or khaki trousers and striped tie." His writing was "conversational prose that conveyed a bracing disdain for sentiment. . . . His scholarship and cultural perspective were never flaunted but were as solid as his journalism. . . . His dignity and stature," Maslin remarked, "were effortless."

After reviewing at *The Boston Phoenix* and the leapfrog year of 1976–77 at *Newsweek*, Maslin joined Canby for what evolved into perhaps the finest one-two punch of critics for one venue that the profession has known. Born in 1949, and with a mathematics degree from the University of Rochester, Maslin's early career was as a rock critic for *Rolling Stone*. She eventually married Benjamin Cheever, the novelist son of novelist John Cheever, and had two sons by him.

Maslin was unimpressed with Hal Ashby's presentation of the life of labor-movement balladeer Woody Guthrie in *Bound for Glory* (1976). "The movie spends two-and-a-half hours and seven million dollars gazing wistfully at a little man in a big country, and it ends up pretty much embalming them both," Maslin wrote in *Newsweek*. That same year, she couldn't take Brian De Palma's *Carrie* seriously. "Combining Gothic horror, off-hand misogyny and an air of studied triviality," Maslin wrote, "*Carrie* is De Palma's most enjoyable movie in a long while, and also his silliest."

A pair of stage adaptations directed by Norman Jewison also left Maslin unimpressed. "*Agnes of God* and *A Soldier's Story* have nothing in common except Norman Jewison, who has given them a similar ponderousness," Maslin wrote in the *Times* in 1985. "*Agnes of God* is, if anything, the slower and more self evident of the two. The director's strength, again, lies in his casting, with Anne Bancroft, Jane Fonda and Meg Tilly sharing what is essentially a three-character melodrama; in unison or in any combination these three actresses cannot help but generate interest. But the material itself, thoroughly unsurprising on the stage, is if anything even more so on the screen. . . . The claustrophobia of the original material was an advantage, and Mr. Jewison gains nothing in lessening it."

Impressed with the skills that wrought eventual Academy Award-winning best picture *Schindler's List* (1993), Maslin wrote, "Mr. Spielberg has made sure that neither he nor the Holocaust will ever be thought of in the same way again." Maslin evaluated Nicholas Hytner's *The Crucible* (1996) as "impassioned and vigorous. . . . The film moves with the dangerous momentum of a runaway train."

Maslin underscored the need for film critics to keep their vocabularies fresh when she talked of the difficulty of not being repetitive. "It's also very hard to describe the way in which things are funny," Maslin said in 1999, when she quit the movie beat at *The New York Times* to review books. "I just got sick of saying 'hilarious.' Even though a lot of things are hilarious. . . . I just felt the paucity of vocabulary. It just sort of beggared the imagination to come up with different ways to say the same thing."

Stability was the hallmark in the 1980s among film critics in New York. While Canby and Maslin were together from 1977 through 1993, and Maslin didn't switch to book criticism until 1999, Kathleen Carroll was the main critic at the *New York Daily News* from 1962 to 1992, overlapped by Rex Reed's 13 years at the same paper as a general arts critic. Judith Crist was the founding film critic of *New York* magazine after the 1967 closing of the *New York World Journal Tribune*, the patched-together daily—on which she was film critic—from several deceased papers after the disastrous newspaper strike of 1966. Meanwhile, Archer Winsten held forth for the *New York Post* into his sixth decade as film critic. He retired in 1986 at the age of 81.

Winsten started reviewing movies in 1936, when FDR won a second term, Jesse Owens starred in the Olympic Games in Berlin, and the Academy Award-winning best picture was Robert Z. Leonard's *The Great Ziegfeld*. Winsten covered the opening of *Gone with the Wind* in 1939. "Our movie critic remained the indestructible Archer Winsten, nearly 80 years old," wrote former *Post* editor Steven Cuozzo in 1996 about the 1980s. "Winsten was a genial, distracted soul with a wispy white beard. . . . I'd point out delicately, 'Archer's a wonderful guy, but he's not the one to cover the youth market.'"

Winsten was old-school to say the least, a daily newspaper critic who honed his craft during contemporary starts by Frank S. Nugent at the *Times* and Howard Barnes at the *Herald-Tribune*—in the heyday of Otis Ferguson and Meyer Levin. The *Post*'s criticism staff relied on durability, since the theatre critic for three postwar decades was Richard Watts, Jr., who had covered silent movies for the *Herald-Tribune*.

"I won't say this is the funniest film you'll see, or that it can please every taste, or many tastes formed more than 30 years ago, but I do say it quite clearly marks the emergence of a comedy group that, given time and opportunity, could brighten, sharpen and broaden American comedy of the next decade or so," Winsten wrote in the *Post* in 1974 about Ken Shapiro's *The Groove Tube* (1974). "It brings together wit, wicked perceptions of human frailty, and a fine, traditional sense of slapstick."

"Mr. Winsten . . . was respected by his colleagues as a consistently solid, intelligent reviewer [and] had a keen eye for excellence," Robert McG. Thomas, Jr., wrote in *The New York Times*. Winsten was an early champion of Robert Rossen's Academy Award-winning best picture *All the King's Men* (1949) and a promoter of European imports. "Indeed, Mr. Winsten became something of a legend in 1943," Thomas reported, "when he was the only local reviewer to praise the great Danish director Carl Dreyer's slow-moving *Day of Wrath*, now widely regarded as a cinematic triumph."

The *Post* eased a variety of film critics alongside Winsten in his final decade, including Frank Rich, Judith Crist, and Rex Reed. Jami Bernard succeeded Winsten, and stayed at the *Post* until 1993. Also reviewing movies at the *Post* in the 1990s and after were Thelma Adams, Michael Medved, David Edelstein, Lou Lumenick, and V.A. "Vince" Musetto, a four-decade *Post* veteran who wrote the paper's most (in)famous headline, "Headless Body in Topless Bar." Edelstein, a 1981 Harvard graduate who had been a devotee of Pauline Kael's, eventually became chief film critic for *New York* magazine in the 21st century. He also reviewed for *The Village Voice*, *Boston Phoenix*, and *Slate* (1996 to 2005), as well as National Public Radio's *Fresh Air* with Terry Gross and *CBS Sunday Morning*.

Bernard was wooed by the competition. "The *Post* tried hard to keep me," Bernard said, after the *New York Daily News* began entreaties to lure the provocative writer. "But the *Post* did a weird thing—they brought in Michael Medved, who is really a conservative commentator in the guise of a film critic. They couldn't promote another critic over me, so Michael and I each reviewed the same movies for a few weeks, side by side, until I went to the *Post* management and said, 'This is ridiculous. Just let me go now.' And they sighed and they did. I had worked there 15 years, grown up there, and the *Post* is truly like a family, so it was very emotional to leave it."

Bernard wrote books about nude scenes in films, her breast cancer survival, and weight loss (*The Incredible Shrinking Critic*), and compiled the most provocative volume in the long book-publishing history of the National Society of Film Critics: *The X List: The National Society of Film Critics' Guide to the Movies That Turn Us On* (2005).

"Acknowledging the timeless appeal of eroticism, members of the National Society of Film Critics extol and explicate the movies they deem the most seductive," wrote Gordon Flagg in *Publishers Weekly*. "Their 80 choices include prestige films that depict sex explicitly (e.g., *In the Realm of the Senses*, *Irreversible*), steamy box-office smashes (e.g., *Basic Instinct*, *Klute*), Hollywood classics (*Laura*, *Gilda*), and porn flicks (*Deep Throat*, *Behind the Green Door*). A few critics fess up to early sexual awakening via such seemingly innocuous fare as *Butch Cassidy and the Sundance Kid* and *Hercules*, or make surprising choices, such as *The Mummy* and the documentary *Ayn Rand: A Sense of Life*. Others sing the praises of sexual icons like Louise Brooks and Ann-Margret. Contributors include some of the best, if not best-known, critics (J. Hoberman, Stuart Klawans, Jonathan Rosenbaum) along with media heavyweight Roger Ebert, who offers a tribute to legendary soft-core director Russ Meyer. Because the selections represent so many genres and nations, the collection has going for it, besides its theme, a variety that most critical compilations lack."

Ebert never had to be an apologist for contributing to what was perceived, in the morality of an earlier era, to be soft-core pornography by writing Meyer's *Beyond the Valley of the Dolls* (1970). In fact, without much spin on his part or anyone else's, Ebert's contribution to the film has been celebrated, and the picture conferred with cult status. Moralizing occurred when the film was released, but has since evaporated. Ebert wrote the picture as a pioneering venture into planned, A-budget sleaze by Twentieth Century-Fox. *Beyond the Valley of the Dolls* concerned a three-girl rock band that came to Hollywood to make it big, and instead gets embroiled with studio executives, drugs, and sex. Campy, raunchy, and overripe in a Russ Meyer sort of way, the film was a top-25 box-office hit of 1970.

Contemporary critics reviled or dismissed the film for the same characteristics that gave it cachet. "Russ Meyer called in a young, Chicago-based movie critic named Roger Ebert to give the screenplay a now-generation gloss," wrote film critic Paul D. Zimmerman in 1970 in *Newsweek*. "Ebert has delivered with a vengeance. When the cast of hundreds isn't smoking grass, they're grooving or getting their heads together or finding out where it's at. They hardly have time to bash a skull or blast away a pair of open eyes." Even Ebert's old pal, Mike Royko, the famous city-side columnist on his paper, the *Chicago Sun-Times*, came away from a special early screening for Ebert's friends with a bad opinion, which he advanced to his readers.

"I believe," Royko wrote, "that every young man is entitled to one big mistake, despite what the alimony court judges might say. And this movie is Ebert's, and I urge you to avoid it. Someday he will write another movie, and I'm confident that it will be excellent. Even if it is dirty, it will be better. I'll be his technical advisor."

But the film became a cult item to the extent that the Los Angeles Film Critics Association presented it two decades later as a special event with Ebert, Meyer, and the cast in attendance for a July 1990 seminar with a standing-room-only crowd at the UCLA Film & Television Archive. Michael Dare, one of the film critics for *LA Weekly*, presided proudly. "While other critics salivated over the prospects of getting Scorsese to discuss *The Last Temptation of Christ*, I daydreamed about seeing *Beyond the Valley of the Dolls* on the big screen again," Dare wrote.

Many film critics have tried to analyze the erotic nature

of films. Ebert, reviewing Zalman King's *Wild Orchid* (1990), wrote, "We engage in a conspiracy of silence about erotic movies. We discuss their plots, their characters, the truthfulness of their worlds. We never discuss whether or not they arouse us— whether we're turned on. Critics are the worst offenders, occupying some Olympian peak above the field of battle, pretending that the film in question failed to engage their intelligence when what we want to know is whether or not it engaged their libido." Bernard's book confronted the issue 15 years later.

While some film critics have written about their sexual orientation, one critic made his gay perspective a main subject in his writing. The Los Angeles-based film critic David Ehrenstein was instrumental in bringing attention to gay films and filmmakers through provocative articles in many periodicals, as well as his chairmanship of the Douglas Edwards Independent/Experimental Film & Video Award Committee for LAFCA. These films included Gus Van Sant's *Mala Noche* (1985) and Jennie Livingston's *Paris Is Burning* (1990).

Ehrenstein was born in 1947 in New York City, the son of a Polish Jew with secular ancestors and an African-American mother. A graduate of the former Pace College, Ehrenstein reviewed for the *Los Angeles Reader* in the 1980s as well as the gay magazine *The Advocate*, and wrote for the *Los Angeles Herald-Examiner* until it folded in 1989. Placing magazine pieces throughout his career, Ehrenstein has been published in *Film Culture*, *Film Quarterly*, *Film Comment*, *Daily Variety*, *The Village Voice*, *Cahiers du cinéma*, *Rolling Stone*, *Sight & Sound*, *LA Weekly*, *Los Angeles Times Book Review*, *The New York Times*, and others. He and companion Bill Reed cowrote *Rock on Film*, and Ehrenstein's magnum opus is *Open Secret: Gay Hollywood, 1928–1998*.

"You'll . . . find sizable, if scattershot, smatterings of old-Hollywood sociology (like where the homosexual watering holes were in the '30s and '40s, and why straights like Bogart blithely frequented them)," wrote Steve Daly in *Entertainment Weekly* about the panoramic *Open Secret*. The reviewer also found "a remarkable, oral-history-style sampling of extended remarks from a host of current industry folk, ranging from big fish (David Geffen) to directors and producers (Gus Van Sant, Clive Barker, Laurence Mark) to in-the-trenches personnel like Steven Dornbusch, a blue-collar grip who dishes on just how graphically gross crew members can get about gay sex."

B. Ruby Rich, the author of *Chick Flicks: Theories and Memories of the Feminist Film Movement* (1998) and chair of the Community Studies and Social Documentation Program at the University of California, Santa Cruz, has often approached film criticism from a lesbian point of view, placing articles with *The Village Voice, San Francisco Bay Guardian, The Nation, The Advocate, Mirabella,* and *Elle.* She is the founding film review editor for *GLQ: A Journal of Lesbian and Gay Studies* and she has served on the selection committees for the Sundance Film Festival and on the juries of film festivals from Toronto to Havana, Sundance to Sydney.

Ehrenstein helped expand the Los Angeles Film Critics Association in the 1980s. Robert Osborne of *The Hollywood Reporter* was the president from 1981 to 1983, followed by two-year stints apiece by Charles Champlin and Kevin Thomas of the *Los Angeles Times* and Univision's Jorge Camara. By the decade's close, LAFCA included Leonard Maltin as well as Peter Rainer and Ehrenstein of the *Los Angeles Herald-Examiner*; Sheila Benson and Michael Wilmington of the *Times*; Kirk Honeycutt of the *Los Angeles Daily News* then *The Hollywood Reporter*; Bob Strauss of the *Daily News*; Duane Byrge of *The Hollywood Reporter*; Henry Sheehan, Andy Klein, and Steven Gaydos of the *Los Angeles Reader*; Jim Emerson of *The Orange County Register*; Michael Dare, Ella Taylor, and, for a time, John Powers and Helen Knode of the *LA Weekly*; and this writer. Others stayed in the group a year or three—John Richardson and David Kronke on the *Daily News*—before moving on.

During the early 1980s, three of the five members of LAFCA's executive committee were at the center of separate imbroglios within the association. Nothing was made of any of these incidents outside LAFCA, as members involved chose not to print them. However, they show that a concerted group of film critics can face the idiosyncratic as well as common challenges that other organizations face, and that the survival of the group, like any group, is based on the resiliency of its members. LAFCA's executive committee in 1981 and 1982 consisted of Robert Osborne of *The Hollywood Reporter* (president), Ruth Batchelor of ABC's *Good Morning America* (executive director), Linda Gross of the *Los Angeles Times* (secretary), Barry Brennan of the Santa Monica *Evening Outlook* (treasurer), and the immediate past president, Dean Cohen of KPFK Radio.

Within two years in separate instances, Brennan was dead and the LAFCA's finances were gone, freelancer Gross had moved briefly to the *Los Angeles Daily News* (then out of reviewing), and Batchelor had quit because of an internal conflict over the televising of LAFCA's awards presentations. Brennan died at age 43 from what was reported in *Daily Variety* as cancer. Afterward, LAFCA's funds, valued at the very least in the tens of thousands of dollars, were never found. Brennan was buried in his native Kentucky.

Gross had been writing regularly for several years for the *Times*'s Calendar section when she joined Charles Champlin and Kevin Thomas on the film beat. She was the envy of practically every other film critic, the recipient of a reviewer's gig on the biggest media outlet in Hollywood's backyard and, for all intents and purposes, the biggest and most important newspaper on the West Coast. She offered *Times* readers a female perspective on a staff that was otherwise all male. She inherited the LAFCA position of secretary in 1981 from Thomas, who had, in turn, inherited it from Champlin. Gross's departure occurred shortly after Sheila Benson arrived on the *Times*'s reviewing staff. Gross was a regular freelancer and not on staff, as were Thomas and Benson. She departed as Benson assumed a direct role over film coverage, as Champlin stepped down from day-to-day reviewing. Michael Wilmington, who had written for *Isthmus* in Madison, Wisconsin, and *LA Weekly*, soon became the *Times*'s third reviewer, after Benson and Thomas.

The duties of the LAFCA treasurer were assumed by Dean Sander, a trusted voice of coal-mine acoustics on KLAC Radio for more than three decades. The secretary's post went to Jack Mathews, who had joined the *Times* after stints at the *Detroit Free Press* and *USA Today*. In 1989, Batchelor's executive director post was eliminated by LAFCA and the vice president's position was created to keep the executive board at a tie-breaking five members.

LAFCA couldn't be blamed for being consistent homers. Among their selections for best picture were Terry Gilliam's *Brazil* (1985) and Christine Edzard's six-hour, two-part *Little Dorrit* (1988), both from Great Britain. The second choice was the result of Benson's agency, as she stumped for the adaptation of one of Charles Dickens's lesser novels. But the big deal over *Little Dorrit* was a fizzle compared to the action over *Brazil*.

The *Brazil* ordination was a brash statement. Gilliam's film was being held from release in America by Universal Pictures, which told the director to cut its European running time from 142 minutes to 125. The studio also wanted the ending changed of the futuristic film about a clerk (Jonathan Pryce) who keeps his dreams alive amid a bleak, oppressive Kafkaesque society, with inspiration from a swashbuckling renegade (Robert De Niro).

Gilliam refused on both counts, and talked of exhibiting the movie in Mexico, bussing Americans across the border to see it. He took out an ad in *Daily Variety* directed at Sid Sheinberg, president of MCA, Universal's parent company. "When are you going to release my movie, *BRAZIL*?" the ad pleaded. On December 16, 1985, LAFCA, for whom Gilliam had screened the movie, announced that *Brazil* won its best picture award, Gilliam was best director, and Gilliam, Tom Stoppard and Charles McKeown had recieved the best screenplay award. Universal eventually shaved 11 minutes off of Gilliam's cut and booked the picture into theatres to the initially brisk business the studio expected to result from the L.A. critics' stand.

But *Brazil* didn't earn back its $15 million cost. Mathews

related Gilliam's story in the book, *The Battle of Brazil*, which included the film's screenplay. Bruce Williamson characterized the book in *Playboy* as "Hollywood's own Hatfields and McCoys." In the *Chicago Tribune*, Gene Siskel said the book "documents in rare detail the back-room haggling and the attempted ego-bashing that is part of the movie business."

Benson's ascendency to a decade of prominence at the *Times* came in middle age, after husbands, motherhood, and criticism written for a small paper in Northern California (the *Pacific Sun* in Mill Valley). Similar to the path taken by Pauline Kael, this career arc also included Kael-like politicking inside LAFCA to elevate the likes of *Little Dorrit*. Benson also colluded the year before in Sally Kirkland's shamelessly infamous campaign through the awards season for the actress's performance in *Anna* (1987). Benson invited the LAFCA critics to her house for the voting, made her feelings known about Kirkland's performance, and garnered enough votes to lift Kirkland to a tie with Holly Hunter for bravura work in *Broadcast News* (1987).

Benson grew up a daughter of the film business in the Los Angeles neighborhood of Westwood. Her mother was Mary C. McCall, Jr., the screenwriter of nearly 50 films and TV shows, from Archie Mayo's *Street of Women* (1932) to William Dieterle and Max Reinhardt's *A Midsummer Night's Dream* (1935), as well as Ann Sothern's *Maisie* films, and a few programmers, such as *Slim Carter* (1957) with Jock Mahoney and *Juke Box Rhythm* (1959) with Jo Morrow. Benson's father was Dwight Franklin, a costume designer on Cecil B. DeMille pictures and others. Benson's first reviews were broadcast over KTIM-AM/FM radio out of San Rafael, California, in the Bay Area. She was the film critic for eight years for the *Pacific Sun* in Marin County.

Benson began writing in 1972 and subsequently placed articles in *TV Guide, Film Comment, Elle, Mother Jones, New West*, and the *Los Angeles Times*, for which she began as a stringer in 1978. She was hired full-time by arts editor Charles Champlin in 1981. Pauline Kael intimated that she helped Benson get the *Times* job.

Reciprocal appreciation was apparent. Benson said that "probably 85 to 95 percent of the reviewers writing now began at the knee of Pauline Kael, and we all smelled and sounded like Pauline. I don't think I do now, but for a long time there was always the matter of comparison with her take on a movie, of feeling, 'Oh, I missed that.' She set the standard to a degree. So did Dwight Macdonald, and . . . James Agee. If you were lucky you learned about Manny Farber.

"Pauline was the one we all cut our teeth on, the one who made it OK to like movies passionately and not just objectively," Benson said in the 1992 book, *Getting Started in Film*. "She made movies accessible and very clear. She's got that great background in philosophy, and she's able to break a film down intelligently, which she loves to do. I think that she can take a position and hold it against all comers, and yet I can disagree with that position passionately. I think that criticism is presenting only the best case one can for one's arguments. There is no right or wrong way to look at a movie. There is no single correct review. There is one person's very best arguments told in plain and forceful language."

Benson, like Kael, occasionally scrapped. Her dust-up on the page with Stephen Farber was significant for her defense of the profession. Farber, who had written for *New West* and *Movieline*, asked in the March 17, 1991, edition of the *Los Angeles Times*, "Why Do Critics Love These Repellent Movies?" He cited critical praise for films about lowdown or horrific characters, such as *The Grifters*; *The Silence of the Lambs*; *After Dark, My Sweet*; and *The Cook, the Thief, His Wife and Her Lover*. "When did critics get the lunatic idea that the greatest movies were the cold-blooded dissections of human venality and depravity?" Farber wrote. "In contemporary film criticism there's no perspective, no sense of what is truly valuable in art, or in life.

"One wouldn't object to critics praising *The Grifters* as an entertaining film noir or admiring *The Silence of the Lambs*' acting and directing. But to call them the best films of the year, as some critics have done, is a travesty. All criticism is subjective, and movie reviews often reveal more about the critics than about the works under scrutiny. If middle-brow pundits of the '50s who honored movies with noble intentions were displaying their own timorousness, one hesitates to think what the appetites of today's critics for tales of angry, maladjusted outsiders tells about them. Their enthusiasm for grotesque violence is as narrow and dubious an aesthetic as the knee-jerk liberalism of their predecessors," Farber wrote.

He concluded that moviegoers were being alienated from reviewers. "Between the monosyllabic gurglings of the TV critics and the frequently demented rantings of the hipper print critics, the level of critical discourse has sunk to a new low," he despairingly asserted. "It's about time that a few people pointed to the rave reviews for a nasty piece of goods like *The Silence of the Lambs* and shouted that the emperors of the press have no clothes."

Benson defended Jonathan Demme's *The Silence of the Lambs* as a feminist story, as "Clarice's odyssey," a brave and intelligent investigation by Jodie Foster's FBI agent. "This is harrowing stuff," Benson wrote, "but it is something audiences understand. It is a touching and a human fear and the reason, I believe, the film resonates as powerfully and as personally as it does—with those able to pull their eyes away from its figures of evil.

"Finally," Benson wrote, "as for Farber's astonishing statement that contemporary film criticism contains no perspective, no sense of what is truly valuable in art or in life, I can only wonder what writers Farber reads—or, more to the point, which ones he doesn't. A very long list can be supplied on request." Be that as it may, Farber had been harping on the issue since April 1981 in *American Film* with "Why Do Critics Love Trashy Movies?"

No Kael-Sarris uproar, and shy of the Ebert-Corliss debate the same year, the Benson-Farber tiff could have used Kael's rapier wit. In all, Benson was further proof of the influence of Kael among critics, as well as proof that women were expressing their opinions on films more and more. Along with Kael and Maslin, Benson was one of America's three leading female critics, whose numbers were growing.

Going back to Evelyn Gerstein in the 1920s and the various incarnations of "Kate Cameron" at the *New York Daily News* from the 1930s onward, and "Mae Tinee" at the *Chicago Tribune* in the decades prior to Gene Siskel, quite a few women worked in the midcentury as film critics, especially in New York (Cecelia Ager at *PM*, Eileen Creelman at the *New York Sun*, Rose Pelswick at the *Journal-American*) and Boston (Marjorie Adams of the *Globe*, Peggy Doyle of the *Record American*, Nora Taylor of *The Christian Science Monitor*).

But as the profession experienced an upswing in the 1980s and 1990s, more women filled major film-review posts. They included Molly Haskell at *Vogue*, Joy Gould Boyum for *The Wall Street Journal* and later *Us* magazine, Julie Salamon at *The Wall Street Journal*, Rita Kempley at *The Washington Post*, Susan Stark of the *Detroit News*, Eleanor Ringel of the *Atlanta Journal-Constitution*, Marsha McCreadie of the *Arizona Republic*, Marylynn Uricchio and then Barbara Vancheri of the *Pittsburgh Post-Gazette*, Carrie Rickey of the *Boston Herald* and then *Philadelphia Inquirer*, Roxanne T. Mueller of the *Cleveland Plain Dealer*, Elfrieda Pantoga of the *Milwaukee Sentinel*, Kathy Huffhines of the *Detroit Free Press*, Yardena Arar of the *Los Angeles Daily News*, and Candace Russell of the *Fort Lauderdale News & Sun-Sentinel*. In 1989, seven women were in both the New York Film Critics Circle and the Los Angeles Film Critics Association. The NYFCC added two women in 2007, Elizabeth Weitzman of the *New York Daily News* and Melissa Anderson of *Time Out New York*, and three more in 2008: Karen Dubin of *Elle*, Dana Stevens of Slate.com, and Stephanie Zacharek of Salon.com.

On the national newsweeklies, the critics endured with a sense of permanence. At *Time* magazine, both critics who had been reviewing movies into the 21st century had been movie critics for four decades. Richard Schickel began reviewing in 1965 and from 1972 at *Time*. When Frank Rich moved to *The New York Times* in 1980, Richard Corliss replaced him. Corliss's editorship of *Film Comment* overlapped with his *Time* job by a

decade, from 1970 to 1990, after which Richard T. Jameson replaced him at the specialty magazine. Corliss had written for the
National Review from 1966 to 1970. A factoid about the *Time*
boys that emerged in the new century was that Corliss placed
movies on his top 10 lists that Schickel rated the worst of the
year, including *Moulin Rouge!* (2001), *Cold Mountain* (2003),
and *Eternal Sunshine of the Spotless Mind* (2004).

Schickel's characteristic professionalism was virtually
Hawksian. His consistently sharp, exacting writing seemed to
presume the national trust. "This unpretentious movie about a
group of American 'advisers' in Viet Nam in 1964, before the
war was thoroughly Americanized, has the virtues of its defects,"
Schickel wrote in *Time* about Ted Post's *Go Tell the Spartans*
(1978). "It is understated, lacking in powerful dramatic incident
and high human emotion, and rather flatly written and directed.
As a result it has about it a realistically antiheroic air that is rare
enough in any movie about any war, and a grubby brutality that
matches memories of the news film that came out of Southeast
Asia in the '60s and did so much to disgust the nation with U.S.
involvement there."

Schickel decided that *Terms of Endearment* (1983), James
L. Brooks's eventual Academy Award-winning best picture, had
an absence of defects, and concluded in *Time* that it needed a
boost. "It deserves some blunt declaration of respect and un-
guarded affection. Therefore," he wrote, "these three: No film
since Preston Sturges was a pup has so shrewdly appreciated the
way with which the eccentric plays hide-and-seek with the respectable in the ordinary American landscape; no comedy since
Annie Hall or *Manhattan* has intelligently observed not just the
way people live now but what's going on in the back of their
minds; and, finally, and in full knowledge that one may be doing
the marketing department's job for them, it is the best movie of
the year."

Corliss happily succumbed to the charms of Lawrence
Kasdan's *The Big Chill* (1983). "This is a movie that can exist
outside the confines of movie genres, with characters whose lives

seep outside the screen frame, who persuade the viewer to care about their pasts and futures," he wrote. ". . . Indeed, the entire film is a kind of sock-hop benefit for Approaching Middle Age. . . . Play the music and let the big chill—the knowledge that we're 'all alone out there, and we're going out there tomorrow'—melt away in the warmth of the feel-good movie of eighty-three."

Jack Kroll joined *Newsweek* in 1963 as an associate editor in charge of arts coverage, and became a jack-of-all-trades, writing and assigning reviews. For many years, *Newsweek*, along with *Time*, did not individually identify reviewers, and Kroll was instrumental in *Newsweek's* decision to place bylines on reviews, including his own. "Allen's growth in every department is lovely to behold," Kroll wrote in *Newsweek* about Woody Allen's *Manhattan* (1979). "He gets excellent performances from his cast. The increasing visual beauty of his films is part of their grace and sweetness, their balance between Allen's yearning romanticism and his tough eye for the fatuous and sentimental—a balance also expressed in his best screen play yet."

Kroll, who died of colon cancer in 2000, worked with Joe Morgenstern, *Newsweek's* film critic from 1965 to 1983, when Morgenstern joined the *Los Angeles Herald-Examiner* as a city-side columnist, and Paul D. Zimmerman, a film critic from 1967 to 1975, when he quit reviewing to write screenplays. Janet Maslin came to *Newsweek* from *The Boston Phoenix* and stayed for a year before leaving for *The New York Times* in 1977. She was followed from the *Phoenix* to *Newsweek* by David Ansen in 1977.

Ansen, who wrote for *The Real Paper* in Boston prior to moving to the *Phoenix*, remained the main film critic at *Newsweek* until 2008, when he accepted a buyout from the magazine amid cost-cutting measures. He has written documentaries on Bette Davis, Elizabeth Taylor, and Groucho Marx. In the October 29, 2007, edition of *Newsweek*, Ansen wrote "7,714 Movies, and Counting," about the list he has kept since 1958, retroactive to 1950, of all the movies he has seen. Sparer and less ceremonial than Peter Bogdanovich's method of typing out an index card per film, Ansen's ongoing tabulation—146 handwritten pages—supplies a trace of his personal anthropology.

"It seemed to have really touched a nerve in a lot of people," Ansen told Denver journalist Marty Mapes. "All of these list makers are coming out of the closet. A lot of the letters said, 'I wish I had kept mine up,' or 'I wish I could find it.' . . . You go back and look at it, and it means different things at different times in your life. How [the movies] influenced you and the people you knew. It reminds you of where you were, what city . . . who you saw it with. . . . It's the diary of my life."

After Ansen was hired by *Newsweek*, he learned that someone had put in a good word for him. "I later found out that Pauline Kael had recommended me," Ansen said. "She had been reading me. She called me up one day actually to say how much she had liked a review. It was a very strange review I had written of *All the President's Men*; it was not written in the conventional way; it was numbered '23 points about *All the President's Men*.' . . . What was funny was that when I went back and looked at my review, I predicted that the movie would date, that the movie would not make sense ten years from [the time of the review]. At the time it seemed that movie could not possibly hold up if you weren't steeped in the moment. I was completely wrong, because the movie holds up very well."

Over his career, on the alternative weeklies and within the *Newsweek*'s tight format, Ansen has written with expressive accessibility. His commentary covered the bases, and he has evinced a knack for pegging the influence of actors and the ways they help or hinder a movie. "There aren't many actors who can portray corn-fed innocence without coyness or cliché, but [Jeff] Bridges sails effortlessly through the part," he wrote in *The Real Paper* about Howard Zieff's *Hearts of the West* (1975). "He's always been easy to underrate because his acting doesn't look like work—he slides into a character body first, no apparent sweat. Lewis Tater doesn't have [the] depth he gave Junior Jackson in *The Last American Hero* (his best performance) but he isn't meant to. Tater is conceived nostalgically—he's as much a figure of small-town American mythology as the adventure heroes he longs to emulate. Bridges gives this innocent abroad flesh, blood and irresistible charm."

Other Ansen judgments cut to the core: Of Milton Katselas's *When You Comin' Back, Red Ryder* (1979), he wrote, "As the crazed, drug-running catalyst Teddy, [Marjoe] Gortner . . . sends off shock waves of artificial energy. . . . He's a hippy Liberace." Studying character actor Scott Wilson's performance in the lead role of Krzysztof Zanussi's *A Year of the Quiet Sun* (1984), Ansen wrote in *Newsweek*, "Wilson, who looks like a softer, more frightened Roy Scheider, has a few near impossible lines to say, such as 'I was an empty man until I met you.' Then you look into his wounded eyes and believe him. . . . This is a very sad story set in a very grim world, yet it leaves you invigorated."

Ansen admired Richard Rush's *The Stunt Man* (1980), writing, "It may be the most original American movie of the year. . . . *The Stunt Man* is at once an exhilarating exercise in pop Pirandello, a bitchily funny satire of filmmakers and a touching moral tale about the perils of paranoia. . . . Rush keeps the audience in a state of almost hallucinatory suspense. It's a sensory, mind-twisting trip that leaves one happily sated."

At *The New Republic*, Stanley Kauffmann has remained the main voice on movies since 1958. While he has reviewed theatre and books, Kauffmann has concentrated on films for most of his tenure. His *New Republic* reviews and essays have been packaged into the most admirably sustained line of anthologies in the profession outside of Pauline Kael, including *A World on Film* (1966), *Figures of Light* (1971), *Living Images* (1975), *Before My Eyes* (1980), *Field of View* (1986), and *Distinguishing Features* (1994).

At *The Nation*, Stuart Klawans became film critic in 1988 and has been a Gibraltar of reason ever since. Klawans has also broadcast reviews on WBAI Radio in New York and written for *The Village Voice*, *Entertainment Weekly*, and other periodicals. Klawans's books include the anthologies *Film Follies: The Cinema Out of Order* (1999) and *Left in the Dark: Film Reviews and*

Essays, 1988–2001 (2002). In the years between the retirement of longtime *Nation* film critic Robert Hatch in the 1980s and the establishment of Klawans, the critics included Terrence Rafferty, James Lardner, and Jonathan Baumbach.

Rafferty was one of the critics Pauline Kael mentored onto *The New Yorker* team after the retirement of Penelope Gilliatt in 1989. Gilliatt, the wife of playwright John Osborne from 1963 to 1968, was a novelist whose film criticism for *The New Yorker* filled the greater summer months—May to September—while Kael presided as film critic the rest of each year. Gilliatt died of alcoholism in 1993.

On March 11, 1991, in an announcement that *The New York Times* reported as "earth-shattering," Pauline Kael said she was retiring as the regular film critic of *The New Yorker*. Although Kael said she would still write occasional pieces, none surfaced except for the introduction to another of her review anthologies, *For Keeps* (1994); that intro was reprinted in *The New York Times*. "I'm frequently asked why I don't write my memoirs," she wrote in the intro. "I think I have."

Kael, who retired at age 72 with allusions to "a bum heart," had been diagnosed with Parkinson's disease in the early 1980s. After her ascendency to film criticism's pinnacle in the 1960s through a series of building skirmishes with filmmakers and other film critics, and following her years at the forefront of the profession in the 1970s, blazing a trail from one controversy to the next, Kael's 1980s were fairly staid. Admirers paid their respects, and the Paulettes were still in tow. "It always bothered me that a writer so independent should surround herself with epigones," wrote Tom Carson in 1991. "One crack about the Paulettes was that they all loved *Driving Miss Daisy* because it was their story."

David Denby admitted his unofficial membership in the Paulettes, and wrote a description of them in *The New Yorker* in 2003. "We were mainly upper-middle-class boys falling out of university and into journalism," Denby wrote about Kael's compulsion to win arguments. "Still, I thought, anyone who loved movies, no matter how protected he was, had the right to an opinion. I was not normally submissive, and neither were any of the others, but we acquiesced in the bullying, in my case with increasing discomfort. The group became a cult that never admitted its existence, a circle that never discussed its exclusions, a set of friends that never acknowledged how much enmity lay outside it, not even after articles had been written fingering her acolytes, complete, in some publications, with mug shots."

Meanwhile, James Wolcott detected that after the retirement, the Paulettes wandered out of theatres into the night, disbursing in nomadic disarray. "Lacking a responsive audience that shares their urgency, the Paulettes are now reduced to writing for second-tier publications, using their underdog status to champion lost causes and pet losers, like the latest Walter Hill film or the career of Eric Roberts," Wolcott wrote in *Vanity Fair*. "They're preaching in a vacant lot. Since for them movie criticism is a calling, the Paulettes are like staunch Catholics stuck in a bad marriage: they can't leave. One Paulette I know was asked to review a book for a Boston paper. 'But that would be writing about *writing*,' he blurted, scandalized by the very suggestion. Writing about writing—aka literary criticism—is something that's been around for three, four hundred years, but to him it was [a] sneaky ploy to mess with his mind. He has since relented and reviewed an actual book. It was a movie book, which made it OK."

Various Paulettes have been identified here and there to occasional consternation. "I am NOT a Paulette!" one critic exclaimed in a pre-show fit in the early 1990s in a Los Angeles screening room. The pejorative aspect of the term "Paulette" has usually driven them underground, where they live by night. "They write as advocates, both feet on the accelerator," Wolcott maintained in a snarky homage, advocating what he claimed to be "the good kind [of trash]—blatant, vital, sexy . . . in danger of being euthanized by the team of Merchant Ivory. Gentility is the enemy—we're drowning in crinoline! They cry. Bring back hot rods and cheap lipstick."

Among film critics and aficionados, naming the Paulettes

was something of a trivia challenge, like remembering every actor who comprised *The Dirty Dozen* or *The Wild Bunch*. By Wolcott's 1997 count, the Paulettes included: Steve Vineberg, Charles Taylor, and Stephanie Zacharek, all of *The Boston Phoenix*; Polly Frost of *Harper's Bazaar* and *Elle*; Peter Rainer of the *Los Angeles New Times*; Michael Sragow of *SF Weekly*; Hal Hinson of *The Washington Post*; and David Edelstein of *Slate*. Of course, lifelong memberships had already been deeded to Joe Morgenstern, David Denby, Terrence Rafferty, and a few select others.

During her last full decade, Kael wielded the power she had left. "Some, like Woody Allen and Warren Beatty, were savaged in print once they dropped out of her good graces," Carson wrote. "At worst, she wasn't far from a film-world version of Walter Winchell, conducting vendettas and boosting intimates." Never very receptive to George Lucas's films, Kael was lampooned by the Lucas/Ron Howard production, *Willow* (1988), in which the villain was "General Kael." The critic panned the big fantasy film, but drolly described the character as an "*homage a moi.*"

Renata Adler reviewed Kael's anthology *When the Lights Go Down* (1980) in *The New York Review of Books* in 8,000 words, calling it "jarringly, piece by piece, line by line, and without interruption, worthless." Adler pointed out Kael's cruelty, redundancy, and arrogance. *Time* referred to this bushwhack as "the bloodiest case of assault and battery in years" amid "the New York literary Mafia."

In his review of *Hooked* (1989) in *The New York Times Book Review*, Robert Sklar wrote, "What is lacking in Miss Kael's criticism, for many, is a clear sense of dialogue—and separation—between reviewer and reader, an admission that more than one response to a film is possible. The first-person voice appears rarely; phrases like 'you feel that' are frequently added when a simple declarative sentence will do. This has the effect of coercing the reader into the either-or position of identifying with or rejecting an opinion that deserves to be debated." Sklar also questioned Kael's allegiance to "vital vulgarity." "It gives the effect," Sklar wrote, "of a highly intelligent critic who downplays ideas. The moviegoer and reader of reviews need ideas as much as anything else."

Kael's detractors always lurked, and even the Paulettes would probably admit that, like Woody Allen's films, her work in the 1980s wasn't as good as the early, funny stuff. David Ansen in *Newsweek* felt that "her tastes in the '80s were more often than not out of synch with the public." Still, Tom Carson wrote, "Even thumbing through the '80s work, I keep having the feeling Kael described in her brilliant review of Norman Mailer's *Marilyn*: 'Just when you get fed up with his flab and slop, he'll come through with a runaway string of perceptions.'"

She could still fire off the one-liners with flair. Michael Apted's *Gorillas in the Mist* (1988) was for Kael "a feminist version of *King Kong*—now it's the gorillas who do the screaming." She felt that Barry Levinson's Academy Award-winning best picture, *Rain Man* (1988), was a "wet piece of kitsch" and "Dustin Hoffman humping one note on a piano for two hours and eleven minutes."

"The fact is [readers] are angry with you if you don't like square movies that have worthwhile, liberal, or open-hearted messages," she told Thomas Murphy of the Associated Press in 1989. "The more sentimental the movie is, the more likely you are to get real hate mail from the readers. The worst hate mail I've had in my 21 years at the magazine was on *Rain Man*. People really fall for that. And they fall for it to the degree that they write letters to the publisher saying I should be fired. That movie is reaching them at a level that has nothing to do with its quality. They want to believe it's doing good somewhere out there. It's doing good for Dustin Hoffman, that's who it's doing good for."

When Richard Corliss reviewed *For Keeps* in 1994, he dragged the new generation's appreciation for Kael out of Quentin Tarantino. The iconic writer-director of *Reservoir Dogs* (1992) and *Pulp Fiction* (1994) recounted, Corliss wrote in *Time*, that when he "was 15, he saw something on TV that changed his life:

Pauline Kael." Tarantino saw late-night NBC host Tom Snyder pressuring Kael toward a tangle about her favorable review
of Philip Kaufman's remake of *Invasion of the Body Snatchers*
(1978). "I thought, 'Who is this wild old woman?'" Tarantino
said. "And soon I was going to the library to find her books. She
was as influential as any director was in helping me develop my
aesthetic. I never went to film school, but she was the professor
in the film school of my mind."

Corliss saved up some riffing for his analysis of the Kael
anthology: "Reading *For Keeps* is like going on a toot with Mary
McCarthy, Belle Barth, and Billie Holiday. It's movie analysis
with a serrated edge; film criticism as stand-up bawdry; intellectual improvisation that soars into the highest form of word
jazz."

When she retired, it was a benchmark in the culture.
"Pauline's retirement marks the end of an era that's actually
been over for more than a decade, but that still echoed faintly
in her familiar voice," wrote John Powers in *LA Weekly*. "Her
work finally matters less for her ideas and judgments than for its
spirit—her passionate belief in absolutely personal criticism, her
awareness that movies and records and books must be understood as we live them, through immediate experience and in the
context of a whole life."

Rafferty, Denby, J. Hoberman, and Michael Sragow con-
tributed film reviews to *The New Yorker* in the early 1990s, and
Rafferty became the full-time critic when Kael retired abruptly in
1991. Rafferty's writing has also appeared in *The Atlantic Month-
ly*, *The New York Times*, and the *International Herald Tribune*.
He was critic at large for *GQ*, and compiled *The Thing Happens:
Ten Years of Writing about the Movies* (1993). A generalist with a
Ph.D. in literature from Cornell University, Rafferty has written
Times articles on Arnold Schwarzenegger's California guberna-
torial campaign and essays on James Dean and World War I, as
well as *Book Review* pieces on Joyce Carol Oates and John Edgar
Wideman. Rafferty has been fascinated by both horror fiction
and horror films.

"*Eyes Without a Face* ends with a shot of Christiane walking off into the distance, surrounded by doves," Rafferty wrote in 2003 in the *Times* about Georges Franju's 1962 horror classic. "It ends in exaltation. This is, to say the least, unexpected, more shocking than the shocks that horror movies are designed to produce. Franju shocks us by embracing and then transcending the grotesque. *Eyes Without a Face* is among the few films in the genre—Carl Dreyer's *Vampyr* (1932) is the only other one I can think of—that holds our attention without any recourse to narrative suspense. We barely care how the story will turn out: the suspense is in the images themselves, in the tension generated by our attempt to resolve the contradictory emotions they arouse."

Rafferty's prose has been uncommonly clear and accessible. "Kubrick's approach is bold, in a rather outdated way," he wrote in *The Nation* about *Full Metal Jacket* (1987). "The recruits chant Marine doggerel in unison, Hartman screams obscenities like incantations, men in white skivvies arrange themselves in symmetrical group compositions—it's all spectacle, ritualized performance, like an avant-garde theater production of the 1960s. (The nearest film equivalent is probably Jonas Mekas's *The Brig*, made in 1964.) Pressed to defend this technique, Kubrick would probably say that there's no way for us to understand something as unnatural as training for war unless we allow him to manipulate and depersonalize us in the same manner: if we put ourselves in his skilled hands, surrender our will and our intelligence, he'll abuse us for our own good.

"Tell it to the Marines, Stanley," Rafferty advised. "These assaultive methods might work—just—if this spectacle were truly autonomous, if the movie ended with the end of basic training. But the story . . . goes on, following a character known as Private Joker (Matthew Modine) to Vietnam around the time of the Tet offensive, and at that point Kubrick's radical surgery on the dramatic conventions doesn't look like such a good idea; he's cut away too much. The characters remain dehumanized, the audience remains desensitized and Vietnam has never seemed farther away."

Rafferty's economy at conceptualizing a filmmaker for the reader, and then saying why the new film is important, is one of his dexterous strengths. "Errol Morris's documentaries have a luxuriant weirdness, a deep unfamiliarity. In his first two films— *Gates of Heaven* (1978), a report on pet cemeteries in California, and *Vernon, Florida* (1981), a loosely assembled collection of tales from a small Southern town, told by rambling coots and half-demented good old boys—his choice of material and his fondness for lingering on the cracked discourse of his interview subjects identified him as a true connoisseur of native eccentricity, a hoarder of oddball Americana. His new movie, *The Thin Blue Line*, shows that he's more than an inspired believe-it-or-not artist.

"Telling the story of a 1976 cop-killing in Dallas, and detailing the process by which a man who is almost certainly innocent was convicted and sentenced to death for the crime (with the likely killer as the prosecution's star witness), Morris burrows into a nightmarish realm of duplicity, faulty perception, and bottomless ambiguity," Rafferty wrote in *The New Yorker*. "The movie is both detached and fanatically intense. Its materials have the heterogeneity, the heedless comprehensiveness, of documents in a dossier: There are interviews with the principals, close ups of key words and paragraphs from the newspaper accounts, courtroom sketches, maps, family-album snapshots of the suspects, diagrams of the crime scenes and of the entry and exit wounds in the victim's body, and a series of eerie reenactments of witnesses' different versions of the murder and the events that led up to it. But this stuff isn't organized in ways that we're used to. *The Thin Blue Line* doesn't have the structure either of *60 Minutes* . . . or of detective fiction, though it borrows elements from both; its form is circular, spiraling, its obsessive, repetitive visual motifs echoed in Philip Glass's hauntingly monotonous score. This is documentary as epistemological thriller."

While Rafferty and later Denby were generally considered worthy of carrying on *The New Yorker*'s film-review tradition, Anthony Lane was young and not a New Yorker, in fact he wasn't even American. Lane was born in 1962, the year that Pauline Kael wrote "Is There a Cure for Film Criticism?" in *Sight & Sound*. Lane became the deputy literary editor of *The Independent* in London in 1989 and, a year later, a film critic for *The Independent on Sunday*. In 1993, Lane was asked by *The New Yorker*'s then-editor, Tina Brown, to join the magazine as a film critic. He wrote pieces on Alfred Hitchcock and Ian Fleming for the magazine. His *New Yorker* reviews, essays, and profiles were published in 2002 as *Nobody's Perfect*, borrowing Joe E. Browne's final line in Billy Wilder's *Some Like It Hot* (1959).

"I prefer a critic who takes things as they come—one at a time, alert to their accidental felicities, good-naturedly witty about their much more common failings, resistant to gaseous (and unprovable) generalizations," Richard Schickel wrote in a review of *Nobody's Perfect*. "These qualities make Lane's occasional angry outbursts (see him on *The Phantom Menace*) the more powerful. Lane is not a perfect critic—I cannot for the life of me understand his affection for *Titanic* or his tolerance for *Apocalypse Now*. But 'right' or 'wrong' he is a pure pleasure to read. And that is the critic's first—and most often failed—obligation."

Lane practically hosts his column like a Noel Coward facsimile with a new TV show. "Anthony Lane is the fizziest critic around," John Updike wrote. "Each paragraph tickles the nose like a flute of champagne. His ebulliently active mind and wonderfully cluttered memory work to make us laugh aloud while he slips in the dirk, its edge painlessly keen, of urbane, humane opinion."

Lane's smooth style and what Manohla Dargis termed his "jokes"—smartly worded leads that engage the reader on the movie at hand—have made him one of the most admired of film critics. "Fellini is dead, Tarkovsky is dead, Bergman sticks to theatre, and Godard is out to lunch," Lane writes in the opening of his review of *Three Colors: Blue* (1993). "All of which leaves European cinema wandering around like a lost kid. Rescue has come in the unlikely shape of the Polish director Krzysztof

Kieslowski—unlikely because a resume of his early career, most of it in documentaries, barely hints at the glories to come. The man who made *The Principles of Safety and Hygiene in a Copper Mine*, fine work though that undoubtedly was, had a long path to tread."

Lane got to the punch line quicker in his review of Jan De Bont's *Speed* (1994). "*Speed* is set in Los Angeles. Most of it takes place on a bus. It is a film full of explosions but bare of any emotional development. Its characters are no more than sketches. It addresses no social concerns. It is morally inert. It's the movie of the year."

After explaining that "watching a Michael Bay film is indistinguishable from having a large, pointy lump of rock drop on your head," Lane remarked that the director's new picture, *Pearl Harbor* (2001), "maintains the mood, pulsing with fervor as it tells a tale familiar to every child in America: How a great nation was attacked and humbled by the imperious pride of Ben Affleck."

"Given the grumpy disarray of film criticism, it should come as little surprise that its dominant figure is *The New Yorker*'s Anthony Lane, who invariably manages to convey delight at having such a cushy gig," wrote John Powers in *LA Weekly*. "As a man who once herniated himself trying to find something fresh to say about Hugh Grant, I can only admire Lane's unflagging ability to pretend that nothing could be more jolly than reviewing *Notting Hill*. His new collection of reviews, *Nobody's Perfect* (great title), exhibits him at his most enjoyable, figure-skating across the world of movies (and books) like a Russian, er, Canadian champion, glittering wit flying up from his blades. He writes the most alluring lead paragraphs of any critic I know, and one can only imagine how much effort goes into making all of this throwaway aperçus seem effortless.

"Nobody says Lane is the best or most knowledgeable, but he's clearly the biggest star," Powers asserted. "His fat new collection was published by Knopf (not a university press). It garnered terrific reviews, including one from *Time*'s film critic

Richard Schickel (whose rave betrayed such a corrupt disdain for the movies, the audience and film criticism itself that I kept wondering if he was actually the third Weinstein brother). . . . In truth, the aristocratic ease that makes Lane so pleasurable to read is inseparable from his limitations. Caught up in the dazzling virtuosity of his leaps and twirls, he rarely breaks through the ice to see what might be swimming around in the chilly deep below; he never forces us to see a director in a brand-new way. He's the ideal reviewer for today's denatured Hollywood product—born, one might say, to dismember *Pearl Harbor*—because very little is at stake in his work beyond the splendors of his own performance. Delight he always does, but can you imagine Anthony Lane ever getting anyone angry?"

Steady, reliable, and informed, David Denby followed long associations with *The Atlantic Monthly* in the 1960s and 1970s and *New York* magazine through the 1980s with a place at his old friend Kael's magazine, *The New Yorker*, beginning in the mid-1990s. The "Rear Window" columnist in *Premiere*, Denby veered from movies with his book output, including *Great Books* (1996); *American Sucker* (2005), about his own faulty investing; and *Snark: It's Mean, It's Personal, and It's Ruining Our Conversation* (2009). Denby's writing on the movies occasionally carried strength of conviction.

"Tim Hunter's *River's Edge* is the most disturbing movie I have seen in the nearly nine years I have held this job," Denby wrote in *New York* in 1987. "Certainly not the best, but the most disturbing. This brilliant, messy little picture, another triumph for the independent film movement, should cause people to argue and celebrate for years—argue over how it could have been done better, celebrate that it was done at all. In recent years, American movies have followed teenagers from school to shopping mall to make-out couch, and some of these pictures have been skillful and charming. But as far as real moral interest or complexity goes, this is the only one that matters."

People Weekly, which Time, Inc., expanded in 1974 from its weekly "People" section of celebrity odds and ends and unusual personality features, started reviewing movies in 1977, and publishing bylined reviews in 1984. Ralph Novak and Peter Travers were its main reviewers. *People* has been a digest of weekly celebrity and personal-interest pieces that function as the feature and entertainment arm of its parent magazine. Time, Inc., became more specific in 1990 with *Entertainment Weekly*, which concentrated on show business. *EW*'s two main critics have been Lisa Schwarzbaum and Owen Gleiberman. Gleiberman was another film critic whose early years were spent with the great feeder system for career film critics, *The Boston Phoenix*.

Gleiberman was also yet another film critic whose inspiration came from Pauline Kael. Gleiberman, who grew up in Ann Arbor and attended the University of Michigan, told Aaron Aradillas of RockCritics.com that he casually read the 1976 edition of *The New Yorker* containing Kael's review of Brian De Palma's *Carrie*.

"I'd never heard of Pauline Kael . . . but I started to read the article just to kill a few minutes," Gleiberman said. "I'd never read anything like it. She seemed to be right inside my head, describing, quite literally, every detail of what I'd felt as I watched the movie. Pauline's writing is a little like crack. You want more. At the time, I didn't think, 'Gee, I'd like to write movie reviews, too,' but that pretty much planted the seed."

Gleiberman was hired at the *Phoenix* by Stephen Schiff and became acquainted with Kael. "She needed to be surrounded by admirers, and she knew just how to play them," Gleiberman said. "At the end of 1983, I got a freelance gig writing for a little paper in New York that Clay Felker had started—it was called the *East Side Express*—and Pauline told me flat-out that she didn't like my work for it. She said, 'You must be getting much better editing at the *Phoenix*.' Well, here's the deal: At that point, I was hardly getting edited at the *Phoenix* at all. Whatever your opinion of my stuff, it wasn't really any different in the two papers. Here was the difference: At the *East Side Express*, I was writing for the first time as a lead critic, reviewing the big movies of each week.

"So Pauline could see, in a way that she hadn't before, how truly different our tastes were—the way, for instance, that I raved about a film like *Star 80*, which she found morally revolting," Gleiberman remembered. "So she withheld her praise to guilt-trip me into falling in line. That's when our friendship ended."

People Weekly and *Entertainment Weekly* were not designed to cut into the business-insider aspects of the main trade papers, *Daily Variety* and *The Hollywood Reporter*. They were tailored for Middle America and its growing appetite for celebrity news and gossip.

Filling the landscape in between the trades and the mainstream magazines were three publications that combined popular appeal with savvy reporting and writing of personality and trend features that fell shy of the intellectualizing of *Film Comment* for an audience that nevertheless understood films: *American Film*, published by the American Film Institute from 1976 to 1987; *Premiere*, published out of New York by the magazine conglomerate, Hachette Filipacchi Media U.S., from 1987 to 2007; and *Movieline*, which was published in Los Angeles from 1989 into the new century, and relaunched online in 2009.

Film critics often wrote for the three magazines, which, in turn, also wrote about them. *Premiere*, edited by Susan Lyne and then Christopher Connelly, elaborated trends about blurb-meisters and film critics becoming screenwriters. Glenn Kenny was *Premiere*'s film critic. *Movieline* was a little more off-the-wall and less adorned, carrying provocative articles by Stephen Farber, Stephen Rebello, Martha Frankel, and the inveterately comedic Joe Queenan.

"In Los Angeles, for several years, under the editorship of Virginia Campbell, *Movieline* was funny, inside, scurrilous and quite convinced that the movie business was a place for scoundrels and frauds," film critic David Thomson wrote in 2000. "The wonder was that vision had taken so long to be realized. *Movieline* could move from the trashy to the expert in a single sentence, and it got under the plastic skin of the business. Now, things have changed. *Movieline* has discovered the young, their clothes and their advertisers. It has gone stale in a year."

The telescoping toward a feature-angle focus, and latterly entertainment as a core of coverage, evinced by the *Time*-to-*People*-to-*EW* evolution, was symptomatic of a general trend, from *Entertainment Tonight* through E! Entertainment Television. The trade papers even created special sections highlighting trends, awards, tributes, anniversaries, and other celebrations, providing new revenue streams. Former *Los Angeles Reader* film critic Steven Gaydos nurtured these sections, first at *The Hollywood Reporter*, then at *Daily Variety*. Established on the trades as the main film critics in the 1990s and later were Duane Byrge at the *Reporter* and Todd McCarthy, a former *Reporter* scribe, at *Variety*.

Like the reporters for the trades, the film critics were hardworking and savvy. Apart from his daily deadline work, Byrge cowrote *The Screwball Comedy Films: A History and Filmography, 1934–1942*, and edited for the American Film Institute *Private Screenings: Insiders Share a Century of Great Movie Moments*. McCarthy has been chief film critic at *Variety* for a generation, and came out of the industry.

Born in Evanston, Illinois, on February 16, 1950, and a graduate of Stanford University, McCarthy was an assistant to Elaine May at Paramount Pictures and director of advertising and publicity for Roger Corman's New World Pictures from 1975 to 1977, during which time he was also writing film criticism for *The Hollywood Reporter*. Like many entertainment writers, film critics included, McCarthy balanced active roles in the industry as he portrayed the industry for both insiders and cineastes. He had been the Hollywood editor for *Film Comment*, and his scholarship went into *Kings of the Bs: Working within the Hollywood System* (1975), a seminal book on Hollywood directors, co-edited with Charles Flynn.

McCarthy cowrote the documentary *Hollywood Mavericks* (1990), and won the Emmy Award for writing *Preston Sturges: The Rise and Fall of an American Dreamer* (1989), which aired on PBS's *American Masters*. McCarthy's great triumph as a filmmaker is *Visions of Light: The Art of Cinematography* (1992), which he wrote and co-directed. The film was named best documentary by the National Society of Film Critics, New York Film Critics Circle, and won an Eddie from the American Cinema Editors.

Visions of Light includes onscreen interviews with dozens of directors of photography—Conrad L. Hall, László Kovács, William A. Fraker, Néstor Almendros, Sven Nykvist, et al.—and pays tribute to other greats, including Gregg Toland and John Alton. It contains clips of 125 films. In *The New York Times*, Vincent Canby described the film as "the vibrant, gloriously documented tale of the evolution of motion-picture photography. . . . It's a vastly entertaining introduction to an art that's not always easy to see."

McCarthy's magnum opus as a writer is *Howard Hawks: The Grey Fox of Hollywood* (1997), an epic biography from Grove Press. "Hawks's life, until now rather an enigma, has been put into focus and made one with his art in Todd McCarthy's wise and funny *Howard Hawks*," *The Wall Street Journal* said. "Excellent. . . . A respectful, exhaustive, and appropriately smartass look at Hollywood's most versatile director," was *Newsweek*'s assessment.

McCarthy's film reviews usually express masterly completeness in logical progression, covering artistic merit, success in the film's perceived mission, and, of course, audience susceptibility and box-office potential. "I look at it first from an artistic point of view," McCarthy said. "Beyond everything else, I try to find the motivation behind the film. I ask, 'Why does this film exist? Why was it made?' Quite a few films, however, are made because the author or director or producer needs to express a point of view. But what's important, and what I try to do as a critic, is to tell you what the film is about. Is it successful at saying what it is trying to say?"

McCarthy's leads, always pithy summations, bolded, and atop the reviews, have been in direct service to *Variety*'s industry readership. "*The Client* is a satisfactory, by-the-numbers child-in-jeopardy thriller that will fill the bill as a very commercial hot weather popcorn picture," McCarthy packed into his lead of Joel Schumacher's film. "Lackluster, if faultlessly professional, in terms of filmmaking and performance, this third adaptation of a John Grisham bestseller to hit the big screen within less than a year's time typically has enough narrative meat on it to pull audiences in and keep them attentive. But unlike *The Firm* and *The Pelican Brief*, both of which had superstar casts to propel them past the $100 million domestic B.O. mark, this one will have to sail more on the author's rep alone, spelling very strong but perhaps less than towering business."

Renny Harlin's *Driven* (2001), written by its star, Sylvester Stallone, received this reception from McCarthy: "There seems to be no escaping the inherent cliches of auto racing pictures. Almost invariably, they fall into the same predictable pattern of pretty people moving from one track to another, drivers competing with each other in cars by day and over available young women after hours, with the constant spectre of sudden injury or death looming over all concerned. *Driven*, a souped-up, big-canvas actioner with a notably cheesy look to it, reps the latest manifestation of the genre's apparent built-in limitations. B.O. for pics set in this milieu is normally reliable but unspectacular, a pattern that should continue with this Warner Bros. release."

Of the other writers who have critiqued movies for *Daily Variety*, Emanuel Levy was akin to McCarthy in that he maintained his worth at the trade paper as a critic while forging an ambitious, multifaceted career as an author and academic. His Ph.D. at Columbia University was earned under instructors including Andrew Sarris and he taught at the New School for Social Research and Arizona State, among others. Levy has written books on John Wayne, George Cukor, Vincente Minnelli, independent films, and the Academy Awards. *And the Winner Is: The History and Politics of the Academy Awards*, first published in 1987, has been reprinted several times under several titles as one of the standard sources on the Oscars' history.

Levy might hold the record for memberships in film

critic organizations and related groups, having been president of the Los Angeles Film Critics Association, and a member of the National Society of Film Critics, Broadcast Film Critics Association, and International Federation of Film Critics as well as the Hollywood Foreign Press Association. Levy has also served on the juries of at least 45 film festivals, including Cannes, Venice, and Montreal.

Levy's great contribution to film criticism has been a paean to his former mentor. *Citizen Sarris, American Film Critic: Essays in Honor of Andrew Sarris* was published by Scarecrow Press in 2001, containing pieces by Molly Haskell, Elisabeth Weis, Roger Ebert, David Thomson, Leonard Maltin, Richard Schickel, Charles Champlin, Richard Corliss, Henry Sheehan, Kenneth Turan, Phillip Lopate, Todd McCarthy, Gerald Peary, Michael Wilmington, Caryn James, Dave Kehr, Levy himself, and other critics. Filmmakers contributing pieces included Martin Scorsese, Budd Boetticher, John Sayles, Curtis Hanson, and Peter Bogdanovich. This tribute volume, born in a conversation between Levy and Wilmington, allowed film critics reverence for the importance of one of their own. It also allowed some filmmakers the opportunity to comment in return on one of the not insignificant boosters to their careers.

"I consider Andrew Sarris to be one of the most fundamental and valued teachers," Scorsese wrote in *Citizen Sarris*. "His writings led me to see the genius in American movies at a time when the cinema was considered a mindless form of entertainment, worthy of serious attention only if it came from Europe or Asia. Sarris's passion, his enthusiasm, his wonderful ability to articulate for me and many others as well as what we unconsciously felt about the styles of various directors played a truly pivotal role in my life. For that, I'll always be grateful."

One of the more unusual books about film critics also concerned Sarris, and was written by his wife, Molly Haskell. Morose lamentation may have been feeding the field, but critical issues in the late 1980s for Haskell and Sarris turned into a critical condition. Sarris contracted an encephalitic virus that required him to spend six months in a hospital, during which he was afflicted with paralysis and memory loss.

The resulting infirmity was recounted in diary-like form in *Love and Other Infectious Diseases: A Memoir* (1990), perhaps the most deeply personal look inside the lives of film critics. "I wanted to write about my relationship with Andrew in the context of illness and identity," Haskell told *Publishers Weekly*. ". . . My thought was that I had been engulfed by marriage, and I had to chart how I retook possession of myself." Margaret Carlson wrote in *Time* that "Haskell uses Sarris' illness as a lantern by which she can shine a light on the dark corners of her life: . . . what it is like to be married to an acknowledged expert in her field . . . and all the complications and compensations of love." Haskell eventually nursed Sarris back to health.

A book by Sarris also circulated. This was the history *You Ain't Heard Nothin' Yet: The American Talking Film, History and Memory, 1927–1949*, released in December 1999. The book touches on Ford, Hitchcock, Chaplin, and Welles; Garbo, Bogart, Bergman, Tracy, and Katharine Hepburn; MGM, Paramount, RKO, Warner Bros., Twentieth Century-Fox and the other studios.

The book went deep into long obscured genre issues. "Discussing the gangster film, [Sarris] moves beyond the standard *Little Caesar-Public Enemy-Scarface* trilogy and makes us yearn to see the ones that largely have eluded history—*The Doorway to Hell, Quick Millions, Blood Money*," wrote Sarris's longtime colleague Richard Schickel in the *Los Angeles Times Book Review*. "We are not talking cultishness here. Or idiot savantry. We are talking the kind of profoundly engaged, even romantically inflamed criticism any art requires if its traditions are to live on in ways that are useful and informative to the present—and to the future."

The world of film criticism that Sarris wrought flourished in the 1980s, as movies were a big portion of the alt-weeklies' coverage. Their critics' voices were often hyper-skeptical and savage, as well as uncannily intuitive and informed. J. Hoberman inherited the mantle of the *Voice*'s lead critic from Sarris. Working at first with Sarris and Haskell at the *Voice*, Hoberman gradually through the 1980s built a dedicated following developed from his deeply impassioned and strongly analytical sense about movies. Hoberman's first review for *The Village Voice* was of David Lynch's *Eraserhead* (1977), and he has since been a kind of inspirational voice of intelligence and strength through the long years alongside such other excellent *Voice* film critics as Tom Allen, Amy Taubin, Michael Atkinson, and Dennis Lim.

"Although I'm sure it would horrify Hoberman to hear this," said Manohla Dargis, a former New York University student of Hoberman's who eventually became a film critic for *The Village Voice*, *LA Weekly*, *Los Angeles Times*, and *The New York Times*, "there are writers who now slavishly write in imitation of Jim's style, much as an older generation imitates the late Pauline Kael in voice and prejudice. The thing is that although Jim's imitators can, to a modest degree, approximate his style, they're simply nowhere as smart. They also don't get that he has a definite worldview and that his style dovetails with that worldview."

Welcoming bends and warps to genre conventions, Hoberman has been a deep-thinking generalist with a scholar's long view and a film geek's reference memory. "A superior entertainment," he called Joe Dante's *The Howling* (1981), "as creepy, witty and suggestive as its disreputable genre would warrant." Hoberman called Ivan Passer's *Cutter's Way* (1981) "a bitter neo-noir with an unexpected bonanza of B-movie virtues," and he explained it as "ultimately less a murder mystery than it is a sensual meditation on the mysteries of friendship and fate, power and personal responsibility." A rougher neo-noir case came in 1986: "Robust in its sleaziness, John Frankenheimer's *52 Pick-Up* is the ultimate guilty husband movie," Hoberman wrote.

The genre of *Full Metal Jacket* (1987) was more Stanley Kubrick than war. "Neither ecstatic napalm d'or spectacle nor personal unburdening, this is one distanced film—directed as if gazing through the wrong end of a telescope from the perspective of 2001," Hoberman wrote in *The Village Voice*. "What fools these insects be? *Full Metal Jacket* seems to have been made with less burning conviction than disciplined revulsion. Joker [Matthew Modine] must be speaking for his creator when, at the end of the film he proclaims, 'I am in a world of shit, but I am alive and I am not afraid.'"

Hoberman joined forces with one of the other master film critics to have risen and flourished through a career in the alternative press, Jonathan Rosenbaum of the *Chicago Reader*, for the compendium *Midnight Movies* (1991), one of the classics of cult-film appreciation—"still the best book on the topic," according to *Daily Variety* in 2005. After Dave Kehr moved to the *Chicago Tribune* in 1986, Rosenbaum took over as lead film critic of the *Reader*. Rosenbaum's book output includes *Moving Places: A Life at the Movies* (1980), described on the critic's Web site as "an experimental memoir about growing up in a family of film exhibitors in small-town Alabama during the 1950s, interrogating the role played by movies in shaping a life and consciousness." Rosenbaum edited Orson Welles and Peter Bogdanovich's oral history, *This Is Orson Welles* (1998).

In the best tradition of the great film critics, Rosenbaum has consistently sought out the unfairly obscured or marginalized movies and filmmakers. Overshadowed in Chicago by Siskel and Ebert, Rosenbaum seemed nevertheless comfortable in his alternative-paper niche, much like Andrew Sarris in New York or Michael Ventura in Los Angeles, left to his own devices and considerable talents in order to contribute mightily to the record.

"Given the difficulties he had in the '70s and '80s getting his films made and seen, Charles Burnett seemed in danger of becoming the Carl Dreyer of the black independent cinema—the consummate master who makes a film a decade, known only to a small band of film lovers," Rosenbaum wrote in 1998. "Seven years passed between *Killer of Sheep* (1977) and *My Brother's Wedding* (1984), and then another six before *To Sleep With Anger* (1990), which tried and failed to make a dent in the mainstream, as did *The Glass Shield* (1994). But Burnett's output has gradually accelerated, and in the mid-'90s he produced two near miracles. *When It Rains* (1995), a 12-minute masterpiece financed by European TV, remains as hard to see as his two first features, but *Nightjohn* (1996), a wonderful feature made for the Disney Channel, is being revived."

Rosenbaum could both try and rally efforts for a neglected talent like Burnett and weigh in on big Hollywood subjects. Like Hoberman and Ventura and a few other alt-weekly critics—Ty Burr, David Chute, Peter Keough, and David Edelstein out of *The Boston Phoenix*— Rosenbaum saw the big picture.

"I was finishing school, and a friend told me that Carolyn Clay at *The Boston Phoenix* was looking for a third-string theater critic," Edelstein said. "I got a try-out and then voila: I was a professional, earning a grand $35 a review while teaching on the side. Carolyn was a blast—I've never since had an editor who'd add puns to my pieces.

"Then the film section needed a fourth-stringer and Stephen Schiff gave me a shot. Schiff was a huge influence on my voice," Edelstein recalled. "His style back then had a lot of Pauline Kael, but it was more fluid and magisterial, and he knew how to let the air out with snarky punchlines. Owen Gleiberman was second string and was very supportive, too. I still recall, fondly, Donkey Kong, debate about movies, and endless pints of Bass Ale with Owen after the section was closed. David Denby and David Chute had been at the *Phoenix* before my time, and Mike Sragow came at the end of my tenure. I missed my pals Charlie Taylor and Stephanie Zacharek by a few months. It was a great place to apprentice."

From a 2007 perspective, the *LA Weekly* achieved the age of 30 along a bumpy ride. In a look back on the publication at three decades, film critic John Powers called the paper's first film critic, Michael Ventura, "the single most important writer in the history of this newspaper" as well as "the most original film critic of my generation."

Ventura's classics in the *Weekly* included an obituary/commentary on John Wayne's lasting mythic importance and a piece on Steven Spielberg's "dwindling imagination," connected to *Indiana Jones and the Temple of Doom* (1984). "What made Ventura's criticism extraordinary was his faith in his own perceptions," Powers wrote. ". . . Maileresque in its baroque pithiness, Ventura's movie criticism was so profoundly personal—so unlike everybody else's in style and ambition—that I never picked up one of his reviews without a sense of high drama."

Despite Powers's regard for Ventura and the *Weekly's* proving ground for many writers and film critics, including mainstay F.X. Feeney and future *New York Times* film critic Manohla Dargis, John Powers and Ella Taylor have been the voices most associated with the paper's film criticism throughout its history. Powers wrote a regular Hollywood column for Britain's *Sight & Sound* and was a critic at large on National Public Radio. Powers left a Georgetown University teaching position in 1985 to become a film critic at the *LA Weekly*.

Powers has been an adventurous writer with opinions that work like ammonium carbonate on lazy readers. An entertaining wiseacre, he noted that Francis Coppola resumed his middle name (Ford) for *The Godfather Part III* (1990), and wrote, "This Godfather doesn't equal either of the first two; there are fewer transcendent moments, more clinkers, and the pacing feels both sluggish and rushed. Yet it's always absorbing because Coppola's ambition is so grand and his conviction so genuine—like *Part II*, this movie revises what's come before. *The Godfather Part III* may be disappointing when you're watching it, but in your head it's likely to start turning into a masterpiece—the conception, anyway, is nothing short of magisterial."

Film editors at the *Weekly* included Helen Knode, who married novelist James Ellroy after saying she was bored with movies, and Ella Taylor, a former TV critic and media sociology teacher at the University of Washington. Taylor, in charge from 1989 to 1991, remembered Powers—whom she called "an extraordinarily lucid and fluent writer on just about any topic you can think of (he wrote a definitive essay on Pauline Kael . . .)"—trying to convince her to run his one-word review of a

Child's Play sequel: "Upchucky." Powers fleshed out that succinct evaluation at her request. However insistent an editor, Taylor certainly was a writer of some elegance, whose criticism also
appeared in *The Atlantic Monthly*, *The Village Voice*, and *Mirabella*. Taylor returned to writing film reviews at the *Weekly* in
1995 after the 1993 mutiny there, during which she and most of
the paper's writers walked out in support of editor-in-chief Kit
Rachlis's battle with management.

Facile and fierce on the feminist watch without the rabble-rousing of, say, Helen Knode, Taylor zeroed in on Diane
Ladd's performance as a fearsome mother in David Lynch's *Wild
at Heart* (1990). "It's as though Lynch has poured all his fear and
loathing of controlling mothers (or just mothers) into Marietta,
and Ladd seethes and steams, flexes her lurid nails and tosses
her metallic blonde curls as she turns loose her demonic former
lover," Taylor wrote. "Marietta's an overwrought cross between
Blanche DuBois and Cruella De Vil."

The most representative film critic at the *Weekly*'s head-
to-head competition, the now defunct *Los Angeles Reader*, was
Henry Sheehan, who also served as president of the Los Angeles Film Critics Association, and contributed to *Film Comment*,
Sight & Sound, *Atlantic Monthly*, *Daily Variety*, the *Chicago
Reader*, *Chicago Journal*, *The Boston Phoenix*, *Boston Globe*, *LA
Weekly*, and *The Hollywood Reporter*. From 1986 to 1991, Sheehan upheld the *Reader*'s reviewing tradition of long think pieces,
the modus operandi of his predecessors Dan Sallitt, Myron Meisel, David Ehrenstein, and Andy Klein. The *Reader*'s critics also
included Blake Lucas and Steven Gaydos.

An incisive critic whose in-depth analyses have included
unique examinations of the careers of Steven Spielberg and Clint
Eastwood, Sheehan has often been thorough and dead-set in his
opinions. Sheehan's two-part 1991 essay in *Film Comment*, "The
Panning of Steven Spielberg," cuts deeply into the filmmaker's
flawed heroes. "[I]n fragments, that story is the story of nearly
every Spielberg film. . . . Although Spielberg's films are usually
described as warm or even exhilarating and euphoric, their most

prevalent temper is anxiety," Sheehan wrote. "Every Spielberg hero from *Duel* onward is, to one extent or another, worried that he is failing at some essentially male role, either lover or father. In *Hook*, these twin fears are mirrored in Peter, who is plainly a poor father and who, less conspicuously, wants to retreat from the issue of sex in general."

Sheehan took over as film critic of the *Orange County Register* when Jim Emerson, his predecessor, returned to the Seattle area, and eventually became editor of Microsoft's Cinemania Web site. From 1993 to 2002, Sheehan reviewed for the *Register*, and beginning in 1986, has been a regular panelist on KPCC-FM's *Film Week*, a live, hour-long Friday discussion broadcasting film criticism on new releases. Other critics joining host Larry Mantle on the show's revolving lineup have included Peter Rainer, Andy Klein, Jean Oppenheimer, Lael Lowenstein, Claudia Puig, Wade Major, and animation scholar Charles Solomon.

Both Rainer and his predecessor as the main film critic at the *Los Angeles Herald-Examiner*, Michael Sragow, have occasionally been elusive figures. Both are among the most admired film critics of their times, writers of common sense and skepticism, purveyors of facilitative language that bridges frank talk with intellectual discourse, always with hard-to-please constitutions, but ultimately possessed of true love for the cinema. They are also the great gypsies of film criticism, crisscrossing the nation to new challenges.

Sragow and Rainer represent the film critics of vocational entrenchment, those who have been critics most of their adult lives, worked hard to stay film critics, and been successful as such. Judith Crist and Rex Reed, once they had attained the post of film critic, stayed in the vocation for at least half a dozen venues apiece on TV and in magazines and newspapers. This was in the Film Generation years, when the position of film critic still had some mystery and glamour for the nation at large, and films were being accepted as art.

Some major film critics who began in the late 1960s and early 1970s proved themselves outstanding cineastes, writers, and valuable employees—even icons—at their papers and magazines: Vincent Canby, Roger Ebert, Gene Siskel, Janet Maslin, David Denby, Jay Carr, Gary Arnold, Bruce Williamson, et al. They kept on keeping on as film critics. The vocation was for them something on which to spend a lifetime. Sragow and Rainer also dedicated their careers to film criticism; it's just that, to paraphrase Bogart, fate, occasionally, takes a hand—or ambition kicks in. The geography of Sragow's and Rainer's professional lives requires an atlas.

Sragow began his career at *Boston* magazine, and has been the official film critic at the *Los Angeles Herald-Examiner* (1978–1981), *Rolling Stone* (1981–1983), *Boston Phoenix* (1983–1985), *San Francisco Examiner* (1985–1992), *Seattle Weekly* (1995–1996), *SF Weekly* (1997–1999), and the *Baltimore Sun* (2001 onward). Sragow has also been among the most prolific writers among film critics, as a frequent contributor to *The Atlantic Monthly* and the Arts & Leisure section of the Sunday *New York Times*, and has contributed movie notes and film stories to *The New Yorker* since 1989. He placed articles in *Mother Jones, Esquire, Harper's, American Film, Film Comment, Sight & Sound, The Nation, The New Republic,* and others.

"Philip Kaufman's *Henry & June* is a gorgeous piece of work—a tough-minded, ironical, tremendously enjoyable vision of sex, love, and creation and the roving, improvisatory life of the expatriate artist in Paris circa 1931," Sragow wrote in the *San Francisco Examiner* in 1990. Sragow's four-star review of Gavin Millar's *Dreamchild* (1985) in the *Examiner* is credited with making that film a hit in the Bay Area while it did slight business elsewhere in the United States. Upon the death of Sam Peckinpah in 1985, Sragow eulogized the director in the *Boston Phoenix*: "When an instructive artist like Peckinpah works all out, he touches on eternal mysteries. He brings us such a full understanding of tragedy that we feel both purged by pity and terror and haunted by the question, 'What was it all for?' *The Wild Bunch* is Peckinpah's answer."

Rainer replaced Sragow in 1981 as the film critic at the

Herald-Examiner and stayed the decade, until the *Herald* folded in 1989. David Chute shared reviewing and other film-beat chores from 1981 to 1986, and David Ehrenstein and Andy Klein also reviewed. Also on staff in the 1980s were former and future film critic Joe Morgenstern, who was a city-side columnist, and future film critic Elvis Mitchell, who covered TV. The city's number two daily after the *Times*, the *Herald-Examiner* had been in decline since the 1960s, when it was the largest afternoon daily in the U.S. with a circulation of 700,000—known for crime, entertainment, and sports coverage, and for colorful writers.

Rainer wrote about films with an introspection and dexterity that belied a daily deadline. He had magazine style on one of the inkiest sheets in the land, and placed features and essays throughout his career with *The New York Times Magazine*, *Vogue*, *American Film*, *Premiere*, *Connoisseur*, and other periodicals. He made TV appearances on *Nightline*, *ABC World News Tonight*, *CBS Morning News* and CNN, and was chairman of the National Society of Film Critics in the late 1980s and early 1990s.

Apprehending *Shoot the Moon* (1982), a marital breakup story, Rainer wrote in the *Herald-Examiner*, "Howard Hawks once said that he would only direct a tragedy if he saw no way to make it a comedy. Alan Parker and Bo Goldman have it both ways in *Shoot the Moon*. It's a sorrowful film, but it expresses the human comedy. Watching it, you're amazed at what love and lovelessness can do to people, how it can warp them into monsters and rag dolls and buffoons. This movie is saying the same things the screwball comedies were saying, only in a different key: It's saying that on some essential level, human beings are bewilderingly inadequate to the demands of love. They can't handle it."

Rainer didn't recognize the environs of William Friedkin's *To Live and Die in L.A.* (1985), calling it "a deep-set nutcase movie. You get the feeling that the filmmakers responsible for it are working out of some manic, militarized zone for which they alone hold the map." In 1987 in the *Herald-Examiner*, he reasoned that "Robert Altman doesn't make movies like anybody else, so I suppose it makes sense that his stinkers are as one-of-a-kind as his great films. *Beyond Therapy* . . . isn't like other bad movies. But make no mistake, it's a nose-pincher. . . . You can't even take the movie's lack of seriousness seriously." In the lead of his *Herald-Examiner* review of *Empire of the Sun* (1987), Rainer wrote, "I hope Steven Spielberg's *Empire of the Sun* wins him that damn Oscar so he goes back to making movies that give real and lasting pleasure to people."

Glib on the air and a believer in the axiom that comedy is hard, Rainer has promoted certain comedic films and performances. He successfully argued, for instance, for Steve Martin's performance in *Roxanne* (1987) to gain the best actor award (in a tie with Jack Nicholson for *Ironweed* and *The Witches of Eastwick*) from the Los Angeles Film Critics Association. As a filmmaker, Rainer has coproduced documentaries for the Arts & Entertainment Network on Sidney Poitier and the Hustons.

"For more than three decades, Woody Allen has directed movies on the average of about one a year," Rainer wrote in 2001. "Even when he doesn't really have anything to make a movie about, he makes one anyway. This isn't necessarily such a terrible thing: As marking-time movies go, I much prefer the goofball nothingness of, say, *Manhattan Murder Mystery* to the furrowed-brow meaningfulness of films like *September* or *Alice*. Allen is at his best when he's closer in spirit to Brooklyn than to Sweden. He's earned a right to his doodles, but he's sure been doodling a lot lately—remember *Celebrity* and *Everyone Says I Love You*? His latest comedy, *The Curse of the Jade Scorpion*, is so thin that if you squint at the screen sideways it might disappear."

After the *Herald-Examiner* ceased in 1989, Rainer was hired by the *Los Angeles Times* onto a reviewing roster crowded by Sheila Benson, Kevin Thomas, and freelancer Michael Wilmington. With the addition of Rainer, the quartet wasn't the happiest of film-review staffs, and rumbled into gossip coverage, primarily about alleged fights between head film critic Benson and film desk editor Jack Mathews, who began selecting the films that she would review. The situation became messier when, according to

Los Angeles magazine, Mathews skipped over Benson, Rainer, and Thomas with the plum assignment of reviewing Coppola's *The Godfather Part III* and gave it to Wilmington.

The logjam was alleviated when Benson retired from the *Times* in 1991, and Kenneth Turan assumed the head critic's role. Wilmington soon moved to replace Dave Kehr as the head film critic for the *Chicago Tribune*. Rainer was let go in a staff shake-up in 1995, leaving Thomas as the enduring film critic from past decades.

Rainer became film critic of *Los Angeles* magazine in 1996, succeeding David Thomson and, earlier, Rod Lurie. "Being a critic is one of the classiest ways I know of to be disreputable," Rainer said. "It's a kid's dream with an adult twist. You get to sit in the dark and widen your eyes and then afterwards you try to make sense of it all." In 1997, Rainer became lead film critic for the *Los Angeles New Times*, one of an upstart chain of new alternative weeklies, which bought and amortized the *Los Angeles Reader*. It was Rainer's fourth reviewing post in Los Angeles within seven years.

In 1998, Rainer was runner-up for the Pulitzer Prize in criticism for his *New Times* reviews, specifically, according to the citation, "for his versatile and perceptive writing about film," on such movies as *Titanic, L.A. Confidential, Good Will Hunting,* and *Hamsun.* Book critic Michiko Kakutani of *The New York Times* won the Pulitzer that year for criticism. Rainer was the first West Coast film critic recognized by the Pulitzer board, and only the sixth film critic ever cited for winning or placing second.

Rainer became the film critic of *New York* magazine that same year, succeeding David Denby. Rainer stayed in that post into 2004, when he was replaced by *Entertainment Weekly*'s Ken Tucker, a longtime TV critic. In 2006, Rainer took over for David Sterritt as film critic of *The Christian Science Monitor.* Sterritt, an educator and author, had been on the staff at the Boston-based *Monitor* for 37 years, most of those as film critic. The former editor-in-chief of the *Boston Phoenix*, film critic for

National Public Radio's *All Things Considered*, and Boston-area theatre critic for *Variety*, Sterritt had written books about the Beat Generation in film and edited books of interviews on Jean-Luc Godard, Robert Altman, and Terry Gilliam for the University Press of Mississippi, which honored him by publishing *Guiltless Pleasures: A David Sterritt Film Reader* in 2005.

Rainer and Sterritt had each been chairman of the National Society of Film Critics, which, like the other film critics organizations, was expanding. The three major critical groups were growing so large with new critics added each year that the back-room aspect of the voting procedures grew toward town-hall debates. The Los Angeles Film Critics Association grew from 25 to nearly 50 members within 15 years. The New York Film Critics Circle was just shy of tripling its membership—originally solely the city's daily newspaper film critics—by 2008. Historian Tom O'Neil in 2002 characterized the old days of these groups with humorous if vague intrigue.

"The voting conclaves are so mysterious—and regarded by many as being so sacred—that it may seem as if the critics are powwowing to pick a pope, but in fact their secret antics can be quite devilish," O'Neil wrote. "Fistfights, 'screams of dissenters,' 'fierce laments,' tears and wanton drunkenness have all been reported at conclaves in the past. In 1975 a voting session of the national society got so rowdy that *New York Times* writer Roger Greenspun suffered a heart attack. Bosley Crowther, a longtime chairman of the New York circle, once commented: 'to put it bluntly, the voting sessions of the critics have sometimes been nigh unto brawls.'"

The NYFCC, which has a large overlap with the National Society of Film Critics, was nearly a snoozefest at its 1989 meeting, as member Georgia Brown reported in her insider's profile, "Bite the Ballot," in *The Village Voice*. The critic, who chastised the group in the piece for neglecting her pick for best picture, Spike Lee's *Do the Right Thing*, was "depressed by the tedium, by the lack of warmth" at the 1988 meeting, but returned anyway, and noted the new meeting was marked by "bland and oppressive silence." Brown's piece mulled over Pauline Kael's pervasive influence, and she identified members David Denby of *New York*, David Edelstein of the *New York Post*, and Terrence Rafferty of *The Nation* and *The New Yorker* as "perennially registered 'Paulettes.'"

"*Do the Right Thing* came out during Kael's summer leave from *The New Yorker*," Brown wrote. "Terrence Rafferty (ablebodied critic at *The Nation* deputized by Kael) was trusted to do the right thing. According to an anecdote reported by Phillip Lopate in his *New York Woman* profile of Kael, 'the Lady in the Dark' . . . Kael was miffed after getting a phone call at her home in the Berkshires reporting that Sheila Benson of the *Los Angeles Times* ("And to think I recommended her for that job!") had just given *DTRT* a rave. (The L.A. critics, meeting the same day as our group in a city far away, voted *DTRT* best picture.)"

After absorbing Brown's impressionistic piece, Richard Corliss explained the New York and National Society groups in 1990 in *Premiere*. The NYFCC "is no cutting edge outfit," he wrote. "It is a middle-aged finger that points, ever so decorously, toward Oscar night," quite a change from the nature of the group in the rebellious 1930s. "Georgia Brown . . . charged the critics with sins of racism, social myopia, artistic sclerosis, terminal stodginess, senility . . . I forget what all. What happened was, as often does in groups of strong-minded but not like-minded individuals, is that votes fell from the extremes to the center. Some NYFCC members passionately liked *Do the Right Thing*, and some passionately disliked it. So *My Left Foot*, a mild, minor film that nobody could hate was chosen. Apathy won the day."

Kael, meanwhile, deployed the Paulettes in National Society bivouacs. "In the National Society voting one can see the fine, finagling hand of Pauline Kael as it waves benediction at certain of her favorite films and as a substantial number of younger critics follow her lead," Corliss wrote. "In the voting for the 1988 awards, *The Unbearable Lightness of Being* won for best film largely through her agency. Not many members bothered to show up for the meeting, and enough of those who did pushed the Philip Kaufman drama through.

"At the 1989 session, Kael's sympathies were known to be with the Vietnam War drama *Casualties of War*, whose director, Brian De Palma, had lost a close vote by the NYFCC," Corliss continued. "As I recall, Kael did not put De Palma's name on her ballot, and he hardly placed in the National Society's voting. Someone said later that she had simply forgot to include De Palma. The anecdote is revealing and comforting: it indicates that even where critics are concerned, you can't always believe in conspiracy theories. So forget about critics as snipers and anarchists. Read us for whatever entertainment and insight we bring to our work."

Corliss lamented the passing of the National Society's heyday when John Simon came to the annual meeting with a fully loaded verbal arsenal. "Gone are the days when our sainted scourge, John Simon, would take target practice on critics proposed for membership," he wrote. ". . . Once he and another critic goaded each other into a near fistfight, a confrontation memorialized in Wilfrid Sheed's 1970 novel *Max Jamison*. (The fictional critic Jamison on his colleagues: "'You're all self-important asses. Or threadbare clowns. Or pretentious hacks. . . .'" The room was rimey with contempt; he had never seen such mutual loathing in one group.') Alas, those choleric times have passed, just as the headlines of the '60s gave way to hangover. The splendid Simon may have mellowed, too. At last year's NYFCC meeting, he contented himself with observing that in *Music Box*, Jessica Lange 'spoke atrocious Hungarian.'"

Critics fighting critics, and studios fighting critics were long-established brands of skirmishes, when an innovative filmmaker took a feud with a film critic public. Filmmakers were used to the studios fighting in their stead, as Twentieth Century-Fox did for Tyrone Power in the 1930s against *The New York Times*'s film critic, Frank S. Nugent, and as Warner Bros. did for Delmer Daves and Fox did for Joseph L. Mankiewicz and Elizabeth Taylor in the 1960s, both against the *New York Herald-*

Tribune's film critic, Judith Crist. But James Cameron went it alone, and after assuming Oscar's throne, he unleashed an attack on *Los Angeles Times* film critic Kenneth Turan, which the paper seemed to promote.

On March 21, 1998, Turan wrote the essay entitled, "You Try to Stop It," on the eve of the Academy Awards. Turan saw *Titanic* as a marking point in multiplex culture, writing that "the flip side of *Titanic's* ability to draw hordes of viewers into the theaters is the question of where these viewers have been for the past several years. In its unintentional understanding of how narrow an audience net movies cast over the American public, *Titanic* is not an example of Hollywood's success, it's an emblem of its failure . . . how desperate the mainstream audience . . . has become for anything even resembling Old-fashioned entertainment. [The audience has been] deadened by exposure to non-stop trash."

Cameron aped his own screenplay for *Titanic* (1997) at the Academy Awards that year by declaring himself "the king of the world!" when he won the best picture Oscar, the final of 11 statuettes won by the film. Kenneth Turan had panned the mega-hit in his *Los Angeles Times* review before he wrote about the film as a cultural phenomenon. Not sufficiently satisfied at his kingly dominion over Hollywood, Cameron took Turan's opinion personally, as if the *Times* critic were the only person in America who thought the film was mediocre.

"I have shrugged off Kenneth Turan's incessant rain of personal barbs over the last few months, since he is clearly not a big enough man to admit when he is wrong," Cameron wrote in a letter to the *Times*, "and it has been amusing to watch him dig himself into a deeper hole each time he tries to justify his misanthropic sensibility with regard to *Titanic*." The 1,200-word letter was printed on the front of the *Times* Calendar section on March 28 under the headline, "He's Mad as Hell at Turan." "But it's time to speak when Turan uses his bully pulpit not only to attack my film, but the entire film industry and its audiences."

Fortified by the Oscars, Cameron wrote, "In Turan's private reality, the vast majority of the worldwide audience and the majority of Hollywood screenwriters are wrong, and only he is right. . . . Poor Kenny. He sees himself as the lone voice crying in the wilderness, righteous but not heeded by the blind and dumb 'great unwashed' around him. Turan's critical sensibility is the worst kind of ego-driven elitism. . . . Nobody's interested in the vitriolic ravings of a bitter man who attacks and rips apart movies that the great majority of viewers find well worth their time and money. Turan has lost touch with the joys of film viewing . . . and no longer serves a useful purpose. . . . Give us a critic who actually likes movies. . . . Forget about Clinton—how do we impeach Kenneth Turan?"

The *Times* devoted a full page to "*Titanic* Letters." Humorist and actor Orson Bean chimed in, "I find myself saying, 'Ken Turan liked it, but let's give it a shot anyhow.'" Film critics Wade Major and Gene Shalit supported their fellow critic. "I salute Turan for his lucid, impressive and persuasive essays," Shalit wrote. "I hope producers and critics will be influenced by him, and will take the thumbs out of their eyes." Actor Jesse Vint and director Ted Post gave their two cents. The debate was covered by *The New York Times* and *The Washington Post* and was reported from coast to coast by The Associated Press.

More than 300 more letters, faxes and e-mails poured in. The *Times* reported that the tide had turned: 220 of the missives were pro-Turan, 63 in Cameron's favor, and 18 were sitting on the fence. The paper printed some, then declared a moratorium on the issue. Turan remained unimpeachable, at least into the next century.

Turan arrived on the West Coast from posts at *TV Guide* and *The Washington Post* to ostensibly run the *Los Angeles Times Book Review* in 1990. He became established as the paper's lead film critic shortly thereafter. Shelby Coffey III had arrived to run the editorial side of the L.A.-omnipotent *Times* from *The Washington Post* at the end of the 1980s, and Turan followed, gaining the catbird's seat as the city's lead critic after inside fulminations resulting in Sheila Benson resigning, and secondary critics Peter

Rainer and Michael Wilmington moving on to new pastures.

Born October 27, 1946, in Brooklyn, New York, Turan was educated at Swarthmore College and Columbia University. He became a reporter in 1968 at the *Fremont News-Register* in California, and joined *The Washington Post* as a sports writer the following year. Turan became a staff writer for the *Post's Sunday Magazine* in 1972, then a Style section feature writer and cultural critic in 1975, and reigned as book review editor from 1978 to 1986.

His early film criticism was written for the Madison, Wisconsin-based *The Progressive* from 1972 to 1980, and *New West/California* and *Gentlemen's Quarterly* in the 1980s, and was broadcast on National Public Radio's *All Things Considered* and CBS Radio. Turan's books include *The Future Is Now* (1972), with William Gildea, about the Washington Redskins; *Sinema: American Pornographic Films and the People Who Make Them* (1974) with Stephen F. Zito; and *Call Me Anna* (1987), actress Patty Duke's autobiography.

Turan's leads were akin to good movie openings, by drawing the reader in and making him or her want to know more. "As shocking yet haunting as a Diane Arbus photograph, disturbing because it was so unmistakably human, *Crumb* makes it difficult to look away," was his entry to his review of Terry Zwigoff's 1995 documentary about cartoonist R. Crumb. "Not even Leo Tolstoy's dictum that 'Every unhappy family is unhappy in its own way' is adequate preparation for the unsettling personal dramas that unfold in this remarkable film."

"In an age of known quantities, *Jesus' Son* is almost indefinable," Turan wrote in the *Times* about Alison Maclean's 1999 independent film. "In a sea of one-note symphonies, this touching feature is bleak and comic, heartbreaking and affirmative, romantic and tragic, gimlet-eyed and sympathetic, all at the same time. It's the sweetest, most punishing of lowlife serenades, a crawl through the wreckage created by, protagonist FH informs, 'people just like us, only unluckier.'"

In one of his occasional public explorations into the profession of film critic, Turan talked about second-guessing himself, particularly about his indifference to a Mexican film that others had highly touted, Alejandro González Iñárritu's *Amores Perros* (2000). Recalling the 1967 fate of Bosley Crowther, relieved as film critic of *The New York Times* for missing the boat on *Bonnie and Clyde*, Turan wrote, "It's easier to find a seat on the critical bandwagon, a safe haven in which you don't have to worry about being behind the curve and the last to applaud the latest phenomenon, anointed in large part because designating phenoms is one of the things critics most like to do. In a blurb-happy atmosphere where no film ad is without a quote, however dubious, calling the work a triumph, reviewers often seem to feel that it's only by resorting to hyperbole themselves that they can call attention to a worthy film."

Turan said Roger Ebert told him to reference Robert Warshow's *The Immediate Experience* and re-read a classic passage to re-affirm personal conviction regarding any film in question. The essence of Warshow's essay was that what he or any critic or any person saw on the screen, and what he or that person felt and thought about it, were reactions as valid as the next person's, whether that next person was a critic or not. "A man goes to the movies," Warshow wrote. "The critic must be honest enough to admit that he is that man."

Testimonials to the dedication of film critics from the halcyon days of Vernon Young, Manny Farber, and Andrew Sarris on forward to Dave Kehr and Jonathan Rosenbaum, must include the trekking of the auto-less Michael Wilmington across the length and breadth of Los Angeles to screenings and festivals, art houses and campuses. Often carrying a leather satchel and knowing nighttime bus schedules by heart—and sometimes accompanied by his equally dedicated mother—Wilmington was enchanted by movies, and one of the few to have served as film critic for a decade or more each on two of the nation's largest dailies. Wilmington was with the *Times* from 1984 to 1993, and from 1993 through 2006 at the *Chicago Tribune*. In 2000, he wrote a personal "Reverent 'Thank You'" to 10 movies that influenced him.

"Every movie critic can thank the movies for his or her profession, of course—and also for providing a rich, imaginative life and an entry to many different worlds," Wilmington wrote in the *Chicago Tribune* (reprinted in the *Los Angeles Times*). "And many of us—critics or not—can thank the movies for changing our lives in some way. Each of the following movies, in some way, changed mine." The films in descending order were Ben Sharpsteen's *Dumbo* (1941), Alfred Hitchcock's *Vertigo* (1958), Vittorio De Sica's *The Bicycle Thief* (1949), Akira Kurosawa's *The Seven Samurai* (1954), Frank Capra's *It's a Wonderful Life* (1946), Gene Kelly and Stanley Donen's *Singin' in the Rain* (1952), Howard Hawks's *To Have and Have Not* (1944), Luis Buñuel's *Belle de Jour* (1967), Spike Lee's *Do the Right Thing* (1989), and Orson Welles's *Citizen Kane* (1941).

"From a very young age, my mother took me to the movies whenever possible—not easy for her since she was a single, working mother without much money," Wilmington said in 2001. "The first movies I remember were *Cinderella* and *Samson and Delilah*. I was about four years old and fascinated with movies from that time on."

Wilmington's review of the Academy Award-winning *Platoon* (1986) put the reader in a foxhole. "Oliver Stone's *Platoon* is a Vietnam War film that hits you like a rolling wave from a long-ago battle zone: a blood tide of rage and pain. It's a furious, blistering film. Like Arthur Penn's *Bonnie and Clyde* and Sam Peckinpah's *The Wild Bunch* in their day, it's a movie that sums up a whole national mood, that seethes with bitterness and bloody poetry, that shows such explosive anger and roaring impact you can't dodge it, can't even look away from it, can't evade the blows."

Stone's driven and flawed heroes were compared by Wilmington in his review of *Talk Radio* (1988). Eric Bogosian's shock jock contained "the same mixture of honesty and sleaze, high aspiration and character as James Woods's reporter in Stone's *Salvador*," Wilmington wrote. "Like that character, Champlain

[Bogosian] is a catalyst; he drags out the truth, the dark sides. But he's become a beast in public to win his ratings. And he's become a beast in private as well. He tears his life and ideals to shreds. Honesty becomes a gig, and cynicism a crutch."

Wilmington's descriptions were palpably about his vivid viewing experience, and could travel like Manny Farber screeds, unexpectedly on two wheels for a bend down a side street, but with a momentum all their own. "This is a movie that tears up your nerves," Wilmington wrote in the *Los Angeles Times* about William Friedkin's *To Live and Die in L.A.* (1985). "Both cinematographer Robby Muller and editor Bud Smith work you over brilliantly. . . . Friedkin's L.A. . . . is a Darwinian world, clogged with trash, hard as a brick, soaked with evil. It's film noir blanched."

At the *Los Angeles Times*, Kevin Thomas largely covered independent and foreign films in the 1990s, while Turan reviewed the studio product. "You know, it's not at all important that people agree," said Thomas, who had been reviewing films for the *Times* since 1962, "it's the quality of the argument that matters." Thomas watched the comings and goings of critics at the paper from the days when Philip K. Scheuer was the lead film critic, through Champlin's entire tenure, the days of Benson and Rainer, and for nearly two decades alongside Kenneth Turan.

Thomas has been one of the longest continually serving staff film critics at a single daily newspaper. "I'm extremely fortunate to work with Kenny," Thomas said of Turan. "We complement each other. He's very well cast as the first-string critic, and frankly, I'm pretty well cast as the other. I get the kick, the psychic income, of creating audiences for the offbeat stuff."

A second-generation *Times* man, Thomas or his father had been continually working at the paper since 1937. Kevin Thomas rose from copy boy to stringer to film critic. While he had to take a buyout from the Tribune Company, owner of the *Times*, at the end of 2005, Thomas continues to review films on a freelance basis.

"Filmmakers in the indie, experimental, foreign, avant-garde or, until very recently, documentary fields desperately need critics," wrote Kirk Honeycutt, film critic and reporter for the *Los Angeles Daily News* and *The Hollywood Reporter*. "Lacking money for a promotional campaign and forced to rely on word-of-mouth, these filmmakers have found no better friend over the past 40-plus years than Kevin Thomas of the *Los Angeles Times*.

"His love of avant-garde and experimental films led him to be the only *Los Angeles Times* critic to review films by Kenneth Anger and Andy Warhol. Since 1984 his 'Special Screenings' column in the *Los Angeles Times* has been the lifeblood for venues that exhibit films for brief runs or even one night. In short, no one in the Los Angeles critical establishment has done more to create an awareness and appreciation of film culture than Kevin Thomas," Honeycutt wrote in tribute to his colleague for the Los Angeles Film Critics Association.

Oftentimes, Thomas couldn't stem the ennui that greeted worthwhile films that weren't given the studio push, including the private investigation rituals of Arthur Penn's underrated *Night Moves* (1975) or Ivan Passer's deeply felt *Cutter's Way* (1981). Thomas judged *Night Moves* in the *Times* to be "a stunning, stylish detective mystery in the classic Raymond Chandler-Ross Macdonald mold. A tough yet vulnerable private's eye's investigation of murder becomes a quest for his own identity and a pursuit for truth that cuts through many layers of social strata. It all ends with a wry sense of irony over the eternal treachery of human nature and of one's own illusions."

Saving small, worthwhile pictures as much as possible from oblivion had always been a job of the film critic. But arriving in the 1990s amid the cacophony of blurbmeisters and junketeers was a lot of big noise about the big movies from the big studios, which further marginalized the small pictures. Fighting for a small film was overridden by publications that saw starry blockbusters with big box-office potential as bandwagons to join, as movies that the masses would be most interested in seeing. Their critics were nudged toward going Hollywood, joining the junkets, forgetting about the foreign-language films when opportunities for recording the words of wisdom from the fonts of Arnold Schwarzenegger or Sylvester Stallone presented themselves.

"Movie criticism has become a cultural malady," James Wolcott wrote in *Vanity Fair* in 1997, "a group case of chronic depression." David Denby wondered in *The New Yorker* in 1998 why the public doesn't attend the movies that the critics champion, and mulled over Wolcott's notion: "Wolcott himself thought that critics were becoming chronic whiners, and a friend has said to me that 'movie critics are like spotted owls,' by which he means that the fate of so specialized a creature will never stir a general outcry. True enough, but notice the flaws. . . . If a species is threatened, it may be a sign that something is degraded in the environment. . . . Critics and moviegoers live together in the same forest, not in separate habitats.

". . . In the past decade, the selling of movies has grown both deafening and senseless. A medium that was once the movies' feared rival, television, now functions as a busy ad-pub division of Hollywood," Denby offered. "Oprah, Barbara, Kathie Lee—and, of course, MTV and E!—compete with one another for the sell-the-picture 'interviews' with the stars; and cable outlets run promotional 'documentaries' about the making of a new film. As for print journalism, a good many editors, feature writers, and hack critics—these last handing our rave quotes like free candy on the streets—have simply been pressed into the marketing operation for movies."

The flood tide of promotion "overwhelms the voice of a good critic," Denby complained, adding that the power of studio promotional departments means that "The dog is not being wagged by the tail, but by the fleas on the tail," and that "the marketing-and-promotion system is now less a means of bringing products to consumers than a law of existence, a metaphysics of momentum which either turns the critic into a huckster or reduces him to a crank."

"Now, in the *Armageddon* age, gloom engulfs the field," Janny Scott wrote in *The New York Times* in 1998. "Some critics, like David Denby . . . feeling drowned out by the din of the Hollywood marketing machine, seem despondent to a degree verging on despair. Column inches dwindle while movies multiply. Worthwhile films cannot get distributed. What can be worth saying, some critics wonder, about *Lethal Weapon 4*? . . . 'If you're talking about movies as an art, you're just out of it. . . . The business conversation is the hip conversation, the knowing conversation, the dinner-table conversation.'"

Jonathan Rosenbaum's book, *Movie Wars: How Hollywood and the Media Conspire to Limit What Films We Can See* (2000), concentrated on the problem. "Junkets and what they produce have never been a secret, but even as sophisticated writer as *Time* art critic Robert Hughes was shocked when he went to see *Star Wars: Episode I: The Phantom Menace* with his girlfriend's kids in 1999 and discovered that it wasn't what the hoopla had promised. He complained in the *New York Daily News* that George Lucas had 'managed to broker, or more exactly, enforce a situation by which hundreds of thousands of promotional words have been churned out and published about *The Phantom Menace* by writers who were specifically forbidden by Lucas to see it; and the said writers went right along with it, because, in the end, the tail of Hollywood was wagging the ass, if not the whole dog, of journalism.'

"What's surprising about Hughes' outrage," Rosenbaum went on, "is the implication that if all these journalists had seen *The Phantom Menace* weeks in advance they might not have written the same sort of promotional blather. But Lucas had the entertainment press on its knees, proving that a critical reading of the movie was irrelevant to what the mass media saw as its duty. To my mind, the fawning over *The Phantom Menace* was no more egregious or grotesque than the front-page coverage accorded to, say, Oliver Stone's *JFK* or the American Film Institute's 'One Hundred Best American Films' in *The New York Times*, or the kind of promotional reviews *Schindler's List* and *Saving Private Ryan* received almost everywhere in the U.S. when they came out.

"Media overkill of this kind was fully operational well before *The Phantom Menace* was a gleam in Lucas's eye, though his movie may have made it more obvious," Rosenbaum wrote. "*Newsweek* ran a cover story on it complaining about the overkill, though it fully acknowledged that it was part of it—unlike *Time*, which simply went along with the drift."

In the drift was Jim Whaley of *Cinema Showcase*, a WPBA-TV production at the PBS affiliate in Atlanta. *Premiere* looked into this rave-review machine, who was suddenly quoted large in the early 1990s on studio ads and posters everywhere. The magazine put aside all of Whaley's wildly enthusiastic quotes about his top 10 picks for 1991 to study his assessments of films that didn't make his list.

Michael Apted's *Class Action* was for Whaley "the most powerful film of the year," but undeserving of top-10 status. Wolfgang Petersen's *Shattered* was "the best screen thriller in years," while Martin Scorsese's remake of *Cape Fear* was "the most astounding film thriller of the past decade," and John Frankenheimer's *Year of the Gun* "ranks with the best thrillers in film history."

This bumper crop of thrillers, which didn't deserve top-10 status but surely would have a lasting impact on the history of crime films, was joined by *Mobsters*, which Whaley said "joins *The Godfather* and *Goodfellas* as one of the greatest gangster films ever made!" Whaley was a sucker for romance as Barbra Streisand's *The Prince of Tides* was "one of the most deeply moving films of our time," not to be outdone by Joel Schumacher's *Dying Young*, which Whaley felt compelled to label "the most deeply touching love story of our time."

Charles Fleming of *Daily Variety*, writing under the 1992 headline "Phantom Crix Are Flogging Flicks," said that studio publicity people called Whaley an engaging fellow and "only one snidely refers to him as 'the best quote sucker we have.' But few can say where *Cinema Showcase* airs; even fewer claim to have seen it." Whaley's outsize comments ceased abruptly; he died in 1992 of a heart attack at age 44.

Los Angeles Times media critic David Shaw wrote that on a randomly selected date in February 1999, his paper was "filled with movie ads featuring big, bold rave notices from the likes of Cathy Cogan of MJI's Big Picture, Ron Brewington of the American Urban Radio Network, Susan Granger of SSG Syndicate, Patti Spitler of WISH-TV and Bonnie Churchill of the National News Syndicate." Cogan, Brewington, and Churchill were Los Angeles-area entertainment journalists. Spitler was an anchor and entertainment reporter at WISH-TV, the CBS affiliate in Indianapolis, for more than two decades. Granger was a child actress who became a journalist; she is the daughter of film producer S. Sylvan Simon, once head of production for Columbia Pictures.

Fleming investigated ads for the World War II drama *A Midnight Clear* from InterStar Releasing/Beacon/A&M Films. The ads carried quotes from Dr. Joy Browne of Daynet Radio Network, Chuck Wilson of *Flickers*, Daphne Davis of *American Woman*, Dale Winogoura of *Frontiers*, Shari Roman of *In Fashion* and Nancy Kapitanoff of *Pulse*. "For the record," Fleming found, "*In Fashion* and *American Woman* are limited-circulation versions of *Cosmopolitan*; *Pulse* is a magazine put out by the Tower Record company; *Frontiers* is a gay men's magazine. None of the current issues, available on newsstands, features film reviews." Wilson's *Flickers* was "one man's notes on movies and other life obsessions," and Daynet was a radio network.

Susan Granger was quoted as representing AMC or AMC/CRN International. She didn't do on-air reviews on the cable network and didn't write them for the network's magazine. Jeff Craig of *Sixty Second Preview* was another so-called critic who suddenly appeared to be on every other movie ad. He was actually a Westport, Connecticut, businessman who owned a radio show heard on 200 stations nationwide. He wasn't even writing his own blurbs.

Doing that was Joey Berlin, a Los Angeles-based freelance writer who eventually founded the Broadcast Film Critics Association with Rod Lurie. "Jeff does six radio programs a day," was Berlin's explanation to Fleming. "He can't be everywhere."

"Serious critics deride these people as 'quote whores,' quasi-journalists eager to see their names in print and equally eager, perhaps, to show their gratitude to the studios that fly them, free of charge, to New York or Los Angeles two or three dozen times a year, wine and dine them and provide them with access to the stars," David Shaw wrote.

A 57-minute documentary, *Junket Whore* (1998), directed by Debbie Melnyk and produced by Rick Caine, aired and defined studio-journalism collusion on Bravo. Doing the majority of the talking in the film about the junket circuit was Rod Lurie, which was only fitting, several critics thought, because Lurie often did most of the talking on the junket circuit.

(The film also depicted and/or quoted such journalists and critics as Sam Rubin, Bob Thomas, Jack Mathews, Peter Bart, Roger Ebert, John Anderson, Virginia Campbell, Gene Siskel, Chris Connelly, Rita Kempley, Leonard Maltin, Joe Leydon, Kenneth Turan, Edward Guthmann, Marie Salas, Lisa Hintelmann, and Mike Clark.)

"The most pathetic aspect of this giveaway culture is how easily journalists are bought off," wrote Sharon Waxman in *American Journalism Review*. "Junket journalists are one thing, ersatz critics are another. With nothing more than the prospect of seeing their name in print, a whole stable of film critics—often freelancers or writers for small radio operations—are prepared to provide studios with quotes for use in film ads. These 'critics' will concoct quotes for films they do not intend to critique, may send studios advance copies of their reviews and in some cases are not critics at all, except for the purposes of film blurbs."

Roger Ebert and David Denby's shared view that studio marketing was marginalizing film critics fed a sense of professional malaise. Others went further in explaining the decline as sinister and a done deal. "What the studios and conglomerates have done," said screenwriter-director Paul Schrader, who was a film critic in the 1960s and early 1970s, "is to make a contract between the marketing departments and the audiences and to somehow get the critic out of the influence business."

Some critics changed their styles because of the blurb-meisters. "What all this blurbing has done is kind of devalue the currency of criticism," said film critic Kenneth Turan of the *Los Angeles Times* in 1997. "It's made me think twice about us-ing such words as 'masterpiece' or 'best ever' that have been so overused in ads, and used in such a knee-jerk fashion by the blurbmeisters. There's probably no film out there that some crit-ic somewhere hasn't called a 'masterpiece.'"

Turan's point was illustrated in the *OC Weekly* in De-cember 1999, when 36 critics were singled out for stamping the label "masterpiece" on 27 films during the year, no matter if that use was for wordplay and not face value. Roger Ebert called *Three Kings* "some kind of weird masterpiece" in the *Chicago Sun-Times*. Gary Arnold considered *The Blair Witch Project* "the shoestring-budget masterpiece" in *The Washington Post*. Such tried and trusted critics, for better or worse, tagged films with that label, including Richard Corliss, Richard Schickel, Michael Wilmington, Lisa Schwarzbaum, Tom Carson, Jeff Simon in the *Buffalo News*, Steven Rosen in the *Denver Post*, Joanna Connors in the *Cleveland Plain Dealer*, and Henry Sheehan in the *Orange County Register*.

Studio flimflammery extended to the truncating of le-gitimate reviews. Studio marketers would retrieve or misuse a quote from a negative review. Merrill Schindler, a Los Angeles food critic who once reviewed movies for the *Los Angeles Herald-Examiner* and *Los Angeles* magazine, wrote of a forgotten film that "the burning of this movie would be a boon to mankind," and later an ad for the film declared, "A boon to mankind!" Andy Klein of the *Los Angeles Reader* wrote that the Los Angeles TV-horror show host who starred in her own movie, *Elvira, Mistress of the Dark*, was "supposed to be coming across as charmingly exuberant," but "she is only obnoxious." The print ads quoted him as saying "Charmingly exuberant!"

"Studios and distributors say we don't matter, yet are so anxious for our certification that they ransack our reviews for

usable quotes," wrote *Baltimore Sun* film critic Michael Sragow
in 2001. "Every critic has his favorite story to tell on the matter. Oddly enough, mine was not with a studio picture but an
art-house movie that opened when I was writing in Los Angeles:
Peter Brook's *Meetings with Remarkable Men* (1979). It was a
biography of cult leader G.I. Gurdjieff, and I said it wanted to
be taken as an inspirational film. Naturally, in the ads the next
day, there appeared the single word: "'Inspirational!"—Michael
Sragow, *L.A. Herald-Examiner.*'"

    In some cases, the studios just got rid of critics. Jeffrey
Wells, a Los Angeles-based freelancer, was blackballed by Columbia Pictures for a story he wrote in the *Los Angeles Times* on
John McTiernan's *Last Action Hero* (1993), generally regarded
in retrospect as one of Arnold Schwarzenegger's worst films, but
one in which Columbia had sunk something like $100 million.
Columbia threatened to pull advertising if Wells's name appeared
again. Rod Lurie said he was banned for life from Warner Bros.
for recycling a description of Danny DeVito as a "testicle with
arms" in his review of Norman Jewison's *Other People's Money*
(1991).

    The end result of the buy-off junkets, the blurbmeisters
working at full fraud, and the media overkill on TV was the
obscuring and obfuscating of the true critical voices. *Los Angeles
Times* film critic Peter Rainer singled out the failure of the critically acclaimed Alfonso Cuarón film *A Little Princess* (1995) as
a victim of the "Hollywood marketing juggernaut." He wrote,
"Hollywood can be indicted for many crimes but the indictment here is with people who claim to hunger for heartfelt, inspiring, nonviolent family fare, and then, with *A Little Princess*
around, line up for *Casper* and clobberfests like *Die Hard with a
Vengeance* instead," partially because the kids were "bombarded
by *Casper* trailers and *Casper* toy tie-ins."

    Kids of all ages were influenced by the marketing over-
kill. "You can't get college kids interested in going to any sort of
daring movie now," complained Pauline Kael in 1989. "They're
perfectly willing to sit through the same old crap, a larger ver-

sion of what they've seen on television all their lives. They may even resent it if they go see a film that has subtitles, or that has any kind of complexity."

Meanwhile, the lack of insightful movies and the changing critical landscape prodded some critics to change their focuses. J. Hoberman came to film criticism for aesthetics in previous decades, but began looking at the political, historical, and sociological aspects of movies. Rainer tried that idea, too, but gave up on it. "It's just if that's the only way that you can really sink your teeth into movies time and time again, you become famished," he told *The New York Times*. "Because so much of what brought us into movies as budding critics was the wonderfulness of movies, not the social context." Rainer also thought the new plurality of critics was a problem.

"We live in an age when film criticism, or what passes for it, has never been more ubiquitous," Rainer wrote in 1992. "Our newspapers and magazines, our airwaves, are heady with the gabble of screening-room scribes and soothsayers. And yet there may be a neutralizing effect in all this ubiquity; for many in the mass audiences, criticism has become a kind of hum in the background of the moviegoing event. It is perceived as a part of the overall media blitz. (Some reviewers, feeling insufficiently stroked, are not above conspiring in the blitz. These socko blurbs are all-of-a-piece with the movies' ad copy.)

"The Hollywood studios, despite their increasing reliance on market research test screenings and demographic flowcharts, still fancy they need critics to help sell their movies. (The independent film companies certainly need them.) But they're not too worried: with so many critics writing reviews now, it's a cinch that any movie, no matter how putrid, will draw a few blurbable reviews," Rainer wrote in the introduction to *Love and Hisses: The National Society of Film Critics on the Hottest Movie Controversies*. "For the incurious legions who automatically equate a movie's popularity with its worth and feel no need to move beyond that equation, criticism—real criticism, that is, practiced with taste and intelligence —may be close to irrelevant anyway," he continued. "Virtually all the major media outlets now feature weekly rankings of the five or ten top-grossing films; these lists, which both reflect and determine a movie's media push, have become the nation's true critics of choice. They carry a the-People-have-spoken certitude that regular critics can't hope to match."

The knowledge about the backgrounds of movie production became part of the "cool" discussion. "Today we live in a world in which most American taxpayers cannot correctly identify either of the senators from their state but can readily recall how much money Cannon Films spent on *Superman IV: The Quest for Peace*," Andy Borowitz wrote in *Premiere*, also citing the money angle from a pauper point of view. "Just as costly Hollywood films are lambasted for their profligacy, so these shoestring efforts are praised for their inventiveness." Borowitz cited John Sayles's $60,000 *Return of the Secaucus Seven* (1980) for ushering in the I'm-broke spin, which has been parlayed by publicists to sell movies by such bargain-basement stylists as Robert Townsend, Robert Rodriguez, and Quentin Tarantino. "In the end, you have to judge a movie and not the backstory," Rainer said. "Sometimes, poverty is used as a selling point." And sometimes fabrications are used.

"*Mad* magazine, hanging in there after all these years, recently sent subscribers an issue wrapped in a mailer covered with blurbs for *Mad* itself," Denby wrote. "The best blurb: '"Every once in a while a magazine comes along. This is such a magazine."—Hecky Peckersmith, Peckersmith Press.' You may wonder how someone like Hecky can possibly survive as a movie critic. But who's going to tell him he's a fake? The movie companies? The newspaper or the TV station that employs him and obviously finds him useful? Hail Hecky! Junketing twenty weekends a year in good hotels in Los Angeles and New York, Hecky Peckersmith hardly seems like an absurd man. On the contrary, he knows what he's doing. And if Peckersmith is happy, and if his editor or his producer doesn't much care how silly he is, then why make a fuss?

"One makes a fuss," Denby declared, shifting gears, "because honest praise is devalued when the studios fill the ads with manufactured raves; the language of criticism has become so debased that the public may not notice any difference between the ads for *L.A. Confidential* and those for trash like *Kiss the Girls. . . .*

"Critics seldom make things happen, but they can spark the dialogue, the good talk that is one of the prime pleasures of moviegoing," Denby went on. "Aroused, they may long find a way of preaching to their readers, and so they examine small bits of evidence—the spoor and flower of an entertainment system—and offer their modestly immodest commentary on the moral life in the country. If they forget that all this matters, too, when bad movies triumph and good ones falter, they will amount to little more than horseflies on the great rump of movie commerce."

Even though there were some critics fights in the 1990s—Ebert vs. Corliss, Benson vs. Farber—there weren't any heavyweight tussles. In the *San Diego Reader*, Duncan Shepherd found the film-criticism landscape as barren as the films: "And just as the desire on the production end narrows the range of available movies, it likewise reduces the amount of personal bias tolerated in the critical sphere, the idiosyncrasy, the specialization, the factionalism that formerly gave criticism its vitality: French aesthete vs. British humanist, Hollywood mainstreamer vs. New York undergrounder, auteurist vs. semiologist, Kael vs. Simon, Kael vs. Sarris, Kael vs. anyone. The whole shooting match has pretty well died away. The stray sniper rarely squeezes off a round anymore."

However, a couple of film criticism's battlefields were internal—inside publications. Two film critics resigned their posts in protest in the 1990s, Pat Dowell at *Washingtonian* magazine and Joseph McBride at *Daily Variety*. Dowell gave Oliver Stone's *JFK* (1991) a three-and-a-half-star review, calling it "a brilliantly crafted indictment of history as an official story." Her editor, Jack Limpert, spiked the review, because he thought *JFK* was "the dumbest movie about Washington ever made . . . bizarre, crackpot, just preposterous." Dowell refused to reconsider her view and resigned. Kevin Costner, who played Orleans Parish district attorney Jim Garrison in the film, supported her move, as did the Peter Rainer-chaired National Society of Film Critics, which issued a statement.

"Limpert's decision, based upon his admitted disagreement with the review's content, promotes censorship over freedom of speech and strikes a blow to the critical discourse so vital to a free expression of ideas," said the society's statement.

McBride called Phillip Noyce's *Patriot Games* (1992) an "ultraviolent, fascistic, blatantly anti-Irish" film and "a right-wing cartoon of the current British-Irish political situation." The review prompted Paramount Pictures to pull its ads from *Daily Variety*. "That was hardly an unprecedented reaction," McBride wrote, "but my editor-in-chief, former Paramount executive Peter Bart, reacted by writing a letter to Paramount Communications Chairman and Chief Executive Marvin S. Davis apologizing for my review and promising that I would not be allowed to review any more Paramount films."

McBride was pulled off an assignment to review Paramount's and Penny Marshall's *A League of Their Own* (1992), and then assigned to review children's movies. He received nearly unanimous media support when he defended his First Amendment rights after *The New York Times*—also a former employer of Bart—obtained a copy of the editor's letter. The critic's attorney forced Hollywood's biggest trade paper to resume his client's coverage of mainstream features. "I stuck it out for five months before obtaining a financial settlement from *Daily Variety* and resigning to concentrate on writing books," McBride wrote.

The moaning over the state of the movies reached a nadir when David Thomson became *Esquire's* film critic in 1996. His first column was entitled "Who Killed the Movies?" He points to the blockbuster syndrome after Spielberg and Lucas loosed *Jaws* and *Star Wars* in the 1970s. "He could be the caretaker of *Sunset Boulevard*," James Wolcott wrote of Thomson in *Vanity*

Fair. "It's perversely comic of Thomson to use his opening column to tell *Esquire* readers, in effect, 'the Show's over, folks, go on home.' His elegant fatalism seemed to leave no next move. What do you do for an encore after you've announced your field is dead?"

Wolcott's ultimate suggestion was to tell all of the moaners and whiners to shut up: "At some point persistent gloom becomes so insupportable that something has to give—people get bored with being bored. I can see that, for cinephiles, movies aren't the narcotic they used to be, and I can understand why critics are in the doldrums. I just don't taste cinders and ash in the air. Critics need to get over themselves, and not treat the cinema as their personal cross."

Some of the critics were just going soft, too. *Brill's Content* surveyed the 14 most "blurbed" critics for three months ending in January 20, 1999, to see who gave the greatest percentage of favorable reviews. These weren't the blurbmeisters, but the real deal, the film critics who were established as the big-time players of the field. These were the results:

1. Gene Shalit (12 total reviews), *Today* (NBC), 84 percent favorable.
2. Richard Corliss (12), *Time*, 75 percent favorable.
3. Joel Siegel (28), *Good Morning America* (ABC), 72 percent favorable.
4. Peter Travers (47), *Rolling Stone*, 68 percent favorable.
5. Jay Carr (44), *Boston Globe*, 66 percent favorable.
6. Jeffrey Lyons (44), WNBC-TV (New York) and radio's *Lyons Den*, 61 percent favorable.
7. Michael O'Sullivan (34), *The Washington Post*, 56 percent favorable.
8. Gene Siskel (46), *Chicago Tribune*, 56 percent favorable.

9. Janet Maslin (38), *The New York Times*, 56 percent favorable.
10. Jack Mathews (38), *Newsday*, 55 percent favorable.
11. Roger Ebert (53), *Chicago Sun-Times*, 53 percent favorable.
12. Kenneth Turan (27), *Los Angeles Times*, 52 percent favorable.
13. David Ansen (14), *Newsweek*, 50 percent favorable.
14. Owen Gleiberman (22), *Entertainment Weekly*, 45 percent favorable.

The numbers proved that Ebert certainly was one of the most durable critics. *Brill's* provided labels and commentary on "The Fawning Five" at the head of the list. Shalit was "The King of Schmaltz: If it's on celluloid, chances are this feel-good 'critic' loves it. Favors painfully cheesy puns." Corliss was "The Equivocator: With his poetic sensibility and endless irresolution, Corliss is the thinking man's softy. . . . Dubious calls [are] difficult to find for Corliss, whose mealy-mouthed style—and safe choices—stop him from touting the worst dogs."

Siegel was "The Master of the Obvious: . . . A thesaurus might do him some good. . . . Number of times he used 'great' in a 30-second review of *You've Got Mail*: nine." Travers was "The Sundance Kid: If the film has even the most tenuous indie connection or any art-house aspirations, Travers will gush." Carr was "The Unconditional Lover: When Carr falls head-over-heels for a movie, he has a hard time getting back up. Nearly half of his reviews bestowed a '4' rating, meaning Carr offered virtually boundless approval."

Spy, a superficially brainy and hip New York-based magazine that lived fast and died young, featured Siskel and Ebert on the June 1990 cover with outsized thumbs and asked, "Whose Is Bigger?: How the critical opinions of a few middle-aged dweebs mean millions to movies, restaurants, books and Broadway." Using an inexact formula that doesn't deserve an explanation, the magazine calculated that Siskel was the most powerful film critic in America and was followed, in descending order, by Ebert, Siegel, David Ansen, Shalit, Travers, Gary Franklin of KABC-TV in Los Angeles, Pauline Kael, Richard Schickel, Sheila Benson of the *Los Angeles Times*, Vincent Canby of *The New York Times*, and Corliss.

Ebert didn't take being second lightly. "'How could he have *possibly* edged me out?' whined Ebert when we called to congratulate him on his second-place finish," wrote Eddie Stern of *Spy*. "'I demand a recount,'" Ebert said. "'. . . Did you know that I'm in 190 papers and he's in 16? That I'm on the number-one-rated network station in Chicago and he's on number three? I'm in the [*New York*] *Daily News* and he isn't—that's another million every day. If you add up the *Sun-Times* and the *Daily News*, that's certainly more than the *Chicago Tribune*.

"'[Also], you've added the *Chicago Tribune's* circulation without acknowledging the fact that he doesn't write reviews for them. . . . He writes Siskel's Flicks Picks [short, one-paragraph items], so I would question whether he should get full credit for the *Tribune* at all, since they have another reviewer [Dave Kehr at the time] doing full-length reviews. You have to throw in my book, too.'" Siskel said that his reviews ran in 75 papers, not 16, and *Spy* declined Ebert's appeal. "It doesn't matter to me so much that he's ahead of me," Ebert said, "as long as you mention that it's because he liked *Fatal Attraction* and *I didn't*."

Ebert, the first film critic ever associated with the Pulitzer Prize for criticism, was being joined in Pulitzer discussions by film critics who were also nominated for the prize. In 1995 and 1996, Stephen Hunter of the *Baltimore Sun* became the only film critic to have been a finalist in back-to-back years for the Pulitzer Prize in criticism.

He was but the fourth finalist to be a film critic after Stephen Schiff of the *Boston Phoenix* in 1983, Andrew Sarris of *The Village Voice* in 1987, and Matt Zoller Seitz of the *Dallas Observer* in 1994, and the fifth film critic ever associated with the prize (Ebert won it in 1975, when finalists weren't announced).

Hunter was born in 1946 and graduated from North-western University in 1968. He spent 1969 and 1970 in the U.S. Army, stationed in Washington, D.C. He had been a copy editor for the *Sun*'s Sunday edition for a decade before becoming a film critic in 1982. A writer of thriller novels, such as *Point of Impact* and *Target*, Hunter was lured away from the *Sun* by *The Washington Post* in 1997.

"Here's one way to look at it: Man is a meaning-seeking creature," reads Hunter's lead to his *Post* review of Atom Egoyan's *The Sweet Hereafter* (1997). "Pitiful being, he cannot accept the random cruelty of the universe. That is his biggest failing, the source of his unhappiness and possibly of his nobility as well. He paws through disasters with but one question for God: Why? And God never answers.

"He certainly doesn't answer in . . . *The Sweet Hereafter*, which watches a mad, vain scrambler seeking to impart his own meaning on someone else's terrifying disaster. As derived from the intense Russell Banks novel, the story follows lawyer Mitchell Stephens (Ian Holm) on his peregrinations through a western Canadian town where a school bus has recently fallen through the ice, drowning 14 children and leaving an enamel of grief as blinding as the snow that blankets the place.

"This lawyer: greedhead or pilgrim of pain?

"This town: victim of horrid coincidence or of God's vengeance?

"This story: remembered myth or spontaneous occurrence?

"The answer to the questions is: All of the above. And one more thing is certain, and that is uncertainty. The movie is of the mode called postmodernism, which no one understands but everyone recognizes."

While Hunter and a few other critics stretched their talents to encompass fiction, and Denby and a few others wrote on subjects other than the movies or entertainment, several others added to film biography. Joseph McBride produced three exhaustive and definitive filmmaker biographies, *Frank Capra: The Catastrophe of Success* (1992), *Steven Spielberg: A Biography* (1997), and *Searching for John Ford: A Life* (2001), and had previously written or compiled essential studies on Orson Welles and Howard Hawks, as well as a 1975 book entitled *John Ford*, written with Michael Wilmington.

More than a dozen books have been written on Spielberg, but McBride's reflects the deepest kind of research and a sharp ability to separate fact from legend. "All future biographers will have to stop here first, likewise, all movie lovers who want to understand Spielberg and his place in film history," wrote F.X. Feeney in the *LA Weekly*. McBride's *Searching for John Ford: A Life* is simply a masterly biography, and a culmination of McBride's skills as a reporter, film critic, and longtime Ford scholar. A descendent of Irish forebears by way of Milwaukee, Wisconsin, McBride brought focused enlightenment with his superbly researched analyses of Ford's films, folded into the facts, relationships, and developments in Ford's life, enlarging on the great artistic sensibility behind the grinding cussedness and compulsive blarney of his contrary subject.

The other major classics to have been published about American films and filmmakers in the 1980s and 1990s include Pauline Kael's *5,001 Nights at the Movies* (1982), Todd McCarthy's *Howard Hawks: The Grey Fox of Hollywood* (1997), and Peter Bogdanovich's *Who the Devil Made It* (1997). Most of the books authored by Kael, Stanley Kauffmann, Roger Ebert, and Leonard Maltin were published in the 1980s and 1990s. Overall references, such as Ephraim Katz's *The Film Encyclopedia* (1979) and the various capsule-review guides, were momentarily dwarfed by *Videohound's Golden Movie Retriever*, edited by Martin Connors, Jim Craddock, and others in 1991.

Adorned with the drawing of a pooch in shades, it would seem to be a part of the dumbing down happening throughout American movie culture. Its publicity and even its front-page blurbs by 2001 made it clear that this annual franchise was going after Maltin's audience by incorporating more information in each movie's entry—awards, cinematographer, etc. "If you're going to purchase one video guide for your home or library, this is it," enthused *Library Journal*. "It is the inclusion of ten separate indexes that push this work to Number One." By the 21st century, the Internet Movie Database (IMDb) and other online sources would make most of the book guides obsolete.

However, one guide would never be obsolete. David Thomson, a Briton transplanted to America, produced exhaustive biographies on David O. Selznick and Orson Welles, as well as the confounding item known as *Warren Beatty and Desert Eyes: A Life and a Story* (1987), comprised of chapters of the actor's biography alternating with a lurid novel. A former instructor at Dartmouth College who has written for *Film Comment*, *The New York Times*, *Movieline*, *Los Angeles* magazine, and *The New Republic*, Thomson's greatest contribution to the film criticism field has been *A Biographical Dictionary of Film*, a selective reference to major talents covered by the author's personal essays.

First published in London in 1975 by Secker & Warburg as *A Biographical Dictionary of Cinema*, the volume was updated and reprinted to acclaim by Knopf in 1980, 1994, and 2002. Reverent and deliberative, Thomson's opinionated entries often don't match with history's accepted critical notions. Thomson retains little respect for Charlie Chaplin or John Ford, but he lionizes Cary Grant and Robert Mitchum. Thomson's summations of actors are acute and often definitive. Grant was "the best and most important actor in the history of the cinema." And Mitchum was, simply, in Thomson's final analysis, "untouchable."

"*Schindler's List* is the most moving film I have ever seen," Thomson deposits into the body of his discussion of Steven Spielberg in the 800-page-plus opus. "That does not mean it is faultless. To take just one point: the reddening of one little girl's coat in a black-and-white film strikes me as a mistake, and a sign of how calculating a director Spielberg is. For the calculating reveal themselves in those few errors that escape. I don't really believe in Spielberg as an artist: I don't believe that much soul or doubt is there, or that much heartfelt trust in the organic meaning of style. But *Schindler's List* is like an earthquake in a culture of gardens. And it helps persuade the viewer that cinema—or American film—is not a place for artists. It is a world for producers, and showmen and Schindlers. The closest that *Schindler's List* comes to art may be in aiding Steven Spielberg to back into the upheld coat of his own mysterious, brilliant, actorly nature. The film works so well because he is Schindler, and 1993 has been his 1944."

Thomson had a great knack for pegging his subjects with terrific exactitude. "The movies are fake," he writes, "and [Robert] De Niro is hanging on by his broken fingertips, for he seems as averse to charm as a lurcher dog." Thomson does reference his standards, as Jeff Bridges "is as close as the modern era has come to Robert Mitchum," and Matt Damon has the "promise of an intelligent sourness not seen on screen since the days of Holden and Mitchum."

With the third edition came uncommon praise. Former *New Yorker* editor Robert Gottlieb, for whom Pauline Kael had worked, became Thomson's editor at Knopf. "I trust David's opinions more than I trusted Pauline," Gottlieb said, aligning his loyalties at the time. The *Minneapolis Star Tribune* pointed out that Roger Ebert had a Pulitzer Prize to his credit, "but David Thomson he is not."

Like Robert Warshow, Peter Bogdanovich and other essayists whose books qualify them as essential contributors to the film-opinion discussion, Thomson wrote little film criticism for periodicals, which did, however, include *Los Angeles* magazine and *Esquire*. Mostly because of the personally composed reference work, a great classic to be sure, Thomson is considered by some a giant of film criticism. "Not since another Englishman before him, Kenneth Tynan, wrote the *Observer* and *New Yorker* essays that became *Profiles,* has a critic reached into the illusory world of movies and pulled out such immediate human truths," Emily Green wrote in the *Los Angeles Times Magazine* in 2005.

Roger Ebert traced the initial eliminations of film critics

at major papers in the 1990s as symptomatic of an effort to court the public. The papers' managers wanted their critics to reflect, rather than influence, public opinion, part of what was referred to by some critics as the "dumbing down" of movie criticism. Indeed, wrote David Shaw in the *Los Angeles Times*, both Dave Kehr at the *New York Daily News* and Howie Movshovitz at the *Denver Post* "lost their jobs because their editors thought they were too highbrow for their readers." The newspapers themselves were disappearing in the first wave before the Internet's death knell in the 21st century. Publications that went out of business in the 1980s and 1990s were: the *Los Angeles Herald-Examiner*, *Baltimore News-American*, *Philadelphia Bulletin*, *Buffalo Courier-Express*, *The Pittsburgh Press*, *Washington Star*, *Chicago Daily News*, *St. Louis Globe-Democrat*, and *Houston Post*. Two-paper mergers formed the *San Diego Union-Tribune*, *Atlanta Journal-Constitution*, and *Milwaukee Journal Sentinel*.

Joe Leydon was one of the critics who lost his reviewing outlet. He was film critic of the *Houston Post* from 1982 to 1995. A New Orleans native who graduated from Loyola University, he has reviewed films for MSNBC.com, NBC affiliate KPRC-TV, the *Houston Press*, and *San Francisco Examiner* since the paper folded. He became a film critic and regional correspondent for *Variety*, communications director for *Cowboys & Indians* magazine, contributing writer for *MovieMaker* magazine, and an adjunct professor at University of Houston and Houston Community College. A casualty of the *Post*, Leydon used existing contacts and freelance gains from the past to continue; he wrote for *Motion Pictures*, *Stereophile Guide to Home Theater*, the *Los Angeles Times*, *Newsday*, *New York Daily News*, *Boston Globe*, and *Nashville Tennessean*.

The late 1990s was also a time when the fashionableness of midsize papers having their own critics was beginning to be perceived as a luxury that had run its course; the wire services provided Vincent Canby's or Roger Ebert's reviews in cost-effective package deals with other features. News services such as Knight-Ridder, Copley, Chicago Tribune, McClatchy, and others syndicated a few critics nationally, such as Ebert, Canby, Bob Strauss, David Elliott of the *San Diego Union*, and Michael H. White of the *Fort Worth Star-Telegram*. The year-end top-10 lists were still endemic to the profession on midsize papers, which had their own film critics produce top-10 lists.

Director Ang Lee and screenwriter/star Emma Thompson's *Sense and Sensibility* made practically everyone's 1996 list, including those of Rod Dreher of the *Fort Lauderdale Sun-Sentinel*, Joe Baltake of the *Sacramento Bee*, Soren Anderson of the *Tacoma News-Tribune*, Barry Caine of the *Oakland Tribune*, Donald La Badie of the *Memphis Commercial Appeal*, Margaret A. McGurk of the *Cincinnati Enquirer*, Judith Egerton of the *Louisville Courier-Journal*, and Jeff Simon of the *Buffalo News*. In the coming decade, many film critics of papers with 50,000 to 150,000 circulation would be shifted to other newsroom posts or pushed out of jobs that were purged by management.

The decline of print operations continued into the new century. While there were more film critics than ever, especially on the Internet, the level of discourse sadly seemed to sag. "We're sort of in the golf years now—a very staid cultural environment," Janet Maslin told the *Los Angeles Times* in 1999.

THE GREAT WAKE: THE 21ST CENTURY

Pauline Kael died 10 years and six months after retiring from *The New Yorker*, at her home in Great Barrington, Massachusetts, on September 3, 2001. She was 82. The eulogies were legion.

David Denby, who had become a *New Yorker* film critic, said, "She had an enormous impact on a whole generation of critics. She opened a lot of doors to different ways of writing about movies. There was no simple set of rules for her. You had to respond with everything you had, not just what you knew about movies but what you knew about painting, literature, life, other people. That was what made the writing so three-dimensional, so engaging. People felt a need to argue with it, to rethink it themselves. She was enormously provocative in that way."

Elaine Woo characterized Kael as the "high priestess of film criticism" in the *Los Angeles Times*. Several critics felt a need to write about how and why they became "Paulettes," including Denby and Paul Schrader. The latter had been introduced to Kael by Paul Warshow, the son of long-deceased film critic Robert Warshow, author of *The Immediate Experience*. The day after they met—Schrader was in his late teens—Kael told him he should not become a minister but a film critic.

"Pauline was a complex mentor," Schrader wrote in *Film*

Comment. "On one hand, she infused your life like a whirlwind, dominating your thinking, affecting your personal relationships, demanding fealty; on the other, she could not respect anyone who could not stand up to her. Love her too little and she attacked you, love her too much and she disregarded you. It was a formula for heartbreak, a heartbreak I think the acolytes felt more deeply than the mentor."

Kael had resisted public honoraries, but on her 80th birthday in 1999, there occurred what Schrader characterized as a "convocation of the tribes" at Great Barrington. "Most, if not all" of the attendees, Schrader said, had shared the ritual of arguing with Kael and harbored "emotions as conflicted as my own."

"From the first generation," Schrader wrote, "there were David Denby, Joe Morgenstern, and I; from the second, Terry Rafferty and Meredith Brody; from the third, David Edelstein (and others I've neglected to mention). [Kael friend] James Hamilton took a group photo and mailed it to all the participants. It hangs in my office."

Music and film critic Howard Hampton wrote, "Her sometimes grandiose claims and pronouncements were a way of throwing down the gauntlet, as movies themselves were at their best: bolts of lightning meant to shake people out of their habits and complacency, reminding them not only of how rich art ought to be but life as well. Pauline was the most vital, joyous, tough-minded person I've ever known or writer I've ever read."

Michael Sragow described her writing in terms of the organic variety of performance art in her own field of study. "She was a writer and critic of enormous vitality and emotional depth," Sragow said. "Like method actors, she was in the moment as a critic." Manohla Dargis wrote, "She didn't just make writing about the movies and the world seem possible, she made writing itself seem possible."

The old guard came back out with appreciative eulogies again in August 2008, when Manny Farber died at the age of 91. The inspirations that Kael and Farber were to many film critics still did not stem the fact that the profession that they had both seized, manipulated, and redrew in their own idiosyncratically fierce and brazen ways had fallen on rocky times. The malaise that shrouded film criticism at the close of the 20th century became an increasingly downward spiral through the first decade of the 21st century. The same trends that affected the 1990s deepened into part of an overall effect. It was easy to blame the movies. Big franchises like *Batman* and *Pirates of the Caribbean* thrived along with binge sequel-itis like *Saw* and *The Fast and the Furious*.

"Claiming that the quality of Hollywood's output has set another new low has become a depressing annual event, not just among cineastes, but among hard-bitten industry professionals as well," wrote Roger Smith, a film and media consultant, in the January/February 2001 edition of *Film Comment*. Leonard Maltin, writing later that year in *Playboy*, lamented, "This summer we had *The Mummy Returns*, *Dr. Doolittle 2*, *Rush Hour 2*, *Scary Movie 2*, *Jurassic Park III* and *American Pie 2*. . . . The claim that studios are just giving audiences what they want to see is a lot of baloney. . . . Customers take what they can get. And, if anyone's paying attention, the biggest hits every year are originals—the kinds of movies that set trends, make stars, and inspire imitations. It doesn't take a genius to understand that without a steady stream of new material, where will tomorrow's sequels come from?" Maltin concluded.

Kenneth Turan, film critic of the *Los Angeles Times*, could have been summing up the attitude many film critics had taken in the final decades of the 20th century into the 21st when he pinpointed the once creeping notion that became a prevailing hazard of the craft: critics see too many bad movies. "All those movies whose ads you skim in the Sunday paper and say, '*No way* I'm seeing that one,' the critic has suffered through," Turan wrote. "True, that's just part of the job, but experiencing all that detritus couldn't help but have deleterious effects: a junk-film diet makes movies that are so-so seem like masterpieces.

"Even more insidious in that regard is the feeling you

get when you realize that way more than half of what you're viewing not only isn't any good, it isn't even worth your time," Turan continued. "When that happens, you have two choices: you can get another job or you can unconsciously compromise your standards. Since I would be a pathetic fool to be wasting all my time watching trash, you say to yourself, it follows logically that what I'm watching must be worthwhile. Clear to you, kemosabe, but not necessarily to anyone else."

The perception the film critic profession still carried with it was the notion of cushy fun and glory in a Hollywood playland. Film critics themselves vouch for the fact that they live the good life in a dream job. But the complaints of Maltin and Turan come after decades in the business. The same genre retreads and gadget-driven summer blockbusters can dull the senses and the vocabulary.

"Of course, these are disillusioned days for film critics," John Powers wrote in the *LA Weekly* in 2002. "I don't mean the happy hacks and quote whores who scarf shrimp at press junkets, refer to 'Gwyneth' as if they actually know her and repay studio freebies with idiot blurbs ('*XXX* is Triple X-citing!'). I mean the serious folks, to adopt the Bushian locution, who remember when being a film critic wasn't just a cool job (It still is) but the catbird seat in an era when movies electrified the culture, Andrew Sarris and Pauline Kael battled for the souls of the young, and preferring Godard to Truffaut (or vice versa) was a way of announcing who you were. Now, critics seem shell-shocked that they've lost this privileged status—their space is being devoured by articles on digital media or no-carb diets—and they must actually fight to make themselves heard.

"Sad to say, most film critics are better at feeling beleaguered than at fighting (what would you expect from people who spend their lives in the dark?)," Powers wrote. "Hanging out with other critics, I'm always startled how many actually grumble at having to go to Cannes (ah, the horrors of the Riviera), feel personally insulted at having to write about Adam Sandler, or sink into clock-punching passivity—they only want to review the big movies that are put in front of them.

"Terrified of appearing to care too much (which *can* get you fired), most critics have been cowed into aiming low," Powers decided. Of course, the blame for bad movies can be laid, like always, at the feet of the studios, along with the blame for marketing tricks that changed the movie-reviewing landscape with the creation of blurbmeisters, and the intensified use of junkets to compromise the press.

However, an abdication of press responsibility to sustain good print criticism during a print-industry sea change to court public allegiance also occurred. Newspapers went soft in the 1990s on big blockbuster films as a survival measure. This decision to sustain the revenue streams from studio advertising departments included influencing critics to shy away from the intellectual and aesthetic discussions on movies, which were becoming more arcane to young and general readers, and to focus more on data about production costs and box-office weekends, and to collude in the studio-regulated cult of celebrity.

The interview feature with Hugh Jackman or Nicole Kidman or Christina Ricci—or even directors Oliver Stone or Peter Jackson—became more important than any evaluation that a critic might have on a film's merit. The personality coverage brings Hollywood stardust closer to Anytown, USA, and also joins in the celebratory nature of the high-budget event film, which looks to open wide and big on the target weekend, creating the buzz on the hot multiplex topic, a film that has been presold by TV-ad bombardment and often fast-food franchise toy tie-ins.

"The CelebCult virus is eating our culture alive, and newspapers voluntarily expose themselves to it," complained Roger Ebert in 2009. "They want to devote less space to considered prose, and more to ignorant gawking." Ebert had, like dozens of other entertainment newspaper journalists, written hundreds of feature stories on movie stars tied to movie releases. His view had obviously changed.

Decreased editorial space has been a problem on all papers, for which "downsizing" has several meanings, including the actual reduced size of broadsheets. "When all news divisions are pared down to the core, and it seems when you can't fully cover a presidential campaign, a movie critic might seem like a luxury," said Carrie Rickey in 2008. The film critic of the *Philadelphia Inquirer* for more than two decades, Rickey added, "Papers are managing contraction right now."

The preludes to pending newspaper funerals included an upswing in "service journalism" in all sections of newspapers, which squeeze down, among many things, criticism. "Editors everywhere have been affected by the influence of service journalism to the point where you find them asking why critics are going on at such length when all the readers really want to know is—should they go to the movie or not?" said Leah Rozen, film critic of *People* since 1997.

The money discussion incrementally became the hip discussion after Francis Ford Coppola's *The Godfather* (1972) generated long queues outside theatres, then William Friedkin's *The Exorcist* (1973), and especially Spielberg's *Jaws* (1975) had patrons lining up around corners for tickets. The blockbuster syndrome had invaded Hollywood in a huge way. The media took notice and editors wondered how many millions were being made. The moguls began searching for the next dynamic property to hype into a $100-million-plus hit.

George Lucas's *Star Wars* (1977) and its sequels and Spielberg's *Raiders of the Lost Ark* (1981) and the other Indiana Jones movies firmed up franchise-marketing concepts. The weekend box-office grosses, once solely reserved for Monday reports in the film-industry trade papers, *Daily Variety* and *The Hollywood Reporter*, began being logged weekly in the mainstream media by the 1980s. Told what pictures the biggest audiences were attending, filmgoers wanted inside the loop. The blockbuster syndrome begat the lemming syndrome. Some film critics were particularly upset by the late 1980s as their impact was being eroded by dollar signs and numbers on TV and in newspaper reports.

Gene Siskel of the *Chicago Tribune*, in particular, had

lobbied for years to get both weekend grosses and what movies cost to make out of the mainstream media, where they only become marketing tools. Speculation on the costs of James Cameron's movies *Terminator 2: Judgment Day* (1991) and *Titanic* (1997) became entertainment-page staples for weeks. *Los Angeles Times* columnist Steve Lopez applied Oscar Wilde's adage to the movies in 2001: "We know the price of everything and the value of nothing."

"I was watching a show like *Access Hollywood* . . . and they were interviewing the director [Brett Ratner] of *Rush Hour 2* and talking about the gross receipts," said Jill Stein, a lecturer at UCLA's LeRoy Neiman Center for the Study of American Society and Culture. "He was being congratulated," she told Lopez, on the $66 million box-office weekend when the director's own greatest expectations would have put the take at around $45 million.

"And it had nothing to do with the content or quality of the movie," Stein said. The critical response was that the film was mixed to insufferable—telling audiences that it was just more or worse hyperactive hijinks by Jackie Chan and Chris Tucker from *Rush Hour* (1998). But the sequel's financial success and that of the other brainless summer hits of 2001 reinforced the notion that serious critics were less effective than ever. Their voices were drowned in blurbmeister cacophony.

But the biggest reason that the situation for film critics reached critical condition was the fact that the Internet, which had been siphoning readers away from newspapers and magazines for more than a decade, was more than just stronger than ever; it had taken over movie coverage in the first decade of the 21st century.

The sites are legion: the Internet Movie Database (IMDb), Rotten Tomatoes, Movie City News, Fandango, E! Online, CHUD, IGN Film Force, Yahoo! Movies, Movies.com, etc. Blogs are everywhere, and many of the surviving print critics, including Roger Ebert, began contributing mightily to the blogosphere.

The triumph of cyberspace technology was aided by logic: Newsprint costs were exorbitant, advertising revenue was better spent elsewhere than on print, and it was the "green" thing to do in an increasingly environmentally aware age. And, of course, more people find easy access, great latitude, and enormous value in the Internet. The Pew Research Center for the People & the Press in Washington, D.C., published a 2008 survey that showed more people relied on the Internet for news than newspapers.

The mass-market movie magazines ceased. The general-appeal movie magazines that carried an insider edge, giving readers credit for film knowledge, went out of business. *Movieline* transformed into *Hollywood Life* in 2003, and then disappeared. *Premiere* published its last print edition in April 2007, and with that event, longtime Hollywood business reporter Anne Thompson judged that "the epitaph for long-form movie journalism may well have been written."

From 1995 to 2006, *Premiere*'s circulation dropped from 616,000 to 492,000. The magazine's advertising dollars dropped by 25% in 2006 alone. "An ad in *Premiere* was no good use of ad money anymore," Michael Moses of Universal Pictures' publicity department told Thompson. "We're reaching fans in so many other dynamic ways." The genre-specialty magazines—*Cinefex*, *Fangoria*—are still published and *Film Comment* continued in the new century under the editorship of Gavin Smith, who replaced Richard T. Jameson. *Film Comment* retained its central-forum status for literary-minded filmgoers, but its oasis status now came with no other oasis to travel onward toward.

"I think anyone who cares about language has to admit to a certain amount of demoralization that the written word is being slowly displaced as are feature films losing their place of primacy in our culture," Andrew Sarris said in 2008. "But then I remind myself that I'm not trying to influence the course of human events. I'm writing for readers who read me, and I'm still enjoying it enormously."

That aspect of the critic-reader bond in newspaper opinion writing, which has tied such iconic local columnists as Herb

Caen of the *San Francisco Chronicle*, Jack Smith of the *Los Angeles Times*, and Mike Royko of the *Chicago Sun-Times* to their cities, also gave certain critics great local cachet—Ebert and Siskel in Chicago, Gary Arnold for *The Washington Post*, Jay Carr at the *Boston Globe*.

"The great fun of reading a critic regularly is figuring out his or her likes, biases, quirks," said Stephen Whitty, film critic of the *Newark Star-Ledger* and a former chairman of the New York Film Critics Circle. "The great advantage of having a local reviewer is that he or she understands the likes, biases, or quirks of their readers. There's a relationship that develops, and it's specific to the newspaper and its audience. That's an intimate bond, and at some papers, it's going to be lost."

The independent producers and distributors, with fringe or foreign product, lose as well. "In each city there is a mosaic of voices with each reflecting the personality of the town and the readership," Tom Bernard of Sony Pictures Classics told *The New York Times*. "For us, a movie like *The Lives of Others*"—the German-language Oscar-winner for best foreign film in 2006 —"was dragged along by critics until people realized that it was one of the best movies of the year."

Joe Morgenstern, film critic for *The Wall Street Journal*, elaborated on that point in 2008. "Print journalists have become for the most part irrelevant to studio production, but we are more useful than ever for independent films. Because regardless of what people say about the new media, old reliable—and young reliable—movie critics are still very much needed to support independent films."

Scott Rudin, who produced the Academy Award-winning best picture *No Country for Old Men* (2007), concurred. "For those of us who are making work that requires a kind of intellectual conversation, we rely on that talk to do the work of getting people interested," Rudin said. He called the loss of film critics "a dire situation." Tom Bernard charted movie attendance declines in Boston, Seattle, Washington, D.C., Miami, and Chicago and tied it to the exits of certain critics in those cities.

The Tepper School of Business at Carnegie Mellon University in Pittsburgh studied the situation and determined that critics can have considerable influence on the box-office performance of specialty films. For the study, Peter Boatwright of the Tepper School compiled data that included weekly revenue and number of screens for a sample of 466 films released between December 1997 and March 2001, and correlated it with the reviews of 46 individual and widely accessible film critics. Several factors were taken into account, but Boatwright's study focused on measuring the extent to which unique reviews by specific critics influenced the box office. The results showed that early championing of a small film can accelerate attendance at lesser-known films.

These critics influenced the timing—the early success in the release run—the study determined, not the totals. "Reviewing the Reviewers: The Impact of Individual Film Critics on Box Office Performance" determined that the most influential of the 46 critics were Owen Gleiberman of *Entertainment Weekly*; Manohla Dargis, then of the *Los Angeles Times*; Michael Wilmington, then of the *Chicago Tribune*; and Lawrence Van Gelder, then of *The New York Times*.

And sometimes these critics couldn't help the small productions at all. "It has long been axiomatic in the business that big-budget, big-star movies are impervious to bad reviews," Roger Smith, of *Film Comment*, wrote. "In 2000, it now seems that smaller 'art-house' pictures are impervious to good reviews, although not to poor ones. Such movies can earn near uniform critical raves, and still fail to reach the low box-office hurdle—$5–$10 million—that constitutes a hit in this marketplace.

"Such pictures as *Two-Family House*, *A Family Affair*, *Tigerland* and *Girl on the Bridge* all received wildly positive notices, yet died in theaters. When *Topsy-Turvy* tops out at $6 million, and *Boys Don't Cry* at $11 million, with an Academy Award for best actress [Hilary Swank] thrown in for the latter, it demonstrates how little impact critics have," Smith averred. "The beneficiary of extraordinary reviews, *Wonder Boys* still hasn't cracked the $20 million level after 42 weeks in release, despite an un-precedented second bite at the theatrical apple."

The power of critics had declined all around, and was de-tectable in other ways. A rave review by Pauline Kael or Vincent Canby or Charles Champlin could, in the 1970s, boost a film or help a career. "A great review could get somebody another movie, and those days have sadly disappeared," said film critic Elvis Mitchell. "But the world of that kind of filmmaking has disappeared, too. I mean, I think we have to bemoan that more than this demise of film criticism."

More newspapers closed, including the *Cincinnati Post*, in which Nick Clooney wrote a column; the *Seattle Post-Intel-ligencer*, where William Arnold had been the movie critic; and the *Rocky Mountain News*, which had been the longest ongoing business in Colorado, dating to 1859. Many newspapers down-sized, including the *Los Angeles Times*, *Chicago Tribune*, *Washing-ton Post*, *Boston Globe*, *Pittsburgh Post-Gazette*, *Atlanta Journal-Constitution*, and *St. Louis Post-Dispatch*.

In 2009, David Poland of Movie City News compiled a list of professional film critics—those being paid full-time, presumably with benefits, to critique movies. The number was 117 in the United States, not far off Roger Ebert's estimation in the 1980s that there weren't many more than 100 people in the country reviewing movies for a living. Even though the voices of critics had multiplied exponentially via the Internet, the number of these critics who succeeded in getting paid for their expertise had not changed. The faces, however, had.

As newspapers have searched for ways to cut costs, review staffs received a big hit. Along with movie critics, longtime re-viewers of theatre, art, architecture, and all modes of music have been eliminated from newspaper staffs across the United States. Doug McLellan, the editor and founder in 1999 of artsjournal. com, estimated that in 2009 about half of the 5,000 newspaper staff positions in America involved with writing about the arts had been eliminated in four years.

"A lot of publications are dispensing with movie critics," Richard Schickel told *Variety* in 2008. "The people who run newspapers and magazines never liked us much, and they like us even less now." The standard opening for the TV show *At the Movies* in the 1980s depicted Roger Ebert and Gene Siskel grabbing copies of the latest editions of their papers, the *Chicago Sun-Times* and *Chicago Tribune*, respectively, tossed off delivery trucks. Anne Thompson nostalgically recalled that program opener in 2008, as if it was something like the first television-sized microwave. "How quaint," she wrote.

Since 2006, those who have lost their jobs as film critics because of layoffs, firings, buyouts, retirement, job elimination, reassignment, paper closings, or other methods were: John Anderson, *Newsday*; David Ansen, *Newsweek*; William Arnold, *Seattle Post-Intelligencer*; Michael Atkinson, *Village Voice*; Jami Bernard, *New York Daily News*; Ed Bradley, *Flint Journal*; Mark Burger, *Winston-Salem Journal*; Carina Chocano, *Los Angeles Times*; Robert Denerstein, *Rocky Mountain News*; David Elliott, *San Diego Union-Tribune*; Phoebe Flowers, *South Florida Sun-Sentinel*; Jack Garner, *Rochester Democrat and Chronicle*; David Gathman, *Elgin Courier-News*; Stephen Hunter, *Washington Post*; Glenn Kenny, *Premiere*; Terry Lawson, *Detroit Free Press*; Nathan Lee, *Village Voice*; Barbara Lester, *Fort Lauderdale CityLink*; Dennis Lim, *Village Voice*; Jack Mathews, *New York Daily News*; Rob Nelson, *Minneapolis-St. Paul City Pages*; Bruce Newman, *San Jose Mercury News*; Betsy Pickle, *Knoxville News Sentinel*; Mary F. Pols, *Oakland Tribune* and *Contra Costa Times*; Steve Ramos, *Cincinnati CityBeat*; Jonathan Rosenbaum, *Chicago Reader*; Eleanor Ringel-Gillespie, *Atlanta Journal-Constitution*; Bob Ross, *Tampa Tribune*; Matt Zoller Seitz, *The New York Times*; Gene Seymour, *Newsday*; Matt Soergel, *Florida Times-Union*; Bob Strauss, *Los Angeles Daily News*; Jan Stuart, *Newsday*; Ella Taylor, *LA Weekly*; George Thomas, *Akron Beacon Journal*; Kevin Thomas, *Los Angeles Times*; Desson Thomson, *Washington Post*; Glenn Whipp, *Los Angeles Daily News*; Michael Wilmington, *Chicago Tribune*; and Philip Wuntch, *Dallas Morning News*. Critics who died during the same period included Bill Muller of the *Arizona Republic* and Joel Siegel of *Good Morning America*.

Wholesale disregard for people of expertise, critics who had spent years amassing their knowledge and honing their craft, was rampant. They were expendable, and occasionally replaced by less costly staffers who agreed to fill the void because it was a cool sideline to be a movie critic. "It is scary," said Ansen, who accepted a buyout along with 100 other *Newsweek* employees in 2008. "It's a lot like a return to the hard old days when I was growing up when anybody could be a movie critic and they'd take somebody off the sports desk. It's a profound diss to the knowledge and expertise of a lot of good critics out there."

Superb writers and educators with deep knowledge of culture and the arts, such as John Simon and Stanley Kauffmann, would never make it through the resume-weeding process in this cultural climate, probably would have never been allowed out of their academic boxes to gain footholds at publications of any generalist nature. They wouldn't be tolerated, even if they volunteered to file their reviews for free.

Yet one critic's diss is another's fix. "This de-professionalization is probably the best thing that could have happened to the field," suggested John Podhoretz, film critic of *The Weekly Standard* and editor of *Commentary*. "Film criticism requires nothing but an interesting sensibility. The more self-consciously educated one is in the field—by which I mean the more obscure the storehouse of cinematic knowledge a critic has—the less likely it is that one will have anything interesting to say to an ordinary person who isn't all that interested in the condition of Finnish cinema. Amateurism in the best sense will lead to some very interesting work by people whose primary motivation is simply to express themselves in relation to the work they're seeing—purer critical impulse than the one that comes with collecting a paycheck along the way."

Apparently, the great knowledge and encyclopedic recall of some critics—based on the thousands of dark hours and miles of celluloid—indicates obsolescence to some, well, educated moviegoers. The exactitude and historical comparisons and contrasts that have enriched the analyses of Andrew Sarris, Jonathan Rosenbaum, Dave Kehr, Michael Wilmington, and J. Hoberman might as well be jettisoned from cultural discourse, heaved onto the *Fahrenheit 451* bonfire.

"My experience lately has been that editors don't want 'experts,'" said Kehr, who was fired by the *New York Daily News* in 1998, yet still writes a weekly video/DVD column in *The New York Times*. "'Populism' has become the buzzword. They want standard Joes who won't have some 'pointy-headed' reaction and just want to flop out on the couch before movies and TV."

Robert Morast of Inforum.com in Fargo, North Dakota, published an interview with Associated Press film critic Christy Lemire in 2009 that grilled her on what he characterized as her largely negative reviews. "The AP's film critics can't stand to give a film a positive review," Morast wrote. "Rather than asking if she can write a positive review, it's more fitting to try to understand what she, and other critics, want from movies," indicating not only a disconnect between critics and the heartland, but a bedrock belief that critics are chronically misunderstood. "Mostly, we want to be surprised and entertained," Lemire tactfully replied.

Younger readers don't want to devote time to the big think-piece, the incisive, multi-page review, the kind that used to be a regular epic for such alt-weekly film critics as Henry Sheehan, John Powers, Michael Sragow, Hoberman, and Rosenbaum. A quick critical consensus can be had by a visit to RottenTomatoes.com, the same way a TV advertisement offers a spot look at a picture, with a car wreck and a joke. The source of the viewpoints in a consensus take is never determined. Even if some of those particular opinions came from James Verniere at the *Boston Herald*, Gary Thompson at the *Philadelphia Daily News*, or Robert W. Butler at the *Kansas City Star*, it really doesn't matter if a consensus is only what's perceived as required.

"There is a general inability amongst many viewers to separate hack critics from the established critical voices," Felicia Feaster wrote for Creative Loafing Atlanta in 2001. What's more, there's often no effort to make any distinction between evaluative or promotional information, according to Dana Polan, a professor of cinema studies at New York University. "A lot of what people are reading about film today [on Web sites and message boards] is indistinguishable from press releases and publicity material," Polan said. Younger moviegoers don't make the distinction. The studios, said *Los Angeles Times* film critic Kenneth Turan, have "accepted as gospel that the young-adult audience is their bread and butter. So, they're not in the mass-entertainment business anymore. They're in the certain-demographic business. It's a calculated choice."

Manohla Dargis, film critic of *The New York Times*, takes a pragmatic view of the young audience. "When I was a kid, I never listened to an adult, so why should we expect kids to listen to critics who are the same age as their parents?" Dargis said. "I had a rich intellectual life, yet I didn't read reviews. They weren't even on my map.

"The real problem is even if a kid wants [guidance] today, what they will find, overwhelmingly, is noise about celebrities and meaningless numbers indicating what big movie 'won' the weekend box office," Dargis said. "Who talks about film as something greater than a vehicle for celebrity and consumerism? Very few, I think."

The rise of the Internet critic created a galaxy of cyberspace arbiters, none bigger than Harry Knowles, a blazingly red-haired, 300-pound Austin, Texas, film geek who was mentored by Internet-news pioneer Matt Drudge, has made TV appearances with Roger Ebert, and been labeled "the most powerful independent voice in movie criticism since Pauline Kael" by no less than *The Times* of London. Knowles's Web site, Ain't It Cool News, contains reviews of movies by its creator since 1996 that usually reference his own experiences about anything along with ample amounts of profanity, followed by a trail of blog hogs.

"I was not a fan at all of *The Da Vinci Code*," Knowles writes in his lead to Ron Howard's sequel, *Angels & Demons* (2009). "I wasn't an offended Catholic—I just didn't like the story. I just never got swept up in it. But I loved elements of it. I love the Hardy Boys aspect of it. The clue that leads to a clue that leads to another clue. . . . I love mysteries—but I never felt there was a drive to the story.

"In *Angels & Demons*, it kinda feels like a Michael Crichton novel in the way it is constructed," is an example of a typical Knowles comparison, as he always seeks to reach the widest common denominator to connect to his audience. "There's a series of time limits till something BAD is going to happen. There's crisis upon crisis upon crisis—all of which ramps up the tension level. And I never have a grotesque silliness like 'the direct descendent of Jesus' as a twist."

Whatever grotesque silliness he has had, his work is read, or interpreted, by millions. Knowles's experiences and his rise on the media landscape were chronicled in the autobiography *Ain't It Cool?: Hollywood's Redheaded Stepchild Speaks Out*, published in 2002 by Warner Books, with a foreword by Quentin Tarantino.

"The worst thing about Harry Knowles is that he's perfectly reflective of the taste of predominantly young America in terms of movies," *Variety* editor and former film critic Steven Gaydos said in 2000. "He loves the garbage movies, the big stupid movies and the little stupid movies. It's so middlebrow, just like the E! online Web site or *Entertainment Weekly* or Mr. Showbiz; they just reflect the taste of the public, which frightens the hell out of me."

The screeds against the lowbrow and middlebrow Internet critics and their legions of bloggers included one by Armond White in *Film Comment* in 1992. "The future refinement of movie reviewing will shed any scholarly indulgences, leaving the essential, practical activity of judging a film's content by the demographics of the audience (called speaking for the people)," White wrote, "and then playing to the Nielsens. . . . Competing with the constant barrage of ad-like copy, popular film discourse has fallen to the level of lay opinion typified by the off-the-cuff glibness of TV anchor-desk reviewers or the various sets of dueling assholes. . . . Editors rarely have, and don't ask for, expertise in the field. Unlike reviewing in the other arts, where a familiarity with the forms' history and significant works is assumed prerequisite, there are film critics who've never seen more than a couple Griffith films, or can't tolerate Godard, let alone having heard of Lev Kuleshov. . . . Professionalism has slackened. . . .

"Anyone can do film criticism when the only reason assigned to it is consumerism," White continued. "That's the great leveler; the right to purchase makes every opinion, every desire, every purpose equal: Kitsch is art, and Woody Allen is Ingmar Bergman. Once standards of taste and intelligence have been devalued," White emphasized, "there's no need for critics. Each filmgoer must decide for him/herself. Call it intellectual anarchy. Maybe when criticism—the organized, articulated thinking about films—improves, the movies will, too."

There has never been a standard for film criticism beyond the barriers of whom the critics' groups subjectively allow as members via democratic vote. As White points out, there's a film critic in every home and at every job site. Movies are a constant and ready source for conversation everywhere. And the great paradox is that, while there are as many people earning all or portions of their income as film critics than ever before, they are largely less astute, shrewd, and educated than their predecessors. At the very least, fewer of today's critics can intelligently and lucidly express their opinions of a new film within the context of the themes, directors, genres, and other movies of the past.

In the 1990s, the annual carping about yet another lousy movie year became a seasonal ritual for film critics, whose calendar year begins with awards season, and is capped by Hollywood's Christmas, the Academy Awards. On the way to the Oscars, the three main critics groups—the National Society of Film Critics, New York Film Critics Circle, and Los Angeles Film Critics Association—dole out awards as do other geographically organized critics groups in Chicago; Boston; St. Louis; Detroit; San Francisco; Kansas City; Phoenix; Las Vegas; Dallas/Fort Worth; Austin; Washington, D.C.; Florida; Utah; the southeastern U.S.;

central Ohio; southeast Michigan; and elsewhere. The Broadcast Film Critics Association also bestows year-end movie awards on the usually televised Critics Choice Awards. With nearly 100 members of mostly out-of-town press, the broadcast critics carry many members of the junket press, which do the studios' bidding by traveling on studio money to press-conference-like interviews of filmmakers and performers in pending releases.

Other, newer groups, often comprised of overlapping memberships include the Online Film Critics Society, Internet Film Critics Association, New York Film Critics Online, African American Film Critics Association, Women Film Critics Circle, and the International Federation of Film Critics, formed in 2008 in Munich, Germany, with a Russian president (Andrei Plakhov) and American members (connected through the New York offices of Elisabeth Weis of the National Society of Film Critics) that includes Mike Goodridge, Harlan Jacobson, Robert Koehler, Vincent Musetto, and B. Ruby Rich.

In addition, the usual suspects keep awarding as they always have, some on television, with the usual pomp and glitz: the Hollywood Foreign Press Association's Golden Globes, the Independent Spirit Awards, the People's Choice Awards, the Screen Actors Guild Awards, the Directors Guild of America Awards, and honors from the NAACP, Blockbuster Entertainment, MTV, the American Film Institute, along with Web sites, water-cooler confabs, houses of correction, and film geeks typing to their own tunes online. To say that the meaning of movie awards has been generally diluted by their proliferation is more than an understatement.

"It would be nice to think of ourselves as the climax to a series of playoffs," said Bruce Davis, the executive director of the Academy of Motion Picture Arts and Sciences in 2001. "But the fact is that these awards tend to involve the same films, the same people presenting them, the same people receiving them, and I think we would be naïve to think that the specialness of our event was being eroded by the proliferation of these early-year, film-award shows."

In 2007, awards season carping between hardware-bestowing groups created some fussbudgets. Jack Mathews of the *New York Daily News* called the New York Film Critics Circle's awards-voting system "corrupt." Richard Corliss summed up the NYFCC's activities in *Time* as "we're essentially passing notes to one another, admiring our connoisseurship at the risk of ignoring the vast audience that sees movies and the smaller one that reads us." *LA Weekly* film editor Scott Foundas called Oscar predictions, which year-by-year have eaten up more mainstream entertainment news space, cyberspace, and soundbites, "pseudo-journalistic white noise."

Oscar blogger Scott Feinberg of And the Winner Is. . . called the Hollywood Foreign Press Association "one of the most corrupt, pathetic, kowtowing groups of awards voters imaginable." Columnist Patrick Goldstein in the *Los Angeles Times* claimed, "The root of all this evil, of course, is that everyone writes entirely too much about the Oscars (my newspaper included)."

After the Oscars, critics settle into the summer blockbuster months, when the sequels and special-effects-driven action epics are unveiled by studio marketing departments with the fatuous grandiosity and repetitive dullness of a May Day Parade in the Khrushchev era. Autumn, the season of guarded hope, arrives as the studios offer modestly budgeted pictures of supposed integrity, bringing us human issues, fine acting and candidates for the next awards season.

The year culminates with the month-long crunch season, when critics cram in overstuffed holiday releases like plates of turkey to beat voting deadlines for the coming awards season. They watch and/or review multiple contenders in back-to-back-to-back days. At any time, mental exhaustion may hit critics. It's a contagious byproduct of the studio-marketing rush to beat well-advertised deadlines to maximize any year-end release's box-office take during its debut weekend.

The standardization of the movie year's cycle, along with sequel-itis and awards from Podunk, are all symptomatic of serious film criticism's ineffectiveness. *Film Comment*'s Roger Smith,

taking a stab at trendspotting the five things that are not going to matter anymore in Hollywood in the new century listed
"marketing bucks," "creative issues," "who's in charge," and "the
movies themselves"—all these after the No. 1 thing that won't
matter: "reviews."

The critical reception of Steven Spielberg's *A.I.: Artificial
Intelligence* (2001) was a case in point. It was the first Spielberg
movie to be generally loved by critics and generally avoided by
the public. The science-fiction entry was developed by Stanley
Kubrick and passed on to Spielberg prior to Kubrick's death in
1999. It grossed $80 million after a month in release; long gone
are the days when the $100 million mark signified a great box-
office success.

"Is our aging critical elite terminally out of touch with
regular moviegoers?" Patrick Goldstein asked in the *Los Angeles
Times*. "Were their critical antennae overwhelmed by the one-
two punch of Spielberg and Kubrick? Or were they simply grad-
ing on the curve, giving *A.I.* high marks simply because it was
one of the few movies this year that had higher aspirations than
putting fannies in the seats?" Critics see so many bad movies
that when one arrives with aspirations and a pedigree, they can
overreact. Many of the top critics came of age or developed critical acumens in the 1970s, when Pauline Kael was their all-but-
consecrated spiritual queen, and the *Godfather* films and *Chinatown* were both critical and box-office hits.

"And the critics who grew up under the spell of those
films can't help but feel a deep yearning for the go-for-broke passion that's largely absent in today's films," Goldstein surmised,
concluding, ". . . Maybe that's why, in the end, I can't fault critics for occasionally giving a wet kiss to an aging heavyweight.
They've got their standards and they're sticking to them, even
though they're writing about a medium that sold its soul to the
box-office devil long ago."

Of course, the critics *were* older. By 2000, nearly a decade after Kael retired, most of the critics who evolved as nationally known voices in film criticism throughout the 1970s passed

the half-century mark. Roger Ebert of *Siskel & Ebert & the Movies* and the *Chicago Sun-Times* was 58; Kenneth Turan of the *Los Angeles Times*, 54; Todd McCarthy of *Daily Variety*, 50; Rex Reed, 62; Joel Siegel, 57; Richard Schickel, 67; David Denby, 57; and Leonard Maltin, a fresh 49.

There was one ultra-fresh newcomer who showed up on ads, but nowhere else. A ridiculous fiasco impacted film reviewing when *Newsweek* reported in May 2001 that "David Manning" of the *Ridgefield Press* in Ridgefield, Connecticut—whom Sony Pictures had quoted in advertising for its films *Hollow Man* (2000), *Vertical Limit* (2000), *The Animal* (2001), and *A Knight's Tale* (2001)—didn't exist. The critic was fabricated by the studio's marketing department. "Manning" raved that Heath Ledger, the lead actor in *A Knight's Tale*, was "this year's hottest new star!" *The Animal*, "Manning" maintained, was "another winner!" After "Manning" was revealed to be a hoax, a spokeswoman for Sony said, "It's embarrassing and wrong and we will take the appropriate action." The "Manning" blurbs were then removed from the studio's ads.

Peter Rainer, film critic for *New York* magazine and the chairman of the National Society of Film Critics, said that the "Manning" episode was the end result of junketeer culture, the studio-paid weekend jaunts by writers and critics at midsize papers and magazines, radio and TV stations, and some Internet Web sites. Happy for the free rides to Hollywood and the chances to chat up the stars, the junketeers were usually more than happy to give the movies good reviews and allot ample page space and airplay to the star features. The junket circuit evolved into a studio marketing standard by the 1990s.

"It's been demonstrated in the past that studios will, in effect, create the kind of reviews they want by cultivating junketeers, who then provide quotes for the ads," Rainer said. "Studios are in the business of getting good press now and if critics are perceived as not being part of 'the team,' they are marginalized. There are cadres of blurb-meisters who will do their bidding. This is the logical extension of that. They have taken out an added insurance policy by creating their own critic. Where they slipped up was in not creating their own newspaper."

Newsweek's John Horn, a former Associated Press writer in Hollywood, researched junketeers' blurbs and stumbled upon the nonexistent "Manning." The blurbmeisters, Horn felt, were "undermining the integrity and value of real critics." One of the main blurbmeisters for years, Joey Berlin, felt that the unmasking of the Sony non-critic improved the junketeers' reputations.

"I think it is outrageous," said Berlin, then president of the Broadcast Film Critics Association and a regular junket rider for nearly two decades for various outlets, including Copley News Service, and Jeff Craig's *Sixty Second Preview*, for which Berlin wrote the almost always praise-filled review copy in lieu of Craig. "It's not a huge surprise. Personally, from our perspective, we feel kind of vindicated in a way. If film critics were so compliant"—meaning willing to supply studios with quotes before their reviews were published—"then maybe [the studios] wouldn't have to resort to this to get their quotes."

However, studios usually resort to any strategy to maximize a hit, especially in its first weekend of release. "After the junkets yield their fluff, the ad designers go to work," wrote Steve Persall, film critic for the *St. Petersburg Times*. "Purchased words like 'hysterical' (*Crocodile Dundee in Los Angeles*) and 'a twisted masterpiece' (*Say It Isn't So*) are hyped with exclamation points. Meanwhile, the bylines of quoted reviewers get tinier, in an effort to play down names like Dannah Feinglass from something called Burly Bear Network, who believes *Saving Silverman* is 'funnier than *There's Something About Mary*.'"

A main offender became CNN's talk-show anchor, Larry King, whose tersely exclaimed praise became conspicuous on movie posters. He called D.J. Caruso's *Two for the Money* (2005) "the best movie about gambling ever!" Robert De Niro's *The Good Shepherd* (2006) was deemed "the best spy movie ever!" Had King seen every other spy and gambling movie to determine the base value of his statements, and had he any experience in judging movies beyond being a fan? "I know they're only looking for a catchphrase," King said about studio marketers seeking out his pearls of wisdom, so he happily provided them. "I'm not a critic!" he told the *Los Angeles Times*.

He was and is, however, Larry King, a famous TV face whose uncomplicated rave reactions in very few words might convince another regular Joe or Larry to buy a ticket. "All I can say is that moviegoers are smart enough to see through the charade," Patrick Goldstein beneficently reasoned in the *Times*. "If you need Larry King to tout your picture, why bother with any blurbs at all?"

The one legitimate film critic who maintained a high poster presence, along with Jeff Craig, Larry King, and Susan Granger, was Peter Travers of *Rolling Stone*. "When *Rolling Stone* interviewed writers for the critic's job that eventually went to Peter Travers, the magazine made it known that it wanted its reviewer to be featured in newspaper ads, according to numerous journalists," Allan Wolper wrote in the "Ethics Corner" column in *Editor & Publisher* in 2004. "The reasoning was obvious: *Rolling Stone* saw the blurbs as free advertisements for itself, as well as a selling point with studio ad agencies. Travers has made it big in Blurb Journalisim, by some counts second only to Roger Ebert and Richard Roeper, the two 'Thumbs Up' guys."

Travers is perhaps the most notable monthly critic to the public, because his positive reviews of independent films are often used in studio advertising. Of Karyn Kusama's *Girlfight* (2000), he wrote, "Michelle Rodriguez smolders with the beauty and intensity of a born star, and director Kusama keeps her fearlessly on her feet with a movie that ducks no punches . . . . Final decision: They're both champions." Stephen Frears's *High Fidelity* (2000), with John Cusack as an independent music store clerk, "hits all the laugh bases, from grins to guffaws," Travers wrote.

Rita Kempley, a film critic of *The Washington Post*, retired after 25 years in January 2004, the same month that Wolper's article appeared. She was told years before by an ad agency that her career would suffer if she didn't become more quotable. "I guess they couldn't figure out how to blurb me," Kempley said.

Junkets became so endemic to the Hollywood system after the turn of the new century that they could be siphoned for product. In one case, a junket regular who was known for dominating roundtable discussions, Rod Lurie, the former film critic of *Los Angeles* magazine who had been co-president of the Broadcast Film Critics Association, became a successful film-maker by writing and directing *The Contender* (2000), which garnered Oscar nominations for Joan Allen and Jeff Bridges. And a junket became the backdrop for a major film, *America's Sweethearts* (2001), starring Billy Crystal as a studio public rela-tions agent, John Cusack and Catherine Zeta-Jones as movie stars married to each other, and Julia Roberts as their gofer. The film bombed.

By providing airfare, ground transportation, hotel rooms, meal expenses, and gift bags to reviewers, who then write favor-able reviews for their movies, Sony, Disney, Twentieth Centu-ry Fox, Warner Bros., and other studios have gone against the grain of accepted business practices, including the Federal Trade Commission's mandates. Rules stipulate that when endorse-ments promote a product, the company using the endorsement must disclose all the financial participants. The basic reasoning by studio marketers was the adage that any publicity is good publicity. "They will never penalize somebody for writing a bad review," said Gabriel de Lerma, a Latino journalist and junket rider. "They don't care what you write as long as you write a piece. They get mad if you go to a [junket] and don't write a piece." Said Keith Woods of the Poynter Institute for Media Studies in St. Petersburg, Florida: "When studios bring journal-ists out, it guarantees coverage. Even if the coverage is negative, it's a positive for the studio. It's publicity. That's what the money is being spent on."

Also diluting the power of critics in the new century is the fact that there are so many of them, at least so many who consider and call themselves critics, from junketeers to dot-com writers to members of the enduring and embattled Hollywood

Foreign Press Association to the members of the Florida, Chicago, and Texas critics associations. But more people than ever before are interested in Hollywood and the scenes behind the movies. The media overload requires more disseminators of "news" and reviewers on radio, TV, and the Internet, whether they call themselves critics or not.

Despite more critics on the landscape, members of the old guard abided. Andrew Sarris was again cited, as he was in 1987, by the School of Journalism at his place of employ, Columbia University, as a runner-up for the 2000 Pulitzer Prize for "his informed and enlightening criticism." If the appearance of a conflict of interest came from Columbia University's desire to reward those who were justly deserving or not, many film followers felt that the recognition for Sarris was overdue. This marked the sixth time that a film critic was a non-winning finalist since the announcements of Pulitzer runners-up began in 1980.

Sarris, who was still teaching full-time at Columbia at age 72 and had been writing in the *New York Observer* since 1989, took up an offer in November 2000 to introduce two of his favorite films, Ernst Lubitsch's *The Shop Around the Corner* (1940) and François Truffaut's *Shoot the Piano Player* (1960), at the Los Angeles County Museum of Art. The Directors Guild of America, which had a vested interest in keeping the auteur theory alive as it anticipated future contract battles with the Writers Guild of America over the possessory credit held by directors— e.g., "A film by John Frankenheimer," "A Spike Lee joint"— joined in the Sarris celebration. The DGA hosted Sarris and his film-critic wife during the Los Angeles weekend festivities with "Dialogue on Film: A Weekend with Andrew Sarris and Molly Haskell." Bill Desowitz, writing in the *Los Angeles Times*, dubbed Sarris and Haskell "the Nick and Nora Charles of film critics" after the jaunty Dashiell Hammett characters played famously by William Powell and Myrna Loy in *The Thin Man* (1934) and its sequels.

The new decade brought two film critics the Pulitzer Prize, the only ones in the profession besides Roger Ebert—

despite nine instances of film critics as runners-up. Stephen Hunter won in 2003 after he had moved to *The Washington Post* from the *Baltimore Sun*, and Joe Morgenstern of *The Wall Street Journal* won in 2005 after being a runner-up in 2002. (The other film critic runner-up in the new century was Ann Hornaday of *The Washington Post* in 2008.)

A 1953 graduate of Lehigh University, Morgenstern had been a foreign correspondent for *The New York Times* before becoming a theatre and movie critic for the *New York Herald-Tribune* in 1959, on a staff that included Judith Crist, Otis L. Guernsey, William K. Zinsser, and Paul V. Beckley. In 1965, Morgenstern became a movie critic for *Newsweek*, then a columnist for the *Los Angeles Herald-Examiner* from 1983 to 1988. Morgenstern's scriptwriting included director Randal Kleiser's TV movie *The Boy in the Plastic Bubble* (1976), starring John Travolta, and episodes of *Law & Order*. He joined the *Journal* in 1995 and remained based in Santa Monica. Morgenstern, once married to actress Piper Laurie, was notable for having reversed his opinion on *Bonnie and Clyde* in 1967, and writing that reversal from pan to rave in *Newsweek*. He had been a close friend of Pauline Kael's since that time.

Morgenstern's wide and sleek vocabulary within a succinct style has been a career-long constant. Exposition was never mundane in his care, as in his *Newsweek* review of *Woodstock* (1970): "Director Michael Wadleigh and an adept crew of cameramen have shot and assembled a fascinating, overlong, ear-splitting and screensplitting chronicle of the events that transpired on and around Max Yasgur's cow farm . . . Havens, with his Carborundum voice and ceaseless splay of guitar strums . . . Jimi Hendrix wringing out of his guitar the most martial version imaginable of 'The Star-Spangled Banner,' complete with rockets red glare, dive bombers, bugle calls, and the shrieks of women and children."

Morgenstern's Pulitzer citation read that his win, based on 2004 work, was for "his reviews that elucidated the strengths and weaknesses of film with rare insight, authority and wit."

Among the reviews that the *Journal* submitted to the Pulitzer board was Morgenstern's take on director Mel Gibson's controversially bloody 2004 version of a Passion play.

"Mel Gibson has said that he wanted *The Passion of the Christ* to show the enormity of Christ's sacrifice through scenes so shocking as to push us 'over the edge,'" Morgenstern wrote. "The film does that, though where we land depends on who we are. Some will be inspired by the message of love and hope that emerges from torture depicted in hideous detail. I found myself stunned, then horrified, then defensively benumbed, by a level of violence that would, in another genre, be branded as pornographic. No one who watches Mr. Gibson's dramatization of Christ's final hours will come away unaffected by its intensity.

"His direction combines the fluency of modern techniques—the craftsmanship is impressive—with a central performance, by Jim Caviezel, that sometimes evokes the primal, ecstatic style of the silent era. Yet this work of manifest devotion, financed by Mr. Gibson himself, is overwhelmed by his obsession with physical suffering to the exclusion of social, political and metaphysical context."

While Sarris and Morgenstern were celebrated in the new century, the role of elder statesman came to Richard Schickel as easily as his smooth and direct prose flowed in *Time*. He commented on books, movies, critics, and controversies during a prolific and rich career. He was sounded out on various topics. When the Directors Guild of America faced a barrage of criticism in 2000 for throwing away another touchstone of movie history when it changed the name of its career honorary from the D.W. Griffith Award to the Lifetime Achievement Award—because of the overt racism in the egregiously heroic presentation of the Ku Klux Klan in his classic *The Birth of a Nation* (1915)—Schickel, the author of *D.W. Griffith: An American Life*, told the *Los Angeles Times*, "By any standard, [Griffith] was a racist.

"There are people who instinctively react, 'Oh, God, it's just political correctness,'" Schickel said. "There's some truth in that, I suppose. But on the other hand—I guess I can say this as

Griffith's not entirely admiring biographer, I don't mind if they are renaming the [DGA] award. His attitude is manifest in that film and is undeniable."

Schickel's longevity and pervasiveness on the critical landscape was such that by the turn of the 21st century, he was speaking as 1) Griffith's biographer; 2) a longtime member of the DGA as a documentary filmmaker; and 3) a founding member of the 34-year-old and 53-member National Society of Film Critics, which had inflamed the Griffith flap by drafting a statement deploring the DGA's action as the discarding of a piece of significant history.

"The recasting of this honor, which had been awarded appropriately in D.W. Griffith's name since 1953, is a depressing example of 'political correctness' as an erasure, and rewriting, of American film history, causing a grave disservice to the reputation of a pioneering American filmmaker," read the Peter Rainer-chaired National Society's response. Among the critics supporting the statement was an African American, Armond White, of the *New York Press*. "It's ridiculous to rewrite history that way," White said. But the DGA, traditionally and demonstrably the most powerful guild in Hollywood, had its way.

Speaking of the old guard, the bimonthly *Film Comment* continued to stay eclectic and occasionally quite foreign to anyone wanting to read about Hollywood. Written by a mix of newly cycled-in voices and an established cadre of scribes, *Film Comment* doesn't deserve the "old guard" crack since it has remained vital and consistently open to the new. The Film Society of Lincoln Center has operated the magazine for half a century, issuing news, reviews, features, valentines, diatribes, and manifestos with wit and heart as the critics who function in the best tradition of mostly accessible arbiters of the state of the art to the educated cineastes. This long-form packager of the zeitgeist has usually been less throat-throttling than the often as-thoughtful and as-skeptical urban lifestyle weeklies whose critics sometimes appear on the magazine's pages.

Gavin Smith was *Film Comment*'s first new editor of the

21st century and the repeat bylines among contributors have belonged to, among others, Harlan Kennedy, Kathleen Murphy, Dave Kehr, Robert Horton, Kent Jones, Peter Hogue, Armond White, Michael Atkinson, Jim Emerson, Michael Wilmington, Richard Schickel, Gregory Solman, Donald Phelps, Nicole Armour, Chris Chang, Jonathan Rosenbaum, Chuck Stephens, Mark Olsen, Paul Arthur, and others.

While the one perceptible bias at *Film Comment* seems to be an effort to cover the Film Society of Lincoln Center's New York activities, other prevailing prejudices were alleged among film critics. In 2008, a study by Dr. Martha M. Lauzen of the Center for the Study of Women in Television and Film at San Diego State University found that 70 percent of the movie reviews in the top 100 newspapers were written by men. Almost half of those papers (47%) did not run reviews by women.

Still, prominent publications boasted women critics, led by Manohla Dargis at *The New York Times*, Claudia Puig at *USA Today*, Leah Rozen at *People*, Lisa Schwarzbaum at *Entertainment Weekly*, Betsy Sharkey at the *Los Angeles Times*, Ann Hornaday at *The Washington Post*, Carrie Rickey at the *Philadelphia Inquirer*, Barbara Vancheri at the *Pittsburgh Post-Gazette*, and others.

Clearly chief among them is Dargis. She joined *The New York Times* from the *Los Angeles Times* in the summer of 2004, after the New York paper named A.O. Scott the lead film critic. Elvis Mitchell resigned from the review staff as a result, creating the opening. In the 1990s, following Vincent Canby's exit from the film beat, various critics reviewed alongside Janet Maslin and after. Maslin moved to review books in 1999, and Caryn James and Stephen Holden were the most frequent other bylines, as were Mitchell from 1998, Walter Goodman, Lawrence Van Gelder, Anita Gates, Tom Buckley, Dave Kehr, Ned Martel, and Dana Stevens.

Dargis had only been at the *Los Angeles Times* for about a year. The hiring by the New York paper was viewed by the Los Angeles sheet as the centerpiece of a raid that saw other L.A. cultural staffers defect to the paper of record. *The New York Times* allowed Dargis to remain living in Los Angeles and also offered her the latitude for essays as well. "About the worst thing about living in Los Angeles outside of the lack of decent public transportation is the lack of avant garde film venues," Dargis said. "Filmforum is about the only L.A. organization that screens avant-garde films on any sort of consistent basis."

Dargis began writing for *The Village Voice* in 1987, concentrating at first, like her mentor, J. Hoberman, on the avant-garde. She had taken a class taught by Hoberman in the Masters in Cinema Studies program at New York University. In 1994, Dargis moved to Los Angeles to write for *LA Weekly*'s film section, which she took over the following year from Elizabeth Pincus, bringing in new writers and expanding coverage. "I never wanted to be a critic," Dargis said. "My first great surprise was that you could read a movie like a book. My second was that you could earn a living as a critic—that still surprises me."

Provocative and uneasy to please, she became what she called "queen of hate mail at the *Weekly*—one of the paper's longtime copy editors told me I had received more hate mail than anyone in the paper's history, which is kind of bizarre." Dargis was hired away by the *Los Angeles Times* in 2002, and stayed a year reviewing with Kenneth Turan and Kevin Thomas, then made the leap to *The New York Times*.

Manohla Dargis was born in April 1961 and grew up in New York's East Village. "If I tell you the truth it'll sound absurd, but my parents were bohemians, and as a consequence, my favorite movies at age eight were François Truffaut's *Jules and Jim* and *Orphee*, by Jean Cocteau. I was not taken to any Disney movies."

Dargis offered that *The Wizard of Oz* (1939) remains more than a movie to her. "It's not just an aesthetic object—it's also a childhood object," she told *Los Angeles* magazine. "It's like an old blanket. I appreciate its sense of melancholy and loss. It's profound."

In 2002, she said, "I don't read most of the New York press anymore and I find as time goes by I'm not reading as many film critics, either. I still read *The New Yorker* because I envy David Denby's words and Anthony Lane's jokes. I read my smart friend John Powers . . . and I try to keep up with Hoberman and Jonathan Rosenbaum from the *Chicago Reader* because they're two of the few American critics from whom I consistently learn something new about movies. It's the same reason I read my friends Amy Taubin and Kent Jones . . . [in] *Film Comment*."

Dargis said that she keeps an open mind about movies, even when she has disliked the filmmaker's previous works. "The day I stop being hopeful is the day I quit reviewing movies," she said. However, her reputation precedes her. "She's the critic you love to read," Patrick Goldstein wrote, "just as long as you're not reading about your movie.

"It's an open secret in indie Hollywood that no one wants Manohla Dargis to review their movie, fearing that the outspoken critic will tear their film limb from limb," Goldstein wrote in the *Los Angeles Times*. "It's the ultimate backhanded compliment, since what they really fear is Manohla's persuasiveness—that she'll write a review whose combination of vitriolic snarkiness and intellectual heft will actually persuade high-brow moviegoers to drop the film from their must-see list. (To be fair, she can be equally passionate about films she loves; for example, *Synecdoche, New York*, or anything by David Lynch.)

"The production chief of one indie studio once was so infuriated by a string of negative Dargis reviews that he vowed to keep Manohla away from all of his future screenings, even if that meant stopping all of our critics from seeing his movies. I told him it was a bad idea since it would only make Manohla a hero to critics everywhere, further increasing her clout. When he was still running Miramax, Harvey Weinstein, stung by Manohla's lash on any number of reviews, begged me to persuade her to have lunch with him. Harvey no doubt thought he could influence her with his considerable charm. She politely refused."

Stephen Daldry's *The Reader* (2008) was a contender for the best picture Oscar. For Dargis, it was a manipulative fraud. "You have to wonder who, exactly, wants or perhaps needs to see another movie about the Holocaust that embalms its horrors with artfully spilled tears and asks us to pity a death camp guard," she wrote.

Dargis's review in *The New York Times* of *Nothing But the Truth* (2008), written and directed by former film critic Rod Lurie, spared no mercy for a once fellow journalist. "I'm not sure what Mr. Lurie, whose previous films include *The Contender*, an exploration of female power and its threat, believed he was saying in his new film. *Nothing But the Truth* has nothing much at all to do with the historical record, which wouldn't be bad if it offered something persuasive and worthwhile in return, like a reckoning of journalism and its abuses. It shows Mr. Lurie ambitiously trying out some bold compositions, notably two-shots in which one character's head looms in the foreground while the second person blurs into the background, and a commensurate level of narrative ambition that goes awry in the execution. Truly, the greater problem is not the facts but the delivery."

A.O. Scott, born on July 10, 1966, joined *The New York Times* as a film critic in January 2000. Previously, he was a Sunday book reviewer for *Newsday*, and a frequent contributor to *Slate*, *The New York Review of Books*, and many other publications. Scott graduated with a B.A. degree in literature (*magna cum laude*) from Harvard College in 1988 and was a grad-school dropout from Johns Hopkins University in Baltimore. He has also served on the editorial staffs of *Lingua Franca* and *The New York Review of Books*.

"I have vivid memories of going to see *Willy Wonka and the Chocolate Factory*, but *Fantasia* is the movie that blew my mind," Scott remembered in 2009. "I realized how much a movie could do—it didn't even have to tell a good story to grab hold of you. Probably the first movie of feeling in over my head was *Play It Again, Sam*—early Woody Allen. I must have been eight or nine. It had a great blend of jokes that a kid could get—low comedy, slapstick—and then this great sophistication about setting and relationships. It was the first movie that awoke the idea in me that there were wonderfully rich and complicated things you could think and talk about in films."

While he had been mostly a book critic, Scott was contacted by *The New York Times* to apply for the paper's film criticism post. "Figuring I had a) no shot and b) nothing to lose, I said, 'Why not?'"

In the new century, Scott is interested in what blogging will come to mean for film criticism. "A critical perspective on the arts you care about is important and worthwhile and necessary. If criticism were to cease as an activity, a lot would go with it." Criticism, he said, can "provoke and stimulate thought and argument. Not just to say a work is good or bad, but in a coherent, lively way to share thoughts and impressions and create a virtual dialogue. What's intriguing about the Internet is that it's an actual dialogue."

Considering Mel Gibson's *The Passion of the Christ*, Scott wrote, "What makes the movie so grim and ugly is Mr. Gibson's inability to think beyond the conventional logic of movie narrative." Scott called Gabriele Muccino's *Seven Pounds* (2008) one of "the most transcendently, eye-poppingly, call-your-friend-ranting-in-the-middle-of-the-night-just-to-go-over-it-one-more-time crazily awful motion pictures ever made." In a 2009 *New York Times* review, Scott wrote, "The title of Barry Levinson's new movie *What Just Happened* is not phrased as a question, but if it were, it would demand another question in response, 'Who cares?'"

Scott may have more humor than any of his predecessors at the *Times*—funny, telling, and analytic—as in this 2007 review: "Don't be fooled though. Underneath the surface of racial and sexual button pushing, behind the brandished guns and bared breasts, is a heart of pure, buttery cornpone. Like *Hustle & Flow*, *Black Snake Moan* joins a dubious stereotype of black manhood to an uplifting, sentimental fable. In the earlier movie the hero was a soulful pimp with dreams of hip-hop glory. This time he is a retired blues singer with woman troubles and a vegetable farm. Really, though, the character, played with his usual fearsome wit by Samuel L. Jackson, is a tried-and-true Hollywood stock figure: the selfless, spiritually minded African-American who seems to have been put on the earth to help white people work out their self-esteem issues. No doubt *Black Snake Moan* is a provocative title, but a more accurate one might be *Chaining Miss Daisy to the Radiator in Her Underwear*."

While he can be loose and express predilections for indie and foreign titles, Scott also complies with *The New York Times* standard of framing the movie year with expressive opinions, bedrock sense, and film-genre and pop-culture knowledge, as in this capsule on his selection of *Million Dollar Baby* (2004) for the best picture of the year: "A year after releasing the overpowering *Mystic River*, Clint Eastwood tops it with a boxing melodrama that is quiet, loose-limbed and every bit as powerful— a work of unassuming directorial mastery that includes three resonant, lived-in performances, from Morgan Freeman, Hilary Swank and Mr. Eastwood himself, who has never been better. Rather than dance around the clichés of the fight picture, which is one of the hoariest standards in the Hollywood songbook, Mr. Eastwood reminds us of the deep human emotions and aspirations in which they originate."

Scott and Dargis have their adherents and their detractors. Their five years together might constitute the last great hurrah of newspaper criticism as the Internet age advances, and print disappears. Still, however, someone has to be a critic:

"Its lead critics, A.O. Scott and Manohla Dargis, have yet to establish the kind of bulkhead that Canby and Maslin had during their tenure at the *Times*, but that is partly because neither Scott nor Dargis has a particular mainstream sensibility," Anne Thompson wrote. "Both are canny careerists, though, as well as elegant writers who often seem more interested in crafting arcane intellectual arguments than reaching out to their readers. Thus when Scott or Dargis champions a small movie such as *Gunner Palace* or *The Notorious Bettie Page*, it has little impact."

At least *The New York Times* was attempting to live up to its reputation as the paper of record regarding film criticism in the 21st century, something it did not do at the outset of the

20th century. And despite the ample testimony catalogued to this point of the tragic, waning epoch of good, informed, literate, and well-expressed print film criticism, this decline is both a matter of form and medium, and symptomatic of a generally accepted decline in, and respect for, literacy.

Papers, delivery trucks, and newsstands will continue to disappear as cyberspace gains the upper hand and news dissemination becomes entirely electronic. The ability to communicate opinion has increased with Web sites and blogs, while the capability to do so in the literary tradition—with style, wit, in-depth analysis, and historical context—has not been as evident in cyberspace as in the print era. The decline in literacy has certainly played a part in film criticism's dilution, but it is simply too pandemic a subject for this parochial discussion beyond the fact that it is a major factor.

One view is that with technology providing immediate communication, the impatient wait for the big think piece on the big movie—one of the few among the hundreds that might warrant an epic response—isn't worth it.

In his fifth decade as a film critic, Roger Ebert has adapted to the blogging era of his trade with some enthusiasm, and may be the greatest exponent of the opinion that film criticism is not only very much alive, but lively and doing well in cyberspace. To his view and that of many others, film criticism has not hopelessly and irrevocably declined, but changed. Many more opinions are available than ever before. These opinions can be crunched like numbers, plus or minus, by opinion-tallying Web sites such as Rotten Tomatoes, for a consensus on the weekend's multiplex choice.

The fact of the matter is that contemporary film criticism in its highbrow to lowbrow forms, written about all eras of movie history, can be readily found (and quickly accessed) on the Internet, from capsule reviews to the standard-length periodical assessments, to the more deeply probing essays.

It is found on obscure blogs, such as Thoughts on Film, or on major ones like Ain't It Cool News from the font of film geek

Harry Knowles; in transcendent commentaries on the personal Web sites of such film-criticism masters as Dave Kehr, Jonathan Rosenbaum, Henry Sheehan, and others; on news organization Web sites; and on sites dedicated to criticism's collation.

A page might be borrowed here from the observations of Andrew Sarris. Most movies, he once reminded us, are bad, and have always been bad. But there are enough movies every year—10 or 20—that he can recommend as the best of the lot. The same might be said of the critics who pass judgments on these creations, especially in the cyberspace era. Much of the criticism out there is bad and—as the evidence compiled between these covers points out—has in the past often been considered mostly bad. But some film critics remain who sort the issues with sense of style and purpose, with historical context, and in a literate way in a literary tradition. The reader just has to care enough, about film criticism as much as film itself, to find them.

BIBLIOGRAPHY

BOOKS

Abel, Richard, ed. *Encyclopedia of Early Cinema*. London: Routledge, 2005.

Adler, Renata. *A Year in the Dark: Journal of a Film Critic 1968–1969*. New York: Random House, 1969.

Agee, James. *Agee on Film: Reviews and Comments*. New York: McDowell, Obolensky, Inc., 1958.

Agee, James, and James Harold Flye. *Letters of James Agee to Father Flye*. New York: George Brazilier, 1962.

Agee, James, and Walker Evans. *Let Us Now Praise Famous Men*. Boston: Houghton Mifflin, 1941.

Alexander, Shana. *Happy Days: My Mother, My Father, My Sister & Me*. Garden City, NY: Doubleday, 1995.

Alpert, Hollis. *The Dreams and the Dreamers: Adventures of a Professional Moviegoer*. New York: The Macmillan Company, 1962.

Alpert, Hollis, and Andrew Sarris, eds. *Film 68/69: The National Society of Film Critics Write on Film 68/69*. New York: Simon & Schuster, 1969.

Atkinson, Michael, ed. *Exile Cinema: Filmmakers at Work Beyond Hollywood*. Albany: State University of New York Press, 2008.

Basinger, Jeanine. *Anthony Mann*. Boston: Twayne Publishers, 1979. Reprint, expanded edition, Middletown, CT: Wesleyan University Press, 2007.

Beaton, Welford. *Know Your Movies*. Los Angeles: Howard Hill, 1932.

Beaver, Frank Eugene. *Bosley Crowther: Social Critic of Film, 1940–1967*. Ann Arbor: University of Michigan Press, 1970.

Belford, Barbara. *Brilliant Bylines: A Biographical Anthology of Notable Newspaperwomen in America*. New York: Columbia University Press, 1988.

Berges, Marshall. *The Life and Times of Los Angeles: A Newspaper, a Family, and a City*. New York: Atheneum, 1984.

Bernard, Jami. *Breast Cancer, There and Back: A Woman-to-Woman Guide*. New York: Grand Central Publishing, 2001.

———, ed. *The X List: The National Society of Film Critics' Guide to the Movies That Turn Us On*. New York: Da Capo Press, 2005.

Blades, Joseph Dalton, Jr. *A Comparative Study of Selected American Film Critics, 1958–1974*. New York: Arno Press, 1974.

Bogdanovich, Peter. *Allan Dwan: The Last Pioneer*. New York: Praeger Publishers, 1971.

———. *John Ford*. Berkeley: University of California Press, 1968. Reprint, 1978.

———. *Who the Devil Made It?: Conversations with Legendary Film Directors*. New York: Ballantine Books, 1998.

Bogdanovich, Peter, and Jason Shinder, eds. *The Best American Movie Writing, 1999*. New York: St. Martin's Griffin, 1999.

Bogle, Donald. *Bright Boulevards, Bold Dreams: The Story of Black Hollywood*. New York: Ballantine Books, 2005.

Brantley, Will, ed. *Conversations with Pauline Kael*. Jackson: University Press of Mississippi, 1996.

Braudy, Leo, and Marshall Cohen, eds. *Film Theory and Criticism: Introductory Readings*. New York: Oxford University Press, 1999.

Brown, John Mason. *Seeing Things*. New York: McGraw-Hill, 1946.

Byrge, Duane, ed., with the American Film Institute. *Private Screenings: Insiders Share a Century of Great Movie Moments*. Collingdale, PA: Diane Publishing, 1995.

Byron, Stuart, and Elisabeth Weis, eds. *The National Society of Film Critics on Movie Comedy*. New York: Grossman Publishers, 1977.

Bywater, Tim, and Thomas Sobchack. *Introduction to Film Criticism: Major Critical Approaches to Narrative Film*. New York: Longman, 1989.

Canby, Vincent, Janet Maslin, and the Film Critics of *The New York Times*. *The New York Times Guide to the Best 1,000 Movies Ever Made*. Edited by Peter M. Nichols. New York: St. Martin's Griffin, 2004.

Cardullo, Bert, ed. *Conversations with Stanley Kauffmann*. Jackson: University Press of Mississippi, 2003.

———, ed. *The Film Criticism of Vernon Young*. Lanham, MD: University Press of America, Inc., 1990.

Carney, Raymond. *American Dreaming: The Films of John Cassavetes and the American Experience*. Berkeley: University of California Press, 1985.

Carr, Jay, ed. *The A List: The National Society of Film Critics' 100 Essential Films*. Cambridge, MA: Da Capo Press, 2002.

Chamberlain, Dorothy, and Robert Wilson, eds. *In the Spirit of Jazz: The Otis Ferguson Reader*. New York: Da Capo Press, 1997.

Champlin, Charles. *Back There Where the Past Was: A Small-Town Boyhood*. Syracuse, NY: Syracuse University Press, 1999.

———. *The Flicks: Whatever Happened to Andy Hardy*. Los Angeles: Ward Ritchie Press, 1977. Reprint, as *The Movies Grow Up, 1940–1980*. Chicago and Athens, OH: Swallow Press/Ohio University Press, 1997.

———. *Hollywood's Revolutionary Decade: Charles Champlin Reviews the Movies of the 1970s*. Santa Barbara, CA: John Daniel and Company, 1998.

Ciccone, F. Richard. *Royko: A Life in Print*. New York: Public Affairs, 2003.

Cocks, Jay, and David Denby, eds. *Film 73/74: An Anthology by the National Society of Film Critics*. Indianapolis: Bobbs-Merrill Company, 1974.

Cooke, Alistair, ed. *Garbo and the Night Watchmen: A Selection from the Writing of British and American Film Critics.* London: Cape, 1937. Reprint, London: Secker & Warburg, 1972.

Corliss, Richard. *Talking Pictures: Screenwriters in the American Cinema.* Woodstock, NY: Overlook Press, 1974.

Coursodon, Jean-Pierre, and Pierre Sauvage. *American Directors.* New York: McGraw-Hill, 1983.

———. *American Directors.* Vol. 2. New York: McGraw-Hill, 1983.

Crist, Judith. *Judith Crist's TV Guide to the Movies.* New York: Popular Library, 1974.

———. *The Private Eye, the Cowboy and the Very Naked Girl: Movies from Cleo to Clyde.* New York: Holt, Rinehart and Winston, 1968.

Crowther, Bosley. *The Great Films: Fifty Golden Years of Motion Pictures.* New York: G.P. Putnam, 1967.

Cuozzo, Steven D. *It's Alive!: How America's Oldest Newspaper Cheated Death and Why It Matters.* New York: Crown Publishers, 1996.

Davis, Francis. *Afterglow: A Last Conversation with Pauline Kael.* Cambridge, MA: Da Capo Press, 2002.

Decherney, Peter. *Hollywood and the Culture Elite: How the Movies Became American.* New York: Columbia University Press, 2005.

Denby, David, ed. *Awake in the Dark: An Anthology of American Film Criticism, 1915 to the Present.* New York: Vintage, 1977.

———. *Film 70/71: Members of the National Society of Film Critics Write on Film 70–71.* New York: Simon & Schuster, 1972.

———. *Film 71/72: Members of the National Society of Film Critics Write on Film 71–72.* New York: Simon & Schuster, 1972.

———. *Film 72/73: An Anthology by the National Society of Film Critics.* Indianapolis: The Bobbs-Merrill Company, 1973.

Dickstein, Morris. *Double Agent: The Critic and Society.* New York: Oxford University Press, 1996.

Duberman, Martin. *The Worlds of Lincoln Kirstein.* New York: Random House, 2007.

Ebert, Roger. *Awake in the Dark: The Best of Roger Ebert.* Chicago: University of Chicago Press, 2006.

———. *I Hated, Hated, Hated This Movie.* Kansas City: Andrews McMeel Publishing, 2000.

———. *Roger Ebert's Movie Home Companion.* Kansas City: Andrews and McMeel, 1985–1993.

———. *Your Movie Sucks.* Kansas City: Andrews McMeel Publishing, 2007.

———, ed. *Roger Ebert's Book of Film: From Tolstoy to Tarantino, the Finest Writing from a Century of Film.* New York: W.W. Norton & Company, 1997.

Ehrenstein, David. *Open Secret: Gay Hollywood, 1928–1998.* New York: William Morrow, 1998.

Ellis, Jack C., Charles Derry, and Sharon Kern. *The Film Book Bibliography 1940–1975.* Ann Arbor: University of Michigan, 1975.

Ernst, Morris, and Pare Lorentz. *Censored: The Private Life of the Movies*. New York: Cape & Smith, 1930.

Farber, Manny. *Negative Space: Manny Farber on the Movies*. New York: Praeger Publishers, 1971. Also published as *Movies*. New York: Hillstone, 1971.

Fethering, Dale, and Doug Fethering, eds. *Carl Sandburg at the Movies: A Poet in the Silent Era, 1920–1927*. Metuchen, NJ: The Scarecrow Press, 1985.

Gabler, Neal. *Life: The Movie: How Entertainment Conquered Reality*. New York: Alfred A. Knopf, 1999.

Gebert, Michael. *The Encyclopedia of Movie Awards*. New York: St. Martin's Press, 1996.

Gelb, Arthur. *City Room*. New York: G.P. Putnam, 2003.

Haberski, Raymond J., Jr. *"It's Only a Movie": Films and Critics in American Culture*. Lexington: University Press of Kentucky, 2001.

Halliwell, Leslie, ed. *The Filmgoer's Companion*. New York: Hill & Wang, 1970.

Hanson, Patricia King, and Stephen L. Hanson. *Film Review Index, Volume 1: 1882–1949*. Phoenix, AZ: Oryx Press, 1986.

———. *Film Review Index, Volume 2: 1950–1985*. Phoenix, AZ: Oryx Press, 1986.

Harrison, Louis Reeves. *Screencraft*. New York: Chalmers Publishing Company, 1916.

Haskell, Molly. *From Reverence to Rape: The Treatment of Women in the Movies*. New York: Holt, Rinehart and Winston, 1973.

———. *Love and Other Infectious Diseases: A Memoir*. New York: William Morrow, 1990.

Heinzkill, Richard. *Film Criticism: An Index to Critics' Anthologies*. Metuchen, NJ: The Scarecrow Press, 1975.

Hoberman, J. *Vulgar Modernism: Writing on Movies and Other Media*. Philadelphia: Temple University Press, 1991.

Hoberman, J., and Jonathan Rosenbaum. *Midnight Movies*. New York: Harper & Row, 1983.

Hochman, Stanley, ed. *From Quasimodo to Scarlett O'Hara: A National Board of Review Anthology, 1920–1940*. New York: Frederick Ungar Publishing Co., 1982.

Horak, Jan-Christopher, ed. *Lovers of Cinema: The First American Film Avant-Garde, 1919–1945*. Madison: University of Wisconsin Press, 1995.

Huffhines, Kathy S., ed. *Foreign Affairs: The National Society of Film Critics' Video Guide to Foreign Films*. San Francisco: Mercury House, 1991.

Hunter, Stephen. *Now Playing at the Valencia: Pulitzer Prize-Winning Essays on Movies*. New York: Simon & Schuster Paperbacks, 2005.

Hyman, Stanley Edgar, ed., with Allen Tate. *William Troy: Selected Essays*. New Brunswick, NJ: Rutgers University Press, 1967.

Jacobs, Lewis. *The Rise of the American Film*. New York: Teachers College, Columbia University, 1968.

———, ed. *The Compound Cinema: The Film Writings of Harry Alan Potamkin*. New York: Teachers College, Columbia University, 1977.

Jameson, Richard T., ed. *They Went Thataway: Redefining Film Genres: A National Society of Film Critics Video Guide*. San Francisco: Mercury House, 2000.

Kael, Pauline. *Deeper into Movies*. Boston: Little, Brown and Company, 1973.

———. *5,001 Nights at the Movies: A Guide from A to Z*. New York: Holt, Rinehart and Winston, 1991.

———. *For Keeps*. New York: E.P. Dutton, 1994.

———. *Going Steady*. Boston: Little, Brown and Company, 1970.

———. *Hooked*. New York: E.P. Dutton, 1989.

———. *I Lost It at the Movies*. Boston: Little, Brown and Company, 1965.

———. *Kiss Kiss Bang Bang*. Boston: Little, Brown and Company, 1968.

———. *Movie Love: Complete Reviews 1988–1991*. New York: Plume, 1991.

———. *Raising Kane and Other Essays*. London: Marion Boyars Publishers, Ltd., 1996.

———. *Reeling*. Boston: Little, Brown and Company, 1976.

———. *The State of the Art*. New York: E.P. Dutton, 1985.

———. *Taking It All In*. New York: Holt, Rinehart and Winston, 1984.

———. *When the Lights Go Down*. New York: Holt, Rinehart and Winston, 1990.

Kael, Pauline, Herman J. Mankiewicz, and Orson Welles. *The Citizen Kane Book: Raising Kane*. Boston: Atlantic-Little, Brown and Company, 1971.

Kammen, Michael G. *The Lively Arts: Gilbert Seldes and the Transformation of Cultural Criticism in the United States*. New York: Oxford University Press, 1996.

Katz, Ephraim, Fred Klein, and Ronald Dean Nolen, eds. *The Film Encyclopedia*. 3rd ed. New York: Harper Perennial, 1998. First published 1979.

Kauffmann, Stanley. *Before My Eyes: Film Criticism and Comment*. New York: Harper & Row, 1980.

———. *Field of View: Film Criticism and Comment*. New York: PAJ Publications, 1986.

———. *A World on Film: Criticism and Comment*. New York: Harper & Row, 1966.

Kauffmann, Stanley, and Bruce Henstell, eds. *American Film Criticism: From the Beginnings to Citizen Kane*. New York: Liveright, 1972.

Keough, Peter, ed. *Flesh and Blood: The National Society of Film Critics on Sex, Violence, and Censorship*. San Francisco: Mercury House, 1995.

Klawans, Stuart. *Film Follies: The Cinema Out of Order*. London and New York: Cassell, 1999.

Knight, Arthur. *The Liveliest Art*. New York: The Macmillan Company, 1957.

Knowles, Harry, with Paul Cullum and Mark Ebner. *Ain't It Cool?: Hollywood's Redheaded Stepchild Speaks Out*. New York: Warner Books, 2002.

Koszarski, Richard. *An Evening's Entertainment: The Age of the Silent Feature Picture, 1915–1928*. Vol. 3, *History of the American Cinema*. New York: Charles Scribner's Sons, 1990.

Kracauer, Siegfried. *Theory of Film: The Redemption of Physical Reality*. New York: Oxford University Press, 1960.

Kunkel, Thomas, ed. *Letters from the Editor: The New Yorker's Harold Ross*. New York: Modern Library, 2001.

Landis, John, and Jason Shinder, eds. *The Best American Movie Writing, 2001*. New York: Thunder's Mouth Press, 2001.

Lane, Anthony. *Nobody's Perfect: Writings from The New Yorker*. New York: Alfred A. Knopf, 2002.

Lane, Tamar. *What's Wrong with the Movies?* Los Angeles: Waverly Company, 1923.

Langdale, Allan, ed. *Hugo Münsterberg on Film: The Photoplay: A Psychological Study and Other Writings*. New York: Routledge, 2001.

Laskin, Emily, ed. *Getting Started in Film*. Englewood Cliffs, NJ: Prentice-Hall/ American Film Institute, 1992.

Levy, Emanuel. *And the Winner Is: The History and Politics of the Oscar Awards*. New York: Continuum, 1991. Also published as *Oscar Fever: The History and Politics of the Academy Awards* in 2001, and as *All About Oscar: The History and Politics of the Academy Awards* in 2003.

———, ed. *Citizen Sarris, American Film Critic: Essays in Honor of Andrew Sarris*. Lanham, MD: The Scarecrow Press, 2001.

Lim, Dennis, ed. *The Village Voice Film Guide: 50 Years of Movies from Classics to Cult Hits*. Hoboken, NJ: John Wiley & Sons, Inc., 2006.

Lindsay, Vachel. *The Art of the Moving Picture*. New York: The Macmillan Company, 1915. Reprint, New York: Liveright, 1970.

Lopate, Phillip, ed. *American Movie Critics: An Anthology from the Silents Until Now*. New York: Library of America, 2006.

Lorentz, Pare. *Lorentz on Film: Movies from 1927 to 1941*. New York: Hopkinson and Blake, 1975.

Lounsbury, Myron Osborn. *The Origins of American Film Criticism, 1909–1939*. New York: Arno Press, 1973.

———, ed. *The Progress and Poetry of the Movies: A Second Book of Film Criticism by Vachel Lindsay*. Lanham, MD: The Scarecrow Press, 1995.

Macdonald, Dwight. *Against the American Grain: Essays on the Effects of Mass Culture*. New York: Random House, 1962.

———. *Dwight Macdonald On Movies*. Englewood Cliffs, NJ: Prentice-Hall, 1969.

Maltin, Leonard, ed. *TV Movies*. New York: New American Library, 1969. References also made to subsequent New American Library editions through 1984. Also published as *Leonard Maltin's TV Movies*, 1985 and 1986, and as *Leonard Maltin's TV Movies and Video Guide*, 1986 through 1991. Published from 1992 through 2007 by New York: Plume.

Maltin, Leonard, Spencer Green, and Luke Sader. *Leonard Maltin's Movie Encyclopedia: Career Profiles of More Than 2,000 Actors and Filmmakers, Past and Present*. New York: Dutton, 1994.

Manchel, Frank. *Film Study: An Analytical Bibliography.* Vol. 1. Rutherford, NJ: Fairleigh Dickinson University Press, 1990.

Mathews, Jack. *The Battle of Brazil*. New York: Applause Theatre & Film Books, 1987.

McAuliffe, Kevin Michael. *The Great American Newspaper: The Rise and Fall of The Village Voice*. New York: Charles Scribner's Sons, 1978.

McBride, Joseph. *Frank Capra: The Catastrophe of Success.* New York: Simon & Schuster, 1992.

———. *Searching for John Ford: A Life.* New York: St. Martin's Press, 2001.

———. *Steven Spielberg: A Biography.* New York: Simon & Schuster, 1997.

———, ed. *Focus on Howard Hawks.* Englewood Cliffs, NJ: Prentice-Hall, 1972.

———, ed. *Persistence of Vision: A Collection of Film Criticism.* Madison: Wisconsin Film Society Press, 1968.

McBride, Joseph, and Michael Wilmington. *John Ford.* London: Secker & Warburg, 1974. (Published in U.S. by Da Capo Press in 1975.)

McCann, Richard Dyer, and Edward S. Perry. *The New Film Index: A Bibliography of Magazine Articles in English, 1930–1970.* New York: Dutton, 1975.

McCarthy, Todd. *Howard Hawks: The Grey Fox of Hollywood.* New York: Grove Press, 1997.

McCarthy, Todd, and Charles Flynn, eds. *Kings of the Bs: Working within the Studio System.* New York: E.P. Dutton, 1975.

Merrill, Hugh. *Esky: The Early Years at Esquire.* New Brunswick, NJ: Rutgers University Press, 1995.

Morgenstern, Joseph, and Stefan Kanfer, eds. *Film 69/70: An Anthology by the National Society of Film Critics.* New York: Simon & Schuster, 1970.

Münsterberg, Hugo. *The Photoplay: A Psychological Study.* New York: D. Appleton and Company, 1916. Reprinted as *The Film: A Psychological Study.* New York: Dover, 1970.

Münsterberg, Margaret. *Hugo Münsterberg: His Life and Work.* Whitefish, MT: Kessinger Publishing, 2007.

Murray, Edward. *Nine American Film Critics: A Study of Theory and Practice.* New York: Frederick Ungar Publishing Company, 1975.

O'Neil, Thomas. *Movie Awards: The Ultimate, Unofficial Guide to the Oscars, Golden Globes, Critics, Guild & Indie Honors.* New York: Perigee, 2003.

Pechter, William S. *Twenty-four Times a Second: Films and Film-Makers.* New York: Harper & Row, 1971.

Phelps, Donald. *Covering Ground: Essays for Now.* New York: Croton Press, 1969.

Pizzitola, Louis. *Hearst Over Hollywood: Power, Passion and Propaganda in the Movies.* New York: Columbia University Press, 2002.

Plimpton, George, and Jason Shinder, eds. *The Best American Movie Writing, 1998.* New York: St. Martin's Press, 1998.

Polsgrave, Carol. *It Wasn't Pretty, Folks, but Didn't We Have Fun?: Esquire in the Sixties.* New York: W.W. Norton & Company, 1995.

Potamkin, Harry Alan. *The Eyes of the Movies.* New York: International Pamphlets, 1934.

Rafferty, Terrence. *The Thing Happens: Ten Years of Writing About the Movies.* New York: Grove Press, 1993.

Rainer, Peter, ed. *Love and Hisses: The National Society of Film Critics Sound Off on the Hottest Movie Controversies.* San Francisco: Mercury House, 1992.

Reed, Rex. *Big Screen, Little Screen*. New York: The Macmillan Company, 1971.

———. *Do You Sleep in the Nude?* New York: New American Library, 1968.

———. *Valentines and Vitriol*. New York: Delacorte, 1977.

Rehauer, George. *Cinema Booklist*. Metuchen, NJ: The Scarecrow Press, 1974.

Rich, B. Ruby. *Chick Flicks: Theories and Memories of the Feminist Movement*. Durham, NC: Duke University Press, 1998.

Roberts, Chalmers M. *The Washington Post: The First 100 Years*. Boston: Houghton Mifflin, 1977.

Roberts, Jerry. *The Great American Playwrights on the Screen*. New York: Applause Theatre & Film Books, 2003.

———, ed. *Mitchum, In His Own Words*. New York: Limelight Editions, 2000.

Roberts, Jerry, and Steven Gaydos, eds. *Movie Talk from the Front Lines: Interviews with Filmmakers by the Los Angeles Film Critics Association*. Jefferson, NC: McFarland & Company, Inc., 1995.

Rosenbaum, Jonathan. *Essential Cinema: On the Necessity of Film Canons*. Baltimore: Johns Hopkins University Press, 2008.

———. *Movie Wars: How Hollywood and the Media Conspire to Limit What Films We Can See*. Chicago: A Cappella Books, 2000. Reprint, Chicago: Chicago Review Press, 2002.

Sargent, Epes Winthrop. *Technique of the Photoplay*. New York: Moving Picture World, 1913.

Sarris, Andrew. *The American Cinema: Directors and Directions, 1929–1968*. New York: E.P. Dutton, 1968. Reprint, New York: Da Capo Press, 1996.

———. *Confessions of a Cultist: On the Cinema, 1955–1969*. New York: Simon & Schuster, 1971.

———. *The Primal Screen: Essays on Film and Related Topics*. New York: Simon & Schuster, 1973.

———. *You Ain't Heard Nothin' Yet: The American Talking Film, History & Memory, 1927–1949*. New York: Oxford University Press, 1998.

Scheuer, Steven H., ed. *TV Movie Almanac & Ratings*. New York: Bantam Books, 1958. Reprinted and updated as Bantam editions *TV Key Movie Reviews and Ratings*, 1961, and *TV Key Movie Guide*, 1966, and later as annual editions of *Movies on TV*.

Schickel, Richard. *D.W. Griffith: An American Life*. New York: Simon & Schuster, 1984.

———. *Film on Paper: The Inner Life of Movies*. Chicago: Ivan R. Dee, 2008.

———. *Matinee Idylls: Reflections on the Movies*. Chicago: Ivan R. Dee, 1999.

———. *The Men Who Made the Movies*. New York: Atheneum, 1975.

———. *Second Sight: Notes on Some Movies, 1965–1970*. New York: Simon & Schuster, 1972.

Schickel, Richard, and John Simon, eds. *Film 67/68: An Anthology of the National Society of Film Critics*. New York: Simon & Schuster, 1968.

Seldes, Gilbert. *The Seven Lively Arts*. New York: Harper, 1924. Reprint, Champaign, IL: Sagamore Publishing, 1957.

Sheed, Wilfrid. *Max Jamison*. New York: Farrar, Straus and Giroux, 1970.

Sherwood, Robert E. *Robert E. Sherwood: Film Critic*. New York: Revisionist Press, 1973.

Shuman, R. Baird. *Robert E. Sherwood*. New York: Twayne Publishers, Inc., 1964.

Sillick, Ardis, and Michael McCormick. *The Critics Were Wrong: Misguided Movie Reviews and Film Criticism Gone Awry*. New York: Carol Publishing Corporation, 1996.

Simon, John. *Acid Test*. New York: Stein & Day, 1963.

———. *Movies into Film: Film Criticism, 1967–1970*. New York: The Dial Press, 1971.

———. *Paradigms Lost: Reflections on Literacy and Its Decline*. New York: Clarkson N. Potter, Inc., 1980.

———. *Reverse Angle: A Decade of American Films*. New York: Clarkson N. Potter Inc., 1982.

Slattery, William J., Claire Dorton, and Rosemary Enright. *The Kael Index: A Guide to a Movie Critic's Work, 1954–1991*. Englewood, CO: Libraries Unlimited, 1993.

Slide, Anthony. *Aspects of American Film History Prior to 1920*. Metuchen, NJ: The Scarecrow Press, 1978.

———, ed. *Selected Film Criticism, 1896–1911*. Metuchen, NJ: The Scarecrow Press, 1982.

———, ed. *Selected Film Criticism, 1912–1920*. Lanham, MD: Rowman & Littlefield Publishers, Inc., 1982.

———, ed. *Selected Film Criticism, 1921–1930*. Metuchen, NJ: The Scarecrow Press, 1982.

Snyder, John J. *James Agee: A Study of His Criticism*. New York: Arno Press, 1977.

Snyder, Robert L. *Lorentz: Pare Lorentz and the Documentary Film*. Norman, OK: University of Oklahoma Press, 1968.

Sontag, Susan. *Against Interpretation and Other Essays*. New York: Farrar, Straus and Giroux, 1966.

Spiegel, Alan. *James Agee and the Legend of Himself*. Columbia, MO: University of Missouri Press, 1998.

Sragow, Michael, ed. *James Agee: Film Writing and Selected Journalism*. New York: Library of America, 2005.

———, ed. *Produced and Abandoned: The National Society of Film Critics Write on the Best Films You've Never Seen*. San Francisco: Mercury House, 1990.

Sterritt, David. *Guiltless Pleasures: A David Sterritt Film Reader*. Jackson: University Press of Mississippi, 2005.

Sterritt, David, and John Anderson, eds. *The B List: The National Society of Film Critics on the Low-Budget Beauties, Genre-Bending Mavericks, and Cult Classics We Love*. Cambridge, MA: Da Capo Press, 2008.

Swanberg, W.A. *Citizen Hearst*. New York: Charles Scribner's Sons, 1961.

Taylor, Greg. *Artists in the Audience: Cults, Camp, and American Film Criticism*. Princeton, NJ: Princeton University Press, 1999.

Thompson, Howard. *The New York Times Guide to Movies on TV*. Edited by Richard J. Anobile. Chicago: Quadrangle Books, 1970.

Thomson, David. *The Biographical Dictionary of the Cinema*. London: Martin Secker & Warburg, Limited, 1975. Also published as *The Biographical Dictionary of Film*, New York: William Morrow and Company, Inc., 1976, and New York: Alfred A. Knopf, 1994 and 2002.

―――. *Rosebud: The Story of Orson Welles*. New York: Alfred A. Knopf, 1996.

Turan, Kenneth. *Never Coming to a Theatre Near You: A Celebration of a Certain Kind of Movie*. New York: Public Affairs Books, 2004.

Tyler, Parker. *The Hollywood Hallucination*. New York: Simon & Schuster, 1970.

―――. *The Shadow of an Airplane Climbs the Empire State Building: A World Theory of Film*. Garden City, NY: Doubleday, 1973.

―――. *Underground Film: A Critical History*. London: Secker & Warburg, 1971.

Variety. *Variety Film Reviews, 1907–1984*. 18 vols.

Walsh, John Evangelist. *Walking Shadows: Orson Welles, William Randolph Hearst, and Citizen Kane*. Madison, WI: Popular Press, 2004.

Warshow, Robert. *The Immediate Experience: Movies, Comics, Theatre, and Other Aspects of Popular Culture*. New York: Doubleday, 1962. Reprint, Cambridge, MA: Harvard University Press, 2001.

Weis, Elisabeth, ed. *The National Society of Film Critics on the Movie Star*. New York: Viking Press, 1981.

Welles, Orson, and Peter Bogdanovich. *This is Orson Welles*. Edited by Jonathan Rosenbaum. New York: HarperCollins, 1992.

Wendt, Lloyd. *Chicago Tribune: The Rise of a Great American Newspaper*. Chicago: Rand McNally & Company, 1979.

Wilson, Robert, ed. *The Film Criticism of Otis Ferguson*. Philadelphia: Temple University Press, 1971.

Woods, Frank E. *History of the Motion Picture: Introduction to the Photoplay*. Los Angeles: University of Southern California and the Academy of Motion Picture Arts and Sciences, 1929.

Young, Vernon. *Vernon Young on Film: Unpopular Essays on a Popular Art*. Chicago: Quadrangle Books, 1972.

Zinsser, William K. *Seen Any Good Movies Lately?* Garden City, NY: Doubleday, 1958.

PERIODICALS, REPORTS, ETC.

Alpert, Hollis. "Are Movie Critics Necessary?" *Saturday Review*, October 13, 1962.

―――. "Case of Crowther." *Saturday Review*, September 23, 1967.

―――. "The Movies and the Critics." *Saturday Review*, December 26, 1964.

Anderson, Jon. "Siskel and Ebert: Success, at the Movies." *Riverside Press-Enterprise*, October 13, 1985.

Aradillas, Aaron. "The Girl Can't Help It: Interview with Jami Bernard of the New York *Daily News*." RockCritics.com, May 15, 2009.

———. "Owen Gleiberman Takes the Long Way Home; a RockCritics.com Interview." RockCritics.com, May 2004.

Bakshy, Alexander. "The Movie Scene: Notes on Sound and Silence." *Theatre Arts Monthly*, February 1929.

Basuroy, Suman, and Wagner Kamakura. "Reviewing the Reviewers: The Impact of Individual Film Critics on Box Office Performance." *Quantitative Marketing and Economics*, December 2007.

Bates, James, and Jen Pollack Bianco. "The Movies' 'Riveting!' Blurb Mill." *Los Angeles Times*, March 24, 1997.

"Battle of the Titanic Egos, Cont'd." *Los Angeles*, February 1991.

Beaton, Wilford. "A Real Tail on a Bronze Bull." *Saturday Evening Post*, September 21, 1929.

Beaufort, John. "We Prefer the Beautiful and True to the Ugly and False . . ." *Journal of the Screen Producers Guild*, April 1955.

Benesch, Connie. "Ebert on Ebert." *Los Angeles Times*, Calendar section, January 3, 1988.

———. "'TV Critics Aren't Lowering Standards.'" *Los Angeles Times*, Calendar section, January 3, 1988.

Benson, Sheila. "Why Do Critics Love These Repellent Movies? Counterpoint: Sometimes Arresting, Intelligent Films Happen to Be about Seamy Subjects." *Los Angeles Times*, March 17, 1991.

Berkeley, Christopher. Review of *The Lively Arts: Gilbert Seldes and the Transformation of Cultural Criticism in the United States*, by Michael G. Kammen. H-PCAACA, H-Net Reviews, April 1997.

Bogdanovich, Peter. "Bogie in Excelsis." *Esquire*, September 1964.

———. "The Kane Mutiny." *Esquire*, October 1972.

Borowitz, Andy. "Cost Critics." *Premiere*, January 1988.

Borrelli, Christopher. "New Show Thumbs Its Nose at Quality Criticism." *Chicago Tribune*, August 17, 2008.

Brown, Georgia. "Bite the Ballot: The Great Film Critics Circle Tour." *The Village Voice*, January 9, 1990.

Buck, Jerry. "The Gene and Roger Show: Dissention is Glue Holding It Together." *Riverside Press-Enterprise*, September 4, 1986.

Bugge, Karen. "Thomas Gets a Kick From Creating Audiences for Offbeat Films." *Among Ourselves* [*Los Angeles Times* in-house newsletter], date unknown.

Burnett, Colin. "Going to the Theatre at the Movies: Re-Examining the Film Criticism of Otis Ferguson." *Senses of Cinema*, January 2003.

Byron, Stuart. "The War of the Movie Critics." *New York*, July 17, 1978.

Callenbach, Ernest. "U.S. Film Journalism—A Survey." *Hollywood Quarterly*, Summer 1951.

Cameron, James. "He's Mad as Hell at Turan: James Cameron Gets the Last Word on Our Critic's *Titanic* Commentary." *Los Angeles Times*, March 28, 1998.

Cameron, Kate. "Tell the Reader Where to Get the Best Return on His Money . . ." *Journal of the Screen Producers Guild*, April 1955.

Campbell, Russell. "Potamkin's Film Criticism." *Jump Cut*, no. 18 (August 1978).

Cardullo, Bert. "An Interview with Stanley Kauffmann." *Bright Lights Film Journal*, February 2004.

Carney, Raymond. "A Critic in the Dark: The Corrupting Influence of Vincent Canby and *The New York Times*." *The New Republic*, June 30, 1986.

Carr, David. "Now on the Endangered Species List: Movie Critics in Print." *The New York Times*, April 1, 2008.

Carr, Harry, Edwin Schallert, Katherine Lipke, Norbert Lusk, Philip K. Scheuer, Kevin Thomas, and Charles Champlin. "Judgment Days: The Reviews," *Los Angeles Times*, 125 Years/Hollywood Commemorative Edition, May 21, 2006.

Carson, Tom. "We Found Her at the Movies." *Entertainment Weekly*, March 22, 1991.

Champlin, Charles. "Critic at Large: Scheuer: An Aisle Seat on History." *Los Angeles Times*, February 23, 1985.

Chute, David. "The Fine Art of Red-Neck Reviewing: Joe Bob Briggs's Bad Taste Finally Got Him Fired." *American Film*, September 1986.

Cohen, Harold V. "It's Easy to Be a Movie Fan . . . It Is Not So Easy to Be a Critic." *Journal of the Screen Producers Guild*, April 1955.

Coniff, Kimberly. "'We Loved It!': How Critical Are Hollywood's Critics?" *Brill's Content*, April 1999.

Corliss, Richard. "All Thumbs or, Is There a Future for Film Criticism?" *Film Comment*, March/April 1990.

———. "Manny Farber: Termite of Genius." Time.com, August 26, 2008.

———. "The Secret Life of Critics." *Premiere*, December 1990.

———. "That Wild Old Woman." *Time*, November 7, 1994.

———. "Then Again." *Film Comment*, May/June 1990.

Crist, Judith. "Against the Groin." *Journal of the Producers Guild of America*, December 1967.

"Critic Around the Clock." *Newsweek*, March 27, 1967.

"Critic's Goodbye." *Time*, December 10, 1945.

"Critics: The Pearls of Pauline." *Time*, July 12, 1968.

Crowther, Bosley. "Critic Hollers Help!" *The New York Times*, April 23, 1967.

———. "There Can No More Be Rules for Reviewing, Than Rules for the Making of Great Films . . ." *Journal of the Screen Producers Guild*, April 1955.

Dargis, Manohla. "They Lost It at the Movies: Critics Who Were Never Left in the Dark." *LA Weekly*, November 26, 1998.

Denby, David. "The Moviegoers: Why Don't People Love the Right Movies Anymore?" *The New Yorker*, April 6, 1998.

———. "Personal History: My Life as a Paulette," *The New Yorker*, October 20, 2003.

Desowitz, Bill. "Critic Andrew Sarris, Still a Champion of Directors." *Los Angeles Times*, November 29, 2000.

Drevets, Tricia. "Siskel & Ebert." *Editor & Publisher*, October 17, 1987.

Ebert, Roger. "All Stars or, Is There a Cure for Criticism of Film Criticism?" *Film Comment*, May/June 1990.

———. "Roger Ebert's Journal: Death to Film Critics! Hail to the CelebCult!" Suntimes.com, November 26, 2008.

———. "Roger Ebert's Journal: Remembering Gene." Suntimes.com, February 17, 2009.

———. "A Thumb's Up for This Oscar-Night Performance." *Los Angeles Times*, April 4, 1994.

Edelson, Sharon. "Unethical Culture: Critics Cornered." *Premiere*, November 1989.

"Editorial: Critic of Honor." *Film Heritage*, Fall 1967.

Ehrenstein, David. "The Pronouncements of Pauline." *Los Angeles Times Book Review*, October 9, 1994.

Emerling, Ernest. "Can Critics Make or Break Them?" *Journal of the Screen Producers Guild*, April 1955.

Ephron, Nora. "On Pauline Kael." *New York Post*, May 11, 1966.

Erickson, Steve. "Dave Kehr: An Interview." *Senses of Cinema*, June 2001.

———. "Interview with Manohla Dargis." *Senses of Cinema*, 2002.

Farber, Manny. "Underground Films." *Commentary*, November 1957.

———. "White Elephant Art vs. Termite Art." *Film Culture*, Winter 1962/1963.

Farber, Stephen. "The 2nd Time Around: Do Movie Critics Ever Reverse Their Opinion When They See a Film a Second Time?" *Movieline*, October 1993.

———. "Why Do Critics Love These Repellent Movies?" *Los Angeles Times*, Calendar section, March 17, 1991.

———. "Why Do Critics Love Trashy Movies?" *American Film*, April 1981.

Ferguson, Otis. "Case of the Critics." *New Republic*, February 2, 1942.

Finke, Nikki. "That Giant Sucking Sound: *NY Times* Goes After *LA Times*' Dargis, Leeds." *LA Weekly*, June 25–July 1, 2004.

Fleischer, Matthew. "Once the Best Alt-Weekly in the Nation, *LA Weekly* Tightens Its Belt." *LA Weekly*, January 14, 2009.

Fleming, Charles. "Phantom Crix Are Flogging Flicks," *Variety*, May 11, 1992.

———. "Then There's Those Who Break the Rules." *Variety*, May 11, 1992.

Friedman, Mark. "Hollywood Foreign Press Cuts Charitable Donations, Blames Writers Guild." FoxNews.com, August 4, 2008.

Garcia, Jane. "Kael Force." *Movieline*, July 14, 1990.

Geffner, David. "DGA News: Citizen Sarris." *DGA Magazine*, March 2001.

Gibbs, Wolcott. "Kingdom of the Blind: Reviewing Moving Pictures." *Saturday Review of Literature*, November 17, 1945.

"The Golden Age of Cinema?" *OC Weekly*, December 10–16, 1999.

Goldstein, Patrick. "The Big Picture: Critics' Voices Become a Whisper." *Los Angeles Times*, August 15, 2006.

———. "The Big Picture: The End of the Critic?" *Los Angeles Times*, April 8, 2008.

———. "The Big Picture: King of the Blurbs." *Los Angeles Times*, February 13, 2007.

———. "The Big Picture: Manohla Dargis: The Critic as Movie Killer." *Los Angeles Times*, December 10, 2008.

———. "The Big Picture: Reviewers' *A.I.* May Be Aging, Irrelevant." *Los Angeles Times*, July 17, 2001.

———. "Commentary: The Film Blurb Prize Goes to . . ." *Los Angeles Times*, January 6, 2009.

———. "TV Film Critics Go for the Glitz. Roll Clip, Please." *Los Angeles Times*, Calendar section, January 3, 1988.

Green, Emily. "Little Big Man: David Thomson." *Los Angeles Times Magazine*, May 1, 2005.

Grobel, Lawrence. "*Playboy* Interview: Siskel & Ebert: A Candid Conversation with Film's Cattiest Critics as They Take on the Stars, the Studios, the Ratings and—Most of All—Each Other." *Playboy*, February 1991.

Groening, Matt. "Life in Hell: How to Be a Clever Film Critic." *LA Weekly*, 1985.

Guimond, L.F. "A Valued Critic Passes." *Boxoffice*, January 18, 1936.

Hampton, Howard. "Pauline Kael, 1919–2001: Such Sweet Thunder." *Film Comment*, November/December 2001.

Harmetz, Aljean. "As the Golden Globes Turn: The Hollywood Foreign Press Assn. Knows How to Party, but All It's Wanted Lately Is to Be Respected in the Morning." *Los Angeles Times*, Calendar section, January 23, 2000.

Harper, Dan. "Vernon Young: Unpopular Critic of a Popular Art." *Senses of Cinema*, December 2000.

Hersey, John. "A Critic at Large: Agee." *The New Yorker*, July 18, 1988.

Hoberman, J. "Termite Makes Right." *The Village Voice*, May 20–26, 1981.

Hogan, William. "A Critic's Function Is to Protect the Public from Tired, Indifferent Film Fare." *Journal of the Screen Producers Guild*, April 1955.

Horn, John. "A Rising Star on Hollywood's Awards Circuit?" *Los Angeles Times*, December 14, 2004.

Hornaday, Ann. "Manny Farber; Movie Critic Had Reputation as a Maverick." *The Washington Post*, August 20, 2008.

Hubler, Richard G. "Opinion and the Motion Picture." *Screen Writer*, October 1946.

"Insider: The Last of Sheila?" *Los Angeles*, July 1990.

James, Clive. "How to Write About Film: American Movie Critics." *The New York Times*, June 4, 2006.

"John Beaufort Is Dead; Theatre Critic Was 79." *The New York Times*, September 18, 1992.

Johnson, G. Allen. "Z Channel Made Stars Behind the Scenes." SFGate.com, November 26, 2004.

Jones, Kent. "The Throbbing Acuity of Negative Space." *Film Comment*, March/April 2000.

Kael, Pauline. "Circles and Squares: Joys and Sarris." *Film Quarterly*, April 1963.

———. "Is There a Cure for Film Criticism?" *Sight & Sound*, Spring 1962.

———. "Raising Kane." *The New Yorker*, February 20 and 27, 1971.

———. "Trash, Art, and the Movies." *Harper's*, February 1969.

———. "Why Are Movies So Bad? Or, the Numbers." *The New Yorker*, June 23, 1980.

"Key Critic." *Time*, July 1, 1957.

Kitses, Jim. "Negative Space." *Film Comment*, 1971.

Knight, Arthur. "How to Rate a Critic." *Saturday Review*, December 26, 1964.

———. "Only a Fraud Would Pretend That Personal Bias Doesn't Exist." *Journal of the Screen Producers Guild*, April 1955.

Koch, Stephen. "The Cruel, Cruel Critics." *Saturday Review*, December 26, 1970.

Kroll, Jack. "The Monitor." *Newsweek*, March 29, 1971.

Lardner, John. "Last Word." *Screen Writer*, December 1945.

Larrabee, Eric. "Reflections in a Puddle." *Harper's*, January 1961.

Lee, Chris. "Critic Ben Lyons Gets Many Thumbs Down." *Los Angeles Times*, December 28, 2008.

Leyda, Jay. "James Agee—a Poet Filmwright." *Film Culture*, no. 4 (1955).

Leydon, Joe. "*For the Love of Movies: The Story of American Film Criticism.*" *Variety*, March 27, 2009.

Lopez, Steve. "Points West: Critical Acclaim for the Boffo Bottom Line." *Los Angeles Times*, August 8, 2001.

Lorentz, Pare. "The Critics." *Judge*, August 29, 1931.

———. "Looking Back." *McCall's*, November 1939.

Macdonald, Dwight. "After Forty Years of Writing About Movies, I Know Something About Cinema and Being a Congenial Critic." *Esquire*, July 1969.

———. "Agee and the Movies." *Film Heritage*, Fall 1967.

Macklin, F. Anthony. "Editorial: The Accusers." *Film Heritage*, Winter 1966–67.

———. "Editorial: The Perils of Pauline's Criticism." *Film Heritage*, Fall 1966.

———. "Editorial: Return to Meaning." *Film Heritage*, Summer 1967.

———. "Pauline Kael: Tangents Become Thesis." *Commonweal*, June 28, 1968.

Marsh, W. Ward. "We Are the Bastards in the Field of Criticism . . ." *Journal of the Screen Producers Guild*, April 1955.

Matza, Michael. "A Discriminating Mind to Guide Video-Movie Junkies." *Riverside Press-Enterprise*, November 6, 1988.

McBride, Joseph. "Mr. Macdonald, Mr. Kauffmann, and Miss Kael." *Film Heritage*, Summer 1967.

———. "Rough Sledding with Pauline Kael." *Film Heritage*, Fall 1971.

McLellan, Dennis. "Gary Franklin, 79; Popular Film Critic on Local TV." *Los Angeles Times*, October 4, 2007.

———. "Joel Siegel, 63; Film Critic on ABC's *Good Morning America*." *Los Angeles Times*, June 30, 2007.

Means, Sean. "Movies: Fewer Critics and Less Space May Be Hurting Indie Filmmakers." *Salt Lake Tribune*, March 22, 2008.

Mermelstein, David. "Vet Critics Adapt to Challenging Times: They Still Make Their Marks Despite Downsizing." *Variety*, December 16, 2008.

"Mincing a Dead Horse." *Time*, November 10, 1958.

Mitchell, Sean. "Inside the Celluloid Triangle: Moviemakers, Movie Critics and You." *Los Angeles Times*, Calendar section, October 21, 1999.

Moore, Roger. "America's Movie Critics—117 Still Standing." *Orlando Sentinel*, March 4, 2009.

———. "A Dying Breed . . . (Paid) Movie Critics." *Orlando Sentinel*, November 22, 2006.

Morast, Robert. "Criticized AP Film Critic Defends Herself." Inforum.com, May 22, 2009.

Morgenstern, Joseph. "The Moviegoer." *Newsweek*, February 23, 1970.

———. "Perils of Pauline." *Newsweek*, May 20, 1968.

Murphy, Thomas. Associated Press Report on Pauline Kael, April 7, 1989.

Natale, Richard. "Influence Aided Hollywood, Fans and Other Critics." *Los Angeles Times*, February 24, 1999.

Nelson, Valerie J. "Hollis Alpert." *Los Angeles Times*, December 4, 2007.

Niroumand, Mariam. "A Vulgar Modernist: An Interview with J. Hoberman." *Cineaste* 19 (1992).

"Obituaries: Loretta King." *The New York Times*, October 22, 2008.

Obituary of "Barry Brennan." *Daily Variety*, July 31, 1985.

O'Neil, Tom. "Award for Best Drama Goes to Critics Groups." *Los Angeles Times*, December 8, 2001.

Oney, Steve. "The Critics: Six L.A.-Based Reviewers on the Movies That Move Them." *Los Angeles*, February 2009.

Osborne, Robert. "Rambling Reporter." *The Hollywood Reporter*, April 22, 1983.

Paletz, David. "Judith Crist: An Interview with a Big-Time Critic." *Film Quarterly*, Fall 1968.

"Paid Death Notices: Paul V. Beckley." *The New York Times*, December 5, 2008.

Peary, Gerald. "Women Film Critics." *Boston Phoenix*, February 2006.

Pechter, William S. "Two Movies and Their Critics." *The Kenyon Review*, Spring 1962.

"The Perils of Pauline." *Newsweek*, May 30, 1966.

Persall, Steve. "Best Critic Ever . . . (Invented by a Studio)." *St. Petersburg Times*, June 15, 2001.

Phelps, Donald. "Essays of a Man Watching." *Moviegoer*, Summer 1963.

————. "James Agee as Film Critic." *Film Culture*, no. 4 (1955).

Podhoretz, John. "Thinking on Film: The Way the Wind Is Blowing for Newspaper Movie Critics." *The Weekly Standard*, May 18, 2009.

Pollock, Dale. "Critical Eye." *Los Angeles Times*, Februay 13, 1982.

Potamkin, Harry Alan. "Film Novitiates, Etc." *Close Up* 7, no. 5 (1930).

Powers, John. "A Letter at 3 PM: On Michael Ventura, *LA Weekly*'s Bogart in Cowboy Boots." *LA Weekly*, 30th Anniversary Edition, December 5–11, 2008.

————. "Manny Farber: A Critical Eye for Termite Art." National Public Radio, August 22, 2008.

————. "On the Rise of Anthony Lane: Andy and Pauline Get Laid." *LA Weekly*, September 13–19, 2002.

————. "Pauline Kael and the Rise and Fall of the Movies." *LA Weekly*, April 5–11, 1991.

Proffitt, Steve. "Bob Thomas: A Modest Man Watches the Stars, from Joan Crawford to Johnny Depp." *Los Angeles Times*, March 21, 1999.

Rainer, Peter. "Little Lost *Princess*." *Los Angeles Times*, June 1, 1995.

Rayner, Richard. "*American Movie Critics*." *Los Angeles Times Book Review*, March 5, 2006.

Reynolds, Christopher. "Firey Theatre Critic John Simon Ousted." *Los Angeles Times*, May 11, 2005.

"Rigors of Criticism." *Time*, December 1, 1967.

Roberts, Jerry. "Duo All Thumbs on Awards." *Weekly Variety*, March 7–13, 1994.

————. "Movie Maven Maltin: Critic Gives New Meaning to Word 'Busy.'" *Torrance Daily Breeze*, October 16, 1990.

————. "On-Air Talent Speaks Volumes." *Daily Variety*, September 6, 1996.

Rosenbaum, Jonathan. "On Film: Junket Bonds: Critics and Studios Are Hopping into Bed Together and the Results Are Hard to Watch." *Chicago Reader*, November 17, 2000.

Rosenberg, Howard. "The Eberts: The New Awards for Fawning." *Los Angeles Times*, March 23, 1994.

————. "When Siskel's Thumb Turned, Millions Got the Message." *Los Angeles Times*, February 24, 1999.

"Ruth Batchelor, Songwriter, 58." *The New York Times*, July 29, 1992.

"The Sad Case of a Raving Cinemaniac: The Gush-a House," *Premiere*, May 1992.

Sanson, Kevin. "Publishing: *Tribune* Film Critics Talk Shop." *Tribune News*, March 27, 2005.

Sarris, Andrew. "Auteurism Is Alive and Well and Living in Argentina." *Film Comment*, July/August 1990.

————. "The Movieness of Movies." *December*, Spring 1965.

————. "Notes on the Auteur Theory in 1962." *Film Culture*, no. 27 (Winter 1962/1963).

Schallert, Edwin. "The Los Angeles Critic Is in a Particularly Responsible Position . . ." *Journal of the Screen Producers Guild*, April 1955.

Scheuer, Philip K. "Four Decades as the *Times* Movie Critic." *Los Angeles Times*, Calendar section, March 26, 1967.

"Scheuer Writes '30' to 40-Year Career as Film Critic." *Daily Variety*, March 27, 1967.

Schickel, Richard. "*The Film Snob's Dictionary.*" *Los Angeles Times Book Review*, March 19, 2006.

———. "Film on Paper: When the Critic Met the Tramp." *Los Angeles Times Book Review*, May 15, 2005.

———. "A Movie Critic on Movie Critics." *Harper's*, January 1970.

———. "The Perils of Pauline." *Los Angeles Times Book Review*, November 18, 2001.

———. "Review: *I Lost It at the Movies.*" *The New York Times Book Review*, March 11, 1965.

———. "The Reviewer Re-Viewed: A Conversation between Andrew Sarris and Richard Schickel." *DGA Magazine*, March 2001.

Schrader, Paul. "Pauline Kael, 1919–2001: My Family Drama." *Film Comment*, November/December 2001.

Scott, A.O. "Roger Ebert, the Critic Behind the Thumb." *The New York Times*, April 13, 2008.

Scott, Janny. "A Steady Critical Eye on Film's Shifting Currents." *The New York Times*, June 28, 1998.

Sennwald, Andre. "Gory, Gory, Hallelujah! Being an Inquiry into the Cinema's Recent Trend." *The New York Times Magazine*, January 11, 1936.

"Sennwald's Death Laid to Gas Fumes." *The New York Times*, January 13, 1936.

Shales, Tom. "TCM Offers Clutterless Classics." *The Washington Post*, April 9, 2001.

Shaw, David. "Thumbs Up or Down on Movie Critics?" *Los Angeles Times*, March 20, 1999.

Shaw, Robert. "Hearstian Criteria for Movie Critics." *Screen Writer*, September 1945.

Shepherd, Duncan. "Big Appetite." *San Diego Reader*, February 15, 1991.

Siegel, Joel. "On *Agee on Film.*" *Film Heritage*, Fall 1967.

Sigal, Clancy. "A Gee-Whiz Reporter Is Still as Relaxed and Serious." *Los Angeles Times*, April 18, 2006.

Simon, Jeff. "Siege of Film Critics Gets Worse." *Buffalo News*, April 15, 2008.

Simon, John. "Everybody's a Critic." *Los Angeles Times Book Review*, March 24, 2002.

———. "James Agee." *Film Heritage*, Fall 1967.

———. "Let Us Now Praise Dwight Macdonald." *Commonweal*, October 17, 1969.

Sklar, Robert. "'The Good Ones Never Make You Feel Virtuous.'" *The New York Times Book Review*, March 19, 1989.

Smith, R. "Five Things Hollywood Looks at." *Film Comment*, March/April 2001.

Sragow, Michael. "Commentary: The Perils of Critical Mass: Reviewing Films Is a Balancing Act, but Easier in a Bold Workplace." *Los Angeles Times*, July 24, 2001.

———. "Manny, It Wasn't a Lot of Bunk." *Baltimore Sun*, August 22, 2008. Also printed as "A Prescient, Pungent Artist-Critic," *Los Angeles Times*, August 25, 2008.

Stern, Eddie. "The Critics & the Cashbox: What the Opinions of a Few Quasi-Intellectuals Mean to the Incomes of America's Cultural Elite." *Spy*, June 1990.

Strauss, Bob. "Siskel and Ebert's 500th TV Show." *Los Angeles Daily News*, June 15, 1989.

Strauss, Theodore. "No Jacks, No Giant Killers." *Screen Writer*, June 1945.

Taylor, Ella. "Between the Frames; How Two Refugee Academics and a Gaggle of Moonlighting Novelists Shaped a Golden Age of *Weekly* Film Criticism." *LA Weekly*, December 4, 2008.

Thackery, Ted, Jr. "Philip Scheuer, Ex-*Times* Film Critic, Dies, Witty, Gentle Writer Bridged Eras of Silent and Talking Movies." *Los Angeles Times*, February 19, 1985.

"This Never Happened to Regis Philbin." *Los Angeles*, July 1979.

Thomas, Kevin, A.D. Murphy, and Arthur Knight. "Why Critics Criticize." *Action*, January/February 1969.

Thomas, Robert McG., Jr. "Archer Winsten, 92, Movie Reviewer at *The Post*, Dies." *The New York Times*, February 23, 1997.

Thomas, William C. "Meet the Press." *Journal of the Screen Producers Guild*, April 1955.

Thompson, Anne. "Criticism's Status Quo Getting Thumbs Down." *The Hollywood Reporter*, June 2, 2006.

———. "Risky Business: N.Y. Still Reigns." *LA Weekly*, July 1989.

———. "That's a Wrap for Movie Magazines: Long-Form Entertainment Journalism Pushed Aside." *Daily Variety*, April 5, 2007.

———. "Times Changing for Film Critics: Younger Generation Shuns Print for Web." Variety.com, April 3, 2008.

"*Times* Critic at Large Sheila Benson Retires." *Los Angeles Times*, December 7, 1991.

"Titanic Letters: Readers React—Strongly—to Critic Turan." *Los Angeles Times*, March 28, 1998.

Tucker, Ken. "Rule of Thumb: TV's Reigning Movie Critic Roger Ebert Lands a New Balcony Buddy, Richard Roeper. Can He Fill Siskel's Hallowed Seat?" *Entertainment Weekly*, September 22, 2000.

Turan, Kenneth. "Critiquing Movie Critics—Why Some Watchdogs Become Blind." *Los Angeles Times*, Calendar section, October 21, 1990.

———. "How a Film Critic Can't Go Wrong: A *Times* Reviewer's Rule: Trust Your Instincts About a Movie." *Los Angeles Times*, July 7, 2008.

———. "Perspective: Film Critic, Review Thyself." *Los Angeles Times*, Calendar section, April 22, 2001.

"The TV Film Critics: A Scouting Report." *Los Angeles Times*, Calendar section, January 3, 1988.

Van Gelder, Lawrence. "Pauline Kael: Provocative and Widely Imitated *New Yorker* Film Critic, Dies at 82." *The New York Times*, September 4, 2001.

Warshow, Robert. "The Gangster as Tragic Hero." *Partisan Review*, February 1948.

———. "Movie Chronicle: The Westerner." *Partisan Review*, March/April 1954.

Waxman, Sharon. "Fade to Black: When It Comes to Managing the News and Keeping the Press in the Dark, the Movie Industry Is in a League of Its Own." *American Journalism Review*, June 1997.

———. "Suicide Reveals Strife in Group behind Globes." *The New York Times*, December 20, 2005.

Weddle, David. "The Trouble with Harry: Internet Geek Harry Knowles." *Los Angeles Times Magazine*, September 3, 2000.

Welkos, Robert W. "Awards Shows Are Inundating Oscar." *Los Angeles Times*, September 4, 2001.

———. "Debating an Icon's Genius, Racism." *Los Angeles Times*, February 1, 2000.

———. "Sony Says It Will Take Action Over Fake Critic." *Los Angeles Times*, June 5, 2001.

Welkos, Robert W., and Rachel Abramowitz. "Scathing Review of Junkets." *Los Angeles Times*, July 20, 2001.

White, Armond. "Two Thumbs Down." *Film Comment*, May/June 1990.

———. "What We Don't Talk About When We Talk About Movies: Armond White Takes Aim at the Critics Who Write with Their Thumbs." *New York Press*, May 1, 2008.

Wilmington, Michael. "10 Films That Merit a Reverent 'Thank You.'" *Los Angeles Times*, December 1, 2000.

Wolcott, James. "Hall of Fame." *Vanity Fair*, June 1998.

———. "Waiting for Godard." *Vanity Fair*, April 1997.

Wolper, Allan. "Two Thumbs Down on Blurbing, U.S.A." *Editor & Publisher*, January 2004.

Woo, Elaine. "Manny Farber, 91; Iconoclastic Film Critic and Artist." *Los Angeles Times*, August 21, 2008.

———. "Pauline Kael, Influential Film Critic, Dies at 82." *Los Angeles Times*, September 4, 2001.

———. "Vincent Canby; Sophisticated, Wry Film Critic for *NY Times*." *Los Angeles Times*, October 17, 2000.

Young, Vernon. "I've Been Reading These Film Critics." *Hudson Review*, Summer 1968.

"Youth Movement." *Newsweek*, December 4, 1967.

Zoglin, Richard. "It Stinks; You're Crazy." *Time*, May 25, 1987.

INDEX